# Gian Carlo Menotti

Gian Carlo Menotti. From the general iconography collection, Music Division, Library of Congress. Courtesy of the Music Division, Library of Congress.

# Gian Carlo Menotti

## A Bio-Bibliography

Donald L. Hixon

Bio-Bibliographies in Music, Number 77

GREENWOOD PRESS
Westport, Connecticut • London

Library of Congress Cataloging-in-Publication Data

Hixon, Donald L.
  Gian Carlo Menotti : a bio-bibliography / Donald L. Hixon.
      p.   cm.—(Bio-bibliographies in music, ISSN 0742-6968 ; no. 77)
  Includes bibliographical references and indexes.
  ISBN 0-313-26139-3 (alk. paper)
  1. Menotti, Gian Carlo, 1911—Bibliography.  I. Title.  II. Series.
ML134.M533 H59  2000
780'.92—dc21          99-054384
[B]

British Library Cataloguing in Publication Data is available.

Copyright © 2000 by Donald L. Hixon

All rights reserved. No portion of this book may be
reproduced, by any process or technique, without the
express written consent of the publisher.

Library of Congress Catalog Card Number: 99-054384
ISBN: 0-313-26139-3
ISSN: 0742-6968

First published in 2000

Greenwood Press, 88 Post Road West, Westport, CT 06881
An imprint of Greenwood Publishing Group, Inc.
www.greenwood.com

Printed in the United States of America

The paper used in this book complies with the
Permanent Paper Standard issued by the National
Information Standards Organization (Z39.48-1984).

10 9 8 7 6 5 4 3 2

To Elbert, Nellie, and Don

# Contents

| | |
|---|---|
| Preface | ix |
| Acknowledgments | xi |
| Biography | 1 |
| General References (G1-G227) | 19 |
| Works and Performances (W1-W90) | 53 |
| Appendix A: Chronological List of Works | 293 |
| Appendix B: Genre List of Works | 297 |
| Author Index | 301 |
| Performer Index | 311 |

# Preface

*Thanks solely to the example of Menotti's success in the 1940s, dozens of operas spouted forth from other composers hoping to hit the jackpot. The effort persists after five decades, and it's safe to state that Menotti, whatever his own final worth, violently altered the nature of lyric theater here, and by extension, throughout the globe.* [Rorem, Ned. "In Search of American Opera." *Opera News* 65 (July 1991): 8]

This volume contains the same components as most others in Greenwood Press' series, "Bio-Bibliographies in Music." Its organization has been modified from that found in other volumes, however, to better serve the reader by eliminating the need to continually navigate from one chapter to another in order to discover all information related to Menotti's creative output.

The volume opens with a brief biography. Biographical material on Menotti is abundant and readily available and there is little need in cloning data found among the plethora of secondary sources already cited here.

General references by and about Menotti and his music follow, without regard to particular compositions. In order to enable the reader to discern societal perceptions and their evolution with the passage of time, entries in this section are arranged in *chronological order*.

The bulk of this volume presents several distinct but interrelated elements in one place. First is a list of Menotti's works and performances, arranged *alphabetically by the title of the work*. Included here are the year of the work's composition, publisher, duration, performance resources, and, often, historical, dedication, and manuscript location data. Then follows a bibliography of writings about the specific work, *arranged chronologically*. Data on premiere and other selected performances of the work follow, including date, place, and identification of performers. Performances are arranged *chronologically*. Special emphasis has been placed on performance reviews, and excerpts from such reviews follow each individual work, again in *chronological order*. A discography of recordings of Menotti's works follows the inventory and bibliography of performances for each work, with entries arranged *alphabetically* by the name of the performer or performing group. Next follow chronological and genre appendices. The volume concludes with two indexes. The author index assists readers wishing to locate writings by specific authors. The performer index provides access by the names of performers and performing groups. In both indexes, entries refer not to page numbers, but rather to citation numbers, e.g., G121, W74.2, etc.

Throughout the various interlinking bibliographies found in this volume, space considerations allowed only a representative selection among the ubiquitous cache of writings about Menotti's involvement in Spoleto's *Festival of Two Worlds* and Charleston's *Spoleto Festival U.S.A.* Concerns of space, in addition to those of taste and decorum, did not allow wallowing in the mire of the sometimes insensitive remarks bearing on the artistic and administrative squabbles associated with Menotti's relinquishing of certain commitments to these two endeavors. It is felt that what has been here included is both adequate and typical.

The cutoff date for inclusion of materials in this volume is 1997. Exceptions include the 1998 Newport Classic Berkshire Opera Company recording of *The Consul* (**W14.68**), the work's first truly complete recording, and, similarly, the 1998 Newport Classic unabridged recording of *Help, Help, The Globolinks!* (**W34.24**).

# Acknowledgments

I regret that a number of attempts to reach Gian Carlo Menotti himself proved unsuccessful. Many other persons, however, assisted greatly with various stages of preparation of this volume, and I would hereby like to offer my most sincere gratitude and appreciation to the following individuals: *Joann Alexander-Smith*, General Director, Manitoba Opera, Winnipeg; *Tom Altmann*, Music Librarian, Milwaukee Public Library; *Nedra V. Blanke*, Head, Arts and Literature Department, Orange County Library System, Orlando, Florida; *Dr. Gene Brooks*, Executive Director, American Choral Directors Association; *Roxann Bustos*, Coordinator of Reference Services, Augusta State University; *Roger L. Carroll*, Manager, Fine Arts Division, City of Dallas Public Library; *Kathleen Champ*, Librarian, Fine Arts, Cleveland Public Library; *Kendall L. Crilly*, Music Librarian, Yale University; *Wendy Culotta*, Science Librarian, California State University, Long Beach, Library; *William De Turk*, Anton Brees Carillon Library, Assistant Carillonneur, Bok Tower Gardens, Lake Wales, Florida and Archivist, The Guild of Carillonneurs in North America; *Carolyn Dickinson*, Manager, Fine Arts and Fiction and Literature Department, Salt Lake City Public Library; *Andy Feehan*, Library Service Specialist, Houston Public Library; *Betty D. Goldman*, Bridgeport Public Library, Bridgeport, Connecticut; *Helen Gregory*, Reference Services, Grosse Pointe Public Library, Grosse Pointe, Michigan; *Peggy A. Haile*, Sargeant Memorial Room, City of Norfolk, Department of Libraries; *Ralph Hartsock*, University of North Texas Libraries, Denton; *Robert Heriard*, Reference, Earl K. Long Library, University of New Orleans; *Bob Johnson*, Reference Librarian, San Jose Public Library, California Room; *Judy Klinger*, Reference Librarian, Santa Fe Public Library; *David Lasocki*, Music Library, Head of Reference Services, School of Music, Indiana University, Bloomington; *Kathryn P. Logan*, Music and Art Department, Carnegie Library of Pittsburgh; *Patricia E. Mullan*, Supervising Librarian, Art and Music, Berkeley Public Library; *Shraine L. Newman*, Public Relations Coordinator, Karamu House, Cleveland; *Sara J. Nyman*, Special

Collections Librarian, Kansas City Public Library, Kansas City, Missouri; *Mark Palkovic*, Audio Visual Media Librarian, College-Conservatory of Music Library, University of Cincinnati; *Mark Pendleton*, Senior Reference Librarian, Thomas Branigan Memorial Library, Las Cruces, New Mexico; *Carolyn L. Quin*, Department of Music, Riverside Community College, Riverside, California; *Eero Richmond*, Information Services Coordinator, The American Music Center; *Nancy Russell*, Library Assistant, California State University, Long Beach, Library; *Laurie Sampsel*, Head, Music Library, University of Colorado, Boulder; *Darryl Sanford*, Ambler Library, Temple University; *Lynn Schornick*, Artistic Director, Bowen Park Opera Company, and Superintendent of Cultural Arts, Waukegan Park District; *Elizabeth Kathleen Shamp*, Librarian, Fine Arts and Special Collections, Cleveland Public Library; *Wayne D. Shirley*, Music Specialist, Music Division, The Library of Congress; *J. Rigbie Turner*, Mary Flagler Cary Curator of Music Manuscripts and Books, The Pierpont Morgan Library; *Elizabeth Walker*, Librarian, The Curtis Institute of Music; *Mary Jo Warnke*, Director, Spring Green Community Library, Spring Green, Wisconsin; *Carolyn W. Waters*, Reference Department, St. Petersburg Public Library System, St. Petersburg, Florida; *Peter Whidden*, Rare Books Specialist, The Stanford Libraries; *Greg Wibe*, Library Assistant, Information Dispatch, Multnomah County Library, Portland, Oregon; *Wayne Wright*, Associate Director, Research Library, New York Historical Association, Cooperstown, New York; and *Nancy C. Zavac*, Music Librarian, University of Miami.

In addition, I would like to extend my apologies to those whom I have inadvertently neglected to list above.

Finally, I am in debt to my partner, *Don A. Hennessee*, for his gentle and yet persistent encouragement and goading at every step. Without such inspiration, as the cliché goes, this volume would never have seen the light of day.

# Biography

*I have very strong aesthetic ideas. I write my music for the collective unconscious, of what is noblest in man. The composer is not actually creating anything. He is discovering what already exists. We must be humble enough to be searchers; we look for the inevitable. The greatest proof of inevitability is the melodic line. I don't care what anybody says. All great music carries it.[1]*

### Cadegliano

Gian Carlo Menotti was born in Cadegliano, a small town on Lake Lugano in Lombardy, Northern Italy, on July 7, 1911. Gian Carlo was the sixth of eight children born to Alfonso and Ines (Pellini) Menotti. The Menotti family was very prosperous, reaping income from a coffee exporting firm operated by an uncle, Francesco Menotti, and jointly by Alfonso Menotti in Colombia, South America. While Gian Carlo's father was a thriving businessman, his mother was a talented amateur musician.

Menotti's family was one prevailed upon by a certain lunacy. For instance, on precisely the day of his ordination, Gian Carlo's uncle, Francesco, deserted the Roman Catholic priesthood. Another relative, Liline Bianchini, who had taught Gian Carlo to play the organ, experienced religious hallucinations. "This strain of madness in the Menotti family would place Gian Carlo in touch with the strange and disquieting factors upon which he would draw during his creative life."[2] Another influence which was to play an important role in his artistic development may be traced to Pier Antonio, a brother who introduced him to the presentation of puppet shows, a pastime that Gian Carlo soon adopted for himself.

As a youngster, Gian Carlo was deeply religious, having been influenced by the religious ardor of a somewhat eccentric parish priest by the name of Don

Rimoldi, who encouraged children to play games, dance, and sing in the church. Perhaps the greatest influence on Gian Carlo, however, was his mother, Ines Menotti. She saw to it that her children were instructed in the piano, violin, and violoncello, and who also organized evening chamber programs.

From the age of five, Gian Carlo was already busy setting verse to music at the piano. When he was eleven, he wrote his first opera, *The Death of Pierrot*, which was performed as a home puppet show. At the age of thirteen, he wrote his second childhood opera, *The Little Mermaid*, which was based on the Hans Christian Andersen fairy tale.

In 1924, the family moved to Milan, where Gian Carlo's mother enrolled him in the Verdi Conservatory of Music. During his three years in Milan, Gian Carlo attended innumerable operas performed at the Teatro alla Scala. He also developed an insatiable hunger for reading, especially of fairy tales from around the world. He also was fascinated by the strange and unusual, the theatrical, the mystic, and the depraved and warped, a preoccupation that would prove portentous to much of his later music.

### Curtis, Scalero, and Barber

When Menotti was seventeen, his father's death and the subsequent collapse of the family's shipping concern changed his life drastically. Upon Alfonso's death, Gian Carlo and his mother moved to Colombia, where she unsuccessfully tried to save that end of the business. In the fall of 1928, before returning to Italy, his mother took Gian Carlo to the Curtis Institute of Music in Philadelphia. He knew very little English, but brought with him a letter of introduction from Arturo Toscanini's wife recommending him for study with Rosario Scalero, undoubtedly Curtis' most eminent professor of composition. Scalero recalled that "The boy had some stuff in him, but he was most undisciplined and raw." He told Menotti, "I promise you that I will be uncompromisingly severe. Do you promise to put in some very hard work, something that you have never done before?"[3] With some trepidation, Menotti agreed. Scalero's system stressed the study and emulation of great works of the past, and Menotti endured the "torture" of writing motets and other pieces using sixteenth-century imitative counterpoint. Despite his professed agony, he nevertheless became acquainted with self-reliance, resourcefulness, and a thoroughness in mastering the tools of composition.

One of Menotti's classmates while at Curtis was fellow composer Samuel Barber. Their extraordinary rapport brought them together, resulting in a companionship that was to last until Barber's death in 1981. In 1933, after graduating from Curtis, Menotti and Barber lived for several years in Austria where, as Barber later recalled, they "wasted a lot of time going to wild parties."[4] They eventually settled down to work in St. Wolfgang, a small village on Lake St. Wolfgang. It was there that Menotti began work on his first mature opera, *Amelia al ballo*, one of the few operas that he wrote in his native Italian. *Amelia al ballo* was inspired by the Baroness von Montechivsky, whom Menotti had met while in Vienna. The opera was translated into English by George Meade, and the English version, under the title *Amelia Goes to the Ball*, received its premiere in Philadelphia in 1937. The Italian version was first presented in San Remo during the following year.

## Amelia al ballo

*Amelia al ballo* was Menotti's first mature opera, and it is easy to see why it quickly made a name for him. It shows a real gift for melody, a sure hand at orchestration, and a knack for comedy, which is somewhat a rarity among twentieth-century opera. *Amelia* is a lightly satirical work about a wealthy, young, married woman who is intent on going to the season's first ball, no matter what obstacles she encounters along the way. For example, her husband discovers that she has a lover, there is an encounter between the two men in her room, her husband is hospitalized after an injury inflicted by herself, and her lover is imprisoned after she falsely accuses him. None of this deters her from her goal of attending the ball. In keeping with the lightweight theme, the music is rhythmically energetic and pleasantly lyrical in a very conservative tonal language, with only the slightest hints of dissonance. Technically, *Amelia* is in the traditional *buffa* format, with set numbers (*duettino, romanza*, etc.), connected by accompanied recitatives, so that the music is continuous, reminding one of late Verdi and Puccini.

It is in *Amelia* that we find Menotti dealing with the concept of *faith*, a preoccupation that is found in many guises in Menotti's works. In the case of *Amelia al ballo*, Menotti treats the notion of *faith* with an agreeable, disarming charm. Amelia has the *faith* that no matter what else might happen, she *will* go to the ball. Later, in *The Medium*, Menotti deals as much with a *lack of faith* in the personage of Madame Flora, while her trusting clients demonstrate an overwhelming power to *believe*, another one of Menotti's fixations.

At the time of *Amelia al ballo*, opera was unfashionable in some circles, and his teacher, Rosario Scalero, had been very contemptuous of opera. Therefore, Menotti said to himself, "Well, I'll just write this one opera and then I'll start composing all my symphonies, masses, and motets. I guess *Amelia* was the beginning of my end."[5]

Things didn't exactly work out that way, and the success of *Amelia Goes to the Ball* at the Metropolitan Opera and elsewhere led to a commission from the National Broadcasting Company for an opera to be composed specifically for the radio. Menotti's first attempt at "grand" opera was *The Old Maid and the Thief*, a humorous one-act radio opera, which was broadcast in 1939. The work is in 14 short scenes, one being just a brief recitative and aria. A short spoken narrative before each scene, called "Announcements," is used only in radio broadcasts. The action is much more compact and the texture thinner than in *Amelia*, but the same conservative tonal language prevails. A part of *The Old Maid and the Thief* that is often excerpted is the "Ricercare and Toccata" on a theme drawn from the opera. Composed in 1951, the piece is a stylistic exercise having roots in the grand organ compositions of the Italian Renaissance. In terms of its general milieu, it is reminiscent of some of the piano transcriptions by Ferruccio Busoni of Bach's *Chorale Preludes*, particularly "Nun freut euch, lieben Christen g'mein."

In *The Island God*, his 1942 tragic opera in one act, Menotti was concerned with a subject that always captivated him: the relation and contrast between faith and reality, another one of those abstractions that would prove important in Menotti's later works, particularly his operas. Unfortunately, *The Island God* proved one of the worst flops in the history of the Metropolitan Opera, despite magnificent casting that included Leonard Warren and Astrid Varnay; Menotti subsequently withdrew the opera. Since faulty staging contributed to this dismal failure, Menotti decided that thereafter he would insist on directing his operas himself.

## Sebastian

Menotti has long been involved with ballet, and dance was an inspiration for much of his music. His ballet *Sebastian* was commissioned by the Marquis de Cuevas, a wealthy Chilean aristocrat. Edward Caton did much of the choreography for the original production given by the Ballet International at New York's International Theater, but he was not able to finish the project. When the ballet premiered October 31, 1944, the unfinished choreography was disjointed and attracted resounding criticism. Even so, the score was praised and quickly entered the repertoire of several major international ballet companies. *Sebastian* has since been choreographed with great success by both John Butler and Agnes de Mille.

After writing his ballet *Sebastian* (1939), and his *Piano Concerto in A Minor* (1945), Menotti returned to opera with his two-act *The Medium* (1946), a commission by the Alice M. Ditson Fund. *The Medium* is scored for five singers, a dance-mime role, and a chamber orchestra of fourteen players. Like *The Island God*, *The Medium* is concerned with "whether belief was a creative power and whether skepticism could destroy creative powers." A decade in Menotti's creative life separates *Amelia* from *The Medium*, and yet, it was a crucial period of growth. He moved from the charming, if sometimes a little superficial, *opera buffa* to a more probing form of music drama that is as individual as *Amelia* is derivative. *Amelia* has all the spontaneous virtues of a first opera (and some of its defects as well). By the time Menotti reached *The Medium*, he was a man with a message who was out to do more than deftly entertain. With *The Medium*, he began investigating the darkest corners of the human soul.

## *The Medium* and *The Telephone*

The plot of *The Medium* had its origin in a séance Menotti once attended at the invitation of friends, where he was struck by the effectiveness of faith, or lack thereof, in the area of the occult or supernatural. The title character of the opera is Madame Flora, a fake spiritualist who is unable to control the unseen forces she herself sets into motion, à la The Sorcerer's Apprentice. *The Medium* is theatrically very effective and the music, often somewhat dissonant, imparts a macabre, almost morbid atmosphere. Despite the bleakness, Menotti considers *The Medium* as "a play of ideas. It describes the tragedy of a woman caught between two worlds, a world of reality which she cannot comprehend and a supernatural world in which she cannot believe."

Consistent with Italian operatic tradition, *The Medium* contains numerous unforgettable melodies, including the folklike "O, Black Swan." *The Medium* had its premiere at the Brander Matthews Theater at Columbia University in 1946 and it ran on Broadway on a double-bill with his light, one-act "skit with music" curtain-raiser, *The Telephone*, to which he gave the subtitle *L'amour à trois*, for 211 performances in 1947 and 1948 at the Ethel Barrymore Theatre on Broadway. *The Telephone* is the story of a young lover (Ben) who tries to propose to his girlfriend (Lucy), only to be repeatedly frustrated by the ringing of her telephone. In desperation, the would-be lover rushes to the corner drugstore to propose — by telephone, of course! *The Telephone* has cheerful, witty, and bright tonal music. The scoring is particularly light, and Lucy's part is frequently performed in a coloratura style, at one point with trills and slides taking place in the higher compass of the soprano's range.

A revised version of *The Medium* received its premiere at New York's Heckscher Theatre on February 18, 1947. In 1951, Lopert Films released a motion picture of *The Medium*, directed by the composer, and starring Marie Powers as Madame Flora, who had played the role on Broadway, and Anna Maria Alberghetti in the role of Monica. The United States State Department organized a European tour of *The Medium* and *The Telephone* in 1955. Despite the enthusiastic reception by the press of Menotti's double-bill, theater-going audiences did not at first flock to the Barrymore. The total advance sale came to $47.00. No Broadway house had ever before presented anything as musically serious as an opera.[6]

*The Medium* clearly is a tale of degradation, total and hopeless. A spiritualist, Madame Flora, has for years swindled her gullible clients who pitifully try to communicate with their dead loved ones. She shows only disdain for them, but is happy to take their money. During one of her many séances, she suddenly has a terrifying experience which she cannot explain, and she is reduced to a quivering, drunken shell haunted by a fear which she is powerless to name. She suspects all around her and in a fit of hysteria, shoots at a moving curtain which conceals the innocent gypsy boy (Toby) whom she had adopted. Unquestionably, *The Medium* can very easily descend to nothing more than tawdry melodrama. In the right hands, however, its very cheapness deepens its tragedy and heightens its excitement to a harrowing and heart-wrenching experience. Many consider *The Medium*, with its gripping music and memorable tonal-modal, folklike melodies, to be Menotti's finest work. "*The Medium* has been called, and justly, 'a perfect opera.' Unlike *Amelia*, there is not an excessive note in the score. Everything contributes to the story and its gripping tale of a woman trapped by her fears and her doubts."[7]

In 1948, Menotti wrote his ballet, *Errand Into the Maze*, a retelling of the story of Ariadne, for the Martha Graham Company. Between 1948 and 1955, Menotti taught on and off at the Curtis Institute.

## The Consul

Menotti's multifaceted dramatic proficiency, as director, librettist, and composer, brought him a contract from Metro-Goldwyn-Mayer to write film scripts. Even though his scripts were never filmed, one contained the origin of his first full-length opera, *The Consul*, considered by many to be his greatest work. *The Consul* uses the *verismo* of Puccini's day to treat a contemporary situation: the virtual impossibility of obtaining a visa to leave a police state. The opera continues the tradition of *The Medium*. "By that time," says Menotti, "my recitatives began to have a very definite style. Of course, thematically and musically *The Consul* is much stronger than *The Medium*. It's much richer melodically. I felt that in *The Consul*, I was able to give instant life to my characters, which I think is very rare in opera."[8]

The Philadelphia premiere of *The Consul* on March 1, 1950 served as a tryout for a Broadway run that began on March 15, 1950 at the Ethel Barrymore Theatre, where it ran for 269 performances. It proved a great success, and performances continued for about eight months. In the year following its premiere, *The Consul* was produced at La Scala in Milan, and in London, Zürich, Berlin, and Vienna.

Set in a tyrannical, post-World War II police state, the story concerns Magda Sorel's desperate attempts to obtain visas that would allow her oppressed, poverty-stricken family to leave the country and thus achieve some hope for survival (an obvious parallel to *Tosca*). The gut-wrenching poignancy of the story is likely to leave very few dry eyes. One of the most powerful elements of *The Consul* is its deliberate avoidance of specific time or place. The "good guys" might be "we" or "they." Or vice versa. Like *The Medium*, with its dark, unrelentingly grim tone, *The Consul* could easily fall into the abyss of melodrama. Still, Menotti's characters are so real. The story touches the audience's collective hearts deeply. In *The Consul*, "Menotti cleverly arranged plain speech, recitative, arioso and aria . . . into a hierarchy of expression. In the first three echelons of that hierarchy, Menotti occasionally sounds like Janáček . . . In the big climaxes, however, all pretense of modernity drops away in favor of the lush musical language of Puccini."[9] While much of *The Consul* is traditionally tonal (with only a few passages that might be classified as atonal), there is a considerable increase over earlier works in the amount and level of dissonance, such as in the orchestral beginning. Certain of Menotti's more familiar devices are found in *The Consul*, including parallel chords, frequent triads, sequences, and pedal ostinatos. Clearly, the opera is replete with powerful theatrical effects and some of Menotti's strongest and most dissonant music.

*The Consul* received the Pulitzer Prize and the Drama Critics' Circle Award. It has been translated into twelve languages and has been performed in more than twenty countries. In Menotti's native Italy, however, performances generally were greeted with both boos and bravos!

With *The Consul* and his next two operas (*Amahl and the Night Visitors* and *The Saint of Bleecker Street*), Menotti now seemed at the zenith of his creative powers and of public acclaim. Like Puccini, Menotti was a man of the stage. His theatrical expertise and passionately effective music make *The Consul* a ripe work for continual reassessment.

## *Amahl and the Night Visitors*

The head of the NBC Opera Company, Samuel Chotzinoff, suggested that NBC commission Menotti to write an opera. At first, Menotti did not appear interested, and the idea lay dormant for several years. NBC eventually prevailed, however, and Menotti wrote his one-act television opera, *Amahl and the Night Visitors*. A visit to the Metropolitan Museum of Art brought the needed inspiration, when Menotti was deeply impressed by *The Adoration of the Magi*, by the Flemish Renaissance artist, Hieronymus Bosch. Commissioned by NBC, *Amahl* was the first opera written expressly for television. Dealing with a crippled boy healed by the sacrifice of his crutch, *Amahl* is a sentimental Christmas story clothed in easy-listening music. But it would take a hard heart, indeed, to be unmoved by the pleading of Amahl's mother for her poor boy, or by the miracle of Amahl's first unaided steps. Menotti began the opera only weeks before the scheduled broadcast, and rehearsals were begun before the score was finished. It was first televised on December 24, 1951, and because of its tremendous popularity, remained an annual NBC Christmas Eve presentation for thirteen years. The roles in *Amahl and the Night Visitors*, particularly the main part for boy soprano, are written so that they can be performed convincingly by amateurs, including church, college, and community opera groups. The appeal and transparent diatonicism of *Amahl* have helped make it one of the most frequently performed operas of the twentieth century. The music has tonal charm, is diatonic, never dissonant, and offers many memorable melodies. In a survey of American opera companies and colleges and universities and other groups covering the 1976-1977 and 1977-1978 seasons by *Opera News*,[10] *Amahl and the Night Visitors* in its stage adaptation led all other contemporary operas in number of performances, with 587. *The Medium* was second, with 148.

## The Saint of Bleecker Street

After *Amahl and the Night Visitors*, Menotti turned to *The Saint of Bleecker Street*, a full-length piece in the spacious and sober style of *The Consul*. Set in contemporary New York, *The Saint of Bleecker Street* is once more concerned with the struggle between the physical and spiritual worlds. Menotti has said that here he was trying to express the duality in his own character, much as he had done with *The Medium*. Says Menotti,

> I am definitely not a religious man. All the same, I am haunted by religious problems . . . the intense and incandescent faith which nourished my childhood and my adolescence have seared my soul forever. I've lost my faith, but it is a loss that has left me uneasy.[11]

*The Saint of Bleecker Street* was first staged on Broadway in the 1954-1955 season, but it proved a commercial failure. While not as great a public success as *The Consul*, possibly because of the ambiguity of the subject matter (religious faith *vs.* superstition), *The Saint of Bleecker Street* is equally large in concept. Critics generally regarded it as an improvement over *The Consul*, and it received the Drama Critics Circle Award for the best play, the New York Music Critics' Circle Award for the best opera, and the Pulitzer Prize in music (his second) for 1955. *The Saint of Bleecker Street* received performances at La Scala in Milan and at the Vienna Volksoper, and was broadcast on BBC Television in 1957. Many of the performances, including the premiere, were conducted by Thomas Schippers.

## The Unicorn and Maria Golovín

*The Unicorn, The Gorgon, and the Manticore*, a "madrigal fable" commissioned by the Elizabeth Sprague Coolidge Foundation, was given its premiere in Washington, D.C., in October 1956 and was presented three months later by the New York City Ballet. Menotti avoided calling the work a ballet, although dance is an essential element. The model for *The Unicorn* was the late Renaissance madrigal comedy, such as Vecchi's *L'amfiparnaso*, and contains an introduction, twelve madrigals (some *a cappella*), and six instrumental interludes. In its various movements, *Unicorn* provides a virtual catalogue of $16^{th}$-century secular choral devices. The tone of the work, despite $20^{th}$-century resonances, evokes a medieval world in spirit.

1958 proved very eventful for Menotti. On January 26, Samuel Barber's *Vanessa*, with libretto and stage direction by Menotti, had its premiere at the

Metropolitan Opera. Later in 1958, Menotti's *Maria Golovín*, another commission by NBC, received its first production at the Brussels World's Fair. *Maria Golovín* is one of Menotti's own favorites. He feels "very close to it," since it reflects "very much a part" of his own 'suffering.' Unfortunately, audiences did not share Menotti's enthusiasm for the opera. After a frosty reception in Brussels (August 1958), it opened on Broadway in November, but played for less than one week. Nevertheless, it was later broadcast by NBC.

Five months later, in collaboration with Thomas Schippers, Menotti created the Festival of Two Worlds in Spoleto, Italy. The mission of the Festival of Two Worlds was to promote artists, both known and unfamiliar, particularly younger ones, from both sides of the Atlantic, for the presentation of music, dance, poetry, drama, and the other arts. The Festival of Two Worlds proved so successful that Menotti became a beloved figure by the Spoleto citizenry, nearly to the point of veneration. In 1967, Thomas Schippers became the Music Director of the Spoleto Festival, but Menotti continued as President of the organization.

In 1959, Menotti provided librettos for operas by Samuel Barber (*A Hand of Bridge*), and Lukas Foss (*Introductions and Goodbyes*), and he also wrote the incidental music for Jean Cocteau's *La poète et sa muse*. In the same year, Menotti's *A Copy of Madame Aupic*, a nonmusical play, was presented in Paris in an adaptation by Albert Husson. Written in 1943, the play was subsequently presented in New Milford, Connecticut, in 1947.

On March 3, 1963, NBC televised Menotti's opera, *Labyrinth*, written partially to illustrate the possibilities of special camera techniques. Also premiered in 1963 was the cantata *The Death of the Bishop of Brindisi*, concerning the Children's Crusade of 1212 and commissioned by the Cincinnati May Festival. The same year saw the three-act comic opera, *L'ultimo selvaggio*, translated into French as *Le dernier sauvage* and into English as *The Last Savage*. Written for the Paris Opéra, its premiere was given at the Opéra-Comique and it later received a lavish production at the Metropolitan Opera in New York. French and American critics generally were hostile to *The Last Savage*, but Italians loved it. Sensitive to the criticism leveled against the opera, Menotti did not write any traditional operas for several years.

A CBS commission for the 1964 Bath Festival was fulfilled by a church opera in one act, *Martin's Lie*, broadcast in the U.S.A. in the following year. *Martin's Lie* is as much a musical morality play as an opera, and like *The Death of the Bishop of Brindisi*, *Martin's Lie* is built on a recitative that is largely inspired by Gregorian chant. The opera is set in the fourteenth century when, as Menotti explains, "tolerance was considered weakness and cruelty a necessity." It was his first attempt at the kind of liturgical music theater rooted in the Middle Ages of folklore, when moral or Biblical tales were played to an audience whose lack of education kept them from reading the written word. Some critics have viewed it as maudlin, and Menotti admitted that "one day [I] will have to rework *Martin's Lie*."[12]

*Canti della lontananza*, a cycle of seven songs to Menotti's own text, was written in 1961 specifically for soprano Elisabeth Schwarzkopf, who sang it at the premiere in 1967 at New York's Hunter College. The songs were created as authentic *Lieder*, with demanding vocal and piano parts, although the scoring presents a generally tonal line. The composer's text is rich in references to naturalism, fatalism, nostalgia, abandon, and solitude, all tied together with the greatest of elegance and sophistication.

## *Help, Help, the Globolinks!*

*Help, Help, the Globolinks!*, a 70-minute "opera in one act for children and those who like children," was commissioned by the Hamburg Staatsoper, which premiered the work during Christmas of 1968. Globolinks are dangerous and evil creatures from outer space, albeit "with a sense of humor," who are able to penetrate walls and doors without effort. Once you are touched by a Globolink, you cannot talk and you yourself become a Globolink within 24 hours. Globolinks detest art and beauty, and are destined to live only to inhuman, electronic sounds. Tonal music is their only enemy and is the only effective weapon against them. Menotti's message is unmistakable: only beautiful music can save humanity from mechanized art. He summarizes his music as Mme. Euterpova, the music teacher, sings, "Unless we keep music in our soul, a hand of steel will clasp our hearts and we shall live by clocks and dials instead of air and sun and sea."

In June 1967, the Staatsoper production of Stravinsky's *The Rake's Progress*, in a Menotti adaptation, opened at the Metropolitan Opera House. In the next year, Menotti wrote the incidental music for Michael Cacoyannis' production of Shakespeare's *Romeo and Juliet* at France's Théâtre National Populaire.

Menotti's drama without music, *The Leper*, was first performed in Tallahassee, Florida, on April 22, 1970. *The Leper* is the most "confessional" of Menotti's works, an ambivalent polemic urging toleration of deviance only so long as it does not threaten the social order. John Gruen observes: "A careful reading of the play makes it clear that it is pitted mainly against the homosexual, or at least a certain kind of homosexual. This seems quite surprising, coming from Menotti."[13] When approached on the subject of homosexuality, Menotti has said: "My life is an open book; however, I don't like to leave it around."[14]

## *The Most Important Man* and *Tamu-Tamu*

*The Most Important Man* was commissioned by the New York City Opera and received its first performance at the Lincoln Center for the Performing Arts in New York in 1971. Few critics liked *The Most Important Man*, an opera about racial tensions, but Menotti considers it one of his best works, on the par with *The Saint of Bleecker Street*. The opera *Tamu-Tamu*, commissioned by the Ninth International

Congress of Anthropological and Ethnological Sciences, had its premiere at Chicago's Studebaker Theater in September 1973.

In the fall of 1973, Menotti sold "Capricorn," the house he had long shared with Samuel Barber in Mount Kisco, New York, a house where they had lived since 1943. With his adopted son, Chip, Menotti and Barber moved to the Lammermuir Hills of East Lothian, Scotland, near Edinburgh, and there purchased a 1789 country mansion called Yester House.

The Summer of 1976 was particularly busy for Menotti, with four works receiving their premiere performances: *Landscapes and Remembrances*, a cantata; *The Hero*, a Bicentennial comedy; *The Egg* (a companion piece to *Martin's Lie*, for a Washington Cathedral premiere); and his *Symphony No. 1 in A Minor*, "*the Halcyon*," which represents "the most sincere and optimistic days of my youth when the horizon [was] unclouded," and which received its first performance on August 4 at New York's Saratoga Spa State Park.

*Landscapes and Remembrances* is an autobiographical statement of Menotti's forty years of life in America. Each scene represents a specific experience in Menotti's life: Arrival in New York by sea; The abandoned mansion (South Carolina); Parade in Texas; Nocturne (driving at night through the desert); A subway ride in Chicago; Picnic by the Brandywine; An imaginary trip through Wisconsin; Farewell at a train station in Vermont; and The sky of departure (leaving America by plane at sunset).

## Spoleto

In the summer of 1977, the Festival of Two Worlds became a geographical reality with the first season of Spoleto U.S.A. in Charleston, South Carolina, the other of the two worlds. The night before the 1978 Festival of Two Worlds began in Charleston, Menotti attended the premiere of his 25-minute children's opera, *The Trial of the Gypsy*, first performed by the Newark Boys Chorus at the Lincoln Center for the Performing Arts. In spite of the many organizational, managerial, and operational demands on his time, which includes directing plays as well as operas, Menotti nevertheless maintained an active creative career.

Also in the summer of 1977, tenor Placido Domingo was appearing in an Edinburgh Festival production of Bizet's *Carmen*. Menotti invited Domingo and his family to lunch at Yester House, near Edinburgh. At one point, Domingo said, "Gian Carlo, why don't you write an opera for me to sing?" Thus, Menotti's next opera, *Goya*, was conceived, loosely based on the life of the painter. "It is the duality of character, the heroic artist and the timorous human being, that I have tried to capture in the opera. This is the theme of the opera, and this is why it has been so hard to write!" Indeed, *Goya* was "hard to write," because the opera didn't receive its world premiere until nearly nine years later. During its November 15, 1986 premiere, Domingo portrayed the central character and was supported by Victoria Vergera as the Duchess of Alba.

*Missa o Pulchritudo*, for soloists, chorus, and orchestra, is a mass to beauty in which he replaces the Credo with a setting of a poem by St. Augustine. Under its complete title, *Missa o Pulchritudo in Honorem Sacratissimi Cordis Jesus*, it received its first performance in Milwaukee (May 1979) by the Milwaukee Symphony Orchestra and the Bel Canto Chorus.

His most recent operas have been directed toward children, both as subjects and as performers. In addition to *The Egg* and *The Trial of the Gypsy* (mentioned above), 1979 also saw *Chip and His Dog*, with a first performance in Guelph, Ontario, Canada, in May 1979.

## Juana, La Loca

Menotti's first attempt at a historical work of grand proportions is *Juana, La Loca*, which tells the story of the daughter of Isabella and Ferdinand of Spain. It was specifically written as a fiftieth-birthday present for soprano Beverly Sills. Commissioned by the San Diego Opera, with funding by Lawrence E. Deutsch, *Juana, La Loca* had its world premiere in June 1979, in San Diego. Beverly Sills sang the title role in six performances with the New York City Opera beginning on September 6, 1979. The general consensus of the very mixed reviews was that the opera perhaps was a bit inferior, but that it allowed Miss Sills a *tour de force* performance vehicle.

The first four of Menotti's *Five Songs* date from 1981 (with a premiere at the Abraham Goodman House in New York City) and a fifth song was added two years later, receiving its first performance at the Flagler Museum in Palm Beach, Florida on December 12, 1983. The songs present small but eloquent portraits of human experience, of loss, and of a patient yearning for life's end.

Two more children's operas, *A Bride From Pluto* and *The Boy Who Grew Too Fast*, received their first performances in Washington, D.C., in 1982. The latter is the latest of six operas Menotti has written for children and in many ways the simplest in musical form and dramatically the most direct. At the end, Miss Hope, the school teacher, advises us to "Be glad of what you are, whether fat or thin, short or tall, black or white, be glad to be yourself. Don't try to be another. For what you are, nobody else can be."

Since 1954, with *The Saint of Bleecker Street*, Menotti has not been able to echo his earlier popular victories. His later operas have invariably had fewer productions than his earlier ones, and although he has remained active, when one thinks of Menotti, one generally thinks of his works composed before 1955. Some critics have faulted Menotti for his orthodox approach and what they regard as his refusal to develop his own style beyond merely repeating his prior successes. In the

1940s and 1950s, Menotti seemed a logical heir to Puccini, and no other composer from recent generations has reached an operatic public as broad as his.[15]

## Resignation from Spoleto and Recent Activity

In 1993, Menotti resigned in a fury from the Spoleto Festival U.S.A. after a two-year power struggle with the festival's board and management. First the board insisted on including an avant-garde art exhibit Menotti opposed, then it rejected Menotti's chosen successor, his adopted son Francis. When Spoleto Festival U.S.A. announced a shortened season and a $1.7 million deficit in 1994, there were fears that it might not survive its founder. "They think they have learned my formula and can now do away with my presence," mocked Menotti in 1991. Menotti finally resigned in 1993, threatening to take the name of the festival with him. Festival officials insist that they own the name and will keep it. "Mr. Menotti would very much like for us to [change the name]," says Charleston mayor Joseph P. Riley, Jr. ". . .but we want to keep Spoleto Festival as a permanent artistic legacy for him." When questioned about the prolonged battle with Menotti, Riley merely says, "It's just too bad he's not here to bask in the beauty of what his vision created."

Menotti's recent years have continued to be fertile, despite the composer's advancing years. His one-act opera, *The Singing Child*, premiered in 1993 at the College of Charleston with William Cole singing the central role of Jeremy. 1995 saw Menotti's *Gloria*, for tenor, chorus, and instrumental ensemble. The first two movements of his *Trio for Violin, Clarinet, and Piano* received a Spoleto premiere in July 1996 performed by the Verdehr Trio; the final movement followed two months later. *Jacob's Prayer*, for mixed chorus and based on the Book of Genesis, was commissioned by the American Choral Directors Association and received a 1997 San Diego premiere.

Menotti has received numerous prestigious awards and honors. A partial list includes two Guggenheim awards (1946 and 1947), two Pulitzer Prizes (1950 and 1955), a Kennedy Center Honor for lifetime achievement in the arts (1984), the 1986 New York City Mayor's Liberty Award, The George Peabody Medal from Johns Hopkins University (1987), the 1988 Richard Tucker Award, and, in 1991, *Musical America* named him "Musician of the Year."

## Style

Menotti's melodic gifts alone are prodigious and result in a very wide popular, if not critical, appeal. It has been remarked that "No composer of the post-World War II era has found a broader or more enthusiastic public than Gian Carlo Menotti."[16] Indeed, for a generation following the end of World War II, Menotti was the most celebrated opera composer on the scene, rivaling such contemporaries as Poulenc, Britten, Tippett, and Barber. Displaying an instinctive sense for theater, some consider Menotti a direct descendant of such composers as Giordano, Leoncavallo, and, particularly, Puccini. Even his ballet *Sebastian*, or the broadly angular *Piano Concerto*, or the lyrical *Violin Concerto*, along with some of his chamber music, reflect this same melodic facility and the colorful orchestral style shown in his operas. While he has used some modern compositional techniques, such as tape and electronic music in *Help, Help, the Globolinks!*, the very foundation of his music is its eloquent, melodic writing. Unfortunately, because of his many operatic successes, Menotti's orchestral music has been undeservedly neglected. Clearly, his colorful sense of orchestration adds to the overall dramatic impact of his writing. In his best music, Menotti, like Puccini, lends preeminence to the human voice and to effective theatrical moment. Menotti cares about his audience and also about the human voice. He has written: "There is a certain indolence towards the use of the voice today, a tendency to treat the voice instrumentally, as if composers feared that its texture is too expressive, too *human*."

As noted before, much of Menotti's creative energy has gone into the Spoleto and Charleston festivals, administratively and in his directing of plays and operas. Some critics wonder whether Menotti's many commitments to these festivals might have distracted him from his composing efforts. Also, of course, he wrote the libretto for two of Samuel Barber's works, *A Hand of Bridge* and *Vanessa*, and revised Zeffirelli's libretto for Barber's *Antony and Cleopatra*, activities which again drew time from his own composing. It is clear, though, that Menotti is a force so vital and multifaceted that he would not be content to just sit in his studio and write music.

Menotti's music often is in the Italian operatic tradition, although overlaid with some of the intense expressionism of Richard Strauss. Like Puccini, moreover, he is sensitive to new musical techniques that serve his dramatic purposes. Some examples include the high sustained dissonant chord in *The Consul* as Magda turns on the gas stove to commit suicide, the twelve-tone music used to parody contemporary civilization in the Second Act of *Le dernier sauvage*, or the electronic tape representing the invaders from outer space in *Help, Help, the Globolinks!* Another instance is found at the end of Annina's aria in *The Saint of Bleecker Street*, when she relives the Crucifixion and experiences the stigmata. Menotti calls for the striking of an anvil, replicating the sound of the nail being driven into the hands of Christ. Because of the skill of the orchestral writing and the highly expressive melodic curve of the aria, it is particularly stunning moment.

Menotti's melodies are, by and large, tonal, sometimes with a modal flavor, and often easily retained. Many of his more commanding musical gestures, such as the opening of *The Medium*, reflect his avowed fondness for Moussorgsky. There are striking similarities in the first few bars of *The Medium*, for instance, with "Bydło" from *Pictures at the Exhibition*. Sequences and repetitions are common, and aria-like passages tend to be brief so as not to interrupt the dramatic flow. The continuous recitative-like sections set the text with naturalness and clarity. His harmonies are tonal, sometimes utilizing parallel chords over a simple tonal bass. Menotti's orchestration tends to be light and transparent and he writes particularly well for smaller instrumental ensembles. Even when metrical irregularities are used, his rhythms are natural and easily grasped by both performers and listeners. In general, then, his techniques are traditional and conservative, and while some have labeled his style as sentimental or even dull, his best works can be powerful (*The Consul*), or charming (*Amahl and the Night Visitors* or the *Piano Concerto*).

Sadly, changing fashions in the music world have conspired to regard much of Menotti's work, with the possible exception of *Amahl and the Night Visitors*, to be old-fashioned melodrama. Of course, by the same standards, so is *Tosca*, which remains one of the most frequently-performed works in the repertoire. A critical appraisal of Menotti's music has ranged from sincere admiration to the most bitter castigation. "I've lived through a period when it was an anathema to say you liked Menotti," says Menotti himself.

> Sometimes I get a little bitter. The modern generation of critics pooh-pooh my works, but they forget that I revolutionised opera. When I started to write operas it changed everything. What people consider originality is nothing but a tiresome mannerism that enslaves the artist to the point of sterility . . . I believe that originality can only be achieved through a relentless process of self-discovery. If, after baring yourself, you discover that what you have to say is banal and unimportant, at least you have done all that an artist can possibly do.

Gian Carlo Menotti used to be the critics' favorite whipping boy but that hasn't stopped opera companies from staging his operas or audiences all over the world from responding to their undeniable theatricality.[17] Fellow-composer Ned Rorem offers this estimation: "Whether you like his music or not, the fact exists that due to Menotti, and only Menotti, the whole point of view of contemporary opera in America, and perhaps in the world, is different from what it would have been had he not existed."[18]

Some critics maintain that the turning point in Menotti's popularity was hastened by Joseph Kerman's particularly brutal evaluation in his 1988 *Opera as Drama*, in which he expressed his view that "Menotti is a sensationalist in the old style, and in fact a weak one, diluting the faults of Strauss and Puccini with none of their fugitive virtues."[19]

In the end, however, any assessment of Menotti is useless unless you take the theater as your beginning. Steeped in stagecraft, he discovered early the secret of what makes thrilling drama. His command of the stage gives him command of his audience. One feels that Menotti will be remembered and performed more frequently in future generations than many of the composers who found a broader critical acceptance during their lives.[20] Perhaps H. Wiley Hitchcock provided one of the better assessments: "Menotti combined the theatrical sense of a popular playwright and a Pucciniesque musical vocabulary with an Italianate love of liquid language and a humane interest in characters as real human beings; the result was opera more accessible than anyone else's at the time."[21] One especially vitriolic critic may have been right when he recently described Menotti's current status as "deeply unfashionable." However, history is known to be cheerfully and notoriously nonchalant to contemporary judgements in artistic matters. It will be interesting to see how it finally ranks some of the more conspicuous non-conformists of this conspicuously chaotic century. "One hopes that with the cultural climate becoming more receptive to diversity in the tools of creativity, an objective reappraisal of the work of Menotti is on the near horizon."[22]

NOTES

1. Wynne Delacoma, "Political Woes of 1950 Opera Find Parallels in Today's World; *Consul* Is In." *Chicago Sun-Times*, October 13, 1996, SHO, p. 13.

2. John Gruen, *Menotti: A Biography* (New York: Macmillan, 1978), p. 8.

3. Ibid., p. 19.

4. Ibid., p. 24.

5. Ibid., p. 28.

6. Ibid., p. 65.

7. John Ardoin, "Opera Reaches New Heights." *Dallas Morning News*, April 16, 1984.

8. John Gruen, *Menotti: A Biography*, p. 99.

9. Tom Strini, "Lush Music of 'Consul' Contrasts Brilliantly With Somber Setting." *Milwaukee Journal*, October 10, 1993, p. B2.

10. Reprinted in the November 1978 issue.

11. John Gruen, *Menotti: A Biography*, p. 122.

12. Ibid., p. 167.

13. Ibid., p. 199.

14. Ibid., p. 200.

15. Fogel, Henry, "Menotti, Gian Carlo" *in Contemporary Composers*, editors, Brian Morton, Pamela Collins (Chicago: St. James Press, 1992)

16. Ibid., p. 649.

17. John Von Rhein, "Updated Staging Rescues Menotti's *Consul* at Lyric." *Chicago Tribune*, October 21, 1996, p. 2.

18. John Gruen, *Menotti: A Biography*, p. 79.

19. Joseph Kerman, *Opera As Drama* (Berkeley: University of California Press, 1988), p. 264.

20. Henry Fogel, "Gian Carlo Menotti," p. 649.

21. H. Wiley Hitchcock, *Music in the United States: A Historical Introduction*, 3rd ed. (Englewood Cliffs, NJ: Prentice Hall, 1988), p. 230.

22. John Ostendorf, program notes to Newport Classic NPD85621 recording of *The Unicorn, The Gorgon, and The Manticore*.

# General References (G1–G227)

The following references are to general sources concerning Menotti's life, music, and style, but without particular allusion to any particular works. The references are arranged chronologically. When multiple sources were published on the same date, references are arranged alphabetically by the surname of the author or, in instances of unknown authorship, by the first significant word of the title.

G1   Taubman, Howard. "Prodigy Grows Up." *New York Times Magazine* (June 1, 1947): 28+.
"It used to be standard operating procedure for young composers in this country to go abroad to complete their musical studies, but Gian-Carlo Menotti, born in Italy, came here for the most important phase of his education and here he remained to become one of our leading operatic-writers."

G2   Sargeant, Winthrop. "American Opera on Broadway." *Life* 22 (June 9, 1947): 98.
Regarding Menotti's operas, they show ". . . that American opera need not be restricted to the pompous manner and regimental proportions of grand opera . . . and that it can be as swift-moving and suspenseful as any Broadway melodrama."

G3   "Menotti, Gian-Carlo." *Current Biography* (December 1947): 433-435.
General biographical sketch with portrait and selected bibliographical references.

G4   Kubly, Herbert. "Chamber of Horrors in Capricorn." *Theatre Arts* 33 (January 1949): 32-35.

"In America, he has rescued opera from expensive museum-like opera houses and streamlined it back into the people's entertainment which it was in the golden days of opera writing in Italy and Germany."

G5    Menotti, Gian Carlo. "Opera Isn't Dead: a Conference With Annabel Comfort." *Etude* 68 (February 1950): 14-15+.

"My advice to any young composer who is writing for the stage is to study classic and modern staging. I have seen too many operatic scores of young composers who have used libretti written by people who are ignorant of any stage technique later than the time of Victor Hugo."

G6    Taubman, Howard. "Proving Opera Can Be Modern." *New York Times Magazine* (March 19, 1950): 26-30.

Menotti " . . . says he is overcome at intervals with a terrible sense of the urgency of time. 'I wake up and think . . . that I am 38 and have accomplished so little . . . Time is flying, and I must work.'"

G7    "Opera's Heir Presumptive." *Newsweek* 35 (March 27, 1950): 82-83.

"Menotti may or may not turn out to be America's first really important operatic composer. That decision does not rest with current critics or audiences. But until somebody else proves a better right to the title, Menotti must be considered the heir presumptive."

G8    Menotti, Gian Carlo. "My Conception of Hell." *Saturday Review of Literature* 33 (April 22, 1950): 29.

"The poet shall forever scream the poems which he never wrote; the painter will be forever obsessed by visions of the pictures which he did not paint; the musician will strive in vain to remember the sounds which he failed to set down on paper . . . For me the conception of hell lies in two words: too late."

G9    Menotti, Gian Carlo. "From the Mail Pouch: Credo." *New York Times*, 2 (April 30, 1950): 9.

Menotti's reply to an April 21, 1950 *New York Times* report of a panel discussion in which he took part, with particular reference to a perceived disagreement between him and Copland on the expectations of audiences when faced with 'modern music.'

G10    Marx, H. "Plans." *Music News* 42 (May 1950): 11.

## General References

G11 "Composer on Broadway." *Time* 55 (May 1, 1950): 64-66.
General biographical article with emphasis on Menotti's operas. "Menotti, who naturally likes his new success but also fears it, tells his friends that he thinks it would be good for his soul if his next opera was a flop. He is giving himself plenty of chance to compose one."

G12 Sargeant, Winthrop. "Wizard of the Opera." *Life* 28 (May 1, 1950): 81-82.

G13 "Menotti in San Francisco and Elsewhere." *Opera und Conzert* (San Francisco) 15 (November 1950): 10.

G14 Rosenwald, H. "Contemporary Music." *Music News* 43 (April 1951): 11.

G15 Taubman, Howard. "Gian-Carlo Menotti." *Theatre Arts* 35 (September 1951): 26-27+.
Says Menotti, "I sometimes wake up and think . . . that I am forty and have accomplished so little. Time is flying. I must work."

G16 Kolodin, Irving. "Cloak Uncovers Menotti." *Saturday Review* 35 (March 1, 1952): 25.
"I affirm at once my esteem for Menotti, and note, further, that the recognition should have been apparent long ago — an oversight due in this quarter, at least, to ignorance."

G17 Lansdale, Nelson. "Menotti Calls the Met a Museum." *Theatre Arts* 36 (May 1952): 30-31+.
Says Menotti, "I can't believe that a country as rich and music-loving as this one is incapable of providing opera managements with the necessary money to make opera a vital, contemporary theater rather than a year-in, year-out revival house of standard favorites." See *G20* for a response.

G18 Menotti, Gian Carlo. "A Plea For the Creative Artist." *New York Times Magazine* (June 29, 1952): 8+.
"Most flagrant of all is the indifferent attitude of the American Government toward creative art. Possessing the most formidable means and material for cultural propaganda, it stubbornly insists upon ignoring the only facet of American culture that would really inspire Europe — the arts." Cf. *Music News* 44 (September 1952): 4-6+.

*22    General References*

G19    "Springfield Menotti Festival." *Musical Courier* 146 (August 1952): 9.
"The first festival dedicated to the works of Gian-Carlo Menotti was presented by the William Spada 'Menotti Repertoire Group,' at the New Court Square Theater, Springfield, Mass., in late May [1952]."

G20    Aulicino, Armand. "In Defense of the Met." *Theatre Arts* 36 (September 1952): 74-75+.
Rudolf Bing and John Gutman answer Menotti's accusation that the Metropolitan Opera is a museum. "We agree with Menotti that the Met is a museum, but don't feel that this is a criticism . . . The Met is a living museum like any good artistic institution." See *G17* for Menotti's remarks that provoked this reply.

G21    "Lord Russell Honoured." *Times* (London), (May 7, 1953): 6.
Announcement that on May 6, 1953, in New York, the National Institute of Arts and Letters elected Menotti, le Courbusier, and Colette as honorary associate members, along with Lord Russell.

G22    "AmerAllegro." *Pan Pipes of Sigma Alpha Iota* 46 (January 1954): 52.

G23    Beard, H. "Letter From Italy." *Chesterian* 29 (July 1954): 22.

G24    "Gian-Carlo Menotti." *Pan Pipes of Sigma Alpha Iota* 47 (January 1955): 57.

G25    Menotti, Gian Carlo. "Notes on Opera as 'Basic Theatre.'" *New York Times Magazine* (January 2, 1955): 11+.
" . . . I maintain that every language is, potentially, equal musically, and it is up to the composer to absorb and illuminate this language in his music."

G26    "Inside Stuff: Concerts." *Variety* 197 (January 19, 1955): 72.
Says Menotti about opera in translation: "I insist that an opera must be dramatically understandable to its audience, and if some musical subtleties are lost in translation, there is still much more that has been gained, dramatically."

G27    "People Are Talking About . . ." *Vogue* 125 (February 1, 1955): 144-145.

G28    Ackart, Robert. "Opera: Style All the While, But What Constitutes Style?" *Musical America* 75 (February 15, 1955): 22-23.
"One of Mr. Menotti's techniques . . . to bring his ideas easily to his listener in the theater is by presenting characters readily recognizable to the

audience, who are not separated from everyday life by high birth, foreign title, or mysterious circumstance . . . a trend, it will be said, toward operatic realism."

G29   Merkling, Frank. "Grass Roots Opera." *Musical America* 75 (February 15, 1955): 24.
In 1950-51, Menotti was represented by at least 357 performances in the United States, of half a dozen works, not counting *Amahl and the Night Visitors*.

G30   Mellers, W. "Music, Theatre and Commerce; a Note on Gershwin, Menotti and Marc Blitzstein." *Score* (London) 12 (June 1955): 71.

G31   Eckertsen, Dean. "From Corelli to Menotti." *Music Journal* 13 (July-August 1955): 13.
" . . . it is difficult to think of any contemporary composer who has more in common with Corelli than Menotti. The reason for this seemingly dangerous statement is the basic simplicity of Menotti's harmonic and melodic texture."

G32   "Virile Music Coming from U.S., Sez Menotti; Has New Opera Ready." *Variety* 199 (August 31, 1955): 60.
Menotti "likes many Continental composers, but feels that intrinsically American music is stronger, with public interest in music about the same on both sides."

G33   Parmenter, Ross. "World of Music: Offer to Menotti." *New York Times*, 2 (April 8, 1956): 9.
The Italian Ministry of Culture has offered Menotti rent-free use of a small theater in either Todi or Sulmona in Italy, for an international arts festival which he hopes to have in place by the summer of 1957.

G34   Menotti, Gian Carlo. "Proposal for an International Arts Festival." *National Music Council Bulletin* 17 (January 1957): 7-8.

G35   "Mr. Menotti on His Future Operas." *Times (London)*, (May 16, 1957): 3.
"His scores have been called insubstantial, but there is no lack of substance in his personality or thought. He is genuinely in search of aesthetic truth. Television may be a diversion to his path, but even the most fastidious epicure must sometimes resort to tinned food."

G36 "Opera Or Music Drama." *Times* (London), (May 24, 1957): 3.
Menotti has noted that " . . . opera should be a meditative art, by which he means that the action is only the starting point of music . . . If this is his creed, it is strikingly at variance with his practice."

G37 Hawkins, Robert F. "Menotti Sets Up 4-arts Festival." *Variety* 208 (October 2, 1957): 14.
"Menotti admitted he would like nothing better than a chance to stage one of his own works at Spoleto, but added that this might happen only in a few years time — or perhaps not at all."

G38 Jolly, Cynthia. "Spoleto." *Opera* (England) 9 (January 1958): 46+.
Article on the formation of the Spoleto Festival. "With a convincing blend of idealism and shrewd practicality which sounds challengingly in the face of skeptical Italian materialism, Menotti is moving into action as cultural ambassador . . ."

G39 Menotti, Gian Carlo. "Festival of Two Worlds." *Music Clubs Magazine* 37 (March 1958): 4-5.

G40 Chapman, Frank. "First Spoleto Festival Major Success." *Musical America* 78 (August 1958): 10.
"Its participants, its sponsors both public and private of both 'worlds' may well be proud of an extraordinary achievement. Long may it prosper."

G41 Jolly, Cynthia. "The Festival of Two Worlds." *Opera* (England) 9 (September 1958): 551-557.
"Recommendations for future years? Warm encouragement to Menotti's plan to turn each year to two completely different and sharply contrasted countries; a plea for a general programme that has a clearer sense of direction — without sacrificing this year's enviably high standards of performance."

G42 Groth, H. "Gian Carlo Menotti and the American Lyric Theatre." *NATS Bulletin* 15 (December 1958): 16-17+.

G43 "For TV's Money Only." *Newsweek* 53 (February 23, 1959): 64.
Says Menotti, "Opera and TV are enemies. Opera requires thought rather than action, and the meditative aria never comes off on television because the audience gets bored with lack of motion on the screen."

G44  Sargeant, Winthrop. "Musical Events: Imperishable Menotti." *New Yorker* 36 (February 27, 1960): 133-134+.
"...Gian-Carlo Menotti is, I think, a truly remarkable composer, and his remarkableness is not the less striking because it is evident to a fairly large and by no means culturally snobbish audience."

G45  Briggs, John. "Menotti . . . Opera Magician." *International Musician* 60 (November 1961): 12-13+.

G46  Casmus, Mary Irene. "Gian-Carlo Menotti, His Dramatic Techniques: A Study Based on Works Written 1937-1954." Ph.D. dissertation, Columbia University, 1962.
From the author's abstract: "The over-all pattern of success and failure as revealed in Menotti's librettos indicates that (a) his talents are better adapted to a form of opera that is small-scale, intimate, and short, (b) he has responded in a superior manner to the challenges of various media, [and] (c) his eclecticism and pragmatic approach have served him well in his rise to popularity as a composer of modern opera."

G47  Yarustovsky, Boris. "Journey to America." *Journal of Research in Music Education* 10 (Fall 1962): 125.
Translation by Richard F. French of an article that appeared in the February 1960 issue of *Sovetskaya Muzyka*. An account of composer Yarustovsky's 1959 visit to the United States under an agreement between the American and Soviet governments. On Menotti: " . . . even his opponents cannot deny Menotti his indisputable theatrical flair."

G48  "Retour de Gian Carlo Menotti." *Musica* (Chaix) 94 (January 1962): 13.

G49  "Pas de surhomme: un medium." *Musica* (Chaix) 97 (April 1962): 10.

G50  Hirsch, N. "Renovateur du drama lyrique: Gian-Carlo Menotti." *Musica* (Chaix) 99 (June 1962): 26-30.

G51  Stern, W. H. "Music on the Air: Commissions For TV." *Music Leader* 94 (August 1962): 6.

G52  Stevens, D. "Italy: Spoleto on the Way Out?" *Music Magazine* 164 (October 1962): 44-46.

G53  Menotti, Gian Carlo. "Reflections on Opera Buffa." *National Music Council Bulletin* 24, 2 (1963-1964): 18.

## 26  General References

G54  Sargeant, Winthrop. "Profiles: Orlando in Mount Kisco." *New Yorker* 39 (May 4, 1963): 49-50+.
General article on Menotti's operas. "He is a very religious man, as the subjects of several of his operas show, but he has a pronounced aversion to the Catholic Church, an institution he believes today to be the enemy of good art and good music."

G55  Parinaud, A. "S. Giancarlem Menottim." *Hudebni rozhledy* 17, 3 (1964): 122-123.

G56  Menotti, Gian Carlo. "I Am the Savage; Gian Carlo Menotti Talks to *Opera News*." *Opera News* 28 (February 8, 1964): 8-12.
General consideration of Menotti's operas, based on an interview that occurred during the U.S. premiere of his *Le dernier sauvage*.

G57  Butler, Henry. "A Measure of Menotti." *Opera News* 28 (February 8, 1964): 27.
"His influence and blessing are upon every composer who sets out to write opera for the theater; more important, he has dedicated his life to hacking a clear path toward that goal."

G58  "Menotti Auditions London Boy Singers." *Musical Events* 19 (April 1964): 11.

G59  "Menotti May Move Festival." *Times* (London), (May 28, 1964): 6.
"Already there are rumours in the Italian press that he is threatening to move the festival from Umbria to his native Lombardy, to Bergamo, to be precise. Menotti admits that this is a possibility . . . unless the financial set-up is made easier for him."

G60  "Spilling the Beans." *Newsweek* 66 (July 5, 1965): 79-80.
Says Menotti, "I'm temporarily withdrawing from the operatic scene. It's too grueling. The agony of opening night, I can't do it."

G61  Matz, Charles A. "Menotti & Pound." *Opera News* 30 (November 20, 1965): 14-15.
Reminiscences of a Venice visit between Menotti and poet Ezra Pound, who had earlier composed an opera (*The Testament*) to the poetry of François Villion.

G62  Chase, Gilbert. "Toward an American Opera" *in America's Music*, by Gilbert Chase. p. 651-654. New York: McGraw-Hill, 1966.

"It took a native of Italy . . . to demonstrate that a skillful blending of nineteenth-century operatic ingredients, spiced with some twentieth-century harmonies and some up-dated elements of *verismo*, would meet with an immediate response from American audiences."

G63 Tricoire, Robert. *Gian Carlo Menotti, l'homme et son oeuvre.* Musiciens de tous les temps, 26. Paris: Seghers, 1966.
General biographical and critical information, with list of works and brief discography.

G64 Edwards, S. "Menotti Without Music." *Music and Musicians* 14 (January 1966): 17.

G65 Worbs, Hans Christoph. *Welterfolge der modernen Oper.* Berlin: Rembrandt, 1967.
Discusses 25 twentieth-century operas, with critical notices of the premieres and 121 stage photographs, including photos of the same scene as staged in several different opera houses.

G66 Worbs, Hans Christoph. "Strawinsky-englisch." *Musica* 21, 4 (1967): 163.

G67 Kay, N. "Menotti, Operatic Master." *Music and Musicians* 15 (March 1967): 28-31.

G68 "Ten $100,000-a-Year Grants to Menotti." *Variety* 247 (July 26, 1967): 75.
Funds to encourage American participation for the next decade in the Festival of Two Worlds were assured through a $1,000,000 guarantee by the Samuel Rubin Foundation of New York, spread over ten years, with $100,000 payable each year. "Donation was given with the hope that the Italian government and private Italian citizens would increase their financial support."

G69 "Menotti Unloads Spoleto Burdens." *Variety* 248 (November 1, 1967): 57.
Massimo Bogianckino appointed general manager of the Festival of Two Worlds, dividing the responsibility for Spoleto with founder Menotti and conductor Thomas Schippers.

G70 Kessler, H. "'Tristan' und Menotti." *Musica* 22, 6 (1968): 467-468.

G71 Prokopiou, Stavros. *Mystics and Revolutionaries of the Apollonian Art: Essays on Music.* Athens: Musical Chronicles, 1968.

28   *General References*

> Sketches the contributions to music of Franck, D'Indy, Stravinsky, Menotti, and A.N. Labelet, a Greek composer. In Greek.

G72   Königsberg, A. "Contemporary American Opera: Menotti and Floyd" *in Music and Contemporaneity: Collection of Articles*, ed. T. A. Lebedeva. Moskva: Muzyka, 1968.

G73   Tompkins, Jimmy. "Menotti's Use of Dramatic Impact in *The Medium.*" M.M. thesis, North Texas State University, 1968.
Includes bibliographical references (leaves 171-172).

G74   "Opera House For Harlem?" *Opera* (England) 19 (February 1968): 96.
Menotti is working with civic, business, and entertainment leaders on plans to build a 1,000-seat opera house as part of a redevelopment project for the community. The company would stress contemporary opera.

G75   "Spoleto: Menotti Hands Over." *Opera* (England) 19 (May 1968): 402.
Menotti relinquishes artistic direction of the Festival of Two Worlds to Massimo Bogianckino, until recently director of the Rome Opera. Menotti remains the festival's president.

G76   "Homeless Opera." *Times* (London), (June 7, 1968): 8.
Menotti: "I feel that contemporary opera is homeless . . . The size and the atmosphere of old opera houses isn't right for contemporary opera. I feel very strongly that there is a whole new audience that is never reached. Opera houses are very inhibiting places for the young."

G77   "Festival musicali in Italia." *Nuova rivista musicale italiana* 2 (July-August 1968): 710-724.
Luciano Berio, Duilio Courir, Gioacchino Lanza Tomasi, and Menotti describe the organizing of music festivals. In particular, discusses the Festival dei Due Mondi, the Festival di Venezia, and the Maggio Musicale Fiorentino.

G78   Killingsworth, Kay. "Menotti Not a 'Message' Boy; Spoleto Wants No Angle-Stuff." *Variety* 251 (July 24, 1968): 27-28.
Says Menotti, "I gave up the artistic direction [of the Festival of Two Worlds] . . . because it was too much for me to handle. But I will certainly continue my activities as president, and I have a number of projects for next year."

G79  Wimbush, Roger. "Thomas Schippers." *Gramophone* 46 (August 1968): 242.

Describes recent activities of the conductor, who said, "Whatever may be said of Menotti, he has the theatre in his blood and it is a tragedy that he has not written a note for four years . . . Our time makes it difficult to cross bridges, and a composer is not easily forgiven a commercial success."

G80  Goléa, Antoine. ". . . et 'Tristan' a Spolete." *Journal musical français*, 174 (November 1968): 18-20.

G81  Rizzo, Eugene. "And We Quote . . ." *High Fidelity/Musical America* 18 (December 1968): MA11.

"More than anything, it is Menotti's theatrical genius — his ability to touch his audiences directly — that has helped put life back into modern opera. Even Stravinsky, who has publicly scorned the younger composer's music and is anything but a close friend, personally asked him to direct a recent revival of *The Rake's Progress.*"

G82  Taubman, Howard. "Roving Troupe in West Adds a Flair to Opera." *New York Times*, (March 1, 1969): 20.

Article on the Western Opera Theater, a branch of the San Francisco Opera. In its first season, it gave a double bill of 'The Old Maid and the Thief' and 'The Medium' in Sacramento (January 1967). "It goes into the ghettos and it plays for labor union audiences. To reach those new audiences it emphasizes credible acting as well as a tightly knit singing ensemble."

G83  Menotti, Gian Carlo. "Point of Contact." *Opera News* 34 (December 27, 1969-January 3, 1970): 8-11.

Says Menotti of opera: "Composers will go on experimenting with its form, and in time they may alter it beyond our wildest imaginings. But in its inmost nature . . . opera will live wherever it can make a proper home . . . theater cannot flourish in museums."

G84  Soria, Dorle J. "This Is What They Said." *High Fidelity/Musical America* 20 (March 1970): 7.

Referring to the role of children in his operas, Menotti says, ". . . I do hope that the new generation will allow me to play with them. There is nothing sadder than a neglected child."

G85  Menotti, Gian Carlo and Leonardo Pinzauti. "A Colloquio con Giancarlo Menotti." *Nuova rivista musicale italiana* 4 (July-August 1970): 712-720.

30  *General References*

>
> Menotti speaks of himself, his music, and the music of his contemporaries, with special reference to Puccini and Schönberg.

G86  Berger, Melvin. *Masters of Modern Music.* New York: Lothrop, 1971.
Collective biography of 14 contemporary composers. Gershwin, Richard Rodgers, and Menotti are discussed under the heading "Music for the many."

G87  Menotti, Gian Carlo. "And Where Do You Run at 60?" *New York Times*, 2 (July 18, 1971): 13.
Menotti remarks on some of his career's disillusionment and bitterness, both of which are "apt to poison one's heart and sour one's smile."

G88  Adam, Klaus. "Gesprächt mit Gian Carlo Menotti." *Oper und Konzert* 10, 3 (1972): 21.

G89  Kanski, J. "Gian Carlo Menotti w Warszawie." *Ruch muzyczny* 16, 4 (1972): 6-7.

G90  Soria, Dorle J. "Scene, Seen and Heard." *High Fidelity/Musical America* 22 (February 1972): MA8.
Menotti, ". . .according to Lincoln Center buzz-buzz, had been slated to take over the Juilliard Opera Theatre, a project which seems stillborn."

G91  Ericson, Raymond. "One World Is More than Two." *New York Times*, 2 (February 13, 1972): 15.
Points up the international character of the Festival of Two Worlds. What started out as an Italian-American project now draws artists from all over Europe, Africa, and the Near and Far East.

G92  Hess, John L. "In Spoleto, a Quake Is a Welcome Diversion." *New York Times*, (March 11, 1972): 10.
Says the manager of one of Spoleto's new hotels: "We owe everything to Gian Carlo Menotti . . . Before, we were just another pretty hill town on the Umbrian circuit. Now people know about Spoleto."

G93  Rogers, Harold. "Spoleto! Rock to Ballet at the Festival of Two Worlds." *Christian Science Monitor*, (July 30, 1973): 12.
Interview with Menotti at the end of the 16$^{th}$ Festival of Two Worlds. "Menotti said that if he were to be born again, he would have nothing to do with Spoleto, 'and I would guard myself against enthusiasm . . . It is my

over-enthusiasm that has ruined me with so many people, critics included.'"

G94     Snyder, Louis. "Noted Composer Plans 'A Great Change' Amid Global Activity." *Christian Science Monitor*, (September 5, 1973): 14.
Interview in which Menotti talks generally about his then-35-year career. "In a man's life, there's always a time for a great change . . . Now the realization has finally come to me: I've been writing too quickly, doing too much, taking on more than I can handle . . . There's a saying of Blake that may have influenced me: 'The road to excess leads to the mansion of wisdom' . . . I hope it will prove true in my case."

G95     Martynov, Ivan. *Prograssivnye tendencii vsovremennoj Žarubeznoj opere.* Moskva: Sovetskij Kompozitor, 1974.
Discusses the evolution of twentieth-century opera against its historical background. Classifies material from each period (1900-17, 1917-45, after 1945) and explores the principal tendencies of operatic composition. Among many others, Menotti is considered.

G96     Fryer, Judith Anne. "Realism: a Major Factor for Menotti's Operatic Style." *Opera Journal* 7, 1 (1974): 10-17.
"This article purposely does not go into the aesthetic nature of Menotti's music . . . By dwelling on realism, the effort is to show how closely akin his music and staging reality really are. With all truths told, it is the stage director who should be listening. Only he can keep alive this aspect of Menotti's style, preserving the music-drama parallels, and insisting upon credible acting."

G97     Grieb, Lyndal. *Operas of Gian Carlo Menotti, 1937-1972: A Selective Bibliography.* Metuchen, NJ: Scarecrow Press, 1974.
References to significant periodical literature, reviews, analyses, and commentaries. Most entries are annotated and include data on performances, productions, and illustrations. *For reviews, see G105, G106, and G108.*

G98     Gruen, John. "'When the New York Critics Damn You . . .'" *New York Times*, 2 (April 14, 1974): 1.
Interview with Menotti regarding recent critical notices. " . . . reviewers have relentlessly, often savagely, relegated Menotti's output to a netherworld of music . . . It is principally for this reason that the composer has now decided to leave America and make his home in Europe."

32   *General References*

G99   Diamonstein, Barbara Lee. "Menotti's Worlds." *Art News* 73 (May 1974): 88-89.
Says Menotti, "I love painters and sculptors so much more than musicians . . . I get along better with artists. With musicians, at least. They are too much limited to their own little group. Painters seem to be much more generous, human and interesting."

G100   Byrne, Kevin. "Spoleto." *Music and Musicians* 22 (June 1974): 6-7.
Says Menotti, "I think what interests me in a piece of music is to see reflected . . . the real identity of the composer, his real feeling, what actually he *is*, and not what he is capable of doing or which way he is capable of startling me."

G101   Cunningham, Eloise. "News From Japan." *Opera News* 38 (June 1974): 10.
In February 1974, Menotti directed *The Consul, The Telephone*, and *The Medium* during the Sixth Annual Opera Festival for the Citizens of Tokyo, as part of the Tokyo Opera Festival. The operas were presented by the Fujiwara Opera Institute, the oldest opera company in Japan.

G102   Kolodin, Irving. "Farewell to Capricorn." *Saturday Review/World* 1 (June 1, 1974): 44-45.
"The latest home that has had its day and gone the inevitable way has long been known to the musical community as Capricorn . . . Within an hour's drive of New York but isolated from distraction . . . It was, until a recent sale, the home of Samuel Barber and Gian-Carlo Menotti."

G103   Beckwith, Nina. "Spoleto Peaks, Menotti Piques; Founder Lost in Umbria Haze." *Variety* 275 (July 10, 1974): 51-52.
Rumor has it that Menotti may withdraw from the Spoleto Festival of Two Worlds. "Spoleto gets funds from Communist-dominated Umbria Region, but this year the Left press has been trumpeting about 'renewal and restructuring' of the festival, 'not liquidating it, but relaunching it in profoundly altered terms,' . . . Which is not cheering to old timers."

G104   Ericson, Raymond. "Bounty of Opera for the Bicentennial." *New York Times*, 2 (November 17, 1974): 21.
Menotti is preparing work for four organizations: the Hawaii Opera Theater (Honolulu), the Philadelphia Lyric Opera, the Washington (D.C.) Cathedral, and the Birmingham (Ala.) Civic Opera. He is even considering a Japanese opera for Tokyo.

*General References* 33

G105   Mercer, Ruby. "*The Operas of Gian-Carlo Menotti, 1937-1972: A Selective Bibliography*, by Lyndal Grieb." *Opera Canada* 16, 1 (1975): 48.
Very brief descriptive review of Grieb's bibliography (G97). A ". . . working reference book . . ."

G106   Zijlstra, Miep. "*Operas of Gian-Carlo Menotti, 1937-1972: A Selective Bibliography*." *Mens en melodie* 30 (June 1975): 189.
Review of Grieb's bibliography (G97). In Dutch.

G107   Beckwith, Nina. "Spoleto Ends; Good Year; but Whither Now Menotti? (Festival of Two Worlds)." *Variety* 279 (July 23, 1975): 35-36.
Menotti has been offered the post of artistic director for next season at La Fenice Opera House in Venice, causing speculation about his continued involvement in Spoleto. "Worry in Spoleto was that festival level and personal touch would suffer from the demands on Menotti's time and energies."

G108   Rohrbaugh, Anne. "*The Operas of Gian Carlo Menotti, 1937-1972: A Selective Bibliography*." *ARBA [American Reference Books Annual]* 7 (1976): 482.
Review of Grieb's bibliography (G97). "It should prove a valuable tool for students, researchers, opera workshop directors and general readers in search of details about Menotti that would otherwise remain obscured."

G109   Ericson, Raymond. "Charleston, S.C., Will be Spoleto, U.S.A." *New York Times*, (March 25, 1976): 42.
Charleston chosen as a site for the annual Festival of Two Worlds, the first season to run from May 25-June 5, 1977. Menotti saw Charleston as "a place of exceptional beauty, where creative and performing artists could function as members of the community during the festival."

G110   Gelatt, Roland. "Spoleto in Charleston." *Saturday Review* 3 (May 1, 1976): 40.
Notice that Spoleto's Festival of Two Worlds, begun in 1958, will launch an American counterpoint in Charleston, May 25-June 5, 1977.

G111   Fleming, Shirley. "Notes: A Summer of Premieres for Menotti." *New York Times*, sect. 2 (May 9, 1976): 17.
Between May and August, 1976, four Menotti works will receive their premieres: *Landscapes and remembrances* (May 18), *The Hero* (June 1), *The Egg* (June 17), and *First Symphony* (August 4). See also *New York Times*, May 30, 1976, sect. 2, p. 13, for a short addendum to this article.

## 34  General References

G112   Wolz, Larry. "Gian Carlo Menotti: Words Without Music." *Opera Journal* 10, 3 (1977): 8-14.
Discusses Menotti's views on opera and composition in general. Includes list of works with dates of composition and a selected list of articles by Menotti.

G113   Gruen, John. "Menotti's Two Worlds." *Opera News* 41 (May 1977): 12-17.
"With the inception of Spoleto U.S.A., America will at last be privy to Menotti's sense of adventure, coming under the spell of an imagination that for twenty years has given the international festival scene an entirely new vision of what creative excitement is all about."

G114   Glueck, Grace. "Spoleto U.S.A." *New York Times*, 6 (May 22, 1977): 20.
Preview of the opening of Spoleto U.S.A. Charleston fits Menotti's original prescription for the Spoleto Festival, which was " . . .to create in a small community an artistic climate which would become essential to the welfare of the town itself . . . to give the artist the dignity of feeling not only welcome, but needed."

G115   Gruen, John. "Menotti's Adventures in the Dance World." *New York Times*, 2 (July 17, 1977): 10.
Says Menotti, "many are the dance works that I have *almost* written . . . At any rate, if *my* ballets don't get written, there are plenty of others which do, and chances are that most of them will sooner or later see the light at either of my two Spoleto festivals!"

G116   Gruen, John. *Menotti: A Biography.* New York: Macmillan, 1978.
For reviews, see *G119, G120, G121, G122,* and *G123.*

G117   Ericson, Raymond. "National Opera Institute Awards Mark Medium's Growth in U.S." *New York Times*, (January 10, 1978): 27.
The National Opera Institute held its first Annual Awards Evening on January 8, 1978, at the Manhattan School of Music, and gave five citations for outstanding service to American opera. Menotti was given the International Contribution Award as founder of the Festival of Two Worlds in Spoleto and the Spoleto Festival U.S.A. in Charleston, as well as for his many successful operas.

G118   Soria, Dorle J. "Artist Life (Central Opera Service Conference in Houston)." *High Fidelity/Musical America* 28 (February 1978): MA5.

In October 1977, the Central Opera Service held its fifteenth conference in Houston, with the theme "Opera, the American Scene: 1977." On the final day, Menotti gave a luncheon address, discussing the role of opera on television. Said Menotti, "I prefer the world of the theater, of flesh and blood . . . [but] Opera can and *must* be televised but it will always be a compromise unless a new kind of opera is written for it."

G119   Honig, Joel. "*Menotti: A Biography* [review]." *Opera News* 42 (June 1978): 10.
Review of Gruen's biography (G116) "Gruen's kaleidoscopic interview will no doubt preempt the literature on Menotti. Nevertheless a truly informal study of his art would be welcome. The biography of this man of two worlds remains to be written."

G120   Yohalem, John. "Successful Heretic." *New York Times*, 7 (June 18, 1978): 15.
Review of Gruen's biography (G116) ". . . Mr. Gruen's emphasis is entirely on the social side and slights many important questions. Not only does he neglect the music in discussing the man, he does not even provide a page listing the works and their dates or a discography."

G121   Smith, Patrick J. "*Menotti*, by John Gruen." *High Fidelity/Musical America* 28 (July 1978): MA39-40.
Review of Gruen's biography (G116) ". . . if Gruen does not finally eliminate the veils that surround the man he does indicate the range of his services to all the arts."

G122   Wechsler, Bert. "*Menotti*, by John Gruen." *Music Journal* 36 (October 1978): 24.
Review of Gruen's biography (G116) ". . . he writes as if he is continuously in fear of the personality of Menotti and wants desperately to be liked by him. This is understandable but not fulfilling."

G123   "Menotti: Still an Enigma." *Variety* 293 (November 29, 1978): 107.
Review of Gruen's biography (G116) "Gruen concludes the bio with the uplift message that Menotti 'is among our major twentieth century composers . . . has given the world yet one more reason for whatever claim it may have for survival and dignity,' but something sad and unspoken underlies the whole thing."

G124   Mueller, L. and Imre Fabian. "Wir muessen eine allgemein verstaendliche Sprache sprechen." *Opernwelt*, Yearbook (1980): 96-97.

*36 General References*

G125    Pfeifer, Ellen. "Old Favorite 'Amahl' Will Warm Your Heart." *Herald American* (Boston), (December 22, 1980)
Menotti's music "derives from the lump-in-your-throat, heart-warming school of music theater. And it is utterly blatant and shameless in the way it manipulates the audience's emotions."

G126    Gruen, John. *Gian Carlo Menotti*. Traduzione di Franco Salvatorelli. Torino: ERI Edizioni Rai, 1981.
Italian translation of Gruen's biography (G116)

G127    Sokol, Martin L. *The New York City Opera: An American Adventure*. New York: Macmillan, 1981.
Day-by-day annals of the New York City Opera, with complete cast listings, as well as numerous general references to Menotti and his operas.

G128    "Names, Dates and Places." *Opera News* 45 (March 14, 1981): 4.
"In addition to approximately 35 percent of his $1 million estate, the late Samuel Barber left fellow composer Gian Carlo Menotti his books, tapes, memorabilia and the lifetime use of his home in Santa Cristina, Italy."

G129    Williams, Barbara S. "Spoleto's Fifth Season: Double Celebration." *News and Courier* (Charleston, SC), (May 17, 1981)
"Note undoubtedly will be taken of Menotti's [70th] birthday throughout the festival from an opening fanfare commissioned in his honor by Piccolo Spoleto and performed by the Brass Quintet to a private party at Seabrook."

G130    Ardoin, John. "Menotti At a Milestone." *Dallas Morning News*, (May 24, 1981)
"It has been said that survival in the arts is everything, and certainly Menotti has survived brilliantly. Neither artistic failure, critical blows or personal disappointments seem to have been able to strike him down, or dull his curiosity and his amazing youthfulness."

G131    "Festival Holds Menotti in its Magic Spell." *Charlotte Observer* (Charlotte, NC), (May 24, 1981)
Remarks made during the 1981 Spoleto Festival U.S.A. Menotti's son, Chip, "wants me to give up all this festival business and be like the Last Savage — find a comfortable cave and get to the work of composing. But what I started as an experiment here is a cage from which I don't think I'll escape alive. The experiment is the life. The cave is the dream."

General References   37

G132  Ardoin, John. "A Welcome Gift." *Opera News* 45 (June 1981): 9-11+.
"To know him is to care deeply about him, to be frustrated and even irritated by him, to be swept up in his dreams and his basic goodness. It is also to know he never asks of others what he does not demand of himself, time and again. Happy [70$^{th}$] birthday, Gian Carlo!"

G133  McDowell, Elsa F. "Piccolo Spoleto Needs a Name Change — Menotti." *News and Courier* (Charleston, SC), (June 4, 1981)
During an interview, Menotti says he welcomes Piccolo Spoleto and encourages Charleston to go ahead with it. He adds, however, that it is important to distinguish between it and the Spoleto Festival. "We make enough mistakes on our own . . . It worries me that we're blamed for Piccolo Spoleto's mistakes, too."

G134  Krebs, Albin and Robert McG. Thomas. "Notes on People: Belated Birthday Award." *New York Times*, 3 (September 9, 1981): 24.
Menotti receives 70$^{th}$ birthday award from Mayor Koch at New York's City Hall.

G135  Terry, Walter. "Menotti on Dance." *Saturday Review* 9 (April 1982): 53.
" . . . with his first exposure to dance in America, Menotti began a major phase of his career that witnessed his fostering of dance both as a composer — collaborating with such dance greats as Antony Tudor and Martha Graham — and as an impresario."

G136  Bridges, John. "Menotti's Spoleto Festival City's Salvation." *Tennesseean* (Nashville), (June 6, 1982)
"Where once there was an occasional carriage tour of idiosyncratic architecture, there is now, according to the Charleston Chamber of Commerce, a $40 million economic impact."

G137  Lane, John Francis. "Spoleto Looks Back Fondly at Quarter-Century Mark." *Variety* 307 (July 28, 1982): 66.
"Menotti has succeeded in making the Spoleto Festival in its original Italian home one of the major cultural events, not only of the Italian summer season but also on the international circuit."

G138  Finn, Robert. "Menotti's Work Speaks Louder than His Critics." *Plain Dealer* (Cleveland), (January 2, 1983)
Interview in Cleveland as Menotti was staging the Cleveland Opera Theater's production of *Amahl and the Night Visitors*. "What I find so distasteful in criticism is the way critics talk about music as 'progressive.'

## 38  General References

There is 'progress,' they say, and you are 'antiquated,' as if art were an industry that always has to be bigger and better. They forget that beauty is an absolute."

G139 Apone, Carl. "Menotti Mixes Music, Humor, Philosophy." *Pittsburgh Press*, (April 5, 1984)
During a lecture given the previous night, Menotti complained that "audiences are terribly polite. They applaud everything. People are afraid to say what they feel about music. Be honest. Go nakedly . . . rather than with preconceived ideas."

G140 Molotsky, Irvin. "Five Receive Kennedy Center Honors For 1984." *New York Times*, 3 (December 3, 1984): 15.
Lena Horne, Arthur Miller, Menotti, Isaac Stern, and Danny Kaye were honored at a reception by President and Nancy Reagan at a White House ceremony. Of Menotti, President Reagan said: "You have always kept your Italian citizenship, but you have spent so much time among us that you should allow us to claim you as an honorary American."

G141 Ardoin, John. *The Stages of Menotti*. Garden City, NY: Doubleday, 1985.
Divides works into 1) early stage, 2) Broadway stage, 3) dance stage, 4) concert stage, 5) television stage, 6) church stage, 7) children's stage, 8) spoken stage, and 9) late stage. *For reviews, see G143, G144, and G145; see also G157.*

G142 Jarrell, Frank P. "Menotti Talks of Audiences, Art for Art's Sake and . . . Jazz." *News and Courier* (Charleston, SC), (May 29, 1985)
Interview at a meeting of the Spoleto Festival U.S.A.'s Board of Directors. Ozey Horton, of McKinsey and Company, an Atlanta-based consulting firm, discussed several options for strengthening the Festival's financial position, including positioning, promotion, and programming. Horton noted that "The festival is now at a crossroads . . . because it is maturing, doesn't have stable financial footing (including a potential for diminished government support) and is facing competition from other arts festivals."

G143 Jones, Robert. "The Gian Carlo Menotti Bible." *News and Courier* (Charleston, SC), (June 30, 1985)
Review of Ardoin's *The Stages of Menotti* (G141) "Lavish, well-reproduced photos add to the value of a very handsome volume. I can hardly see how any opera library could do without it."

G144  Ardoin, John. "Book Corner." *Central Opera Service Bulletin* 26 (Winter 1985-1986): 66.
Brief review of Ardoin's *The Stages of Menotti* (G141) "This lovingly-written tribute is a pastiche of biography, interviews, opera synopses, performance history, photographs and sketches the total effect of which adds up to a comprehensive overview of Menotti's career."

G145  Martin, George. "*Stages of Menotti.*" *Opera Quarterly* 3 (Winter 1985-1986): 135-140.
Review of Ardoin's *The Stages of Menotti* (G141) "It does not even provide a balanced account of Menotti's career. But as a souvenir album of the works, it is likely as fine as we will see."

G146  Stefanovic, Pavle. "Um za tonom." *Muzika*. Beograd: Nolit, 1986.
Collection of essays written between 1950 and 1979, one of which deals with Menotti.

G147  Brownlow, Art. "Menotti and the Critics." *Opera Journal* 19, 1 (1986): 2-15.
" . . . a composer past middle age who suddenly takes on such enormous responsibilities as the Spoleto Festival, would understandably have problems maintaining either the quantity or the quality of his creative output."

G148  Robertson, Nan. "Artists in Old Age: the Fires of Creativity Burn Undiminished." *New York Times*, 3 (January 22, 1986): 1.
"'I loathe my body,' said Gian Carlo Menotti, 74 . . . 'The liver spots, the sagging flesh.' He finds himself more vulnerable, weeping in public at the sight of children, or when memory overcomes him. It embarrasses him, he said."

G149  Montsalvatge, X. "La nueva actualidad de Giancarlo Menotti." *Monsalvat* 137 (April 1986): 12-13.

G150  Khadzhimishev, M. "Za Dzhankarlo Menoti." *Bulgarska Muzika* 37, 9 (1986): 65-66.

G151  "Musiker zweier Welten: Gian Carlo Menotti wird 75." *Orchester* 34 (October 1986): 1093.
General article on Menotti on his 75th birthday.

G152    Trucco, Terry. "In Scotland, a Composer's 85-room Retreat." *New York Times*, 3 (October 2, 1986): 1.
Discussion of Menotti's new home, called Yester, located 18 miles east of Edinburgh, with construction having begun in 1699. "This is a wonderful place to work . . . I'm an optimist. I always expect the best. But this time it's worked that way."

G153    Jalon, Allan. "Menotti Sees Ambivalence in Criticism." *Los Angeles Times*, Calendar (March 27, 1987): 1.
Interview held in Costa Mesa, California. "I wish I'd never started operas . . . It has taken so much time away from my composing . . . I have wasted so much of my time directing other people's work."

G154    Fratani, A. "Menoti rezhisira Vagner." *Bulgarska Muzika* 38, 8 (1987): 65-66.

G155    "Menotti to be Honored in November." *Times-Picayune* (New Orleans), (September 26, 1988)
Menotti, " . . . one of the most popular opera composers of the century, will be honored by a 'Menotti Festival' here in November, instigated and designed by University of New Orleans faculty member Raquel Cortina."

G156    Gagnard, Frank. "Minifest For Menotti." *Times-Picayune* (New Orleans), (October 30, 1988)
Announcement of the upcoming Menotti festival at the University of New Orleans. "What a chance to be able to see, meet and hear a composer of this caliber! . . . And he's coming to town for all to see and hear."

G157    Ardoin, John. "Gian Carlo Menotti: Dialogue V." *Opera Quarterly* 6 (Spring 1989): 39-47.
Explains Ardoin, "My book *The Stages of Menotti* [G141] . . . included four dialogues with the composer that dealt with his craft and career. In the process of collecting the material for these, many other subjects were discussed . . . These form the basis for this fifth and largely biographical dialogue."

G158    Jarrell, Frank P. "Gian Carlo Menotti." *News and Courier* (Charleston, SC), (June 3, 1989)
Menotti: "I'd like to learn more. You know, people often ask me to teach. Well, I have too little time left to teach . . . I'd rather learn. It's much more exciting."

G159  Menotti, Gian Carlo. "I Forgive Goethe, Tolstoy and, Above All, Mozart." *New York Times*, sect. 1 (June 10, 1989): 27.
"No great composer will again appear among us until the young are taught that being a genius is not enough."

G160  Baxter, Robert. "Menotti Busy as Ever at 78." *Courier-Post* (Camden-Cherry Hill, NJ), (November 19, 1989)
Menotti: "If I had $1 million I could build a small theater at my home in Scotland. There I could create a theater school and work with talented youngsters from around the world. Until then, I must keep working here and there."

G161  Webster, Daniel. "Menotti Brings His Favorite Opera Here." *Philadelphia Inquirer*, (November 20, 1989)
Says Menotti: "A composer should really be dead. Operatic producers really don't want the composer around. We are a liability . . . You would think the composer might be a resource. After I'm dead, I will be a resource."

G162  "Loose Opera-Talk." *Spectator* 265 (July 21, 1990): 40-41.
At a recent dinner conversation, Menotti noted how money can influence an artist. He was forced to write an opera for the Shah because he needed the money.

G163  Kozinn, Allan. "Menotti and Spoleto Split on Issue of Artistic Control." *New York Times*, (October 15, 1990): C14.
Menotti quits Spoleto Festival U.S.A., " . . . but would return if its board gave him unchallenged artistic control."

G164  Jarrell, Frank P. "Menotti, Spoleto Boards Reach Tentative Agreement." *News and Courier* (Charleston, SC), (October 17, 1990)
"Ross Markwardt, chairman of the festival's board, said . . . that an agreement in principle has been reached that will assure Menotti's involvement for the rest of his life. The exact nature of that involvement, however, has not been defined."

G165  Chacon, Victor. "'Verismo' in the Works of Gian Carlo Menotti: A Comparison with Late Nineteenth Century Italian Opera." D.M.A. dissertation, University of Washington, 1991.
Discusses *The Medium, The Consul*, and *The Saint of Bleecker Street* in relation to a continuation of the *verismo* strain observed in certain

42   General References

late-nineteenth-century operas, especially *Cavalleria rusticana* and *Pagliacci*.

G166   *Gian Carlo Menotti*. New York: G. Schirmer, 1991.
Includes list of works, p. 24-34.

G167   Kornick, Rebecca Hodell. *Recent American Opera: A Production Guide*. New York: Columbia University Press, 1991.
Considers *The Egg, Goya, The Hero, Juana, La Loca,* and *Tamu-Tamu*. For each, there is a plot summary, selected reviews, and production requirements (characters, voice types, extremes of range), and publisher information in order to obtain full scores and orchestral parts.

G168   Gibbons, Andrew. "In the Eye of the Storm." *Sunday Times* (London), Magazine (April 7, 1991): 9.
Article on Menotti's adopted son, Francis, known as Chip, who says, "I often ask myself, 'Why do I put up with all this?' and come to the conclusion that it's because my father has enabled me to leave a grey and senseless world and enter a world of music, magic and unending beauty."

G169   Page, Tim. "Menotti at Twilight." *Los Angeles Times*, Calendar (May 19, 1991): 6.
Say Menotti, "Great art must have what I call an inevitability . . . I am a neo-Platonist, I suppose. I believe there is a Platonic ideal of beauty, and artists are given a fleeting vision of that beauty."

G170   Menotti, Gian Carlo. "Maestro Lists a Few of His Least Favorite Things." *New York Times*, 2 (May 26, 1991): 21.
"No to those insufferable amateurs who, to quote Samuel Barber, 'approach art without humility.' . . . Yes to those creators who believe in the inevitability of great art — who search for truth rather than novelty — and believe in the Platonic existence of Beauty as an ideal."

G171   Jarrell, Frank P. "Festival's Founder Says He'll Stay If 3 Others Go." *News and Courier* (Charleston, SC), (May 28, 1991)
"After a tense and emotional meeting of the Spoleto Festival U.S.A. board of directors . . . Menotti issued an ultimatum that the general manager [Nigel Redden], board chairman [Ross A. Markwardt], and board president [Edgar F. Daniels] leave if Menotti is to continue with the festival."

G172   Kozinn, Allan. "Menotti Gives Spoleto Festival an Ultimatum: They Go or I Go." *New York Times*, C (May 30, 1991): 13.

Menotti threatens to leave unless Nigel Redden, Ross A. Markwardt, and Edgar F. Daniels resign. "'No change of leadership is going to occur for or during the rest of the festival,' Mayor Riley said. 'I see this as a family argument, something we will work out when the festival is over.'"

G173  Smith, Helen C. "The Sound and Fury Upstaging the Arts." *Journal* (Atlanta), (May 30, 1991)
Menotti has demanded removal of Nigel Redden (general manager), Ross Markwardt (Board Chairman), and Edgar Daniels (Board President). Says Markwardt: "People from different backgrounds need time to become accustomed to each other, and we didn't have that time before an adversarial situation set in."

G174  Jarrell, Frank P. "Concert a Gift for Menotti." *News and Courier* (Charleston, SC), (May 31, 1991)
Preview of the Menotti's 80th birthday celebration. "Since Menotti will be in Italy for the Two Worlds Festival in July, Sunday's concert is a continuation of Charleston's own celebration." Note: performed were the *Fantasia For Cello and Orchestra* and *Sebastian Suite*.

G175  "Geburtstag eines Unzeitgemaessen." *Buehne* (Summer 1991): 9-10.

G176  Honig, Joel. "The Menotti Theorem." *Opera News* 55 (June 1991): 12-15+.
Menotti's current compositional interests and literary projects, with career highlights. "Though disparaged as old-fashioned, his music is still very much of the here and now. 'They have to say I'm a contemporary composer,' he [Menotti] told members of the National Arts Club earlier this year, in accepting their annual gold Medal of Honor for Music. 'I'm still alive.'"

G177  Holland, Bernard. "Spoleto: Family Feud or Haute Finance? (or a Bit of Both?)." *New York Times*, C (June 4, 1991): 11.
"Two separate press offices — one Menottian, the other management-run — have been furiously bending the ears of the national press with their respective viewpoints."

G178  Brown, Steven. "At 80, a Weary Menotti Talks of Slowing Tempo." *Orlando Sentinel* (Orlando, FL), (June 9, 1991)
Menotti: "I could easily go 10 years without doing a note. It becomes too painful when you begin to become aware of your faults, and when your aims are getting higher and higher. It becomes more and more difficult to compose."

G179    Kennicott, Philip. "Martha and Music." *Dance Magazine* 65 (July 1991): 66.
"Naturally, Menotti greatly respects the artistic result of [Martha] Graham's musical imperialism, but there is a hint of irony concerning the self-indulgence that implied."

G180    Rorem, Ned. "In Search of American Opera." *Opera News* 56 (July 1991): 8.
"Thanks solely to the example of Menotti's success in the 1940s, dozens of operas spouted forth from other composers hoping to hit the jackpot. The effort persists after five decades, and it's safe to state that Menotti, whatever his own final worth, violently altered the nature of lyric theater here, and by extension, throughout the globe."

G181    Honan, William H. "Manager of Spoleto Will Quit in Dispute." *New York Times*, C (August 13, 1991): 13.
General manager of the Spoleto Festival U.S.A., who has been engaged in a dispute for the last year with Menotti, announced that Menotti would resign at the end of the season on September 30.

G182    Felten, Eric. "Spoleto Festival's Feuding Leaders Take Center Stage in Charleston." *Insight/Washington Times* (Washington, DC), (August 19, 1991)
"The fight ostensibly is over an art exhibit he [Menotti] loathes . . . The maestro may be trying to turn the reins over to his adopted son, an idea the board abhors."

G183    Roos, James. "Menotti: Opera's Symbol of Youth." *Miami Herald*, (September 15, 1991)
Interview prior to the opening of the September 21 1991 Miami performance of *The Saint of Bleecker Street*. Menotti: "I think one has to be true to himself . . . I don't believe an old man can suddenly change. The only way you can be original is to be unashamedly yourself."

G184    Kozinn, Allan. "Spoleto Festival Resolves its Dispute: Menotti Is Winner." *New York Times*, C (September 17, 1991): 11.
Menotti won his 17-month battle with the festival's board. "At a tense and sometimes fractious three-and-a-half-hour board meeting yesterday . . . 10 of the board's 46 members resigned, and 9 others either decided not to stand for re-election or were not nominated."

G185    Jarrell, Frank P. "Menotti Recovering from Fatigue in Clinic." *News and Courier* (Charleston, SC), (September 18, 1991)
Giancarla Berti, the Spoleto Festival U.S.A.'s new president, was told Menotti "was doing very well and just needs rest. Everyone, it seems, needs to be very protective of him because Gian Carlo just wants to jump out of bed and get back to work."

G186    Barnes, J. "Menotti: The Rural Pen Outmoded." *Royal College of Music Magazine* 89, 1 (1992): 29-31.

G187    Fogel, Henry. "Menotti, Gian Carlo" In *Contemporary Composers*. Editors, Brian Morton, Pamela Collins. Chicago: St. James Press, 1992.

G188    "Opera Diary: Events." *Opera Canada* 33, 1 (1992): 8.
Menotti reasserted control of the Spoleto Festival U.S.A. In November 1991, he announced the selection of some 20 new board members — "Menotti supporters all."

G189    "World Music News (Musical America's 1991 Musician of the Year)." *Music Clubs Magazine* 72, 2 (1992): 24.

G190    McDowell, Elsa F. "New Spoleto Director Says Menotti Is Boss." *News and Courier* (Charleston, SC), (January 16, 1992)
"Marcus L. Overton says his role as executive director of Spoleto Festival U.S.A. will be to facilitate Gian Carlo Menotti's artistic vision . . . only Menotti is artistic director of the Spoleto festival."

G191    McLellan, Joseph. "Smithsonian Official to Lead Spoleto; Marcus Overton Joins Menotti Arts Festival." *Washington Post*, C (January 16, 1992): 1. Theodore S. Stern, chairman of the festival board, announced the appointment of Marcus L. Overton, Director of Performing Arts at the Smithsonian Institution since 1983, as Executive Director of Spoleto Festival U.S.A., ending a year-long dispute over the festival's management.

G192    Kozinn, Allan. "Calm After the Storm at Spoleto?" *New York Times*, H (May 17, 1992): 1.
Power struggle between Menotti and Nigel Redden over control of Spoleto Festival U.S.A. in Charleston.

G193  Brozan, Nadine. "Chronicle." *New York Times*, B (October 28, 1992): 5.
Menotti is named artistic director of the Rome Opera. "This has been very surprising . . . I don't know if I'll be alive in six years, so we made it for three years and then can renew it automatically for three more years."

G194  "Appointments." *Opera* (England) 44 (February 1993): 157.
Notice that Menotti was appointed the new Artistic Director of the Teatro dell'Opera, Rome.

G195  "Menotti's Opera House in the Stables." *World Monitor* 6, 3 (March 1993): 8.
Discusses how Menotti is planning to convert a 19th-century stable block into a $14.2 million opera house on his 18-acre estate outside of Edinburgh.

G196  Keller, James M. "*Samuel Barber: The Composer and His Music* (Oxford Univ. Press, 586 p.)." *Opera News* 57 (June 1993): 52.
Review of Barbara B. Heyman's biography of Samuel Barber. "There is plenty of precedent for ignoring homosexuality in composer biographies. John Ardoin's *The Stages of Menotti* [G141] avoids it entirely until the very end, where Menotti states in an interview that he wants to be buried next to Barber."

G197  Fix, Sybil. "Menotti Wants to Keep Legacy in the Family." *Post and Courier* (Charleston, SC), (July 25, 1993)
"Chip Menotti, Menotti's adopted son, has his father's blessing to succeed him as Spoleto Festival U.S.A. director. Not everyone agrees with his choice . . . If it's not going to be Chip, it needs to be clearly defined and slated now because you can't have the threat of a close-down over a disagreement."

G198  Kozinn, Allan. "Menotti Leaves Spoleto U.S.A." *New York Times*, C (October 26, 1993): 15.
"We have an ideal setting. And we know how to do it. I'm saddened that we are going to continue without Maestro Menotti, but we are going to continue."

G199  Weinraub, Judith. "Spoleto Won't Replace Menotti." *Washington Post*, D (November 6, 1993): 2.
The Board of Spoleto Festival U.S.A. decided not to replace Menotti upon his departure as artistic director. Instead, it named Spiros Argiris as director and principal conductor of symphonic and operatic activities,

while retaining Wadsworth and Joseph Flummerfelt as director of chamber and choral music.

G200    "Manager is Named by Spoleto Festival." *New York Times*, (November 13, 1993): 16.
Milton Rhodes, director of the American Council for the Arts in New York City, appointed director of Spoleto Festival U.S.A., replacing Menotti.

G201    "Menotti Cuts Charleston Ties." *Opera* (England) 44 (December 1993): 1399-1400.
Report that Menotti has severed links with the Spoleto Festival U.S.A. board and management. "Disputes which have occurred over the past few years have been resolved, but now reconciliation seems unlikely."

G202    Redmond, Michael. "Spoletto [sic] Changes the Top Guard after Menotti's Departure." *Star-Ledger* (Newark, NJ), (February 6, 1994)
"With founder Gian Carlo Menotti's having departed, Spoleto's supporters are hopeful that the festival's history of internal disputes and public wrangling is, well, history."

G203    Hyman, Ann. "Spoleto Goes on Without Menotti." *Florida Times-Union* (Jacksonville), (April 10, 1994)
The Spoleto Festival U.S.A. divides its artistic director functions among three musicians after Menotti's departure among three people: Spiros Argiris (director of symphonic and operatic activities), Joseph Flummerfelt (director of choral activities), and Charles Wadsworth (director of chamber music activities). Milton Rhodes took over as general manager about a week after Menotti's resignation, citing irreconcilable differences over when Menotti should step up to artistic director emeritus status.

G204    Honig, Joel. "Passing Time in Spoleto." *Opera News* 58 (May 1994): 10-14+.
"Perhaps the right direction for the festival is up — north, that is . . . Menotti has long dreamed of creating on his grounds in Scotland a chamber opera theater where young artists could be trained and perform. With Edinburgh, and its own festival, barely twenty miles away, such an enterprise could hardly want for audiences."

G205    Oestreich, James R. "Critic's Notebook: the First Spoleto Without Menotti." *New York Times*, C (June 1, 1994): 11.
Remarks on the first Spoleto Festival U.S.A. season after Menotti was replaced as artistic director by Milton Rhodes.

## 48  General References

G206   Oestreich, James R. "Spoleto after Menotti: an Outbreak of Peace." *New York Times*, Living Arts Pages (June 1, 1994): 81.
The Spoleto Festival U.S.A. is no longer under the guidance of founder Menotti.

G207   "Menotti is Dismissed From Rome Opera Post." *New York Times*, (September 17, 1994): 19.
Menotti is dismissed as artistic director. The opera's superintendent, Giorgio Vidusso, said "artistic differences" led him to release Menotti. Last year Menotti broke with Spoleto Festival U.S.A., arguing that corporate sponsors had too much control over it.

G208   Sbisà, Nicola. *Menotti il duca di Spoleto e il suo amico Barber*. Fasano: Schena, 1995.
Includes list of works (p. 35-50) and discography (p. 53-59).

G209   Skowron, Zbigniew. *Nowa muzyka amerykanska*. Studia et dissertationes Instituti Musicologiae Varsoviensis, no. 2. Krakow: Musica Iagellonica, 1995.
Based on the dissertation abstracted as *RILM* 89-5813. Menotti is one of several contemporary U.S. composers discussed.

G210   McLellan, Joseph. "Spoleto, Minus Menotti." *Washington Post*, C (May 27, 1995): 1.
Preview of the 1995 Spoleto Festival. ". . .if it is still a notable festival, it is no longer a 'Spoleto' Festival. Though the Charleston organization has copyrighted the name and has every right to use it, the sound of those words only reminds old fans of Menotti."

G211   "Spoleto Manager Returns." *New York Times*, 1 (July 20, 1995): 27.
Spoleto Festival U.S.A. calls on Nigel Redden, former general manager, to deal with the Festival's financial difficulties. Redden resigned after the 1991 Festival.

G212   Campbell, Mary. "Gian Carlo Menotti's Dream Made a City Prosperous." *Chattanooga Free Press* (Chattanooga, TN), (March 31, 1996)
Menotti doesn't think his operas are performed as often in the 1990s as they should be. "I was the most performed opera composer this century except for Puccini . . . My operas speak to this time."

G213    Page, Tim. "Charleston's Season to Swing: Spoleto Festival Fills the Town with Cool Jazz, Hot Opera and a Warm Welcome." *Washington Post*, Style (May 28, 1996): B1.
Overview of Spoleto, Spoleto U.S.A., and the various administrative squabbles involving Menotti.

G214    Kozinn, Allan. "Critics Notebook: Spoleto at 20: Still Volatile, Still in Menotti's Shadow." *New York Times*, C (June 5, 1996): 13-14.
Menotti ". . . got into the habit of haranguing the board members [of Spoleto U.S.A.] who were footing the bill for the festival, charging them with undermining his artistic prerogatives . . . when Mr. Menotti presented his semiannual list of demands in the fall of 1993, the board accepted the accompanying resignation threat."

G215    Ashley, Dottie. "Wadsworth Adds Depth to Chamber Series." *Post and Courier* (Charleston, SC), ST (June 9, 1996): 10.
Menotti's son, ". . . Chip has said that no one from the Charleston festival can participate in the Festival of Two Worlds. He doesn't want any crossover at all, and apparently Gian Carlo is going along with that."

G216    Higgins, Tom. "An Octogenarian Musical Medium." *Opera Now* (July-August 1996): 23-25.
Interview with Menotti. Discusses the themes and style of some of his operas and mentions his relationships with other musicians, including Toscanini.

G217    "Menotti's Son Becomes Italian Festival President." *Post and Courier* (Charleston, SC), B (July 4, 1996): 10.
"Many of the foundation members, including President Umberto Colombo, predict 'a showdown after the final curtain' this year on the issue of whether the younger Menotti can continue the heritage of his father. But the elder Menotti is standing firm against the government and the municipality of Spoleto . . . 'I will never accept to be told how to create the festival, and politics will be kept out,' Menotti said. 'I would leave if I felt Spoleto didn't want me.'"

G218    Fleming, John. "Many Voices, One Song." *St. Petersburg Times* (St. Petersburg, FL), Floridian; Gala Festival V (July 7, 1996): 1F.
Review of the Gala Festival V, featuring more than 110 gay and lesbian choruses and 5,000 singers from North America, Europe, and Australia, held at the Tampa Bay Performing Arts Center. " . . . Household names in classical music such as David Diamond, Ned Rorem, John Corigliano,

Conrad Susa and Gian Carlo Menotti have all composed commissioned works for gay choruses."

G219    White, Michael. "Menotti: Profit Without Honour." *Independent* (London), Real life (July 7, 1996): 13.
"Above all, the music is humane: it tempers technique with compassion and a generosity of spirit that commands respect."

G220    Ashley, Dottie. "Festival in Italy Marks Menotti's 85th Birthday." *Post and Courier* (Charleston, SC), E (August 4, 1996): 2.
Review of CBS-TV's Jul 29, 1996 birthday celebration at Spoleto. "Menotti's birthday party showed his grandchildren surrounding his lighted cake. Also shown in the segment as Chip Menotti, the maestro's son, who was named artistic director of the Italian festival this summer."

G221    Simon, John. "A Little Lower Than Festive." *National Review* 48 (September 30, 1996): 67-69.
The 39th year of The Festival of Two Worlds was not a good year. Menotti handed the leadership to his son, Francis; Spoleto's mayor wants to gain control, and funding is threatened.

G222    Brooks, Gene. "From the Executive Director." *Choral Journal* 37 (November 1996): 2.
Biography of Menotti and composer Stephen Paulus, who have been commissioned to write works for the Raymond W. Brock Commissioned Composition series. The works will be premiered at the 1997 American Choral Directors Association national convention.

G223    Boyden, Matthew. *Opera: The Rough Guide*. London: Rough Guides, 1997 (p. 569-70).
General biographical and critical information, plot synopses, and very selective recording reviews.

G224    Folk, Lucia. "The Spoleto Festival in the 1990s: Moving Past Menotti." M.A. thesis, School of the Art Institute of Chicago, 1997.

G225    Brooks, Gene. "An Interview with Gian Carlo Menotti." *Choral Journal* 37 (March 1997): 9-15.
Excerpts from an interview conducted November 14, 1996 in Washington, D.C. Comments on the major elements of his compositional style and reports on his interest in writing operas and choral music. Says Menotti, "I

find that some of my best music has been written for chorus and orchestra." Includes list of choral works.

G226　Piccoli, Sean. "Anthology Fever: It's All the Beatles' Fault." *Sun-Sentinel* (Ft. Lauderdale, FL), Arts & Leisure (May 4, 1997): 1D.
Review of the Club Verboten DCC recording. ". . .charts the creative face of gay life in the 20th century, chronicling music by gay talents in multiple genres, as well as songs that gay culture has adopted as its own, regardless of the performer's orientation."

G227　"Playing It Safe." *Columbus Dispatch* (Columbus, OH), Artbeat (June 3, 1997): 8E.
"Without the presence of its charismatic founder and artistic director . . . Spoleto has lost its center, perhaps its soul — and certainly its edge . . . If Spoleto is a metaphor for the arts today, we've hit the banal — bigtime."

# Works and Performances (W1–W90)

*Works* are here listed in *alphabetical order by title*. *Performances* of those works are listed *chronologically*, as are reviews of individual performances. In cases of opera performances, identification of roles are here given in the order and as they appear in the review sources cited. *Recordings* appear in order by performers' names and, unless otherwise stipulated, refer to long-playing recordings (LPs). In the *discography* sections, recording reviews are listed in *chronological* order by the date of the source cited.

### W1   *À L'OMBRE DES JEUNES FILLES EN FLEURS* (1947)

Ballet.
Based on "Within a Budding Grove," from Marcel Proust's *Remembrance of Things Past*.
Was to have been choreographed by Anthony Tudor for the Ballet Theatre; Tudor, however, abandoned the project, and the work was never produced.

### W2   *ALBUM LEAVES* (1959-62)

Sketches contributed pseudonymously to the Festival of Two Worlds (Spoleto)

### W3   *AMAHL AND THE NIGHT VISITORS* (1951; G. Schirmer; 46 min.)

Television opera in one act with libretto (English) by Menotti.

Commissioned by the National Broadcasting Company through Samuel Chotzinoff, the producer of the network's series of television operas.
Inspired by Hieronymus Bosch's *The Adoration of the Magi*.
Cast: boy S, S, T, Bar, 2 B; SATB chorus; dancers
1211/1100/perc/hp.pf/str
*The Library of Congress Quarterly Journal of Current Acquisitions*, vol. 13, no. 1 (November, 1955) lists the receipt during the preceding year of *Amahl and the Night Visitors*. According to Wayne D. Shirley, Music Specialist at the Library of Congress, this is not a manuscript in Menotti's hand but a full score of the opera. *Pierpont Morgan Library* has a "partially autograph manuscript of the full score" (227 p., 48.5 x 32 cm.)

### ♦ ABOUT THE WORK

W3.1  "Menotti to Compose First Opera for TV." *Southwestern Musician* 15 (August 1949): 4.

W3.2  Holde, A. "Amahl und die nächtlichen Gäste." *Musikleben* 5 (December 1952): 374-375.

W3.3  Shanet, H. "Out of the Mouth of Babes." *Music Clubs Magazine* 32 (January 1953): 4-5.

W3.4  "Amahl and the Night Visitors." *Choral Guide* 6 (February 1953): 28.

W3.5  Fryer, Judith Anne. "Guide to the Study and Performance of Three Operas of Gian-Carlo Menotti." Ed.D. dissertation, Columbia University Teachers College, 1974.
From the author's abstract: "The purpose of this study is to provide historical information, analytical material, and practical suggestions for the teaching and performance of selected Menotti operas in secondary schools ... Three operas were chosen for thorough analysis: *The Medium* (1946), *Amahl and the Night Visitors* (1951), and *Help, Help, the Globolinks!*"

W3.6  Marriott, Richard John. "Gian-Carlo Menotti, Total Musical Theatre: A Study of His Operas." Ph.D. dissertation, University of Illinois, 1975.
From the author's abstract: "Menotti is most successful in his chamber operas: *The Medium, The Consul*, and *Amahl and the Night Visitors*. In the successful chamber operas, Menotti's goal of effective theatre is realized; they have complete integration of libretto, music, staging, and above all theatricality — they have the qualities of a consciously dramatic stage play."

W3.7 Kanski, J. "*Amahl/* Menottiego po raz pierwszy w Polsce." *Ruch muzyczny* 25, 3 (1981): 10-11.

W3.8 Ryan, Sylvia Watkins. "Solo Piano Music of Gian-Carlo Menotti: A Pedagogical and Performance Analysis." D.M.A. dissertation, University of Oklahoma, 1993.
Discusses *Poemetti* (1937), *Ricercare and Toccata on a Theme from 'The Old Maid and the Thief'* (1953), and the piano version of *Amahl and the Night Visitors* (1951). This study is intended to serve as a reference work for teachers of contemporary piano literature.

W3.9 Witzke, Ronald. "The Duality of Faith and Skepticism in the Operas of Gian Carlo Menotti: A Dramaturgical Study of *The Medium* and *Amahl and the Night Visitors.*" D.M.A. Performance dissertation, Indiana University, 1997.

♦ SELECTED PERFORMANCES

W3.10 1951 (Dec 24): Telecast on over 35 stations of the NBC-TV network; Thomas Schippers, cond.; with Chet Allen (Amahl), Rosemary Kuhlmann (Mother), David Aiken (Kaspar), Leon Lishner (Melchior), Andrew McKinley (Balthazar), and Francis Monachino (Page)

*Reviews:*

W3.10a "New Menotti TV Opera is Legend of Nativity." *Musical Courier* 144 (December 15, 1951): 13.
Short review of the TV premiere and subsequent Bloomington performance. "The opera, begun six months ago, was written specifically for TV but can also be presented in a theatre."

W3.10b "New Short Opera by Menotti." *Times* (London), (December 29, 1951): 4.
"Amahl was played by a 12-year-old boy, Chet Allen, whose performance has been praised in the New York press."

W3.10c Downes, Olin. "Televised Opera: Menotti's 'Amahl' is a Historic Step in the Development of a New Idiom." *New York Times*, 2 (December 30, 1951): 7.
". . . the fact of its dramatic communication and suitableness for television is hardly disputable."

## 56  Works and Performances

W3.10d   "Three Kings in 50 Minutes." *Time* 58 (December 31, 1951): 30.
". . . although he has some difficult singing (and acting) to do, curly-haired and clear-voiced little Chet Allen . . . carries it off beautifully."

W3.10e   Eaton, Quaintance. "New Menotti TV Opera Has Premiere on Christmas Eve." *Musical America* 72 (January 1, 1952): 3-5.
"The impression thus was one of continuing artistry, and most of the time one even forgot that the cameras were there — the highest compliment television can receive."

W3.10f   Levinger, Henry W. "First Opera Written For Television Bows." *Musical Courier* 145 (January 1, 1952): 5.
". . . a miniature masterpiece which, if this writer is not mistaken, will become a standard offering of the operatic stage at Yuletide. Orchestrated with exquisite delicacy and a rare sense for coloristic effects, it is a moving play."

W3.10g   Hamburger, Philip. "Television: Bravo!" *New Yorker* 27 (January 5, 1952): 56+.
"Musically, 'Amahl' struck me as being Menotti's finest work, a perfect complement to his strange and wondrous tale, and it seemed to contain a depth and range of human feeling that I have missed in some of his earlier pieces."

W3.10h   "Menotti and Television." *Newsweek* 39 (January 7, 1952): 36-37.
". . . the Menotti theatrical touch showed that, with taste and imagination, the future of opera on television is rich."

W3.10i   Kolodin, Irving. "Menotti's 'Amahl' on TV." *Saturday Review* 35 (January 12, 1952): 30.
Regarding Chet Allen: "An expressive face, a fluent soprano voice, and a fourteen-year-old conviction gave to this work an actuality that no art could counterfeit."

W3.10j   Smith, Cecil. "New York Music Critics Make Composition Awards." *Musical America* 72 (January 15, 1952): 6.
On January 1, 1952, the New York Music Critics Circle presented Menotti with a special citation for his *Amahl and the Night Visitors*. A citation was given instead of the customary award "because the members of the circle were eager to express their approval of NBC as well as of the composer."

W3.10k    Cowell, Henry. "Current Chronicle: New York." *Musical Quarterly* 38 (April 1952): 296-298.
Brief analysis and review with one musical example, of the NBC television production. "The simplicity of *Amahl* is still a theatrical rather than an actual simplicity — an imitation of the simple — but it is agreeable and suitable here."

W3.10l    Kirstein, Lincoln. "Television Opera in the U.S.A." *Opera* (England) 2 (April 1952): 198-202.
"The opera received numerous awards and citations, and the executives of N.B.C. must have felt well recompensed for their courage, imagination and foresight."

W3.10m   Hijman, Julius. "Een Televisie-Opera van Menotti." *Mens en melodie* 8 (January 1953): 4-7.

W3.10n    Adler, Peter Herman. "TV and the Arts: 2. Music: The Silent Stepchild." *Saturday Review* 52 (April 26, 1969): 23+.
"Kinescopes of the original production were shown abroad and studied as an example of how effective the television screen can be when it leaves grand opera to the grand opera houses and concentrates instead of intimacy and direct emotional appeal."

W3.11     1952 (Feb 21): Bloomington; Indiana University; School of Music; Ernst Hoffman, cond.; with Ronald Jennings (Amahl), Marilyn Rights (Mother), Jack DeLon/George McKinley (Kaspar), James Serviss (Melchior), Don Vogel (Balthasar), and Don Slagel (Page) ("first staged production"; on a double-bill with *A Parfait For Irene* by Walter Kauffman)

*Reviews:*

W3.11a    "New Menotti TV Opera is Legend of Nativity." *Musical Courier* 144 (December 15, 1951): 13.
Short review of the TV premiere and subsequent Bloomington performance. "The opera, begun six months ago, was written specifically for TV but can also be presented in a theatre."

W3.11b    "Indiana University Presents." *Opera News* 16 (April 7, 1952): 8.
"No easy task to metamorphose a television opera to a stage performance, it displayed the skill of Hans Busch, stage director."

58  Works and Performances

W3.12   1952 (Apr 9): New York; New York City Center; New York City Opera; Thomas Schippers, cond.; with Chet Allen (Amahl), Rosemary Kuhlmann (Mother), Michael Pollock (Kaspar), Lawrence Winters (Melchior), Richard Wentworth (Balthazar), and William Starling (Page) ("first professional production"; on a double-bill with *The Old Maid and the Thief*)

Reviews:

W3.12a   Eaton, Quaintance. "Menotti's *Amahl and the Night Visitors* is Second Novelty of the Spring Season." *Musical America* 72 (April 15, 1952): 5. ". . . in the large house, his [Allen's] voice seemed tiny and piping, and he often forced it to make the necessary climaxes."

W3.12b   Watt, Douglas. "Musical Events: Large and Small." *New Yorker* 28 (April 19, 1952): 91.
"It turned out to be a thoroughly ingratiating little piece, holding the interest for some fifty minutes with a succession of appealing, attractively scored melodies."

W3.12c   Kolodin, Irving. "'Amahl' & 'Elijah' Join 'Parsifal' in the Easter Parade." *Saturday Review* 35 (April 26, 1952): 30.
Menotti ". . . may be reaping the past rather than sowing the future, but his shoot, however slender, puts out leaves and bears fruit."

W3.12d   "Menotti's Amahl Staged at N.Y. City Center." *Musical Courier* 145 (May 1, 1952): 11.
"The warming simplicity of the tender story, and the moving, simple music, which flows from and speaks to the heart, was potently felt in a performance that left little to be desired."

W3.12e   Wyatt, Euphemia Van Rensselaer. "Theater." *Catholic World* 175 (June 1952): 227-228.
"Menotti's music stirs with life and beauty. As always it is completely integrated with his text. *Amahl*, full of fun and tenderness is TV's best gift to the theater."

W3.12f   "Amahl and the Night Visitors." *Life* 33 (December 15, 1952): 102-103. Brief description of the opera with color photographs.

W3.13   1952 (Sep 19): New York; New York City Opera; Thomas Schippers, cond.; with James Sammarco (Amahl), Rosemary Kuhlmann (Mother),

*Amahl and the Night Visitors* 59

Michael Pollock (Kaspar), Lawrence Winters (Melchior), Richard Wentworth (Balthazar), and William Starling (Page) (on a double-bill with *The Old Maid and the Thief*)

W3.14   1953 (Dec 20): New York; NBC Television Opera Theatre; Thomas Schippers, cond.; with William McIver (Amahl), Rosemary Kuhlmann (Mother), Francis Monachino (Page), Andrew McKinley (Kaspar), Leon Lishner (Melchior), and David Aiken (Balthazar) (first commercial color telecast in history)

*Review:*

W3.14a   L., J. "Menotti Opera Makes Television History." *Musical America* 74 (January 1, 1954): 27.
"Very few of the millions who viewed *Amahl* saw it in color, of course, because the number of privately owned color sets is infinitesimal."

W3.15   1953 (Mar 22): New York; New York City Opera; Thomas Schippers, cond.; same cast as W3.13 (on a double-bill with *The Medium*)

W3.16   1954 (Apr 1): New York; New York City Opera; Thomas Schippers, cond.; with William McIver (Amahl), Rosemary Kuhlmann (Mother), Michael Pollock (Kaspar), Lawrence Winters (Melchior), Richard Wentworth (Balthazar), and William Starling (Page) (on a double-bill with Copland's *The Tender Land*)

W3.17   1956 (Sep 29): Farnham, England; Farnham Church House; Alan Fluck, music director; performed by Farnham Grammar School, with Geoffrey Dudley (Amahl) and Julia Beeken (Mother)

*Review:*

W3.17a   "Menotti's Opera at Farnham: Composer Watches Performance." *Times* (London), (October 1, 1956): 3.
"... the star of the evening ... was, of course, Amahl, played by Master Geoffrey Dudley, whose sweet, strong voice and fetching personality deservedly earned him the composer's congratulations."

W3.18   1963 (Dec 14): Hempstead, Long Island, NY; Hofstra University; Dept. of Music; Herbert Beattie, cond.; with Mark Beattie (Amahl) and Madeleine Kahn (Mother)

*Review:*

W3.18a  Storrer, William Allin. "Hempstead, Long Island." *Opera* (England) 15 (February 1964): 98-99.
". . . the production did well in releasing the work from its historical strait-jacket. Now one saw more clearly that it was not necessarily the Christ-child himself, but the vision of good he symbolized, that was needed to give rebirth to mankind (as symbolized in Amahl)."

W3.19  1967 (Dec 26): London; BBC-2 Television; James Lockhart, cond.; with Paul Boucher (Amahl), April Cantelo (Mother), Joseph Ward (Kaspar), Forbes Robinson (Melchior), and Don Garrard (Balthazar)

*Review:*

W3.19a  Jacobs, Arthur. "*Amahl and the Night Visitors*, BBC-2." *Opera* (England) 19 (February 1968): 172.
"It would be difficult to imagine a better cast . . . The location of Amahl's dwelling looked rather odd, but otherwise I could hardly fault the visual projection of the story."

W3.20  1968 (Dec 21): Hamburg; Hamburgische Staatsoper; Matthias Kuntzsch, cond.; with Mathias Misselwitz (Amahl), Kerstin Meyer (Mother), Jerry J. Jennings (Kaspar), William Workman (Melchior), and Noël Mangin (Balthazar) (on a double-bill with *Help, Help, the Globolinks!*)

*Reviews:*

W3.20a  Dannenberg, Peter. "Hamburg: Schöne Bescherung." *Opernwelt* 10 (February 1969): 39-40.

W3.20b  Geitel, Klaus. "Wer hat Angst vor Globolinks?" *Neue Zeitschrift für Musik* 130 (February 1969): 54-55.
Also published in *Orchester* 17 (March 1969):111-112.

W3.20c  Joachim, Heinz. "Hamburg." *Opera* (England) 20 (March 1969): 236-237.
". . . thanks to his [Misselwitz's] vocal qualities, his musicality and surprising dramatic gift held his own astonishingly well in Menotti's affectionate production . . ."

W3.21    1969 (Dec 19): New York; New York City Center; Charles Wilson, cond.; with Robert Puleo (Amahl) and Joy Davidson (Mother) (on a double-bill with *Help, Help, the Globolinks!*)

Reviews:

W3.21a   Honig, Joel. "New York." *Opera News* 34 (February 7, 1970): 32-33.
"The thrice-familiar *Amahl* sounded less interesting than the *Globolinks*, but it had a superior protagonist in Robert Puleo. Still a boy soprano, Puleo sang with adult feeling and acted with charm."

W3.21b   "New York." *Opera* (England) 21 (March 1970): 223-224.
". . . the children attending the performance I heard (matinee, December 26) appeared to dote upon it."

W3.22    1970 (Dec 21): New York; ANTA Theater; Christopher Keene, cond.; with Robert Puleo (Amahl), Nancy Williams (Mother), David Clatworthy (Melchior), Edward Pierson (Balthazar), Douglas Perry (Kaspar), and Joseph Galiano (Page) (on a double-bill with *Help, Help, the Globolinks!*)

Review:

W3.22a   Henahan, Donal. "'Amahl' and 'Globolinks' Performed." *New York Times*, (December 24, 1970): 10.
"The show . . . struck one as rather vulgar and cosmetic much of the time, especially in the Broadwayish dance of the shepherds."

W3.23    1971 (Oct 28): Geneva; Grand Théâtre de Genève; Jean-Pierre Marty, cond.; Orchestre de la Suisse romande; with Jacques Nierlé (Amahl), Kerstin Meyer (Mother), George-L. Miazza (Kaspar), William Workman (Melchior), and Louis Hagen-William (Balthazar) (in a translation by Jean-Pierre Marty; on a double-bill with *Help, Help, the Globolinks!*)

Review:

W3.23a   Bloomfield, Theodore. "Switzerland: Menotti Revival." *Opera* (England) 23 (March 1972): 269.
"It received a somewhat pale performance which did not realize the full emotional impact of this touching work."

62   *Works and Performances*

W3.24   1973 (Dec 9): Brooklyn; St. Theresa of Avila Church; Bay Ridge's Kings Forum for Performing Arts; with Anthony Corretto (Amahl), Barbara Giancola (Mother) (repeated on Dec 16 at Ozone Park, Queens, Church of the Nativity; Dec 23 at St. Patrick's Church in Brooklyn; and Jan 6 at St. Rose of Lima in Brooklyn)

*Review:*

W3.24a   Funke, Phyllis. "Ecumenical Chord Struck." *New York Times*, (December 16, 1973): 144.
Largely biographical sketch of Aldo Bruschi [Musical Director for this production], with some general critical remarks. Said Bruschi: "I feel music is a common denominator. It is the one way for the church to reach all our brethren. It can act as a bridge to realizing the ecumenical dreams set forth by Pope John."

W3.25   1976 (Dec 8): Bremen, Germany; Theater der Freien und Hansestadt Bremen at the Stephanikirche; Johannes Wedekind, cond.; with Christian Dettmers (Amahl), Roswitha Habermann (Mother), Peter Winter (Kaspar), Caspar Bröcheler (Melchior), and Friedhelm Rosendorff (Balthazar)

*Review:*

W3.25a   Asche, Gerhart. "Entkitschtes Werke: Menottis 'Amahl und die Nachtlichen Besucher' in Bremen." *Opernwelt* 18 (1977): 40.

W3.26   1978 (Dec 24): NBC Television; Jesus Lopez-Cobos, cond.; Philharmonia Orchestra; Ambrosian Singers; with Robert Sapolsky (Amahl), Teresa Stratas (Mother), Nico Castel (Kaspar), Giorgio Tozzi (Melchior), Willard White (Balthazar), and Michael Lewis (Page) (released on videocassette by Video Artists International, 69032, 1979, 1 cassette, 52 min.)

*Reviews:*

W3.26a   Shepard, Richard F. "TV: '[Amahl]' Will Return for Christmas after 12 Years." *New York Times*, sect. 3 (May 26, 1978): 26.
Amahl will return in an entirely new production after an absence of 12 years next Christmas Eve as a "G.E. Theater" production, sponsored by the General Electric Company. From 1951-55, the opera appeared live in black and white. From 1956-58, it was presented in color. From

1959-62, the black and white versions were repeated. From 1963-66, its last year before this new presentation, taped reruns in color were presented.

W3.26b  O'Connor, John J. "'Tis the Season For Documentaries." *New York Times*, 3 (December 22, 1978): 32.
"The opera is an exquisite jewel . . . This production is gorgeous in every respect."

W3.26c  Jacobson, Robert. "TV." *Opera News* 43 (February 10, 1979): 51.
"In a role that so easily can turn saccharine, Sapolsky made it vibrant, full of personality, open and real in his adolescent mischievousness, always sympathetic but never going for the sappy."

W3.26d  Hemming, Roy. "Christmas Videos for People Who Think They Hate Christmas Videos." *Video Review* 9 (December 1988): 61-64+
Reviews of selected Christmas movies, including the Video Artists International cassette of *Amahl and the Night Visitors*, recorded from the 1978 NBC television production. ". . . may well be the single work that keeps Menotti from being just a footnote to this century's music history . . . Stratas again proves herself a singing actress with few present-day equals."

W3.26e  Pines, Roger G. "Amahl and the Night Visitors." *Opera Quarterly* 5 (Spring 1987): 123-125.
Review of the Video Artists International video recording of the 1978 NBC film. "You may have tired of *Amahl* after growing up with it, but you will capitulate to its sincerity and appeal in this video performance. It is unfortunate that the recorded sound is so inadequate, for Menotti, Stratas, and their colleagues deserve better."

W3.27  1980 (Nov 15): Vienna; Wiener Staatsoper; Reinhard Schwarz, cond.; Wiener Philharmoniker; with Johannes Strassel (Amahl), Helga Dernesch (Mother), Waldemar Kmentt (Kaspar), Eberhard Wächter (Melchior), and Oskar Czerwenka (Balthazar) (on a double-bill with *Help, Help, the Globolinks!*)

*Reviews:*

W3.27a  "Wiener Premieren." *Buehne* 267 (December 1980): 10-11.

W3.27a  "Wiener Premieren." *Buehne* 267 (December 1980): 10-11.

W3.27b  Klein, Rudolf. "Staatsoper für Kinder." *Opernwelt* 22 (January 1981): 27.

W3.27c  Klein, Rudolf. "Wiener Staatsoper für Kinder." *Österreichische Musikzeitschrift* 36 (January 1981): 38.

W3.27d  Wechsberg, Joseph. "Austria: Menotti and Verdi for Christmas." *Opera* (England) 32 (March 1981): 283-284.
"The reception of the Magi by a crippled boy was very well received in Vienna . . . [Strassel] gave a moving performance and more than a touch of credibility to Menotti's fairy-tale."

W3.27e  Norton-Welsh, Christopher. "Vienna." *Opera News* 45 (March 14, 1981): 38.
"The kings were less caricatured than usual, but of the veteran trio only Waldemar Kmentt as Kaspar was audible enough."

W3.28  1980 (Dec 2): St. Paul; Orchestra Hall; Minnesota Opera; Henry Charles Smith, cond.; members of the Minnesota Orchestra; Dale Warland Chamber Singers; with Benjamin Wright (Amahl), Rosemary Kuhlmann (Mother), David Aiken (Melchior), Richard Knoll (Kaspar), and James Ramlet (Balthazar)

*Review:*

W3.28a  Hawley, David. "Fine Holiday 'Amahl' Opera Stars Cast from 30 Years Ago." *St. Paul Pioneer Press* (St. Paul, MN), (December 3, 1980)
Kuhlman and Aiken are " . . . what could be called 'smart singers,' the kind who know how to use what they've got to the best advantage and with the least strain."

W3.29  1980 (Dec 4): Salt Lake City; Capitol Theatre; Utah Opera; Robert Henderson, cond.; with Darin Gates (Amahl), Laura Garff (Mother), Alan Edwards (Kaspar), Noel Twitchell (Melchior), Gene Larson (Balthazar), and Dave Arnold (Page)

*Review:*

W3.29a  Stowe, Dorothy. "Opera 'Amahl' a Seasonal Treat." *Deseret News* (Salt Lake City), F (December 5-6, 1980): 4.

"Young Gates sang sweetly and without strain . . . He is visually an ideal Amahl, slight and delicate, and a good young actor, direct and unaffected."

W3.30   1980 (Dec 21): Saratoga, CA; Carriage House; Montalvo Center for the Arts; San Jose Community Opera Theater; David Rohrbaugh, cond.; with Brenda Willner (Mother), David Cohen (Amahl), Paul Shoor (Kaspar), Warren Brown (Melchior), and William Marshall (Balthazar) (repeated Dec 23 with different cast at the Montgomery Theatre, San Jose)

*Review:*

W3.30a   Hertelendy, Paul. "An Intimate 'Amahl' by Community Opera." *San Jose Mercury*, (December 22, 1980): 7.
"The production was credible and intimate, juxtaposing the poverty of Amahl and his mother with the gilded luxury of the three Magi, outfitted in the style of a Rembrandt Biblical painting."

W3.31   1980 (Dec 28): Toronto; York Quay Theatre Stage; Harbourfront Theatre; Canadian Opera Company Ensemble; Canadian Children's Opera Chorus; Derek Bate, cond.; with Benjamin Carlson/David Yung (Amahl), Eleanor James/Roålana Roslak (Mother), Ben Heppner/Roger Jones (Kaspar), Viorel Dihel (Melchior), Christopher Cameron (Balthazar), and Vytautas Paulionis (Page)

W3.32   1981: Saskatoon, Sask., Canada; Saskatoon Opera Association; Robert Solem, cond.; with Marjorie Boldt (Amahl), Dorothy Howard Brooks (Mother), Paul Reist (Kaspar), Rick Kreklewich (Melchior), and Dennis Jones (Balthazar) (on a double bill with *Chip and His Dog*)

*Review:*

W3.32a   Popoff, Wilf. "Saskatoon Opera Assoc." *Opera Canada* 22, 2 (1981): 24.
". . . the singing was exceptional . . . and the Three Kings . . . when they sang together, were simply beautiful."

W3.33   1982 (May 5): Nantes, France; Nantes Opera; Guy Condette, cond.; with Fabien Denis (Amahl) and Christiane Cadoul (Mother) (on a double-bill with *The Medium*)

*Review:*

W3.33a    Pitt, Charles. "Nantes." *Opera* (England) 34 (September 1983): 1002-1003.
"... a naïve but touching, poetic work in which Fabien Denis showed precocious talent ... and Christiane Cadoul made a touchingly human Mother."

W3.34    1982 (Dec 3): Norfolk; Norfolk Center Theater; Virginia Opera Association; Peter Mark, cond.; with Kevin Dixon/Jonathan Weaver (Amahl), Adrienne Leonetti (Mother), Howard Bender (Kaspar), Vincent de Cordova (Melchior), Arthur Woodley (Balthazar), and Donald Hartmann (Page) (performed later as school matinees in Charlottesville, Williamsburg, Alexandria, and Roanoke, VA)

*Reviews:*

W3.34a    Green, Judith. "'Amahl' a Treat for the Season." *Virginian-Pilot and Ledger-Star*, (December 5, 1982)
"Children were plentiful in the opening-night audience ... Surely there is no happier way to introduce young people to opera than with this lilting work, whose honest sentiment and melodic grace have made it a classic in just 31 years."

W3.34b    Fahy, Joe. "Menotti Touch." *Norfolk Virginian-Pilot*, (November 25, 1984)
Menotti is preparing the production of *Amahl* for the Virginia Opera Association: "It was written so quickly that Samuel Barber had to help me with the orchestration. In the manuscript of the composition now in the Pierpont Morgan Library, one page is not in my handwriting. And the writing there is Barber's."

W3.35    1985 (Dec 15): Denver; Trinity Methodist Church; Opera Colorado; Denver Chamber Orchestra; with Jeremy Shamos (Amahl), Marcia Ragonetti (Mother), Todd Frizzell (Kaspar), Scott Root (Melchior), and Hao Jiang Tian (Balthazar) (on a double-bill with Robert Downard's *Martin Avdeich*)

*Review:*

W3.35a    Samson, Charley. "Yule Operas Bring Moving Performances." *Rocky Mountain News* (Denver, CO), (December 16, 1985)

"Fifteen-year-old Jeremy Shamos portrayed Amahl with dramatic conviction. His high notes were thin, but his sense of character was secure."

W3.36   1986 (Dec 6): Denver; Trinity Methodist Church; Opera Colorado; JoAnn Falletta, cond.; Denver Chamber Orchestra; with Christopher Merrill/Christian Olson (Amahl), Marcia Ragonetti/Eileen Farrell (Mother), Thomas Poole (Kaspar), Scott Root (Melchior), and Hao Jiang Tian (Balthazar)

*Reviews:*

W3.36a   Giffin, Glenn. "Human Touches Highlight 'Amahl.'" *Denver Post*, (December 6, 1986)
"It is a hit despite its many flaws because it touches a sentimental chord with its audiences . . . If anything, the show bodes well to become a Christmas tradition for the two arts ensembles."

W3.36b   Young, Allen. "'Amahl' Provides an Early Yule Gift." *Rocky Mountain News* (Denver, CO), E (December 7, 1986): 12.
"Christopher Merrill pipes appealingly as Amahl; his stage business went very naturally, showing him to be an adroit performer."

W3.37   1986 (Dec 11): London; Sadler's Wells; David Syrus, cond.; with James Rainbird/David Haeems (Amahl), Lorna Haywood/Phyllis Aver (Mother), John Dobson (Kaspar), Roderick Earle (Melchior), and Curtis Watson (Balthazar) (joint production of the Royal Opera House and Sadler's Wells in association with Youth and Music; on a double-bill with *The Boy Who Grew Too Fast*)

W3.38   1987 (Dec 14): Fair Haven, NJ; Church of the Nativity; Felix Molzer, piano and harp synthesizer; with Will Beekman (Amahl), Shelley Ziegler (Mother), Charles Lawson (Balthazar), Robert Dudley (Melchior), and David Roszel (Kaspar) (also Dec 5 in Little Silver, NJ, at Red Bank Regional High School)

*Review:*

W3.38a   Andersen, Jane Lee. "Opera is Still a Christmas Favorite." *Asbury Park Press* (Neptune, NJ), (December 14, 1987)
Beekman ". . . never forgets his affliction and copes well with a difficult score, gaining confidence and authority as the evening advances."

W3.39   1987 (Dec 20): Orlando, FL; Carr Performing Arts Centre; Orlando Opera Company; Karen Keltner, cond.; Florida Symphony Orchestra; with Greg Sarjeant (Amahl), Sandra Collins (Mother), Harry L. Burney, III (Balthazar), Barry Craft (Kaspar), and Tom McKinney (Melchior)

Reviews:

W3.39a   Brown, Steven. "'Amahl' Is Not the Kind of Role That Singers Can Grow Old With." *Orlando Sentinel* (Orlando, FL), (December 18, 1987)
"Once we have a kid who likes to do this, we like to give them as many opportunities to sing as we can, to help them gain their confidence. They have to prove to themselves that they can do it."

W3.39b   Brown, Rebecca. "'Amahl' Pays Sweet Visit to Orlando." *Orlando Sentinel* (Orlando, FL), Style (December 22, 1987)
"It was Collins who brought the most emotion to this one-act production. Her rich voice was fiercely proud one moment, plaintively tender the next."

W3.40   1988 (Dec 3): New York; Lincoln Center; Alice Tully Hall; Dino Anagnost, cond.; Little Orchestra Society; Orpheon Chorale; American Ballet Theatre School of Classical Ballet; with Jedidiah Cohen/Joel Chaiken (Amahl), Lorna Haywood (Mother), Kevin Maynor (Balthazar), David Lowe (Kaspar), and Thomas Woodman (Melchior)

Reviews:

W3.40a   Elliott, Susan. "Menotti's 'Amahl' Makes Annual Visit." *New York Post*, (December 5, 1988)
". . . Cohen . . . possessed a sweet tone and . . . Lorna Haywood sang with a full, vibrant sound and acted believably."

W3.40b   "'Amahl and the Night Visitors' Is a Splendid Version of the 3 Wise Kings." *New York Tribune*, (December 7, 1988)
". . . Joel Chaiken did a remarkable job filling the space, with diction and stage presence that carried his performance to every seat . . . Haywood brought to the mother's role a robust soprano voice and hearty acting, both fitting the role . . ."

W3.41   1989 (Nov 2): Birmingham, England; Crescent Theatre; Midland Music Makers Opera; Tony Ayres, cond.; with Julian Smith (Amahl) and Valerie Matthews (Mother) (on a double-bill with *Amelia al ballo*)

W3.42    1989 (Dec 12): Washington, DC; John F. Kennedy Center for the Performing Arts; Eisenhower Theater; with Joel Chaiken (Amahl), Suzanna Guzman (Mother), Edward Crafts (Melchior), Paul Gudas (Kaspar), and Alvy Powell (Balthazar) (Kennedy Center Holiday Festival)

*Review:*

W3.42a   Roca, Octavio. "'Amahl' is Tired, and it Wearies Us." *Washington Times*, (December 14, 1989)
". . . the modest size of Tuesday's opening night audience may be a sign that this little 1951 charmer finally may be headed for the neglect it richly deserves."

W3.43    1990 (Jan 6): Biggar, England; Gillespie Centre; Opera West; Raymond Bramwell, cond.; with David Priestley (Amahl), Marilyn de Blieck (Mother), Robert Traynor (Melchior), Henry Walker (Balthazar), and Kevin Tillett (Kaspar)

*Review:*

W3.43a   Monelle, Raymond. "Amahl and the Night Visitors." *Opera* (England) 41 (March 1990): 376.
It was a mistake to " . . . think that real crudity would do in place of the comic rusticity of the shepherds; the chorus were encouraged to stumble, leer and get lost . . . with an effect that was predicably embarrassing."

W3.44    1990 (Dec 7): Salt Lake City; Capitol Theatre; Utah Opera; Byron Dean Ryan, cond.; Utah Chamber Orchestra; with Joseph Heninger-Potter (Amahl), Tricia Swanson (Mother), Dave Arnold (Kaspar), Don Becker (Melchior), William Goeglein (Balthazar), and Greg Griffiths (Page) (on a double-bill with Humperdinck's *Hansel and Gretel,* and preceded by Saint-Saëns' *Carnival of the Animals*)

*Reviews:*

W3.44a   Reese, Catherine. "A New Look for a Holiday Classic." *Salt Lake City Tribune*, (December 7, 1990)
Short non-critical review. "Utah Opera revived a Christmas tradition last season, bringing back Menotti's 'Amahl and the Night Visitors' after a five-year absence . . . [and] this year's edition features many familiar faces. . ."

70    Works and Performances

W3.44b    Stowe, Dorothy. "'Amahl,' an Improved 'Hansel' Offer Double Delight." *Deseret News* (Salt Lake City, UT), (December 10, 1990)
" . . . Heninger-Potter sang Amahl competently but is too large to project the waifish pathos of this character, which by its nature calls for a little boy."

W3.45    1992 (Nov 28): Highgate, North London; Jackson's Lane Community Centre; Opera South; Ian Walker, piano; Cathy Cardozo, oboe; with Toby Pardoe (Amahl), Lisa Nolan (Mother), and Kevin West (Kaspar)

*Review:*

W3.45a    Sommerich, Phillip. "Opera South's Amahl in Highgate." *Musical Opinion* 116 (February 1993): 61.
"The fidget factor is having a good measure of success among young audiences, and Opera South passed that test with flying colours."

W3.46    1992 (Dec 11): New Haven, CT; Sprague Memorial Hall; Morse Recital Hall; Yale Opera; Gary Kudo, piano; Elizabeth Dodson, oboe; with Kelly Clark (Amahl), Cynthia Zielski (Mother), Richard Appelgren (Kaspar), Timothy Truschel (Melchior), Rubin Casas (Balthazar), and Ding Gao (Page)

*Review:*

W3.46a    Colurso, Mary. "Yale Opera Students Have Stars in Eyes over 'Night Visitors.'" *New Haven Register*, (December 6, 1992)
"A cast of Yale graduate students will likely wear simple clothing . . . For example, tuxedos will substitute for the kings' majestic robes. Props will be minimal, scenery nonexistent."

W3.47    1992 (Dec 11): San Juan, PR; Conservatory of Music; Jesús María Sanroma Hall; Opera Workshop; Rosalín Pabón, cond.; with Soraya Hugo/Juan Carlos Lathroun (Amahl), Ana Herrero (Mother), and Jorge Ocasio (Balthazar)

*Review:*

W3.47a    Routte Gomez, Eneid. "'Amahl and the Night Visitors' Pulls a New Miracle." *San Juan Star* (San Juan, PR), (December 10, 1992)
"It will look like a Christmas card . . . for budgetary reasons, the sets will be more suggestive than realistic. But a pox on the budget . . ."

*Amahl and the Night Visitors* 71

W3.48 1992 (Dec 11): Kansas City; Lyric Opera of Kansas City; with Michael Piane (Amahl), Jane Gilbert (Mother), Brian Steele (Melchior), Bruce Barr (Kaspar), Michel Warren Bell (Balthazar), and David Okerlund (Page)

*Review:*

W3.48a Cantrell, Scott. "Lyric's 'Amahl' Fills Well its Role as a Child's Christmas Opera." *Kansas City Star*, (December 12, 1992)
"Even for adults, opera can be a challenging, even an off-putting, medium. But it's hard to imagine a better child's introduction . . . and, nigglings aside, the Lyric Opera production is a fetching one."

W3.49 1994 (Dec 14): New York; Kaye Playhouse; Il Piccolo Teatro Dell'Opera; Anton Coppola, cond.; with Paul Galinas (Amahl), Nan Hughes (Mother), Daryl Henriksen (Kaspar), Sam Kinsey (Melchior), James Butler (Balthazar), and Paul Lamont Green and Justin Holmes (Pages)

*Review:*

W3.49a Kozinn, Allan. "In Performance: Classical Music." *New York Times*, 1 (December 17, 1994): 19.
". . . though its flaws are legion, it does offer some sweetly lyrical music, to say nothing of a grand theme: the redemptive power of generosity."

W3.50 1995 (Dec 8): Dallas; Deep Ellum Opera Theatre; with Brandon Snook/Jayson Allen (Amahl), Jacquelyn Lengfelder/Colleen Bolthouse (Mother), and Joe Don Harper (Kaspar), Jinyoung Jang (Melchior), and Van Anthony Hall (Balthazar) (set in what might be a Palestinian refugee camp, with the three kings represented by a modern Western admiral, a Korean potentate, and an African king in *kennte* cloth)

*Review:*

W3.50a Sime, Tom. "Welcome Guest." *Dallas Morning News*, (December 9, 1995)
". . . both singing and acting are charming, and there are enough design eccentricities to allow for surprises even in this well-worn chestnut."

W3.51 1995 (Dec 15): Lexington; Wesley United Methodist Church; Opera of Central Kentucky; with Valerie Miller (Amahl), Alicia Helm (Mother), and Everett McCorvey (Kaspar), Barry Lawrence (Melchior), and Daniel Koehn (Balthazar) (all cast members were Black except Koehn)

*Review:*

W3.51a  "Non-Traditional Amahl." *Lexington Herald-Leader* (Lexington, KY), (December 10, 1995)
"Opera hasn't always been hospitable to black performers, so it's good to see our local group doing so," says McCorvey.

W3.52  1996 (Nov 15): Hartford, CT; Congregational Church; Richard Einsel, cond.; with Ben Fink (Amahl), and Anna Maria Silvestri (Mother) (Asylum Hill Music Series)

W3.53  1996 (Nov 22): Greensboro; University of North Carolina, Greensboro School of Music; Aycock Auditorium; David Holley, cond.; with Steven Martin (Amahl), Chantal Sosa (Mother), Jesse Padgett (Melchior), Brett Pryor (Balthazar), and George Johnson (Kaspar)

*Review:*

W3.53a  Jones, Tina P. "'Amahl' Gets Gentle Treatment." *News & Record* (Greensboro, NC), Triad/State (November 23, 1996): BG4.
"Music, voices and words can be swallowed up by Aycock Auditorium. Perhaps this gentle, accessible, small opera, with its message of family love and childlike faith, would play out more dramatically in a smaller theater."

W3.54  1996 (Dec 6): Las Cruces; Recital Music Center; New Mexico State University; Don Ana Lyric Opera Company; with Guillermo Quezada, cond.; Las Cruces Symphony; Nicole Lamartine (Amahl), Tammy Jenkins (Mother), John Thompson (Melchior), Marcos Virgil (Kaspar), and Jon Linford (Balthazar)

W3.55  1996 (Dec 7): Spring Green, WI; Gard Theater; Rural Musicians Forum; Bob Willoughby, piano; with Holly Hafermann (Amahl), Nancy Giffey (Mother), Gene Hafermann (Melchior), Mitch Feiner (Balthazar), George Manson (Kaspar), and Ben Greenwood (Page)

*Reviews:*

W3.55a   Smith, Susan Lampert. "Dreaming of a Spring Green Christmas: All the Arts Shine on Stage as the Holiday Season Begins." *Wisconsin State Journal*, Hometown (November 25, 1996): 1B.
"It never ceases to amaze me the amount of incredibly gifted people we have in the area," says Amahl's choral director, Jan Swenson. "We draw on American Players Theater, local arts and craftspeople and musicians."

W3.55b   Greenwood, Don. "Between the Lines." *Home News* (Spring Green, WI), (December 1, 1996)
". . . beyond the descriptive range of the usual superlatives. Without doubt, it was one of the finest and most moving productions on the stage of the Gard in many years."

W3.56    1996 (Dec 7): Anchorage; Sydney Laurence Theatre; Grant Cochran, cond.; Anchorage Concert Chorus; with Aaron Young (Amahl), Sherri Weiler (Mother), Robert Clink (Melchior), Ric Davidge (Kaspar), James Todd (Balthazar), and Matt Fernandez (Page)

*Review:*

W3.56a   Stadem, Catherine. "Sold-out House Sees Divine 'Amahl.'" *Anchorage Daily News*, Lifestyles (December 10, 1996): 8E.
"Sometimes people and place are blessed with just the right combination of voices, actors and musicians — and that is what happened Saturday at the Sydney Laurence Theatre."

W3.57    1996 (Dec 8): Memphis, TN; Christ United Methodist Church; with Matt Giebel (Amahl), Patricia Etienne (Mother), David Aiken (Melchior), Roger Havranek (Kaspar) and Erik Johanson (Balthazar)

*Review:*

W3.57a   "Best Bets." *Commercial Appeal* (Memphis, TN), Playbook, (December 6, 1996): 2E.
"What's new about this is that it's a road show offered by David Aiken, a retired Indiana University professor who sang the role of King Melchior on Broadway and national television in the '50s."

W3.58    1996 (Dec 12): Baton Rouge, LA; Bon Marché Playhouse; Baton Rouge Little Theatre; Mary Bresowar and Eric Andries (pianos); with Gregory

Gauthier (Amahl), Shelia Tate (Mother), Don Hill (Kaspar), Corey Trahan (Melchior), Derrick Vernon (Balthazar), and Jonathan Goodman (Page)

*Review:*

W3.58a  Coco, David. "BRLT Has a Winner with 'Amahl' Staging." *Advocate* (Baton Rouge, LA), People (December 14, 1996): 9E.
"Most church choirs do not have the vocal and technical resources to do justice to Menotti's miracle play . . . a cast that could hardly be bettered."

W3.59  1996 (Dec 18): St. Paul, MN; Ted Mann Concert Hall; Hugh Wolff, cond.; St. Paul Chamber Orchestra; James Sewell Ballet; with Maria Jette (Amahl, danced by Sally Rousse), Bonita Hammel (Mother, danced by Penelope Freeh), Mark Schowalter (Kaspar, danced by Anna Laghezza), Peter Halverson (Melchior, danced by Jesse Hammel), James Ramlet (Balthazar, danced by Christian Burns), and James Sewell (Page) ("The production combines Sewell's traditional ballet choreography with the gestural style of American Sign Language")

*Review:*

W3.59a  Anthony, Michael. "SPCO's 'Amahl' Has Honest Charm; Sewell Ballet Heightens the Tale's Emotions, Keeps its Poignance." *Star Tribune* (Minneapolis), Variety (December 20, 1996): 2E.
"Wisely, Sewell adheres closely to Menotti's clear outlines, allowing the choreography to establish relationships among the characters, while heightening the more emotional moments and never veering from the basic charm and poignance of the tale."

W3.60  1996 (Dec 6): Dallas; Deep Ellum Opera Theatre; Galen Jeffers, piano; with Van Kekanui/Nat Loftin (Amahl), Alice E. Leak/Shelley Crawford (Mother), Ralph Stannard (Melchior), Germaine Darrell Wooten (Balthazar), and Mario Antonio Perez (Kaspar)

*Reviews:*

W3.60a  Taitte, Lawson. "'Visitors' Is a Welcome Guest; DEOT Production Stresses Musical Side of Menotti's Christmas Opera." *Dallas Morning News*, Overnight (December 7, 1996): 41A.

"... Ms. Kekanui has two enormous liabilities in playing Amahl — she's the wrong gender, and she's too old. This is one boy soprano role that really has to be played by a boy soprano. Even the best young woman upsets the work's balance immensely."

W3.60b  Fowler, Jimmy. "Holy Snooze: Not Just the Shepherds Count Sheep in Amahl and the Night Visitors." *Dallas Observer*, (December 26, 1996) "... this version ... is guaranteed to make you snooze this and every other night before Christmas."

W3.61  1996 (Dec 23): Sarasota, FL; Golden Apple Dinner Theatre; with Huck Walton (Amahl), Cynthia Heininger (Mother), Roy Johns (Melchior), Jay Strauss (Balthazar), and Michael Marcello (Kaspar)

*Review:*

W3.61a  Handelman, Jay. "Simplicity Aids a Winning 'Amahl.'" *Sarasota Herald-Tribune* (Sarasota, FL), (December 13, 1996): 22.
"... the music features a maturity rarely heard in the typically saccharine kiddie show. And when Heininger's singing, it's always worth listening."

W3.62  1996 (Dec 27): Raleigh; Memorial Auditorium; Opera Company of North Carolina; Lorenzo Muti, cond.; St. Stephen's Chamber Orchestra; Concert Singers of Cary; with Anthony Roth Costanzo (Amahl), Angelina Reaux (Mother), Douglas Perry (Kaspar), Kevin Deas (Melchior), and Herbert Eckhoff (Balthazar)

*Reviews:*

W3.62a  Tonkonogy, Alwin. "Opera Company Makes Fine Debut with 'Amahl.'" *News and Observer* (Raleigh, NC), C (December 30, 1996): 7.
"If this fledgling company continues to provide the high quality of performance we heard in this production, we will be fortunate. Raleigh needs, and one hopes will support, opera presentations that offer so much."

W3.62b  Credle, Melanie. "Young Professionals Get the Lead in 'Amahl.'" *Herald-Sun* (Raleigh, NC), Preview (December 27, 1996): 5.
Says director Galbraith, "I have raised the overall production level about 10 degrees ... It's a wonderful cast. I'm very proud of it. It's really unprecedented for this area."

76    Works and Performances

W3.63    1997 (Dec 6): Xenia, FL; Xenia Westminster Presbyterian Church; OperaFunatics of the Miami Valley; Xander Subashi (Amahl), Gloria McNamara (Mother), Steve Bleeke (Kaspar), Greg Howard (Melchior), William Caldwell (Balthazar), and Matthew Bone (Page)

♦ DISCOGRAPHY

COMPLETE RECORDINGS

W3.64    Chet Allen (Amahl), Rosemary Kuhlmann (Mother), Andrew McKinley (Kaspar), David Aiken (Melchior), Leon Lishner (Balthazar), Frank Monachino (Page); Chorus and orchestra conducted by Thomas Schippers.
RCA Victor LM 1701 (1952); RCA Victrola VIC 1512 (1970); RCA Educational Records DEM1-0029 (1973), LP, mono.; RCA Gold Seal 6485-4, analog, stereo., Dolby processed, cassette, "digitally remastered analog recording" (1987); RCA Gold Seal 6485-2-RG, analog, compact disc (1987)
Original cast of the 1951 NBC telecast.

W3.65    James Rainbird (Amahl), Lorna Haywood (Mother), John Dobson (Kaspar), Donald Maxwell (Melchior), Curtis Watson (Balthazar), Christopher Painter (Page); Chorus and Orchestra of the Royal Opera House, Covent Garden conducted by David Syrus.
TER Classics CDTER 1124, digital, stereo., compact disc (1987); MCA Classics MCAC 6218, cassette, stereo., Dolby processed (1986); MCA Classics MCA-6218, digital, stereo., LP, 12 in. (1987) ; Musical Heritage Society MHS 512042 [on container, MHS 512042A], digital, stereo., compact disc (1987); Musical Heritage Society MHS 912042L, analog, stereo., LP (1987); Musical Heritage Society MHC 312042H, digital, stereo., compact disc (1987)
Recorded at the Sadler's Wells Theatre, London, Dec 21, 1986.
"Recording based on the first professional staging . . . by The Royal Opera House, Covent Garden."

W3.66    Kurt Yaghjian (Amahl), Martha King (Mother), John McCollum (Kaspar), Richard Cross (Melchior), Willis Patterson (Balthazar), Julian Patrick (Page); Orchestra and chorus conducted by Herbert Grossman.
RCA Victor LM 2762 (mono), LSC 2762 (stereo.) LP (1964)
"Cast of the NBC Opera Company, December 1963 television production."
Recorded in Webster Hall, New York City.

Selections

*Suite*

W3.67  Cleveland Pops Orchestra; Louis Lane, cond.
Epic LC 3819 (mono), BC 1154 (stereo.), LP (1962)
Album title: Music for Young America.
With works by Copland, Riegger, Elwell, and Shepherd.

*Dance of the Shepherds*

W3.68  St. Olaf Choir; Kenneth Jennings, director.
St. Olaf Records E-1070/1, 2 discs, LP, stereo. St. Olaf Records E-1839, digital, stereo., compact disc (1991)
Recorded in Skoglund Center Auditorium on the St. Olaf College campus, Northfield, Minn.
Album title: What Child Is This?: Christmas at St. Olaf College.
Recorded in Skoglund Center Auditorium on the St. Olaf College campus.
With works by Vaughan Williams, Hallcok, Honegger, Bach, Naylor, Distler, Anderson, Rutter, Tschesnokoff, Willan, Herman, Luther, Jennings, Howells, Schultz, and Grechaninov.

*Introduction, March, Shepherds' Chorus*

W3.69  New Zealand Symphony Orchestra; Andrew Schenck, cond.
Koch International Classics 2-7005-4, cassette, analog (1990); Koch International Classics 3-7005-2, compact disc, digital, stereo. (1990)
Recorded at Symphony House, Wellington, New Zealand, October 1989.
With *Sebastian (Ballet Suite)* and Barber's *Souvenirs*.

*Shepherds' Chorus*

W3.70  John Yeakey, bass; Fountain Street Choir; Arthur Kurtze, accompanist; Beverly Howerton, director.
Recorded Publications, LP, stereo. (1962)
Album title: Sing, O Heavens: a Christmas Album.
With works by Burt, Willan, Britten, Adam, Tours, Persichetti, Handel, Thompson, Gevaert, and Nelson.

*"I Walk, Mother"* and *"Do You Really Want to Go?"*

W3.71  Chet Allen, boy soprano, Rosemary Kuhlmann, mezzo-soprano; Orchestra and chorus conducted by Thomas Schippers.
DCC Compact Classics CZS (4)-135 (A28552–A28555), 4 CDs (1997)
". . . from the '20s to the '70s . . . musical entertainment through music composed or embraced by the gay and lesbian culture" – Container.
Album title: Club Verboten.
Concept by Marshall Blonstein, text by Richard Oliver.

### ♦ SELECTED RECORDING REVIEWS

W3.72  Todd, Arthur. "Theatre on the Disc." *Theatre Arts* 36 (June 1952): 6-7.
Brief reviews of then-recent recordings of *Amahl, The Medium, The Telephone, The Consul, Sebastian, Amelia al ballo,* and *The Old Maid and the Thief.*

W3.73  Miller, Philip L. "New Amahl." *American Record Guide* 31 (December 1964): 296.
Review of the RCA Victor recording (LM-2762, mono, and LSC-2762, stereo). "On hearing the playback the composer was delighted, and well he might be, for everything is beautifully in place in this performance."

W3.74  Miller, Philip L. "Original-Cast *Amahl.*" *American Record Guide* 37 (December 1970): 208.
Review of the RCA Victrola VIC 1512 recording. "In a way this recording cannot ever be superseded, and I suspect that at least those with long enough memories will prefer it [over the newer stereo release]. The sound, though pre-stereo, is quite acceptable."

W3.75  Coggi, Anthony D. "Menotti. Amahl and the Night Visitors." *Fanfare* 11 (March-April 1988): 145-146.
Review of the RCA Gold Seal 6485-2 RG (CD) recording. This recording boasts ". . . the personal presence of the composer in the recording studio . . . so the claim of authenticity is . . . valid. . ."

W3.76  Teachout, Terry. "Menotti 'Amahl and the Night Visitors.'" *High Fidelity/Musical America* 38 (April 1988): 68.
Review of the RCA 6485 2 RG recording. "The digitally remastered mono sound is good enough . . . If you liked it then, you'll like it now."

W3.77　　Loomis, George W. "Menotti: Amahl and the Night Visitors." *American Record Guide* 51 (November-December 1988): 60-61.
Review of the Musical Heritage Society MHS 512042 (CD) recording. "I am perfectly happy to recommend this performance . . ., though the more conservative, historically-minded amongst us may incline toward the original version."

W3.78　　Vroon, Donald R. "Menotti: Sebastian Suite." *American Record Guide* 53 (July-August 1990): 71.
Short review of the Koch 7005 recording. "The opera is considered one of his best, and these excerpts definitely add to this record."

W3.79　　Seckerson, Edward. "Barber. Souvenirs, Op. 28 — Ballet Suite. Menotti: Sebastian — Ballet Suite. Amahl and the Night Visitors — Introduction; March; Shepherds' Dance." *Gramophone* 68 (September 1990): 507.
Review of the Koch International Classics 27005-4 (cassette), 37005-2 (compact disc) recording. " . . . Menotti's lovely opening pages are an appetizing reminder of its melodic *tinta*, making one regret that he never saw fit to devise a full symphonic suite from the opera . . . Decent recording, big-boned and open."

W3.80　　North, James H. "Barber: Souvenirs, op. 28. Menotti: Sebastian. Amahl and the Night Visitors: Introduction; March; Shepherd's Dance." *Fanfare* 14 (September-October 1990): 162-163.
Review of the Koch International Classics CD 7005 recording. " . . . these six minutes leave us with the kindest possible thoughts about Menotti."

W3.81　　Saltzman, Eric. "Barber: Souvenirs . . . Menotti: Sebastian, Ballet Suite. Amahl and the Night Visitors. Introduction, March, and Shepherds' Dance." *Stereo Review* 56 (January 1991): 98.
Short mention of the Koch International Classics 3-7005-2.

W3.82　　Grueninger, Walter F. "Barber: Souvenirs and Menotti: Sebastian; Amahl and the Night Visitors." *Consumers' Research Magazine* 74 (February 1991): 43.
Review of recording with the New Zealand Symphony under Andrew Schenck. "Totally idiomatic, never over dramatized, delightful playing. Well recorded in Wellington."

W3.83    Crowe, Jerry. "Songs in the Key of Gay Life; Pop Music: 'Club Verboten' Catalogs the Contribution of the Gay and Lesbian Community to Mainstream Popular Music." *Los Angeles Times*, (April 9, 1997): 1.
Review of the Club Verboten recording. "Though not all were written or performed by homosexuals, the cuts . . . have all made a strong connection to gay and lesbian listeners either because of their lyrical themes or the artists involved."

W3.84    Piccoli, Sean. "Anthology Fever: It's All The Beatles' Fault." *Sun-Sentinel* (Ft. Lauderdale, FL), Arts & Leisure, (May 4, 1997): 10.
Review of the Club Verboten recording. " . . . charts the creative face of gay life in the 20th century, chronicling music by gay talents in multiple genres, as well as songs that gay culture has adopted as its own, regardless of the performer's orientation."

W3.85    Kennicott, Philip. "On Classical Side, 'Club Verboten' Had Predecessors." *St. Louis Post Dispatch*, (June 22, 1997): 4.
Review of the Club Verboten recording. "It's a throwback to include Tchaikovsky and Saint-Saens alongside popular music, but a welcome one."


**W4**    ***AMELIA AL BALLO (AMELIA GOES TO THE BALL)*** (1937; G. Ricordi)

Opera buffa in one act.

### ♦ ABOUT THE WORK

W4.1    Howard, John Tasker and Arthur Mendel. *Our Contemporary Composers: American Music in the Twentieth Century.* p. 207-236. New York: Thomas Y. Crowell, 1941.
"Menotti represents something of a phenomenon in American music; before he was twenty-six he had completed, and seen produced, an opera of such sparkling gaiety and charm that it disarmed all criticism."

### ♦ SELECTED PERFORMANCES

W4.2    1937 (Apr 1): Philadelphia; Academy of Music; Fritz Reiner, cond.; Curtis Student Orchestra; with Margaret Daum (Amelia), Edwina Eustis (Her Friend), Conrad Mayo (Husband), William Martin (Lover), Leonard Treash (Police Chief), Wilburta Horn (Cook), and Charlotte

Daniels (Maid) (English version by George Mead; on a double bill with Milhaud's *Le pauvre matelot*)

W4.3    1939 (Nov 14): St. Louis; St. Louis Grand Opera Association; Laszlo Halasz, cond.; with Florence Kirk (Amelia), Nancy Hitch Fordyce (Friend), Robert Weede (Husband), Giulio Gari (Lover), and Lorenzo Alvary (Police agent) (on a double-bill with *I Pagliacci*)

W4.4    1948 (Apr 8): New York; New York City Opera; Julius Rudel, cond.; with Frances Yeend (Amelia), Walter Cassel (Husband), Marilyn Horne (Lover), Gean Greenwell (Police agent), and Bette Dubre (Friend) (on a double-bill with *The Old Maid and the Thief*)

*Reviews:*

W4.4a    "Opera Can Be Fun." *Time* 51 (April 19, 1948): 50.
". . . no crashing success when produced at the Metropolitan Opera ten years ago . . . [even now] it seemed pretty thin."

W4.4b    Smith, Cecil. "Operatic Gagster." *New Republic* 118 (April 26, 1948): 36-37.
"The music is obviously an importation, and the words, translated from the Italian, are sometimes clumsy in their relation to the music — a fault from which the later Menotti operas are notably free."

W4.5    1949 (Oct 9): New York; New York City Opera; Julius Rudel, cond.; with Frances Yeend (Amelia), Walter Cassel (Husband), Marilyn Horne (Lover), James Pease (Police agent), Rosalind Nadell (Friend) (on a double-bill with *The Old Maid and the Thief*)

W4.6    1951 (Jul 14): Central City, CO; Central City Opera House; Tibor Kozma, cond.; with Eleanor Steber (Amelia), Francisco Valentino (Husband), David Garen (Lover), Margaret Roggero (Friend), and Benjamin Thomas (Chief of Police) (on a double-bill with Suppé's *The Beautiful Galatea*)

*Review:*

W4.6a    Eaton, Quaintance. "Suppé and Menotti Operas Form New Central City Bill." *Musical America* 71 (August 1951): 9.

82  Works and Performances

"More relaxation and polish would have benefitted the reading of the difficult score, heard for the first time in a new reduction for small orchestra."

W4.7   1954 (Mar 24): Milan; La Scala; with Margherita Carosio (Amelia), Rolando Panerai (Husband), Giacinto Prandelli (Lover) (on a triple-bill with Virgilio Mortari's *La figlia del diavolo* and Mario Peragallo's *La Gita in Campagna*)

*Review:*

W4.7a  Brindle, Reginald Smith. "New Operas in Triple Bill at La Scala." *Musical America* 74 (April 1954): 7.
Menotti " . . . was revealed as a master of the theatre, and though the work is twenty years old, it retains its capacity to divert and hold the attention of the public. The work went well and received the unquestioned approval of the Scala public."

W4.8   1963 (May 5): New York; New York City Opera; Felix Popper, cond.; with Beverly Bower (Amelia), John Reardon (Husband), Carl Olsen (Lover), and Arnold Voketaitis (Police Sergeant) (on a double-bill with *The Medium*)

W4.9   1967 (Apr 20): Rome; Rome Opera; Bruno Bartoletti, cond.; with Edith Martelli (Amelia), Giuseppe Taddei (Husband), Ruggero Bordino (Lover), and Giorgio Tadeo (Chief of Police) (presented with works by Verettio and Schönberg)

*Review:*

W4.9a  Bellingardi, Luigi. "Rome." *Opera* (England) 18 (July 1967): 584.
" . . . civilized parody, lightness of touch and natural freshness with its obvious echoes of Puccini and Gallic-type wit, and a fluent sequence of arias and recitatives."

W4.10  1981 (Mar 13): West Palm Beach, FL; Palm Beach Civic Opera; Seymour Schonberg, cond.; with Susan Rada (Amelia), George Massey (Husband), Carlos Manuel Santana (Lover)

*Review:*

W4.10a De Marcellus, Juliette. "West Palm Beach." *Opera News* 45 (June 1981): 40.
Rada " . . . brought off the theatrical projection required by Menotti's music, displaying a superb sense of timing and intelligence in her handling of the eternal feminine."

W4.11 1984 (Apr 13): Dallas; Majestic Theatre; Dallas Opera; Nicola Rescigno, cond.; with Elizabeth Hynes (Amelia), Deidra Palmour (1st Chambermaid), Judith Christin (2nd Chambermaid), Jane Shaulis (Amelia's friend), Malcolm Arnold (Husband), Christopher Cameron (Lover), and Greg Ryerson (Chief of Police) (on a double-bill with *The Medium*)

*Reviews:*

W4.11a Ardoin, John. "Opera Reachers New Heights." *Dallas Morning News*, (April 16, 1984)
"As Amelia, soprano Elizabeth Hynes sang with great lyricism and warmth, and her characterization was part cat and part coquette."

W4.11b Chism, Olin. "Dallas Opera Goes it Alone with Fine Twin Bill." *Dallas Times Herald*, (April 16, 1984)
"Soprano Elizabeth Hynes brought a vivacious presence to the part of Amelia . . . while the rather nerdish bluster of the two men . . . was an amusing counterpoint."

W4.12 1987 (Apr 14): New York; Juilliard American Opera Center; Mark Stringer, cond.; with Jianyi Zhang, Korliss Uecker, Jeffrey Morrissey, and Keith Heimann (performed in Italian; on a double-bill with *Tamu-Tamu*)

*Review:*

W4.12a Davis, Peter G. "Trivial Pursuits." *New York* 20 (May 11, 1987): 64+.
"This is . . . a one-act Italian opera buffa that honorably and cleverly recycles all the conventions of the form as it was practiced from Pergolesi to Wolf-Ferrari."

W4.13 1987 (Nov 5): Philadelphia; Curtis Institute of Music; Herbert Gietzen, cond.; Curtis Student Orchestra; with Maria Fortuna (Amelia), Timothy

Sarris (Husband), Perry Brisbon (Lover), Cheryl Majercik (Friend), Seth Malkin (Chief of Police) (on a double-bill with *The Medium*)

Review:

W4.13a  Webster, Daniel. "Menotti Directs His 'Amelia' and 'The Medium.'" *Philadelphia Inquirer*, (November 7, 1987)
"Maria Fortuna . . . [was] a gifted actress and apt singer. Her voice seemed to start well back in her throat, and much of the text may be back there yet, but no matter. The portrayal was vivid — bursting really . . ."

W4.14  1989 (Nov 2): Birmingham, England; Crescent Theatre; Midland Music Makers Opera; Tony Ayres, cond.; with Lynda Shepherd (Amelia), John Hudson (Lover), Claire Bertram (Friend), and Roderick Easthope (Husband) (English version by George Mead; on a double-bill with *Amahl and the Night Visitors*)

Review:

W4.14a  Smaczny, Jan. "*Amelia Goes to the Ball* and *Amahl and the Night Visitors.*" *Opera* (England) 41 (January 1990): 114-115.
" . . . breath-takingly banal and Menotti's blend of blunt pastiche and overripe verismo lyricism manages to sidestep humour at every stage."

◆ DISCOGRAPHY

COMPLETE RECORDING

W4.15  Margherita Carosio (Amelia), Silvana Zanolli (First Maid), Elena Mazzoni (Second Maid), Maria Amadini (Friend), Rolando Panerai (Husband), Giacinto Prandelli (Lover), Enrico Campi (Police chief); La Scala Orchestra and Chorus; Nino Sanzogno, cond.
Angel ANG 35140, mono (1957); Odeon 3C 063-01334, LP, stereo. (196-?)
Sung in Italian.
Recorded in cooperation with the E.A. Teatro alla Scala, Milan.

SELECTIONS

*Overture*

W4.16   Columbia Symphony Orchestra; Thomas Schippers, cond.
Columbia ML 5638 (mono), MS 6238 (stereo.), analog, LP (1961)
Album title: Opera Overtures.
Program notes by David Johnson on container.
With overtures by Rossini, D'Indy, Mozart, Verdi, Smetana, and Weber.

W4.17   Columbia Symphony Orchestra; Thomas Schippers, cond.
Sony Masterworks Heritage MHK 62837 (analog), compact disc (1997)
Repressing of the 1961 Columbia recording.
With works by Barber, Berg, and D'Indy.

W4.18   Philadelphia Orchestra; Eugene Ormandy, cond.
RCA Victor 15377-B, 78 rpm, mono, 12 in. (194-?); Smithsonian RD 103-6, CD (1995), in series "Great American Orchestras"

W4.19   Warwick Symphony Orchestra [*i.e.,* Philadelphia Orchestra]
Camden CAL 238, mono (1955?)
With works by Liszt, Barber, and McDonald.

*"Amelia cara"*

W4.20   Gianpiero Malaspina, baritone.
Parlophone AT 0275.

*"While I Waste These Precious Hours"*

W4.21   Leontyne Price, soprano; New Philharmonia Orchestra; Nello Santi, cond.
RCA Victor LM 2529, LP, mono.; RCA Red Seal ARL1-2529, LP, stereo. (1978)
Album title: Great Soprano Arias From Mozart to Menotti.
Title on container: Prima donna, vol. 4.
With arias by Mozart, Berlioz, Wagner, Verdi, J. Strauss, Jr., Mascagni, Dvořák, Cilèa, Korngold, and Puccini.

♦ SELECTED RECORDING REVIEWS

W4.22   "Opera-Bouffe *Amelia al ballo.*" *Disques*, 77 (January-February 1956): 78.

*86   Works and Performances*

W4.23   Todd, Arthur. "Theatre on the Disc." *Theatre Arts* 36 (June 1952): 6-7.
Brief reviews of then-recent recordings of *Amahl, The Medium, The Telephone, The Consul, Sebastian, Amelia al ballo,* and *The Old Maid and the Thief.*

W4.24   Briggs, John. "Records: Operas by Menotti and Others." *New York Times,* 2 (December 19, 1954): 10.
Rather non-committal review of the Angel recording. " . . . an affectionate performance."

W4.25   Kolodin, Irving. "From 'Amelia' to 'The Saint.'" *Saturday Review* 38 (January 29, 1955): 37+.
Review of the Angel 35140 recording. "It is sung with practised ease, read with light and skimming dispatch . . . After all, these performers have this vocabulary bred in them as much as Menotti does."

W4.26   Simmons, Walter. "Barber: *Overture* . . . Menotti: *Amelia Goes to the Ball: Overture* . . . " *Fanfare* 21 (November-December 1997): 158-159.
Review of the 1997 Sony Masterworks Heritage recording. " . . . an absolutely sizzling reading, and, for some reason, the 36-year-old recording sounds as if it were made yesterday."


*W5*   *APOCALYPSE (APOCALISSE)*  (1951; G. Schirmer; 24 min.)

Symphonic poem.
3333/6431/timp.perc/cel.2hp.pf/str
Movements: Improperia (*adagio, solenne*) — La città celeste (The Celestial City, *andante sereno*— Gli angeli militanti (The Militant Angels, *allegro ma non troppo*) (The last movement was added after the 1951 premiere)

♦ SELECTED PERFORMANCES

W5.1   1951 (Oct 19): Pittsburgh; Syria Mosque; Victor de Sabata, cond.; Pittsburgh Symphony Orchestra [first two movements only]

W5.2   1952 (Jan 18): Philadelphia; Academy of Music; Victor de Sabata, cond. Philadelphia Orchestra

*Review:*

W5.2a    "Apocalypse." *Philadelphia Orchestra Program Notes* (January 18, 1952): 351+

W5.3     1952 (Jan 22): New York; Carnegie Hall; Victor de Sabata, cond.; Philadelphia Orchestra (with works by Mozart, Schumann, and Strauss)

*Review:*

W5.3a    Sabin, Robert. "Menotti's Apocalypse Has New York Premiere." *Musical America* 72 (February 1952): 204.
"... clever tricks of orchestration and borrowed some of the pungent harmonies and thematic patterns of ... *The Medium* ... The audience applauded ... vehemently, and seemed highly pleased with Mr. de Sabata."

### ♦ DISCOGRAPHY

W5.4     Orchestre symphonique de la R.T.B:F.; Spiros Argiris, cond.
EMS SBCD 6600, compact disc, digital, stereo. (1988)
Recorded at the studios of R.T.B.F. in 1988.
With *Sebastian*.

W5.5     Oregon Symphony Orchestra; James DePreist, cond.
Koch International Classics 3-7156-2H1, digital, stereo., compact disc (1992)
Recorded May 1992 at George Fox College, Bauman Auditorium, Newberg, Ore.
With works by Dello Joio and Lo Presti.

### ♦ SELECTED RECORDING REVIEWS

W5.6     Dickinson, Peter. "Menotti. Apocalypse. LoPresti. The Masks. Dello Joio. Meditations on Ecclesiastes." *Gramophone* 70 (January 1993): 43. Review of the Koch International Classics compact disc. "It comes from the period of Menotti's greatest operatic successes and makes an excellent vehicle for the Oregon Symphony under DePreist."

W5.7     Miller, Karl. "Menotti: Apocalypse." *American Record Guide* 56 (March-April 1993): 111.

88  Works and Performances

>Review of the Koch 7156 recording "It is eloquent, poetic, full of drama and expressive thematic material — wonderful, appealing music . . . DePreist brings out more of the nobility of the score."

W5.8  Stearns, David Patrick. "Apocalypse." *Stereo Review* 58 (April 1993): 96.
>Review of the Koch 3-7156 recording. "It's a vigorous, confident work with a theatricality that occasionally borders on melodrama . . . Committed performances . . . make for satisfying listening throughout."

*THE BEAUTIFUL SNOWFALL*  See:  *A Happy Ending*

W6  *THE BOY WHO GREW TOO FAST* (1982; G. Schirmer; 40 min.)

Opera in one act for young people with libretto (English) by Menotti. Commissioned by OperaDelaware (formerly the Wilmington Opera Society) Cast: S, girl S, boy S, T, T, Mz, Tr, B, non-singing role, children 1+pic.111/1110/timp.perc/pf.syn/str

♦ SELECTED PERFORMANCES

W6.1  1982 (Sep 24): Wilmington; Grand Opera House; OperaDelaware; Evelyn Swensson, cond.; with Denise Coffey (Miss Hope), Miriam Bennett (Lizzie Spender), Sara Hagopian (Mrs. Skosvodmonit), Phillip Peterson (Poponel), Frank Reynolds (Dr. Shrink), Joy Vandever (Miss Proctor), Peter Lugar (Little Poponel), Alan Wagner (Mad Dog), and Thomas Littel (Policeman)

*Reviews:*

W6.1a  Dekom, Otto. "Menotti's New Opera an Enchanting Success." *Wilmington Evening News* (Wilmington, DE), (September 25, 1982) Says Menotti, "Children will not put up with long-winded arias, overtures, interludes and ensembles where words are unintelligible. Therefore, the composer must build an intricate, fragile scaffolding of short, simple melodies."

W6.1b     "Opera Reviews." *Variety* 308 (October 27, 1982): 86.
          "The lead singers were in excellent voice, and Menotti's direction, which had pace and clarity, drew good performances from the 22 local children in the cast."

W6.1c     Floyd, Jerry. "Wilmington." *Opera News* 47 (December 4, 1982): 41-42.
          "A touching, brilliant piece, it has a tuneful, neoromantic score, briskly paced action and an easily understood moral: the composer stresses maintaining one's identity when faced with societal pressures."

W6.1d     Derrickson, Jay. "Wilmington." *Opera* (England) 34 (February 1983): 182.
          "The local talent responded to Menotti's direction with infectious charm, a quality all too lacking in the piece itself."

W6.2      1984 (Jan 23): Cannes, France; Philippe Bender, cond.; with Martine Cakveyri (Teacher), Bernard Jean Mura (Dr. Shrink), Florence Raynal (Mrs. Proctor), Juan Carlos Morales (Terrorist), Cecilia Norick (Poponel), and David Sosnowski and Christophe Auburtin (Little Poponel)

          *Reviews:*

W6.2a     Robertshaw, N. "Third Year Set for Midem Event: Menotti Premiere Is Highlight of Second Classique." *Billboard* 96 (February 11, 1984): 41+.

W6.2b     Neufert, Kurt. "Für Kinder jeden Alters: zwei Opern für junges Publikum von Gian-Carlo Menotti: Europäische Erstaufführungen in Cannes und Lyon." *Opernwelt* 25 (April 1984): 53-54.

W6.2c     Neufert, Kurt. "Menotti und die Oper fuer Kinder — zwei europäische Erstaufführungen in Cannes und Lyon." *Musik und Bildung* 16 (June 1984): 464-465.

W6.3      1985 (Jun 3): Charleston, SC; Queen Street Playhouse; Charleston Opera Company; Robin Zemp, cond.; children's chorus from students of Porter-Gaud, Ashley Hall, and Sullivan's Island Elementary schools; chamber orchestra; with Mary Ann Lee (Miss Hope), Ellen Wingard (Lizzie Spender), Evelyn Swensson (Miss Skosvodmonit), Paul Gee (Poponel), Jonathan Willis Brown (Dr. Shrink), Nancy Eaton Stedman

(Miss Proctor), John Van Dorsten (Little Poponel), and Anthony Deaton (Mad Dog) (Piccolo Festival)

*Review:*

W6.3a    McPhail, Claire. "Children's Opera Is Charming Blend of Fact, Fiction . . . With a Message." *News and Courier* (Charleston, SC), (June 4, 1985)
". . . it provided a charming 50 minutes of fact, fiction and humor packaged with Menotti's undeniable gift for musical composition and storytelling."

W6.4    1986 (Dec 11): London; Sadler's Wells; David Syrus, cond.; with Graham Godfrey (Poponel), Judith Howarth (Miss Hope), Paul Crook (Dr. Shrink), Elizabeth Bainbridge (Miss Proctor), Maureen Morelle (Mother), and Eric Garrett (Terrorist) (joint production of the Royal Opera House and Sadler's Wells in association with Youth and Music; on a double-bill with *Amahl and the Night Visitors*)

*Reviews:*

W6.4a    Sadie, Stanley. "Menotti." *Musical Times* 128 (February 1987): 96.
". . . succeeds on every plane: its lyricism, its appealing harmony, its impressive orchestral writing join . . . to tug to order on the heart-strings."

W6.4b    Taylor, Peter. "Opera and Ballet in London." *Musical Opinion* 110 (February 1987): 38-39.
The role of Poponel " . . . was taken with great zest by Graham Godfrey and the happy gang of schoolchildren were played with much obvious enjoyment by pupils from London schools."

W6.4c    Jacobs, Arthur. "*The Boy Who Grew Too Fast* and *Amahl and the Night Visitors*, Sadler's Wells Theatre." *Opera* (England) 38 (February 1987): 197-199.
"Some innocent pleasure, at least, will have been generated by this first British production. The children . . . were humorous, not silly, making the wish that Menotti had not encouraged such an over-caricaturing of the adult roles . . ."

## ♦ DISCOGRAPHY

W6.5   Judith Howarth (Miss Hope), Graham Godfrey (Poponel), Elizabeth Bainbridge (Miss Proctor), Maureen Morelle (Mrs. Skosvodmonit), Paul Crook (Dr. Shrink), Eric Garrett (Mad Dog); Royal Opera House Orchestra; David Syrus, cond.
Musical Heritage Society MHS 512254T, digital, stereo., compact disc (1988); Musical Heritage Society MHS 512254, digital, stereo., LP (1988); Musical Heritage Society MHS 912254, analog, stereo., LP (1988); Musical Heritage Society MHC 312254/312254Y, analog, stereo., Dolby processed, cassette (1988); TER Classics CDTER 1125, digital, stereo., compact disc (1989)
Recorded in association with The Royal Opera House; recorded at Abbey Road Studios on February 22, 1987.

W6.6   Vocal soloists; children's choruses; Orchestre régional Cannes-Provence-Côte d'Azur; Philippe Bender, cond.
Auvidis AV 4277, LP, stereo. (1984)
French translation by Charles Fabius.
Recorded at the Palais des Festivals de Cannes, Jan 23, 1984.

W6.7   Unidentified vocal soloists.
Musicmasters MMC 40152X/53T, 2 cassettes (1988)
Manufactured by Amreco.
Album title: Chamber music at the Dock Street Theatre.
With works by Kodály, Shostakovich, Dvořák, Mozart, and Vivaldi.

## W7   *A BRIDE FROM PLUTO* (1982; G. Schirmer; 38 min.)

Chamber opera in one act for children with libretto (English) by Menotti. Commissioned by the John F. Kennedy Center for the Performing Arts for its 1982 Imagination Celebration; with a grant from Mrs. Jean Kennedy Smith (trustee of the John F. Kennedy Center for the Performing Arts) and Senator Edward M. Kennedy.
Cast: Bar, Mz, B, 2 S
1(pic)011/1100/timp.perc/pf.syn/2vn.va.vc.db

### ♦ PREMIERE PERFORMANCE

W7.1   1982 (Apr 14): Washington, DC; John F. Kennedy Center for the Performing Arts; Terrace Theater; Lorenzo Muti, cond.; with Nicholas

*92   Works and Performances*

Karousatos (Billy), Robert Keefe (Father), Dana Krueger (Mother), Camille Rosso (Girlfriend), and Pamela Hinchman (Queen of Pluto)

*Reviews:*

W7.1a   Modi, Sorab. "Kennedy Centre." *Opera Canada* 23, 2 (1982): 37.
"Certain it is that you don't have to be a child to appreciate Menotti's latest opus for children."

W7.1b   Floyd, Jerry. "Washington, D.C." *Opera News* 47 (July 1982): 32.
"Miss Hinchman and her Plutonian entourage, including opera's first robot, cavorted with earthlings in Zack Brown's clever sets, a rural American Gothic house interior superimposed at times against a spaceship that delighted everyone."

W7.1c   Lowens, Irving. "Kennedy Center: Menotti A Bride from Pluto." *High Fidelity/Musical America* 32 (August 1982): MA21-22.
"The score, characteristic Menotti salted and peppered with electronic sound effects, is something of a disappointment. However, it does not interfere with the plot line."

W7.1d   Mott, Michael. "Washington." *Opera* (England) 33 (October 1982): 1058-1060.
"Despite excellent casting . . . Menotti's talky text and thin score . . . failed to attach themselves to one's memory."


*W8*   *THE BRIDGE* (1947)

Film script for screenplay contracted with MGM in 1947; never produced.


*W9*   *CANTI DELLA LONTANANZA* (1961; G. Schirmer; 15 min.)

Song cycle for high voice and piano; in Italian.
Movements: *Gli amanti impossibili* (Impossible Lovers) — *Mattinata di neve* (Snowy Morning) — *Il settimo bicchiere di vino* (The Seventh Glass of Wine) — *Lo spettro* (The Specter) — *Dorme Pegaso* (Pegasus Asleep) — *La lettera* (The Letter) — *Rassegnazione* (Resignation)

## ♦ SELECTED PERFORMANCES

W9.1    1967 (Mar 18): New York; Hunter College, Assembly Hall; with Elisabeth Schwarzkopf (soprano) and Martin Isepp (piano)

*Review:*

W9.1a   Movshon, George. "Elisabeth Schwarzkopf, Soprano." *High Fidelity/Musical America* 17 (June 1967): MA17.
"The style prescribed for Miss Schwarzkopf was a near-*parlando*, the accompaniment was a brand of musical chewing gum with no discernible melodic or harmonic distinction."

W9.2    1986 (Dec 13): Brooklyn; Brooklyn Academy of Music; Katherine Ciesinski (soprano) and Jean-Yves Thibaudet (piano) (Spoleto Comes to BAM series)

*Review:*

W9.2a   Crutchfield, Will. "Music: Menotti Program." *New York Times*, 3 (December 15, 1986): 22.
Menotti's ". . . chamber music, though not questing or gripping, has been sensitively conceived, and skillfully and affectionately carried out . . ."

W9.3    1988 (Nov 4): New Orleans; University of New Orleans; UNO University Club Center Ballroom; with Robin Lehleitner Mackin (soprano) and Ronald Brothers (piano) in "Gli amanti impossibili," "Il settimo bicchiere di vino," and "Rassegnazione," and with Nancy Assaf (soprano) and Peter Collins (piano) in "Lo spettro" and "La lettera" (performed during a Menotti Festival, produced by The University of New Orleans and Hispanidad)

## ♦ DISCOGRAPHY

W9.4    Karan Armstrong, soprano; Alfred Lutz, Mischa Salevic, violins; Stephan Blaumer, viola; Klaus Kühr, violoncello; Helga Storck, harp.
Etcetera KTC 1045, compact disc, digital, stereo. (1988)
With *Five Songs* (1981) and *Cantilena e scherzo.*

W9.5    Anne Victoria Banks, soprano; Silva Costanzo, piano.
Nuova Era Records 7122. Compact disc (1992)

*94   Works and Performances*

With *The Telephone* and *Ricercare and Toccata*.

W9.6   Blagovesta Karnobatlova Dobreva, soprano; Elena Mindizova, piano.
Balkanton VKA 11650, LP, analog, stereo. (1985?)
Album title: Pesni ot italianski kompizitori.
Recorded Mar 8-19, 1985, Studio 1 of the Bulgarian National Radio.
With work by Donaudy.

W9.7   Judith Howarth, soprano; Malcolm Martineau, piano.
Chandos CHAN 9605. digital, stereo., compact disc (1988)
Recorded at St. Paul's Church, Knightsbridge, June 28, 1997.
With *Martin's Lie* and *Five Songs*.

♦ SELECTED RECORDING REVIEWS

W9.8   Ardoin, John. "Menotti's Passion Erupts in CD Collection." *Dallas Morning News*, (November 20, 1988)
"Armstrong, however, is not the ideal interpreter . . . Her voice is unsteady and too grainy. At the beginning of her career it was probably an attractive lyric sound."

W9.9   Greene, David Mason. "Menotti: *The Telephone; Ricercare and Toccata on a Theme from The Old Maid and the Thief; Canti della lontananza.*" *American Record Guide* 56 (March-April 1993): 111-112.
Review of the Nuova Era 7122 (Koch) recording. ". . . strikes me as a pleasant salon trifle . . . If you must have the songs (typical Menotti texts) you might try Karan Armstrong on Etcetera: though not ideal, she is preferable to Ms. Banks."


*W10*   *CANTILENA AND SCHERZO* (1977; G. Schirmer; 12 min.)

Quintet for harp and string quartet.

♦ SELECTED PERFORMANCES

W10.1   1977 (Mar 15): New York; Lincoln Center; Alice Tully Hall; with Osian Ellis (harp), James Buswell (violin), Ani Kavafian (violin), Walter Trampler (viola), and Leslie Parnas (cello)

*Review:*

W10.1a Henahan, Donal. "A Tully Party Chez Alice." *New York Times*, 3 (March 17, 1977): 33.
The new work caressed ". . . the ear with sonorities that reminded one of Debussy or Schoenberg (*Verlkärte Nacht*, of course) . . . The work struck one as lovely on its own terms, a haunting visit to old musical ruins, so to speak."

W10.2 1977 (May 24): New York; Lunt-Fontanne Theatre (version choreographed by Martha Graham under title *Shadows*)

W10.3 1986 (Dec 13): Brooklyn; Brooklyn Academy of Music; Barbara Allen, harp; Ridge Quartet (Spoleto Comes to BAM series)

*Review:*

W10.3a Crutchfield, Will. "Music: Menotti Program." *New York Times*, 3 (December 15, 1986): 22.
Menotti's ". . . chamber music . . . has been sensitively conceived, and skillfully and affectionately carried out . . ."

♦ DISCOGRAPHY

W10.4 Marian Rian Hays, harp; San Diego Chamber Orchestra; Donald Barra, cond.
Koch 7215; Koch International Classics 3-7215-2, compact disc, digital, stereo. (1993)
Arrangement for harp with string orchestra.
With *Poema autunnale, Suite in sol maggiore per orchestra e organo*, and *Il tramonto*, by Respighi.

W10.5 Helga Storck, harp; Alfred Lutz, Mischa Salevic, violins; Stephan Blaumer, viola; Klaus Kühr, violoncello.
Etcetera KTC 1045, compact disc, digital, stereo. (1988)
With *Nocturne* and *Five Songs* (1981)

♦ SELECTED RECORDING REVIEWS

W10.6 Fogel, Henry. "Respighi: *Poema autunnale*, for Violin and Orchestra. *Suite in G for String Orchestra and Organ. Il Tramonto*, for Voice and

*96 Works and Performances*

String Quartet. Menotti: *Cantilena e scherzo,* for Harp and Orchestra." *Fanfare* 17 (May-June 1994): 227.
". . . a wonderful discovery, darkly lyrical in its *Cantilena* section . . . they turn in communicative performances."

W10.7   Oliver, Michael. "Respighi: *Poeme autunnale. Suite in G. Il tramonto.* Menotti: *Cantilena e scherzo.*" *Gramophone* 72 (August 1994): 56.
". . . for those who enjoy the voluptuous chromaticisms of his melodic style will find it attractive; it is certainly nicely played."

W10.8   Bond, David. "Respighi: *Autumn poem; Suite in G; Il Tramonto.* Menotti: *Cantilena and Scherzo.*" *American Record Guide* 57 (November-December 1994): 176.
Brief review of the Koch 7215 recording. "Menotti's scherzo offers a perfect addition to this program . . . The performance is sparkling and delightful."

*CAPRICCIO See: Fantasia for Cello and Orchestra*


*W11*   **THE CATALOGUE** (1943)

Satirical rendition of The Curtis Institute of Music's 1943-1944 catalogue (p. 1, 6, 10, and 11), written to honor Mary Curtis Bok.
Scored for three singers (TBB), piano, and bassoon.

♦ PREMIERE PERFORMANCE

W11.1   1943 (Dec 5): Philadelphia; Curtis Institute of Music (at a private Curtis Christmas party not open to the public nor the press; the performers are not noted on the autograph)


*W12*   **A CHANCE FOR ALEKO** (1961)

Television play written early in 1961.
Originally titled *The Chance,* written for CBS' *"Robert Herridge Theatre, "* but never produced.

*W13     CHIP AND HIS DOG* (1978; G. Schirmer; 30 min.)

Opera in two scenes for children with libretto (English) by Menotti.
Commissioned by the Canadian Opera Chorus.
Cast: boy S, mime, 2 A, 2 S, A, 2 non-singing roles; treble chorus
fl.bn./pf/vn.va.vc.db

♦ SELECTED PERFORMANCES

W13.1     1979 (May 4): Guelph, Ont.; War Memorial Hall; University of Guelph; Canadian Opera Company; Canadian Children's Opera Chorus; Bruce Ubukata, piano; David Kent and William Winant, percussion; with David Coulter (Chip), Andrea Kuzmich (Dog), Priscilla Heffernan (Messenger), John Kuzmich, alternating with Ben Carlson (Page), Laura Zarins (Princess), Heidi Hobday (Courtier), Valarie Williams (Doctor), Avril Helbig (Gardener), and Breffni O'Reilly (Scribe) (presented at the Guelph Spring Festival, celebrating the Year of the Child (1979) on a double-bill with Richard Rodney Bennett's *All the King's Men*)

*Reviews:*

W13.1a    Manning, Gerald. "Guelph Spring Festival." *Opera Canada* 20, 3 (1979): 28-29.
"The music is appropriate because it expresses the playful fairy-tale mood of the opera, and because, unlike Amahl, it must be managed by a cast of children. Menotti has written a work . . . which will likely enjoy frequent performing."

W13.1b    Schulman, Michael. "Spring Operas Beguile with Fairytales Old and New." *Performing Arts in Canada* 16, 2 (1979): 25.
". . . should prove even more effective when sung by young professional singers rather than children . . . the many solo parts would tax the vocal resources of most children's choirs."

W13.1c    Roewade, Svend A. K. "Guelph: A Spring Festival." *Opera* (England) 30 (Autumn 1979): 116-117.
". . . it was enjoyed just as much by children of all ages in the audience (this of course includes their parents) as by the children in the cast."

W13.2     1979 (Dec 16): Toronto; Bruce Ubukata, piano; Canadian Children's Opera Chorus; with David Coulter (Chip) and Andrea Kuzmich (Dog) (CJRT-Ryerson Institute's "A Gift of Music" Concert Series)

Review:

W13.2a  Mercer, Ruby. "Toronto: Canadian Children's Opera Chorus." *Opera Canada* 21, 1 (1980): 46.
" . . . a superb performance . . . There was the steady singing and exceptionally clear enunciation of David Coulter . . ."

W13.3  1981: Saskatoon, Sask.; Saskatoon Opera Association; Canadian Children's Opera Chorus; Robert Solem, cond. (on a double-bill with *Amahl and the Night Visitors*)

Review:

W13.3a  Popoff, Wilf. "Saskatoon Opera Assoc." *Opera Canada* 22, 2 (1981): 24.
"The Menotti magic is especially evident . . . sung entirely by children."

W13.4  1984 (Jan 28): Lyon, France; Mark Foster, cond.; with Brigitte Lafon (Chip), Yves Neff (Dog), Aline Dumas (Princess), Fabrice Pothier (Page), Maurice Xiberras (Doctor), and Marc Dufour and Geneviève Lièvre (Comedians)

Reviews:

W13.4a  Neufert, Kurt. "Für Kinder jeden Alters: zwei Opern für junges Publikum von Gian-Carlo Menotti: Europäische Erstaufführungen in Cannes und Lyon." *Opernwelt* 25 (April 1984): 53-54.

W13.4b  Neufert, Kurt. "Menotti und die Oper für Kinder — zwei europäische Erstaufführungen in Cannes und Lyon." *Musik und Bildung* 16 (June 1984): 464-465.

W13.5  1986 (Apr 20): New York; Preparatory Division of the Manhattan School of Music; with Richard Owen, Jr. (Chip), Nick Van Amburg (Dog), Linzie Tynes (Royal Messenger), and Barbara Heller (Princess) (on a double-bill with Peter Maxwell Davies' *The Rainbow*)

Review:

W13.5a  Crutchfield, Will. "Opera: Two by Menotti and Davies." *New York Times*, 3 (April 23, 1986): 19.
The opera " . . . drips with sentimental condescension to the future citizenry of the world."

W13.6    1997 (Jan 17): Kansas City; Johnson County Community College; Theater; a production of Lyric Opera of Kansas City; among the performers will be children for Summer 1996's Opera Camp plus six members of the Lyric's Honors Chorus (on a double-bill with John Davies' *The Three Little Pigs*)

♦ DISCOGRAPHY

W13.7    David Coulter (Chip), Andrea Kuzmich (Dog), Laura Zarins (Princess), Priscilla Heffernan (Messenger), John Kuzmich (Page), Valarie Williams (Doctor), Heidi Hobday (Courtier), Erica Giesl (Cook); Canadian Children's Opera Chorus; Derek Holman, cond.
Aquitaine-CBS Records Canada MS 90567.


*W14*    *THE CONSUL* (1950; G. Schirmer; 120 min.)

Opera in three acts with libretto (English) by Menotti.
Cast: Bar, S, A, B, 2 silent roles, Mz, B-Bar, 2 S, A, T, Bar, S
1(pic)1(ca)11/2210/timp.perc/hp.pf/str
*The Library of Congress Quarterly Journal of Current Acquisitions*, vol. 16, no. 1 (November, 1958) reports receipt of "A most welcome gift . . . from the composer himself, is his pencil draft of the piano-vocal score of *The Consul* . . . The manuscript is not dated, but at the end the composer dashed off the following heartfelt sentiment: 'The End Thank God!' . . . The holograph of a work of such distinction is an acquisition of extraordinary significance." *The Library of Congress Quarterly Journal of Current Acquisitions*, vol. 13, no. 1 (November, 1955) lists the receipt during the preceding year of *The Consul*. According to Wayne D. Shirley, Music Specialist at the Library of Congress, this is not a manuscript in Menotti's hand but a full score of the opera.

♦ ABOUT THE WORK

W14.1    Cowell, Henry. "Current Chronicle: New York." *Musical Quarterly* 36 (July 1950): 447-450.
Analysis of the opera, with musical examples. "The real impact of Menotti's stage works is not due to the music primarily, but rather to the exceptional integration of idea, text, music, and staging, an integration certainly helped in this instance . . ."

W14.2    "*Consul* Will Be Produced in Seven European Countries." *Pan Pipes of Sigma Alpha Iota* 43 (December 1950): 125.

*100 Works and Performances*

W14.3   Smith, Cecil. "Gian-Carlo Menotti: *The Consul.*" *Notes* (Music Library Association) 8 (December 1950): 125-126.
Review of the G. Schirmer vocal score. ". . . he has not improved at all in his two weakest areas, English prosody and melodic characterization. For my taste his first opera, *Amelia Goes to the Ball* remains his best, for when he wrote it he still wanted to be a musician more than he wanted to be a success."

W14.4   Smith, Cecil. "Menotti's *The Consul* Issued in Vocal Score." *Musical America* 70 (December 15, 1950): 34-35.
Review of the G. Schirmer vocal score. ". . . the score offers little evidence that he [Menotti] has taken time to investigate the central issues of operatic composition that still remain outside his purview."

W14.5   Benjamin, Arthur. "The Consul." *Music and Letters* 32 (July 1951): 247-251.
"It is the work of man who feels passionate pity, passionate humanity. Menotti is no ivory-tower composer . . . It is a great achievement on the part of a man of the theatre so to focus a hideous indignity and woe of our times."

W14.6   Kessler, Giovanna. "Intolerant mit 'Intolleranza.'" *Opernwelt* (February 1972): 12-13.

W14.7   Galatopoulos, Stelios. "Intolerant Nono." *Music and Musicians* 20 (February 1972): 10+.
Luigi Nono refuses permission for his opera *Intolleranza* to be performed at the Florence Maggio Musicale because Menotti's *The Consul* is to be given during the same festival.

W14.8   "Spoleto: Political Storm in a Tea-cup." *Opera* (England) 23 (March 1972): 217.
". . . Nono has withdrawn his opera *Intolleranza* from the [Florence] festival on the grounds that 'The Consul is pro-American, conceived during the Korean War' . . . The Rome correspondent to *The Guardian* commented that the attacks on Menotti may not be 'unrelated to the fact that he is being considered for the post of artistic director of the Teatro La Fenice in Venice, which also happens to be Signor Nono's home.'"

W14.9   Henahan, Donal. "Repetition: The Gravy in Which Art Floats." *New York Times*, 2 (June 9, 1974): 13.

Reply to Menotti regarding recent criticism of the composer's newly-revived opera, *The Consul*. "Menotti does not have to like the clichés of music critics; they do not have to like the clichés of 'The Consul.' What, to coin a phrase, could be fairer?"

W14.10  Marriott, Richard John. "Gian-Carlo Menotti, Total Musical Theatre: A Study of His Operas." Ph.D. dissertation, University of Illinois, 1975. From the author's abstract: "Menotti is most successful in his chamber operas: *The Medium, The Consul*, and *Amahl and the Night Visitors*. In the successful chamber operas, Menotti's goal of effective theatre is realized; they have complete integration of libretto, music, staging, and above all theatricality — they have the qualities of a consciously dramatic stage play."

W14.11  Roepke, Gabriela. "Bitter Lot." *Opera Journal* 10, 3 (1977): 3-7. Comparison of Cherubini's *Medea* and Menotti's *The Consul*. ". . . two operas which cannot appear more different at first sight, nevertheless offer many similar aspects."

W14.12  Blum, Michael I. "Gian-Carlo Menotti's *The Consul*: From Concept to Production." Research paper, M.M., Southern Illinois University, Dept. of Music, 1979.

W14.13  Amico, Fedele d'. "La musica e l'impegno." *Nuovo rivista italiana* 14 (July-September 1980): 321-332.
". . . the manner of evaluating a work of musical art in light of certain currents of musical criticism that are tied to political ideology . . . The author illustrates his point by reference to Menotti's *The Consul* and to works by Verdi, Schonberg, and Bartok" — Giancarlo Rostirolla.

W14.14  Ardoin, John. "Menotti Magic." *Dallas Morning News*, (May 22, 1983) Includes remarks made during Menotti's judging for the revamped C.B. Dealey Awards for Young Artists. "I wanted to prove that opera, if presented with the care and love for detail with which a play is presented, could find a new audience and even pay for itself, and no longer depend on subsidization. All of this I think I proved with *The Medium* and *The Consul*."

♦ SELECTED PERFORMANCES

W14.15  1950 (Mar 1): Philadelphia; Shubert Theatre; Lehman Engel, cond.; with Cornell MacNeil (John Sorel), Patricia Neway (Magda Sorel), Marie

*102    Works and Performances*

Powers (The Mother), Leon Lishner (Secret Police Agent), Chester Watson (First Police Agent), Donald Blackey (Second Police Agent), Gloria Lane (The Secretary), George Jongeyans (Mr. Kofner), Maria Marlo (The Foreign Woman), Maria Andreassi (Anna Gomez), Lydia Summers (Vera Boronel), Andrew McKinley (Nika Magadoff), and Francis Monachino (Assan)

*Review:*

W14.15a   Singer, Samuel L. "Philadelphia Premieres Menotti's *The Consul.*" *Musical Courier* 141 (March 15, 1950): 3.
"Menotti's music . . . underscores and highlights the action . . . [but] One believes that Menotti has not yet reached his peak as a composer of serious opera."

W14.16   1950 (Mar 15): New York; Ethel Barrymore Theatre; with same cast as in W14.15.

*Reviews:*

W14.16a   Nathan, George Jean. *The Theatre Book of the Year, 1949-1950: A Record and an Interpretation.* p. 249-254. New York: A. A. Knopf, 1950.
"Patricia Neway is vocally and dramatically the outstanding member of the company. Except for a momentary flatness and uncertainty . . . her performance of the wife contributes a full share toward the music drama's success."

W14.16b   Sabin, Robert. "Menotti's *The Consul* Begins New York Run on Broadway." *Musical America* 70 (March 15, 1950): 7.
". . . not to be missed, even though it may disappoint some of Mr. Menotti's warmest admirers in its more serious aspects as a work of art."

W14.16c   "Consul." *Theatre Arts* 34 (March 1950): 28-29.
General article with audition photographs. "Invitations to the auditions . . . were divided evenly between habitual investors and musical friends of Menotti."

W14.16d   Kolodin, Irving. "Menotti Moves Ahead." *Saturday Review of Literature* 33 (March 25, 1950): 63-63.
"For casual entertainment 'The Consul' will certainly be rewarding. Those with a more exacting standard will mark it as an expanding

instance of Menotti's capacity to dominate a musical-dramatic problem which appeals to him . . ."

W14.16e  Watt, Douglas. "Musical Events: 'The Consul.'" *New Yorker* 26 (March 25, 1950): 54+.
"It even seems trashy at times, in its unblushing appeal to the emotions and in its use of theatrical tricks, but then so are half the operas that have ever been written."

W14.16f  "Red Tape." *Time* 55 (March 27, 1950): 42.
". . . it was . . . Neway whose powerful denunciation aria in the second act stopped the show. When the curtain came down the new Broadway opera had to share the cheers with a new Broadway star."

W14.16g  S., H. "Opera of Our Age." *International Musician* 48 (April 1950): 12.
"The music is, in fact, as much an actor as those people on the stage. So it is lucky that the players are all of virtuoso calibre . . ."

W14.16h  Levinger, Henry W. "Menotti's *The Consul* Bows on Broadway." *Musical Courier* 141 (April 1, 1950): 7.
"Marie Powers, famous for her Madame Flora . . . again was brilliant as the Mother. Her lullaby is a deeply poignant highlight in her excellent delineation."

W14.16i  Krutch, Joseph Wood. "Drama." *Nation* 170 (April 1, 1950): 305.
"The cast . . . is not only excellent but also seems perfectly at home in the somewhat unconventional form."

W14.16j  "'Member of Wedding' 1st Choice of Critics; 'Consul' Top Musical." *Variety* 178 (April 5, 1950): 2.
*The Consul* won the New York Drama Critics' Circle award for the best musical of the Broadway season.

W14.16k  Phelan, Kappo. "Stage: The Consul." *Commonweal* 51 (April 7, 1950): 677.
". . . I do think it would be wise for him to consider that it is again only . . . his wonderful, wonderful cast . . . [that] can any way prove him to be not only a showman but also a musical dramatist."

W14.16l  "'Consul.'" *Life* 28 (April 10, 1950): 61-63.
Review with cast photographs. "Though his music in *The Consul* is not unfailingly distinguished, it unfailingly packs an emotional wallop . . ."

*104  Works and Performances*

W14.16m  Clurman, Harold. "Theatre: Bali Hai." *New Republic* 122 (April 10, 1950): 21-22.
"... well produced, and has an extremely good cast ... [including] Leon Lishner, whose sinister demeanor as Chief Police Agent scared me more than Scarpia ever does in Tosca."

W14.16n  Brown, John Mason. "Man's Inhumanity." *Saturday Review of Literature* 33 (April 22, 1950): 28-30.
"However ill or shrunken the theatre may be, it is a long, long way from dying so long as it possesses the vitality, the imagination, the sympathy, and the skill to make a production such as 'The Consul.'"

W14.16o  "Consul." *Theatre Arts* 34 (May 1950): 17.
"Patricia Neway ... gives an extraordinary performance. She is a fine singer and a brilliant actress who must be considered a front-rank star on the strength of this role alone."

W14.16p  Wyatt, Euphemia Van Rensselaer. "Theater." *Catholic World* 171 (May 1950): 148.
"With unerring instinct as to the dramatic exigency, Menotti's characters combine speech and song and ... only the music relieves the tensity of repetition with which he accents the frustration of the victims of consular bureaucracy ..."

W14.16q  Marx, H. "Menotti's 'Consul' Triumphs on Broadway." *Music News* 42 (June 1950): 25.

W14.16r  Haggin, B. H. "Music." *Nation* 170 (June 3, 1950): 557-558.
Due to pervasive pre-show publicity, "... its success ... was magnified enormously beyond what it would have achieved if it had been produced as an opera in the Metropolitan."

W14.16s  Beyer, William. "The State of the Theatre: Seasonal High Lights." *School and Society* 72 (September 16, 1950): 183.
Patricia Neway's " ... is a genuine theatrical personality and temperament, which is traced in her highly individual, almost stylized movement and arresting plasticity, revealing her vitality of person as well as dynamic artistry."

W14.16t  Thomson, Virgil. "Pathos and the Macabre" *in Music Right and Left* p. 79-81. New York: Henry Holt, 1951.

Reprint of Thomson's March 17, 1950 review of the first New York performance, which originally appeared in the *New York Herald Tribune*. "*The Consul* is a music drama of great power in a production remarkably efficient."

W14.17 1951 (Feb 7): London; Cambridge Theatre; Thomas Schippers, cond.; with Gloria Lane (The Secretary), Patricia Neway (Magda Sorel), Norman Kelley (Nika Magadoff), Elinor Warren (Vera Boronel), and Marie Powers (The Mother) (This performance was brought to London through negotiations by Sir Laurence Olivier)

*Reviews:*

W14.17a "Cambridge Theatre: 'The Consul.'" *Times* (London), (February 8, 1951): 8.
"The opera may not be vocally exacting, but it requires proper singing from all its cast; which it certainly got in a taut performance . . ."

W14.17b "Menotti's Experiment." *Times* (London), (February 16, 1951): 8.
"His experiment is of absorbing interest, but it falls between the two stools of tragedy on the one hand and opera on the other, and remains only a piece of 'good theatre.'"

W14.17c Kirstein, Lincoln. "Menotti's 'The Consul.'" *Opera* (England) 2 (March 1951): 175-178.
". . . a work of distinction, of sincerity in sentiment and of a relentless theatrical efficiency, while its force entirely derives from the fact that it is conceived and realized entirely in musical terms."

W14.17d "Menotti's Opera to Be Withdrawn." *Times* (London), (March 20, 1951): 6.
*The Consul* will be withdrawn from the Cambridge Theatre (London) after the March 31 evening performance since ". . . the present audiences are not sufficiently large to meet heavy costs of an operatic production." *See W14.17e*

W14.17e "The Consul." *Times* (London), (March 24, 1951): 4.
Since the announcement that The Consul was to be withdrawn from the Cambridge Theatre after the March 31 evening performance, ". . . there has been such a steady demand for seats that Sir Laurence Olivier has decided to continue its run for a further period of two or four weeks." *See W14.17d*

W14.17f   Jacobs, Arthur. "The Consul." *Musical Times* 92 (April 1951): 166.
"Led by Patricia Neway . . . the all-American cast sang with tremendous impact and without flaw."

W14.18   1951 (Dec 12): Portland, OR; Playhouse Theatre; Portland Civic Opera Association; Ariel Rubstein, cond.; with Ferne Misner (Magda Sorel), James Duyn (John Sorel), Jean Handzlik (The Mother), Robert McCoy (Secret Police Agent), Catherine Miller (The Secretary), Robert Leppert (Mr. Kofner), Violet Raschio (The Foreign Woman), Mildred Rommel (Anna Gomez), Frances Hoops (Vera Boronel), Dean Lieber (Nika Magadoff), and William Riggs (Assan)

*Reviews:*

W14.18a   Morse, Bob. "'The Consul' Rates Cheers on Pacific Coast Premiere." *Oregon Journal* (Portland, OR), (December 13, 1951)
". . . a performance, while not perfect, can stand on its own as an achievement. . .it can be unqualifiedly recommended."

W14.18b   A., P. "Menotti Gets Around." *International Musician* 50 (March 1952): 11-12.
"Rubstein . . . conducted Menotti's modern, colloquial score with fine insight and understanding, and kept that continuous forward pace so necessary to insure the success of an opera marked by high emotional tension."

W14.19   1951 (Dec 12): Los Angeles; University of Southern California; Carl Ebert's Opera Workshop; Ingolf Dahl, cond.; student orchestra; with Peggy Bonini (Magda Sorel), Katherine Hilgenberg (The Mother), William Vennard (Secret Police Agent), Chris Lachona (Nika Magadoff), and Kalem Kermoyan (Mr. Kofner)

*Review:*

W14.19a   A., P. "Menotti Gets Around." *International Musician* 50 (March 1952): 11-12.
"Menotti with his unerring sense of the theater offers with each part the possibility for flesh and blood characterization, and this opportunity was seized and made the most of by each of the young singers."

W14.20   1952 (Jan 17): Stockholm; Stockholm Opera; Sixten Ehrling, cond.; with Brita Hertzberg (Magda Sorel), Hugo Hasslo (John Sorel), Gertrud

Wettergren (The Mother), Benna Lemon-Brundin (The Secretary), Arne Wirén (Secret Police Agent), and Leon Björker, Arne Hendriksen, Eva Prytz, Ida Quensel, Bette Wermine, and Sven-Erik Jacobsson.

*Review:*

W14.20a  Sandberg, Ingrid. "Menotti's *The Consul* Given First Swedish Production." *Musical America* 72 (July 1952): 12.
"... Brita Hertzberg as a touching Magda Sorel. The rest of the cast was superbly chosen..."

W14.21  1952 (Oct 8): New York; New York City Opera; with Patricia Neway (Magda Sorel), Gloria Lane (The Secretary), Norman Kelley (Nika Magadoff), Maria Marlo (The Foreign woman), Richard Torigi (john Sorel), Mary Kreste (The Mother), Emile Renan (Secret Police Agent), George Gaynes (Mr. Kofner), Vilma Georgiou (Anna Gomez), Edith Evans (Vera Boronel), and Arthur Newman (Assan)

*Review:*

W14.21a  Watt, Douglas. "Musical Events: New Values." *New Yorker* 28 (October 18, 1952): 149.
"The production moved somewhat creakily, on the whole, and the story was less convincing and urgent than I had remembered."

W14.22  1954 (Nov 11): London; Sadler's Wells; Alexander Gibson, cond.; with John Probyn (John Sorel), Olwen Price (The Mother), Denis Dowling (Secret Police Agent), John Larsen (First Policeman), Vernon Rees (Second Policeman), Anna Pollack (The Secretary), Stanley Clarkson (Mr. Kofner), Marjorie Shires (The Foreign Woman), Helen Hillier (Anna Gomez), Rowland Jones (Nika Magadoff), Elisabeth Robinson (Vera Boronel), and Ronald Eddolls (Assan)

*Reviews:*

W14.22a  Rosenthal, Harold D. "Sadler's Wells." *Opera* (England) 6 (January 1955): 52-55.
"... theatrically its impact is something quite out of the ordinary, and Dennis Arundell's production...made no bones about assailing the audience's emotions in the most uncompromising way."

W14.22b  "Sadler's Wells Opera." *Musical Opinion* 78 (January 1955): 203.

108  Works and Performances

W14.23   1956 (Feb 8): London; Sadler's Wells; Alexander Gibson, cond.; with Amy Shuard (Magda Sorel), Anna Pollack (The Secretary), Ava June (The Foreign Woman), Rowland Jones (Nika Magadoff), Sheila Hardie (Anna Gomez), Patricia Johnson (Vera Boronel), Harold Blackburn (Secret Police Agent), and Judith Pierce (The Mother)

Review:

W14.23a   M., W. S. "Sadler's Wells." *Opera* (England) 7 (March 1956): 187-189.
"It is a masterpiece, perhaps, of the musical theatre and as such must find its level amongst such pieces as the works of Orff and Weill . . . As Magda Sorel, Amy Shuard gives a performance that touches greatness more closely than any she has previously given."

W14.24   1957 (Feb 11): Cleveland; Karamu Lyric Theatre; Helmuth Wolfes, cond.; with Zelma George (Magda Sorel)

W14.25   1960 (Feb 14): New York; New York City Opera; Werner Torkanowsky, cond.; with Patricia Neway (Magda Sorel), Chester Ludgin (John Sorel), Evelyn Sachs (The Mother), Regina Sarfaty (The Secretary), Jack Harrold (Nika Magadoff), Joshua Hecht (Secret Police Agent), Arnold Voketaitis (Mr. Kofner), Maria Marlo (The Foreign Woman), Maria di Gerlando (Anna Gomez), Ruth Kobart (Vera Boronel), and Dan Merriman (Assan)

Reviews:

W14.25a   Sargeant, Winthrop. "Musical Events: Imperishable Menotti." *New Yorker* 36 (February 27, 1960): 133-134+.
"Much of the success of last week's revival was due to the sterling dramatic and vocal gifts of Patricia Neway . . . who seems to have expanded the scope and subtlety of her characterization, giving the role a stature that is almost epic."

W14.25b   Merkling, Frank. "Light and Heavy." *Opera News* 24 (March 12, 1960): 27-28.
"It stands as a *tour de force*, a landmark on the road to American opera that has since veered in the direction of *The Ballad of Baby Doe* . . ."

W14.26   1962 (Mar 28): New York; New York City Opera; Werner Torkanowsky, cond.; with Richard Fredricks (John Sorel), Patricia Neway (Magda Sorel), Evelyn Sachs (The Mother), William Chapman

(Secret Police Agent), Marija Kova (The Secretary), George Gaynes (Mr. Kofner), Maria Marlo (The Foreign Woman), Mary Le Sawyer (Anna Gomez), Teresa Racz (Vera Boronel), Norman Kelley (Nika Magadoff), and Fredric Milstein (Assan)

*Review:*

W14.26a   Ardoin, John. "The Consul." *Musical America* 82 (May 1962): 25.
"It is impossible to think of anyone but Patricia Neway as Magda and her portrayal is surely one of the most memorable characterizations of the contemporary lyric stage."

W14.27   1964 (May 2): Vancouver; Vancouver Opera Association; Mario Bernardi, cond.; with Margarita Zambrana (Magda Sorel), Elaine Bonazzi (The Secretary), Dorothy Cole (The Mother), Chester Ludgin (John Sorel), Bernard Turgeon (Secret Police Agent), Alan Crofoot (Nika Magadoff), Peter Van Ginkel (Mr. Kofner), Audrey Glass (The Foreign Woman), Betty Phillips (Vera Boronel), and Marcelle Zonta (Anna Gomez)

*Review:*

W14.27a   Watmough, David. "Vancouver." *Opera* (England) 15 (August 1964): 548-549.
"Bernardi held the score in dutiful subservience to the libretto and, by refusing to indulge in excessive emotionalism at the highpoints of sentimentality in the opera, presented the musical worth of *The Consul* in the most attractive light possible."

W14.28   1966 (Mar 17): New York; New York City Opera; Vincent La Selva, cond.; with Sherrill Milnes (John Sorel), Patricia Neway (Magda Sorel), Evelyn Sachs (The Mother), Herbert Beattie (Secret Police Agent), Beverly Evans (The Secretary), David Smith (Mr. Kofner), Elizabeth Carron (The Foreign Woman), Ludmilla Azova (Anna Gomez), Elisabeth Farmer (Vera Boronel), Gene Bullard (Nika Magadoff), and Jack Bittner (Assan)

W14.29   1966 (Oct 6): New York; New York City Opera; Charles Wilson, cond.; with David Clatworthy (John Sorel), Patricia Neway (Magda Sorel), Evelyn Sachs (The Mother), Leon Lishner, alt. with Joseph Fair (Secret Police Agent), Beverly Evans (The Secretary), David Smith (Mr. Kofner), Julia Migenes (The Foreign Woman), La Vergne Monette

*110  Works and Performances*

(Anna Gomez), Charlotte Povia (Vera Boronel), Gene Bullard (Nika Magadoff), and Jack Bittner (Assan)

W14.30   1968: Tel-Aviv, Israel; Israel Festival; Gary Bertini, cond.; Israel Chamber Ensemble; with Netania Davrath (Magda Sorel), Rema Samsonov (The Mother), Willy Haparnas (Mr. Kofner), Seymour Schwartzman (John Sorel), William Wolff (Secret Police Agent), Carole Rosen (The Secretary), and Neil Jenkins (Nika Magadoff)

*Reviews:*

W14.30a   Pataki, Ladislaus. "Musikfest in Israel." *Orchester* 16 (October 1968): 441.

W14.30b   Gradenwitz, Peter. "Festivals: Israel." *Musical Times* 109 (December 1968): 1144.
"Though excellently performed . . . the work has lost much of its impact since it was first heard in the early 50s . . . and the music too eclectic, too merely illustrative to provoke deeper interest and sympathy."

W14.31   1969 (Jun 10): San Francisco; San Francisco Spring Opera; Charles Wilson, cond.; with Christina Krooskos (The Mother), Joy Davidson (The Secretary), and Jeannine Crader (Magda Sorel)

*Review:*

W14.31a   Jacobs, Arthur. "California Postscripts." *Opera* (England) 20 (August 1969): 690.
". . . despite the composer's taut and convincing production . . . the music no longer seems vital . . . I came away unmoved."

W14.32   1971 (Apr 12): Jaffa, Israel; Alhambra Theatre; Gary Bertini, cond.; with Netania Davrath (Magda Sorel), Joshua Hecht (John Sorel), Leon Lishner (Secret Police Agent), Willy Haparnas (Mr. Kofner), Ilana Bruckmann (The Secretary), and Adi Etzion, Rachel Nachmias, Bibiana Goldenthal (The Foreign Woman), Rema Samsonov (The Mother), and Gerald Stern (Nika Magadoff) (translated into Hebrew by Nissim Aloni)

*Review:*

W14.32a  Frankenstein, Alfred. "Jaffa." *Opera* (England) 22 (July 1971): 632.
"It was one of those performances where teamwork, cond., director and singers may be called ideal. This may well be the true future of opera in Israel."

W14.33  1972 (May 5): Warsaw, Poland; Staatsoper Warschau; Antoni Wicherek, cond.; with Zdislaw Klimek (John Sorel), Krystyna Jamroz (Magda Sorel), Krystyna Szczepanska (The Mother), Marek Dabrowski (Secret Police Agent), Pola Lipinska (The Secretary), Janina Ruskiewicz (Anna Gomez), Bozena Brun-Baranska (Vera Boronel), Zdzislaw Nikodem (Nika Magadoff), and Eugeniusz Banaszczyk (Assan)

*Reviews:*

W14.33a  Greinus, Jochen. "Internationale Maifestspiele 1972." *Oper und Konzert* 10, 6 (1972): 24-28.

W14.33b  Kaczynski, T. "Warszawski 'Konsul.'" *Ruch muzyczny* 16, 5 (1972): 6-7.

W14.33c  Koch, Gerhard R. "Wiesbaden Maifestspiele: Oper aus den Osten." *Opernwelt* (July 1972): 15.

W14.34  1972 (Jul 2): Florence; Teatro Nuovo; Thomas Schippers, cond.; with Virginia Zeani (Magda Sorel), Joy Davidson (The Secretary), Giovanna Fioroni (The Mother), Nico Castel (Nika Magadoff), Giuliana Matteini (Anna Gomez), Flora Rafanelli (Vera Boronel), Gianluigi Golmagro (John Sorel), Gianfranco Casarini (Secret Police Agent), Graziano Del Vivo (Mr. Kofner), and Giorgio Giorgetti (Assan) (Maggio Musicale Fiorentino)

*Review:*

W14.34a  Weaver, William. "Florence." *Opera* (England) 23 (Autumn 1972): 108-113.
"It was a great and deserved success . . . Zeani's intensity and conviction . . . overcame any vocal deficiencies, and the rest of the cast was also on a high level."

112  Works and Performances

W14.35   1974 (Mar 27): New York; New York State Theater; New York City Opera; Christopher Keene, cond.; with Olivia Stapp (Magda Sorel), Sandra Walker (The Secretary), John Darrenkamp (John Sorel), Muriel Greenspon (The Mother), Nico Castel (Nika Magadoff), Judith de Rosa (The Foreign Woman), and Virginia Brobyn (Vera Boronel)

*Review:*

W14.35a  Hughes, Allen. "Durable 'Consul' Revived." *New York Times*, (March 29, 1974): 25.
"This is not music to arouse admiration for rarity of inspiration or refined workmanship, but it makes its points, and it works."

W14.36   1975 (Mar 22): New York; New York City Opera; Christopher Keene, cond.; with John Darrenkamp (John Sorel), Olivia Stapp (Magda Sorel), Muriel Costa-Greenspon (The Mother), Edward Pierson (Secret Police Agent), Sandra Walker (The Secretary), Don Yule (Mr. Kofner), Judith de Rosa (The Foreign Woman), Barbara Hocher (Anna Gomez), John Lankston (Nika Magadoff), Sofia Steffan (Vera Boronel), and William Ledbetter (Assan)

W14.37   1976 (Sep 23): Portland, OR; Portland Opera; Stefan Minde, cond.; with Marvellée Cariaga (Magda Sorel), Alyce Rogers (The Secretary), Chester Ludgin (John Sorel), Norman Paige (Nika Magadoff), and Willene Gunn (The Mother)

*Review:*

W14.37a  Kinkaid, Frank. "Portland." *Opera News* 41 (November 1976): 91-92. Cariaga " . . . dominated the stage, both physically and dramatically."

W14.38   1977 (Mar 18): London; Royal Academy of Music; Duke's Hall; Marcus Dods, cond.; with Christine Taylor (Magda Sorel), Lesley Garrett (The Secretary), Nicola Lanzetter (The Mother), Kevin Hughes (Nika Magadoff), Clare Moll (Vera Boronel), Elaine Williams (Anna Gomez), Timothy Harper (Mr. Kofner), Hilary Reynolds (The Foreign Woman), and Richard Suart (John Sorel)

*Review:*

W14.38a  Forbes, Elizabeth. "Consul." *Opera* (England) 28 (May 1977): 507.

"... still carries a theatrical impact as powerful as the kick of a mule, especially when Menotti himself supervises the production ..."

W14.39   1977 (May 26): Charleston, SC; Gaillard Municipal Theater; production from the Portland Opera Association; Christopher Keene, cond.; with David Clatworthy (John Sorel), Marvellée Cariaga (Magda Sorel), Fredda Rakusin (The Mother), Vern Shinall (Secret Police Agent), Sandra Walker (The Secretary), Gregory Servant (Mr. Kofner), Bibiana Goldenthal (The Foreign Woman), Sylvia Dairs (Anna Gomez), Alice Garrott (Vera Boronel), Jerold Siena (Nika Magadoff), and Boris Martinovich (Mr. Kofner) (Spoleto Festival U.S.A.)

*Reviews:*

W14.39a   Mercer, Ruby. "Charleston: Spoleto U.S.A. '77." *Opera Canada* 18, 3 (1977): 35-36.
"A quick and spontaneous standing ovation at the end of the performance, and wild acclaim for Menotti not only as the composer and director but as the founder and spirit of the Festival itself."

W14.39b   Schonberg, Harold C. "Chamber Music a Hit at Spoleto U.S.A." *New York Times*, (May 28, 1977): 10.
"Some Menotti specialists around here say that this is the finest 'Consul' that has ever been staged."

W14.39c   Jacobson, Robert. "Charleston, S.C. (Spoleto Festival, U.S.A.)" *Opera News* 42 (August 1977): 38.
"... has the virtue of maintaining a 1950 stage style, though it is now verging on the tired routine and the careless in detail ..."

W14.39d   Fleming, Shirley. "Spoleto Festival U.S.A." *High Fidelity/Musical America* 27 (October 1977): MA32-34.
"... left everybody sitting around me in tears, thanks in large part to the searing emotional charge set off by Marvellée Cariaga as Magda."

W14.40   1978 (Aug 12): London; London Coliseum; English National Opera; Howard Williams, cond.; with Ava June (Magda Sorel), Patricia Taylor (The Mother), Ann Howard (The Secretary), Patrick Wheatley (John Sorel), Geoffrey Chard (Secret Police Agent), Stuart Kale (Nika Magadoff), Sally Burgess (The Foreign Woman), Marie McLaughlin (Anna Gomez), John Kitchiner (Mr. Kofner), Shelagh Squires (Vera Boronel), and John Gibbs (Assan)

*Reviews:*

W14.40a  Forbes, Elizabeth. "The Consul." *Musical Times* 119 (October 1978): 881-882.
". . . normally a reticent artist, she [Ava June] can throw off reticence when required, and in Magda's big scene . . . she blew her top quite magnificently."

W14.40b  Blyth, Alan. "Consul." *Opera* (England) 29 (October 1978): 1027-1029.
Williams' " . . . direction was always astute and involved without dipping over into maudlin sentiment, always a danger here . . ."

W14.40c  Goodwin, Noel. "London Coliseum: *The Consul.*" *Music and Musicians* 27 (October 1978): 44-45.
"It is a score to be treated expressively . . . and he [Williams] needed to instil a much greater degree of musical tension . . ."

W14.40d  Taylor, Peter. "Opera in London." *Musical Opinion* 102 (October 1978): 33.
"A very tense new production of the work . . . assured me without any doubt that the opera is still fresh and valid today since the situation it recounts is still with us . . ."

W14.40e  Barker, Frank Granville. "London." *Opera News* 43 (December 2, 1978): 57-58.
". . . there was no doubt that what remains his most substantial theater piece has remarkable dramatic impact. Its message still has validity, the only difference wrought by time being that the dissident has taken over the role of the displaced person."

W14.41  1978 (Nov 12): Gießen, Germany; Herbert Gietzen, cond.; with Michael Willeke (John Sorel), Nancy Henninger (Magda Sorel), Helga Schmidt (The Mother), Nelson Martilotti (Secret Police Agent), Gail Gilmore (The Secretary), Wolfgang Stein (Mr. Kofner), Maria Butschek (The Foreign Woman), Hildegard Berkenhoff (Anna Gomez), Geneviève Perreault (Vera Boronel), Melvin Brown (Nika Magadoff), and Siegfried Lenkl (Assan)

*Reviews:*

W14.41a  Loebe, Bernd. "Auf hohem Niveau — Menottis 'Konsul'; in Gießen." *Opernwelt* 20 (January 1979): 21.

W14.41b   Krause, Manfred. "Aktuell wie je: Gießen: Menotti inszeniert seinen 'Konsul.'" *Orchester* 27 (April 1979): 290-291.

W14.42   1979 (Nov 10): Stockholm; Södra Teatern; Bjørn Hallman, cond.; with Birgit Nordin (Magda Sorel), Margit Rödin (The Secretary), Barbro Ericson (The Mother), and Carl Johan Falkman (John Sorel)

*Review:*

W14.42a   Redvall, Eva. "Stockholm." *Opera News* 44 (February 9, 1980): 34.
". . . proved that excellent performances can turn mediocre staging into something memorable . . . [Nordin] could hardly have been more dramatically convincing, and her normally slender voice seemed to expand with the musical demands."

W14.43   1980 (Oct 28): Atlanta; Atlanta Civic Opera; William Noll, cond.; Atlanta Opera Orchestra; with Marvellée Cariaga (Magda Sorel), Edward Crafts (John Sorel), Carolyne James (The Mother), Emily Golden (The Secretary), and Randy Locke (Nika Magadoff)

W14.44   1981 (Mar 12): Long Beach; California State University, Long Beach; University Theatre; Hans Lampl, cond.; with Keith D. Peters (John Sorel), Charlene Vernelle Capetillo (Magda Sorel), Nancy Graybill (The Mother), Steven Jones (Secret Police Agent), Sheila M. Kearney (The Secretary), David Downing (Mr. Kofner), Elisabeth Pehlivanian (The Foreign Woman), Mary Jo Palencia (Anna Gomez), Marilyn Gabriel (Vera Boronel), Stephen Dublin (Nika Magadoff), and Thomas Clark (Assan)

*Review:*

W14.44a   Michaels, Connie. "Lighting Design for the Production of Gian-Carlo Menotti's *The Consul*." M.A. thesis, Theatre Arts, California State University, Long Beach, 1981.
From author's abstract: "The text is divided into four sections, an introduction; a statement of the problem involved in creating a lighting design . . . the solution to the problem, documenting the evolution of the design . . . [and] An evaluation by the designer of the final product completes the text."

W14.45   1981 (Nov 14): Linz, Austria; Landestheater Linz; Bruckner-Orchester; Roman Zerlinger, cond.; with Althea Bridges (Magda Sorel), Riccardo

*116 Works and Performances*

    Lombardi (John Sorel), Uta Palzer (Mother), Lois White (Secretary), Alfred Werner (Police Agent), Peter Strummer, Jean-Anne Teal, Linda Roark Strummer, Birgit Greiner, Franz Donner (Magician), and Leopold Köppl (Assan).

    *Reviews:*

W14.45a Rudolf, Bert. "Linz." *Oper und Konzert* 20, 1 (1982): 11.

W14.45b Schoenegger, H. "Linz: *Boris* und *Konsul.*" *Buehne* 280 (January 1982): 19.

W14.46 1982 (Nov 23): Oslo; Norwegian Opera; Bjørn Hallman, cond.; with Birgit Nordin (Magda Sorel), Terje Stensvold (John Sorel), Astrid Hellesnes Hukvari (The Mother), Stein Arild Thorsen (Secret Police Agent), Vesla Tveten (The Secretary), and also with Svein Carlsen, Mirjana Dancuo, Irma Urrila, Torhild Staahlen, and Arild Eriksen.

    *Review:*

W14.46a Fossum, Knut. "Oslo: 'Tristan' for the First Time." *Opera* (England) 33 (June 1982): 635.
    Brief review. ". . . a powerful production . . . and . . . a strong cast."

W14.47 1983 (Apr 9): Chicago; Athenaeum Theater; Chicago Opera Theater; Joseph De Rugeriis, cond.; with Susan Hinshaw (Magda Sorel), Judith Farris (The Mother), Kathleen Butler (The Secretary), Louis Otey (John Sorel), Ronald Hedlund (Secret Police Agent), and Jon David Gruett (Nika Magadoff).

    *Reviews:*

W14.47a Rhein, John von. "Getting Nervous with Opera's Most Popular Living Composer." *Chicago Tribune*, (April 10, 1983)
    Interview during a rehearsal. Says Menotti, "In a certain way, I knew that this terrible monster of bureaucratic political oppression, this invisible tyranny, would get worse as the population grew . . . The interesting thing is that in whatever nation it [ *The Consul*] is performed, they always set the consulate in some *other* country."

W14.47b Rhein, John von. "Menotti's Splendid 1949 'Consul' Stops the Clock with its Timeliness." *Chicago Tribune*, (April 11, 1983)

"As for Gian Carlo Menotti's 1949 opera's being dated, one has only to read recent newspaper accounts of political dissidents running afoul of secret police and implacable bureaucracies to refute that tired criticism. Menotti's theme, whether or not one considers it simplistic in the telling, is unfortunately valid."

W14.47c  Samachson, Dorothy. "Chicago." *Opera* (England) 34 (September 1983): 980.
"As staged by the composer . . . the work has an even more poignant, powerful timelessness today than in 1950, when it was first performed."

W14.47d  Rhein, John von. "Chicago." *Opera News* 48 (September 1983): 56.
"Susan Hinshaw turned in a gripping performance . . . and though her cutting soprano was not always steady under pressure, none of the stinging ironies of the text escaped her."

W14.48  1985 (Aug 23): Edinburgh; Leith Theatre; Connecticut Grand Opera; Lawrence Gilgore, cond.; Scottish Chamber Orchestra; with Susan Hinshaw (Magda Sorel), Bibiana Goldenthal (The Foreign Woman), Kathleen Butler (The Secretary), Beverly Evans (The Mother), Ronald Hedlund (Secret Police Agent), and Louis Otey (John Sorel)

*Reviews:*

W14.48a  Monelle, Raymond. "The Consul." *Opera* (England) 36 (Autumn 1985): 45-46.
Hinshaw, " . . . vocally very adequate and a sincere and agonized actress, somehow lacked that last ounce of space and force that would have taken the emotion to its peak."

W14.48b  Johnson, David. "Edinburgh." *Musical Times* 126 (November 1985): 684.
". . . here the universal subject matter is more important than individual self-expression, so if the message has to be put over crudely to reach the masses, that is a legitimate part of the composer's craft."

W14.49  1987 (Mar 30): Manchester, England; Royal Northern College of Music; Opera Theatre; Opera North; Sian Edwards, cond.; with Julia Parrott (Magda Sorel), Adèle Paxton (The Secretary), Bruno Caproni (John Sorel), Stephen Gadd (Nika Magadoff), Sian Wyn Gibson (Vera Boronel), Martin Robson (Mr. Kofner), Amanda Roocroft (Anna Gomez), and Ida-Maria Turri (The Foreign Woman)

*Reviews:*

W14.49a  Duck, Leonard. "The Manchester Scene." *Musical Opinion* 110 (June 1987): 183-184.
"Menotti's mish-mash of Puccini, Britten and Kurt Weill seldom rises above the level of a competent film score and not infrequently sinks below it in a welter of sentimentality."

W14.49b  Kennedy, Michael. "Consul." *Opera* (England) 38 (June 1987): 705-706.
"I just wish all this talent had been expended upon a worthier vehicle, but I was conscious of being in a small minority in thinking that."

W14.50  1988 (Jan 22): Tours, France; Grand Théâtre de Tours; Robert Martignoni, cond.; with Martine Surais (Magda Sorel), Anne Bartelloni (The Secretary), Rita Gorr (The Mother), Yves Bisson (John Sorel), Alain Vernhes (Mr. Kofner), Ivan Matiakh (Nika Magadoff), and Bernard Deletré (Secret Police Agent) (performed in French translation)

*Reviews:*

W14.50a  Parouty, Michel. "*Le consul* a Tours." *Diapason-Harmonie*, 336 (March 1988): 36.

W14.50b  Pitt, Charles. "Tours." *Opera* (England) 39 (April 1988): 474-475.
"It was sad to see this undeniably theatrical piece, which has been successful over much of the world . . . losing its impact. Producers and designers need to rethink it."

W14.50c  Parouty, Michel. "*El consul* en Tours." *Montsalvat*, 160 (May 1988): 48.

W14.51  1988 (Jan 23): Washington, DC; John F. Kennedy Center for the Performing Arts; Washington Opera; Cal Stewart Kellogg, cond.; with William Stone (John Sorel), Badiene Gray (Magda Sorel), Ariel Bybee (The Mother), Emily Golden (The Secretary), Bibiana Goldenthal (The Foreign Woman), Adolfo Llorca (Nika Magadoff), Barbara Hocher (Anna Gomez), David Groth (Secret Police Agent), and Manuel Melendez (Assan)

*Reviews:*

W14.51a  "Superb 'Consul' Cast Outshines a Dull Score." *Washington Times*, (January 25, 1988)

"Memory can be a sly trickster. Even if his derivative melodies were borrowed so long ago that by now they sound like his, the bulk of this 1950 score just sits there inviting giggles."

W14.51b  Jahant, Charles. "Washington." *Opera* (England) 39 (May 1988): 594.
". . . the best production of the season so far . . . as relevant now as it was 30 years ago."

W14.51c  Jahant, Charles. "Washington, D.C." *Opera News* 53 (July 1988): 34-35.
". . . Menotti's talents for the theatrical are stronger than those of his musical inspiration . . . First honors went to Badiene Gray . . . who gave a Magda Sorel of the highest intelligence, emotionally compelling, vocally fine-grained."

W14.52  1988 (Mar 4): Strasbourg, France; Opéra du Rhin; Claude Schnitzler, cond.; with Anne-Marie Blanzat (Magda Sorel), Chantal Dubarry (The Secretary), Madeleine Jalbert (The Mother), Nicole Labarthe (The Foreign Woman), Mireille Alcantara (Anna Gomez), Gisèle Ory (Vera Boronel), Claude Meloni (John Sorel), Paul Guigue (Secret Police Agent), Albert Voli (Nika Magadoff), Philippe Kahn (Mr. Kofner), and Frank Schooten (Assan) (repeated Mar 15 in Colmar and March 18 and 20 in Mulhouse)

*Review:*

W14.52a  Neufert, Kurt. "'Der Konsul': nach wie vor aktuell: Menottis Oper in Straßburg." *Opernwelt* 29 (May 1988): 54.

W14.53  1988 (Spring): Tallin, Estonia; transmitted by Tallin TV; featuring local artists; sung in Estonian; the transmission did not make it clear whether it was filmed in the Estonia Theatre or made in a studio specifically for television.

W14.54  1989 (Mar 11): Passau, Germany; Herbert Morasch, cond.; with Stephen Swanson (John Sorel), Rose Bihler-Shah (Magda Sorel), Adrienne Passen (The Mother), Helmut Kramer (Secret Police agent), Edina Leue (The Secretary), Roland Friedrich (Mr. Kofner), Miyase Kaptan (The Foreign woman), Johanna Stojkovic (Anna Gomez), Ursula Wind (Vera Boronel), Seiji Makino (Nika Magadoff), and Thomas Hermann (Assan)

*Review:*

W14.54a  Stöckl, Rudolf. "Passau: Menotti, 'Der Konsul.'" *Opernwelt* 30 (June 1989): 44.

W14.55  1990 (May 5): Kiel, Germany; Stephan Tetzlaff, cond.; with Mario Taghadossi (John Sorel), Gerda Kosbahn (Magda Sorel), Marita Dübbers (The Mother), Wolfgang Bankl (Secret Police agent), Margaret Russel (The Secretary), Attila Kovács (Mr. Kofner), Ute Raithel (The Foreign Woman), Valerie Errante (Anna Gomez), Kathleen Murphy (Vera Boronel), Tibo Tóth (Nika Magadoff), and Viktor Lederer (Assan)

*Review:*

W14.55a  Asche, Gerhart. "Kiel: Menotti, 'Der Konsul.'" *Opernwelt* 31 (July 1990): 45-46.

W14.56  1990 (Nov 18): Wuppertal, Germany; Stefan Klieme, cond.; with Mildred Tyree (Magda Sorel), Marianne Dorka (The Mother), Theo van Gemert (John Sorel), Jef Vermeersch (Secret Police Agent), Lynne Wickenden (The Secretary), Marek Wojciechowski (Mr. Kofner), Claudia Visca (The Foreign Woman), Doris Brüggemann (Anna Gomez), Dora F. Brockmann (Vera Boronel), Arthur Friesen (Nika Magadoff), and David Rice (Assan)

*Reviews:*

W14.56a  Kirchberg, Klaus. "Wuppertal: Menotti, 'Der Konsul.'" *Opernwelt* 32 (January 1991): 40.

W14.56b  Mail, Jens. "Wuppertal." *Oper und Konzert* 29 (January 1991): 16-17.

W14.56c  Luys, Thomas. "Wuppertal." *Opera* (England) 42 (March 1991): 330-331.
The conductor " . . . was right not to damp down these emotions, since they are an element of Menotti's original, though now rather stale, compositional style, the power of which to convince should not be underestimated."

W14.56d  Richter, Arnd. "Die personifizierte Unmenschlichkeit: Gian Carlo Menottis Oper 'Der Konsul' in Wuppertal." *Orchester* 39 (1991): 279.

W14.57      1991 (May 18): Pittsburgh; Carnegie Music Hall; Pittsburgh Opera Theater; Pittsburgh New Music Ensemble; with Anna Singer (Magda Sorel), Korby Myrick (The Mother), Todd Thomas (John Sorel), Theodora Hanslowe (The Secretary), John Furman (Mr. Kofner), Diane Owens (The Foreign Woman), Cynthia Harding (Anna Gomez), Myrna Paris (Vera Boronel), Howard Carr (Nika Magadoff), Curt Scheib (Secret Police Agent), and Russell Franks (Assan)

*Review:*

W14.57a   Rosenberg, Donald. "Cast Saves Opera Theater's 'Consul.'" *Pittsburgh Press*, (May 20, 1991)
"The production was fortunate . . . to have performers who appeared to believe in Menotti's vision on every level."

W14.58      1991 (Nov 22): New York; New York Historical Society; Elizabeth Hastings, cond.; Joseph A. LoSchiavo, piano; with Raymond Aceto (Secret Police Agent), Joan Tirrel (The Mother), Lorraine DiSimone (The Secretary), Badiene Gray (Magda Sorel), and also with Richard Storm, Veronica Burke, Joy Hermalyn, Gregory Gunder, and Nathan Bahny (a "semi-staged" performance presented by the Istituto della Enciclopedia Italiana and Fordham University)

*Reviews:*

W14.58a   Holland, Bernard. "Menotti: The Consul." *New York Times*, (November 24, 1991): 67.
"Badiene Gray's Magda made volume a metaphor for her strongest emotions and did not shy from the melodrama Mr. Menotti had urged on her."

W14.58b   McKinnon, Arlo, Jr. "New York City." *Opera News* 56 (February 1, 1992): 38.
"The cast was uniformly excellent, making the most of individual moments of focus without overemoting . . . [Gray's] stellar interpretation was finely paced and natural, evoking compassion for a desperate soul . . . "

W14.59      1992 (Apr 23): Würzburg, Germany; Stadttheater; Martin Lichtfuß, cond.; with Alexander Poljakow (John Sorel), Galina Pandowa (Magda Sorel), Eligia Klosowska (The Mother), Dan Muselescu (Secret Police Agent), and Ilca Lopez (The Secretary)

*Reviews:*

W14.59a Riedlbauer, Jörg. "Würzburg: Menotti, 'Der Konsul.'" *Opernwelt* 33 (August 1992): 46-47.

W14.59b "Die tödliche Macht der Bürokratie: Gian Carlo Menottis 'Der Konsul' im Würzburger Stadttheater." *Orchester* 40, n7-8 (1992): 895-896.

W14.60 1993 (Oct 8): Milwaukee; Pabst Theater; Florentine Opera; Joseph Rescigno, cond.; with Pamela South (Magda Sorel), Kathleen Hegierski (The Secretary), Louis Otey (John Sorel), Josepha Gayer (The Mother), and David Groth (Secret Police Agent)

*Reviews:*

W14.60a Strini, Tim. "Lush Music of 'Consul' Contrasts Brilliantly with Somber Setting." *Milwaukee Journal*, News (October 10, 1993): B2.
"South . . . made a believable and sympathetic Magda. Her shoulders sagged and face fell ever so gradually under the wearying weight of life. As Magda faded toward the inevitable suicide, South's singing grew ever warmer and more impassioned."

W14.60b Parsons, Charles. "Milwaukee's Florentine Opera: Menotti *The Consul*." *American Record Guide* 57 (January-February 1994): 39.
"An impressive season opener for an opera company growing rapidly in artistic integrity and popular acclaim."

W14.61 1995 (Mar 3): Monaco; Opéra de Monte-Carlo; Spiros Argiris, cond.; with Stephen Lusmann (John Sorel), Leila Guimares (Magda Sorel), Josepha Gayer (The Mother), Brian Jauhiainen (Secret Police Agent), Emily Golden (The Secretary), Edward Crafts (Mr. Kofner), Bibiana Goldenthal (The Foreign Woman), Leila Chalfoun (Anna Gomez), César Ulloa (Nika Magadoff), and Randal Turner (Assan)

*Review:*

W14.61a Rohde, Gerhard. "Aschenbrödelschicksale." *Opernwelt* 5 (May 1995): 42-43.

W14.62 1996 (Apr 25): Boulder; University of Colorado; Imig Music Theatre; Colorado Lyric Theatre; Robert Spillman, cond.; Terese Stewart and Mutsumi, pianos; with Julie Simson (Magda Sorel), Leslie Remmert (The

Mother), Mark Morgan (John Sorel), Ashraf Sewailam (Secret Police Agent), Brian Gill (Nika Magadoff), Camille Mouch and Gayle Shay (Visa Seekers), and Sarah Sheperd (The Secretary)

*Review:*

W14.62a  Bradley, Jeff. "CU Cast Tops in Cold War Opera." *Denver Post*, Denver & the West (April 27, 1996): B2.
". . . the CU grad student singers were first-rate, especially mezzo-soprano Sarah Sheperd's unfeeling secretary . . ."

W14.63  1996 (Oct 19): Chicago; Civic Opera House; Goodman Theatre; Lyric Opera of Chicago; Richard Buckley, cond.; with Barbara Daniels (Magda Sorel), Richard Cowan (John Sorel), Josepha Gayer (The Mother), Emily Golden (The Secretary), Dale Travis (Secret Police Agent), Barry McCauley (Nika Magadoff), Elena Zilio (The Foreign Woman), Elena Kolganova (Anna Gomez), Jennifer Dudley (Vera Boronel), and Franco Pomponi (Assan) (The Lyric Opera's "Toward the 21$^{st}$ Century" retrospective)

*Reviews:*

W14.63a  Delacoma, Wynne. "Political Woes of 1950 Opera Find Parallels in Today's World; 'Consul' Is In." *Chicago Sun-Times*, (October 13, 1996): 13.
"Tsypin's sets move away from the crumbling cinder block walls and wooden benches typical of the 1940s European atmosphere for many productions . . . " Says Tsypin, "It's set in a fluorescent-lit, harsh, white office . . . It could be an insurance building. It could be anywhere."

W14.63b  Rhein, John von. "Package Deal: Lyric's Updated Staging of 'The Consul' Could Restore Menotti's Image as Well." *Chicago Tribune*, Arts & Entertainment (October 20, 1996): 6.
Says Barbara Daniels, "I have seldom found music that is so challenging in terms of bringing across everything that is in the text . . . And the physical demands approach the athletic. I might be ready to quarterback for the Bears before this show is over."

W14.63c  Ringham, Wynne. "Melody Triumphs in Staging of Lyric Opera's 'The Consul.'" *Chicago Sun-Times*, FTR (October 21, 1996): 32.
"In 'To this we've come' . . . the melody kept returning to its home key, reflecting Magda's inability to escape. Plodding rhythms and dark,

repetitious motifs conveyed the accumulating weight of Magda's frustration."

W14.63d Rhein, John von. "Updated Staging Rescues Menotti's 'Consul' at Lyric." *Chicago Tribune*, Tempo (October 21, 1996): 2.
"'The Consul' has not aged terribly well, and dressing it up in 1990s jogging suits, cellular phones and Rolex watches cannot disguise that fact . . . It's an almost unrelievedly bleak opera with a heart of treacle."

W14.64 1997 (Feb 8): Winnipeg; Manitoba Opera; Winnipeg Symphony Orchestra; Semyon Vekshtein, cond.; with Joanne Kolomyjec (Magda Sorel), Steven Horst (John Sorel), Sandra Walker (The Mother), Jean-Clément Bergeron (Secret Police Agent), Kathleen Hegierski (The Secretary), Torin Chiles (Nika Magadoff), David Watson (Mr. Kofner), Svetlana Sech (The Foreign Woman), Nathalie Morais (Anna Gomez), Lois Watson (Vera Boronel), and Mel Braun (Assan)

*Reviews:*

W14.64a "The Consul." *Jewish Post & News*, (January 29, 1997): 11.
"*The Consul* is a work of heart-breaking tension, both theatrically compelling and deeply compassionate."

W14.64b Manishen, James. "Bleak Drama Upstages Forgettable 1951 Score." *Winnipeg Free Press*, C (February 10, 1997): 5.
"The music is admirable in its technical aplomb, but doesn't function independently enough to elevate this intensely moving story into an unforgettable piece of musical theatre."

W14.65 1997 (Mar 7): Waukegan, IL; Bowen Park Opera Company; Jack Benny Center for the Arts; Goodfellow Hall; Roger Bingaman, music director & accompanist; with John Hacker (John Sorel), Debra DeNoon (Magda Sorel), Mary Zitnik (The Mother), Nicholas Solomon (Secret Police Agent), Robert Andresen (First Plainclothesman), Mike Kalman (Second Plainclothesman), Elizabeth Richardson (The Secretary), Richard Luketich (Mr. Kofner), Sarah Hersh (The Foreign Woman), Meredith Barber (Anna Gomez), Sarah Sheperd (Vera Boronel), William Chamberlain (Nika Magadoff), and Michael Kotze (Assan)

W14.66 1997 (Apr 19): New Orleans; University of New Orleans; Pamela Legendre, cond.; with Thomas M. Irwin, III (John Sorel), Bridget A. Bazile (Magda Sorel), Vickie R. Thomas (The Mother), Gary Lee Randall

(The Secret Police Agent), Peter Hagan (First Plainclothesman), J. Michael Turner (Second Plainclothesman), Sheila McDermott (The Secretary), Jay V. Hall, Jr. (Mr. Kofner), Grace Cho (The Foreign Woman), Jennifer Wise (Anna Gomez), Robin Robertson Polizzi (Vera Boroenl), Arthur Espirita (Nika Magadoff), and Tywon Morgan (Assan)

♦ BRIEFLY NOTED

W14.67 Reich, Willi. "Die europäische Erstaufführung in Basel." *Melos* 18 (February 1951): 53-54. Review of a 1950 Basel production ✚ Joachim, Heinz. "Deutsche Erstaufführung an der Hamburgischen Staatsoper." *Melos* 18 (February 1951): 52-53. Review of a 1950 Hamburg Staatsoper production ✚ Hell, Henri. "Trois etapes du theatre lyrique." *Revue musicale* 211 (March 1952): 7-9. Review of a Paris production at the Théâtre des Champs-Elysées ✚ Paap, Wouter. "Nederlande Opera." *Mens en melodie* 11 (April 1956): 117-119. Review of a Dutch Opera production ✚ Danzuso, D. "'Console' di Menotti al Teatro Massimo di Catania." *Musica d'oggi* 4 (July-August 1961): 180-182 ✚ Kanski, J. "Polska premiera 'Konsula.'" *Ruch muzyczny* 6, 7 (1962): 17 ✚ Baldini, G. "'Il Console' di G. C. Menotti." *Rassegna musicale* 32, 2-4 (1962): 242-247 ✚ Jurik, M. "Cs. premiera Menottiho." *Hudebni rozhledy* 19, 15 (1966): 463 ✚ "Uspesne finale sezony." *Slovenska Hudba* 10, 10 (1966): 466-467 ✚ Ter-Simonyan, M. "Vpervye u nas." *Sovetskaya muzika* 30 (December 1966): 74-77 ✚ Garde, C. O. "Reposiciones en El Colon: 'El Consul' — vibrantes valores teatrales." *Buenos Aires Musical* 22, 360 (1967): 3 ✚ Goury, J. "A Annecy: un 'Consul' Kafkaien." *Opera* (France) 10, 87 (1970): 14-15 ✚ Greinus, Jochen. "Internationale Maifestspiele 1972." *Oper und Konzert* 10, 6 (1972): 24-28. Review of a May 5, 1972 Warsaw production ✚ Benesch, G. "Der Konsul in einer Auffuehrung der Bieler Orchestergesellschaft." *Opernwelt* 23, 4 (1982): 50 ✚ Krakauer, P. M. "Nonn' erubeskite in aegra urbe clamare . . . ? Anmerkungen zur Figur der Mutter in der Oper des 20. Jahrhunderts." *Musikerziehung*, 38 (December 1984): 71-72+ ✚ Atterfors, G. "Konsuln i Karlstad." *Musikrevy* 45, 2 (1990): 65-66.

♦ DISCOGRAPHY

COMPLETE RECORDING

W14.68 Berkshire Opera Company; with Beverly O'Reagan (Magda Sorel), Michael Chioldi (John Sorel), Joyce Castle (Mother); John Cheek (Secret

Police Agent), Emily Golden (Secretary), John Davies (Mr. Kofner), and David Cangelosi (Magician); Camerata New York Orchestra; Joel Revzen, cond.
Newport Classic NPD 85645/2 (1998) 2 compact discs

ABRIDGED RECORDING

W14.69    Marie Powers (Mother), Patricia Neway (Magda Sorel), Gloria Lane (Secretary), Cornell MacNeil (John Sorel), George Jongeyans (Mr. Kofner), Leon Lishner (Chief Police Agent), Maria Marlo (Foreign Woman), Andrew McKinley (Nika Magadoff), Lydia Summers (Vera Boronel), Maria Andreassi (Anna Gomez), and Francis Monachino (Assan); Lehman Engel, cond.
Decca DX 101; Decca DXA 101 (DL 9500-9501), LP, mono (1950)
Series: Decca gold label series.

SELECTIONS

*"My Child is Dead"*

W14.70    Inge Borkh, soprano.
EMI Classics CHS 7697412, CDH 7697452, CHS 7697912A, CDHG 69741, mono., analog, CD (1991); disc 4 of 7.
Album title: The Record of Singing, vol. 4, "From 1939 to the End of the 78 rpm Record (1948-55)."

*"Next! Please, Please"*

W14.71    Benna Lemon-Brundin, Ida Quensel, Brita Hertzberg, Eva Prytz, sopranos; Bette Björling, mezzo-soprano; Arne Hendriksen, tenor; Leon Björker, bass; Kungliche Hovkapellet; Sixten Ehrling, cond.
EMI Svenska C153-35350/8, 7C 153 35357M, LP, mono. (1976)
Produced by the Kungliga Teatern, Stockholm.
Album title: Svensk opera antologi.
Recorded 1952-1969.
Label on discs: EMI Odeon (made in Sweden)
With works by Britten, Berg, Blomdahl, Janáček, and Henricksen.

W14.72    Patricia Neway, soprano; orchestra cond. by Lehman Engel.
New World Records NW 241, LP, stereo. (1978)
Album title: Toward an American Opera, 1911-1954.
At head of title: Recorded anthology of American music.

With works by Herbert, Taylor, Gruenberg, Hanson, and Copland.

### ♦ SELECTED RECORDING REVIEWS

W14.73   Kolodin, Irving. "'The Consul' for Ear Alone." *Saturday Review of Literature* 33 (October 28, 1950): 74.
Review of the Decca DX 101 recording. "The intensity, the power, the insistence of the theatre experience have been remarkably conveyed by Decca in this venture . . . reproduction throughout is remarkable . . ."

W14.74   Todd, Arthur. "Theatre on the Disc." *Theatre Arts* 36 (June 1952): 6-7.
Brief reviews of then-recent recordings of *Amahl and the Night Visitors, The Medium, The Telephone, The Consul, Sebastian, Amelia al ballo,* and *The Old Maid and the Thief.*

W14.75   Paller, Rebecca. "Menotti: The Consul." *Opera News* 63 (January 1999): 71.
"The new CD does have some marvelous ensemble work . . . The Berkshire Opera Company is a fine introduction to an important American work."

## W15    A COPY OF MADAME AUPIC (1947)

Comic drama in three acts.
Written in 1943.

### ♦ SELECTED PERFORMANCES

W15.1   1947 (Aug 27): New Milford, CT; Theatre-in-the-Dale; with Sam Wren (Steve), Walter Armitage (Albert), Thomas Beck (George Norris), Marguerite Lewis (Gogo), Olga Baclanova (Madame Renée Aupic), and Cele McLaughlin (Martha)

W15.2   1959 (Mar 25): Paris; Théâtre Fontaine; with Madeleine Robinson (Madame Renée Aupic)  (revived in a two-act translation by Albert Husson)

## W16    THE DAYS OF THE SHEPHERD (1974)

Ballet in four seasons.

*128 Works and Performances*

Commissioned in 1973 by the Harkness Ballet and as yet unproduced.
Seasons: Winter (Courtship and Games) — Spring (Promises and Farewells) — Summer (Solitude and Encounters) — Fall (Homecoming and Reunions)

**W17   THE DEATH OF PIERROT** (1922)

Opera written when Menotti was eleven years old.
Says Menotti: "Everybody in it sings and plays all the time and dies at the end . . . It was just completely insane." (*See* "Notes and Comments." *New Yorker* 23 (June 7, 1947): 23-24)

**W18   THE DEATH OF THE BISHOP OF BRINDISI** (1963; G. Schirmer; 30 min.)

Dramatic cantata.
Commissioned by the Cincinnati May Festival Association.
Chorus; 2+afl.22+bcl.2/4331/timp.2perc/hp/2pf/str

♦ **SELECTED PERFORMANCES**

W18.1   1963 (May 18): Cincinnati; Music Hall; Max Rudolf, cond.; May Festival Chorus; with Rosalind Elias (Nun), Richard Cross (Bishop) (1963 May Festival)

*Reviews:*

W18.1a   "De Morte et Conscientia." *Time* 81 (May 31, 1963): 40.
". . . Brindisi would have been a triumph anywhere." Said Menotti, "Nothing like this has ever happened to me before. I want the final chorus sung at my funeral."

W18.1b   Bell, Eleanor. "Ohio: Bravos for 'The Bishop.'" *Musical America* 83 (July 1963): 12.
"As hundreds of admiring listeners and chorus members surged into his dressing room to wring his hand and get his autograph, Menotti said, 'I'll never find another audience like this.'"

W18.2   1964 (Oct 21): Boston; Philharmonic Hall; Erich Leinsdorf, cond.; Boston Symphony Orchestra; New England Conservatory Chorus; Children's Chorus of the Catholic Memorial and St. Joseph's High

School Glee Clubs of Boston; with George London (Bishop), Lili Chookasian (Nun)

*Reviews:*

W18.2a   Sargeant, Winthrop. "Musical Events: His Master's Voice." *New Yorker* 40 (October 31, 1964): 231.
"Predictably, this composition turned out to be a deeply sincere and at times somewhat theatrical affair, touching in spots, thunderingly menacing and poetically evocative in others, and written throughout in the simple, communicative style that has made the composer a success with audiences."

W18.2b   Kolodin, Irving. "Music to my Ears: London (Symphony) Calling — Menotti." *Saturday Review* 47 (November 7, 1964): 28.
"Erich Leinsdorf's attentive direction was of positive value to the best portions of the work . . . But he was, later on, limited by what there was in the score itself."

W18.2c   Davis, Peter. "Boston Symphony." *Musical America* 84 (December 1964): 119-120.
"It is surprising that Erich Leinsdorf would take this all so seriously, but the performance presented the work in the best possible light."

W18.2d   Rogers, Harold. "Massachusetts with Little Emotion." *Musical America* 84 (December 1964): 63.
"Mr. London gave poignant expression to the Bishop's torment. Miss Chookasian was lyrically moving as she expressed the nun's consoling remarks."

W18.3    1995 (Feb 14): New York; John F. Kennedy Center for the Performing Arts; Concert Hall; Richard White, cond.; Choral Arts Society; members of the National Symphony Orchestra; with Max Wittges (Bishop), Phyllis Bryn-Julson (Nun); singers from St. Paul's Parish, Baltimore and Walt Whitman Middle School, Fairfax County (on a triple bill with Ralph Vaughan Williams' *Dona Nobis Pacem* and William Grant Still's *In Memoriam*)

*Review:*

W18.3a   McLellan, Joseph. "Choral Arts Society's Powerful 'Bishop.'" *Washington Post*, D (February 21, 1995): 4.

*130 Works and Performances*

"The Choral Arts Society sang with passionate conviction, precise diction and rich, well-balanced tone. Equally impressive were the tonal purity and effective diction of the children's choir . . ."

W18.4  1996 (Jun 26): Spoleto; Cathedral of Santa Maria del Vescovado (Festival of Two Worlds) (also with *Sebastian*, which was performed in the Teatro Nuovo)

*Review:*

W18.4a  "Italian Festival Salutes Its Founder." *BBC Music Magazine* 4 (July, 1996): 14.
In addition to *The Death of the Bishop of Brindisi*, the 39th Festival of Two Worlds will include 200 other events, including grand opera, ballet, and experimental theater.

### ♦ DISCOGRAPHY

W18.5  Lili Chookasian (Nun), George London (Bishop); New England Conservatory Chorus (Lorna de Varon, director); members of the Catholic Memorial and St. Joseph's High Schools Glee Clubs of Boston (Berj Zamkochian, director); Boston Symphony Orchestra; Erich Leinsdorf, cond.
RCA Victor LM 2785, LP, mono, 12 in.; LSC 2785, LP, stereo. (1965) With "Introduction and song of the wood-dove" from *Guerrelieder* by Schönberg.

### ♦ SELECTED RECORDING REVIEW

W18.6  Luten, C. J. "On Record." *Opera News* 29 (April 3, 1965): 34.
Review of the RCA Victor recording. "The presentation is highlighted by beautiful orchestral playing and sensitive singing by George London . . . and Miss Chookasian."

**W19   *LE DERNIER SAUVAGE (L'ULTIMO SELVAGGIO; L'ULTIMO SUPERUOMO; THE LAST SAVAGE)*** (1963; Belwin Mills)

Comic opera in three acts.
Originally commissioned for the Paris Opéra, but changed to the Opéra-Comique.

Originally in Italian titled *L'ultimo superuomo*; French version by Jean-Pierre Marty; English version by George Mead. English title changed from *The Last Superman* via *The Wild Man* to *The Last Savage*.

### ♦ ABOUT THE WORK

W19.1 "Last Superman: Paris Commissions Menotti Opera." *Times* (London), (March 3, 1959): 3.
Note that Menotti " . . . is the first non-French composer to be commissioned by the Paris Opéra for over 100 years. The last foreign operatic commission was given to Verdi."

W19.2 Parmenter, Ross. "World of Music: 'Met' to Mount Menotti Comic Opera about a Superman in Modern World." *New York Times*, 2 (January 22, 1961): 9.
Preview of the opera, to be presented by the Met during the season after next. " . . . Mr. Menotti is doing the libretto, but this time he has written his book in Italian. It will be translated into French for the Paris premiere and into English for the New York one."

W19.3 "Menotti Finishing New Opera." *Times* (London), (February 7, 1961): 14.
The final act is being completed, with a Paris world premiere set for November 1961, followed by a production at the Met during the 1962-63 season.

W19.4 Parinaud, A. "'Io sono l'ultimo selvaggio.'" *Musica d'oggi* 6, 6 (1963): 262-265.
Based on an interview with Menotti.

W19.5 Pincherle, Marc. "Nel regno delle fate: 'L'ultimo selvaggio.'" *Musica d'oggi* 6, 6 (1963): 266-268.
Translated from an article in *Le nouvelles litteraires*, October 31, 1963.

W19.6 Reynolds, M. "Abominable 'Savage.'" *Music and Musicians* 12 (January 1964): 32.

### ♦ SELECTED PERFORMANCES

W19.7 1963 (Oct 22): Paris; Opéra-Comique; Serge Baudo, cond.; with Charles Clavensy (Maharajah), Solange Michel (Maharani), Michele Molese (Kodanda), Xavier Depraz (Mr. Scattergood), Mady Mesplé

(Kitty), Gabriel Bacquier (Abdul), and Adriana Maliponte (Sardula) (first public performance; on Oct 21 there was a private gala for the benefit of Atlantique, an association that provides exchange scholarships for French and American students)

*Reviews:*

W19.7a  "Sad Savage." *Time* 82 (November 1, 1963): 63.
". . . Menotti had fallen well below his usual mark, with a tiresome, lurching, seldom funny libretto and a derivative score that even in its academic jokes was hardly *musique sérieuse.*"

W19.7b  Genêt. "Letter from Paris." *New Yorker* 39 (November 2, 1963): 198-200.
"On the whole, the premiere audience seemed to enjoy itself immensely — all except the critics . . . The Paris music critics have already used Menotti rather as their whipping boy. In their reports on this weeks' Menotti opera, it is they who have been the savages."

W19.7c  Kaufman, Wolfe. "Menotti's 'Last Savage' a Legit Show Decked out as Grand Opera." *Variety* 232 (November 6, 1963): 55+.
Except for Bacquier, "None of the others in the large cast are notable, but all of them underline the realization that what the operatic world needs more than anything are singers who can act and actors who can sing."

W19.7d  Goléa, Antoine. "Caprices d'Euterpe." *Musica* (Chaix), 117 (December 1963): 41.

W19.7e  "Homme Sauvage." *Musica* (Chaix), 117 (December 1963): 11.

W19.7f  Goléa, Antoine. "Lichter und Schatten in Paris, Marseille und Besançon." *Neue Zeitschrift für Musik* 124, 12 (1963): 488.

W19.7g  Jacobs, Arthur. "Menotti in Paris." *Opera* (England) 14 (December 1963): 803-804.
Review of the October 21 private showing. "Under the expert guidance of Menotti himself and of Serge Baudo, the performance went splendidly."

W19.7h  Onnen, Frank. "Parijs: Le dernier sauvage." *Mens en melodie* 18 (December 1963): 371-372.

W19.7i   Soria, Dorle J. "First 'Savage.'" *Opera News* 28 (December 7, 1963): 30-31.
"Witty, romantic and highly enjoyable, the score abounds in beautiful arias, duets and concerted pieces, including a marvelous last-act septet."

W19.7j   "Prima rappresentazione italiana dell' 'Ultimo selvaggio' di Menotti." *Musica d'oggi* 7, 5 (1964): 136-139.

W19.7k   Stein, Elliott. "Paris." *Musical Times* 105 (January 1964): 42.
". . . over three hours long, funny not a minute . . . Parisian critics received [it] . . . with a chorus of irately unconcealed disgust."

W19.8   1964 (Jan 23): New York; Metropolitan Opera; Thomas Schippers, cond.; with Ezio Flagello (Maharajah), Lili Chookasian (Maharani), Nicolai Gedda (Kodanda), Morley Meredith (Mr. Scattergood), Roberta Peters (Kitty), George London (Abdul), and Teresa Stratas (Sardula)

*Reviews:*

W19.8a   Brozen, Michael, ed. "Quote, Unquote." *Musical America* 84 (January 1964): 28.
Interview at Menotti's New York City apartment, prior to the opening of the opera. Said Menotti: "The musical style may surprise New York; I know it shocked the Paris critics . . . After the Met premiere, it is going to be done at La Fenice in Venice, which should be the ideal theater for the work."

W19.8b   Menotti, Gian Carlo. "'Last Savage' Arrives at the 'Met.'" *New York Times*, 2 (January 19, 1964): 13.
"For better or worse, in 'The Last Savage' I have dared to do away completely with fashionable dissonance, and in a modest way I have endeavored to rediscover the nobility of gracefulness and the pleasure of sweetness."

W19.8c   "The Last Savage." *Variety* 233 (January 29, 1964): 70.
"Nothing like this fascinatingly varied fare has ever been seen, it may be guessed, in an opera house."

## 134   Works and Performances

W19.8d   "A Banal Savage." *Time* 83 (January 31, 1964): 33.
Menotti " . . . is a man who is truly touched by life. As his past masterworks nobly demonstrate, a passion for the world can be as much a blessing to the composer as in this case it is a disaster to the comedian."

W19.8e   Harrison, Jay S. "The New York Music Scene." *Musical America* 84 (February 1964): 25-26.
"Considering the elegance of the production, it all should have worked like a charm. That it didn't is a fault to be placed firmly on the Menotti's musico-dramatic doorstep."

W19.8f   Sargeant, Winthrop. "Musical Events: Grand Spoof." *New Yorker* 39 (February 1, 1964): 60-64.
"I couldn't understand a word that Roberta Peters sang . . . until the last act, when, for some mysterious reason, her diction seemed to improve, but she acted the part perfectly . . ."

W19.8g   "Menotti's Eleventh." *Newsweek* 63 (February 3, 1964): 77.
"The Metropolitan audience . . . largely made up of seasoned subscribers who usually resent anything new, loved Menotti's 'Savage.' They laughed happily, and cheered lustily at the end."

W19.8h   Kolodin, Irving. "Music to My Ears: Menotti in India — Vintschger, Varèse." *Saturday Review* 47 (February 8, 1964): 27.
"If *The Last Savage* is but a passing fancy, it shows the Metropolitan company capable of an all-out ensemble effort of high quality."

W19.8i   "Bringing Him Back Alive." *Opera News* 28 (February 8, 1964): 17-20.
Chiefly photographs from the Metropolitan Opera production.

W19.8j   Freeman, John W. "Idyllic Retreat." *Opera News* 28 (February 8, 1964): 24-25.
General discussion, with musical examples, coinciding with the Metropolitan Opera production. The score "reveals Menotti's customary fluent, eclectic style — this time, more than in any of his operas since the first (*Amelia Goes to the Ball*), consciously is the Italian tradition."

W19.8k   Fitzgerald, Gerald. "Cast of the Characters." *Opera News* 28 (February 8, 1964): 13-15.
Remarks concerning their roles from Meredith, Flagello, Gedda, Chookasian, Peters, Stratas, and London, with rehearsal photographs from the Metropolitan Opera production.

W19.8l   "'Last Savage.'" *Life* 56 (February 14, 1964): 66A-66B.
Brief review with photographs from the Met production. "Some critics and stuffy traditionalists have harrumphed about *Savage*. But the box office has been besieged."

W19.8m   Bowen, J. "Menotti's 'The Last Savage.'" *Listen* 1 (March-April 1964): 21-22.

W19.8n   Plussain, Michel. "New Works." *Music Journal* 22 (March 1964): 117-118.
"Menotti's staging is mostly ingenious but more admirable is the ease with which the company accomplishes it."

W19.8o   Stravinsky, Igor. "A Dialogue." *Show* 4 (April 1964): 42.
Stravinsky's appraisal: ". . . the latter ⅔rds of this score should have been composed by feeding the first ⅓ to an IBM machine."

W19.8p   Breuer, Robert. "Mit Menotti zurück zur Natur." *Melos* 31 (April 1964): 134-135.

W19.8q   Osborne, Conrad L. "New York." *Musical Times* 105 (April 1964): 284.
"I am a dedicated non-fan of nearly all of Menotti's 'serious' operas, but I found *Last Savage* a most likeable piece, and will not think it a chore to listen to again."

W19.8r   Sabin, Robert. "New York." *Opera* (England) 15 (April 1964): 241-242.
"No one will be surprised to hear that *The Last Savage* is proving a popular hit. It offers a tissue of toothsome banalities and makes absolutely no demands upon its listeners."

W19.8s   Helm, Everett. "Eintönige Saison." *Neue Zeitschrift für Musik* 125, 5 (1964): 209.

W19.8t   Übel, Ruth. "Von der Metropolitan Oper." *Musica* 18 (July-August 1964): 209.

W19.8u   Sarnette, E. "'Dernier Sauvage.'" *Musique e Radio* 53 (December 1963): 373.

W19.9    1964 (Dec 30): New York; Metropolitan Opera; Robert La Marchina, cond.; with Roberta Peters (Kitty), Teresa Stratas (Sardula), Donald

Gramm (Maharajah), Lili Chookasian (Maharani), and John Alexander (Kodanda)

Reviews:

W19.9a   "The Last Savage." *Variety* 237 (January 13, 1965): 82.
"Managing Director Rudolf Bing materialized to introduce Leontyne Price who interpolated an aria which brought down the house, though she did not sing it with her customary distinction."

W19.9b   Bernheimer, Martin. "Returning *Savage*." *Saturday Review* 48 (January 16, 1965): 22.
"Mr. La Marchina . . . produced plenty of healthy sound and a good measure of spirit too; but in the process lost the crucial delicacy that had illuminated Thomas Schippers' reading."

W19.9c   Mayer, Martin. "In the Face of Odds: *Savage* by Marchina." *High Fidelity/Musical America* 15 (March 1965): 86f.
"The ensemble singing in the third act, beautifully crafted by Menotti, was as good as anyone could ask."

W19.10   1973 (Feb 4): Honolulu; Hawaii Opera Theater; Robert La Marchina, cond.; with John Reardon (Savage), Ruth Welting (anthropologist), Joanna Bruno (Sardula), David Clatworthy (millionaire), Gary Glaze (Kodanda), and William Fleck (Maharajah) (production funded through a grant from the National Endowment for the Arts)

Reviews:

W19.10a  Winters, Lee. "Honolulu." *Opera Canada* 14, 2 (1973): 32.
". . . with the composer in Honolulu to supervise its realization, the almost-unknown score came to life with a nice sense of wittiness and melodic purpose."

W19.10b  Aguiar, William, Jr. "Honolulu." *Opera News* 37 (March 31, 1973): 25.
"In revising some of his musical ideas Menotti has been successful in better communicating the humorous implications of his philosophy and has shrewdly parodied other composers and traditional operatic styles."

W19.11   1981 (May 22): Charleston, SC; Gaillard Municipal Auditorium; Spoleto Festival Orchestra U.S.A.; Christian Badea, cond.; Westminster Cathedral Choir dir. by Joseph Flummerfelt; with Suzanne Hong

(Sardula), Sunny Joy Langton (Kitty), Carolyne James (Maharani), David Clatworthy (Mr. Scattergood), William Stone (Abdul), Roger Havranek (Maharajah), and Tonio di Paolo (Kodanda) (Spoleto Festival U.S.A.; on a double-bill with *Missa O Pulchritudo in Honorem Sacratissimi Cordis Jesus)*

Reviews:

W19.11a "Festival Holds Menotti in its Magic Spell." *Charlotte Observer* (Charlotte, NC), (May 24, 1981)
"The skill showed most clearly in a second-act double fugue where the intricate rhythm for soloists and more than 50 chorus members could have spelled disaster in less capable hands."

W19.11b Rothstein, Edward. "Menotti: Is He the 'Last Savage' in Worlds of Arts and Finance?" *New York Times*, 3 (May 28, 1981): 15.
Includes general comments about the nature of the Festival. ". . . in the three-hour performance, it was the party scene that was most intriguing. Its cliched condemnations of capitalist civilization were ironically connected to the Spoleto Festival itself."

W19.11c "The Last Savage." *Variety* 303 (June 3, 1981): 87.
"This year's new collaboration . . . has achieved improved results, although stated in an outsize arena ill-suited to musical presentation."

W19.11d Ardoin, John. "Menotti's 'The Last Savage.'" *High Fidelity/Musical America* 31 (September 1981): MA32-33.
"There were no big names as such in the cast, as there had been at the Met, but the performance had more naturalness, was more amusing and less pointedly 'operatic,' and it had an easier flow to it."

W19.11e Storrer, William Allin. "Charleston: Menotti's Last Savage (Spoleto Festival)." *Opera* (England) 32 (Autumn 1981): 120.
"All seemed hampered by Menotti's clean but unexacting staging. The production used the Gaillard's shallow stage as well as may be hoped for . . . ."

W19.11f Dolmetsch, Carl. "Charleston: Spoleto U.S.A." *Opera Canada* 22, 4 (1981): 31.
". . . it is one of Menotti's strongest works, musically and dramatically, and has lost none of its topical relevance."

W19.11g   Jacobson, Robert. "Charleston." *Opera News* 46 (October 1981): 34+.
"The ladies appeared the most strongly cast, especially Suzanne Hong as Sardula, her fresh, silvery soprano and charming presence ideal in the role."

W19.12   1982 (Feb 24): Detmold, Germany; Edwin Scholz, cond.; with Pamela Hicks (Kitty), Ameen Dishtchekenian (Sardula), Waclawa Górny (Maharani), Ernst Botkin (Kodanda), Aldo Tiziani (Abdul), Werner Schürmann (Mr. Scattergood), and Christof Sitarski (Mahajani)

*Review:*

W19.12a   Loskill, Jörg. "Zweimal Menotti: Der letzte Wilde in Detmold." *Opernwelt* 23 (April 1982): 49-50.

W19.13   1984 (Jul 7): Spoleto; Teatro Nuovo; Baldo Podic, cond.; Spoleto Festival Orchestra; Westminster Cathedral Choir; with Maria Bolgan (Kitty), Louis Otey (Abdul), François Loup (Maharajah), Gianni Vanzelli (Mr. Scattergood), William Livingston (Kodanda), Ambra Vespasiani (Maharani), and Christina Rubin (Sardula)

*Review:*

W19.13a   Bellingardi, Luigi. "Contrasts at Spoleto." *Opera* (England) 35 (Autumn 1984): 102-103.
"The production . . . combined natural fluency, professionalism and good taste, qualities which are always to be found in Menotti's stage direction."

### ♦ DISCOGRAPHY

SELECTIONS

W19.14   Metropolitan Concert Band (East Detroit, MI); Martin A. Stella, cond. Silver Crest MID-80-16, 2 discs, LP, analog, stereo. (1980)
Album title: 1980 Mid-West National Band and Orchestra Clinic. Recorded at the 34th annual clinic, Chicago.
With works by Bencriscutto, Iannaccone, Dello Joio, Lecuona, Teike, Monti, and Strauss.

W19.15   St. Olaf College Norseman Band; Paul Niemisto, cond.
WCAL RSST-811101, LP (1981)

Album title: Norseman Band "In Concert."
Recorded in Boe Memorial Chapel at St. Olaf College on April 25, 1981, and in Skogland Center at St. Olaf College.
With works by Giannini, Ginastera, Cable, Nielsen, and Chance.

W19.16　National Music Camp High School Symphonic Band; George C. Wilson, cond.
National Music Camp NMC-1967-18, W4RS-2946, analog, stereo., LP (1967)
Recorded in Hill Auditorium, Ann Arbor, Mich.
With works by Nelhybel, Berlioz, Sousa, Grange, Grainger, and Holst.

W19.17　University of Michigan Symphonic Band; William D. Revelli, cond.
Golden Crest CRS-4042, stereo., LP (1980)
Album title: The Revelli years.
With works by Nixon, Gould, Yoder, Prokofiev, Sousa, Sessions, Massenet, and Goldman.

W19.18　University of Michigan Symphonic Band; William D. Revelli, cond.
Franco Colombo SP 102, analog, mono, LP (1968), BP 102, analog, stereo., LP (1970)
Series: Educational record reference library. Band program, 2.
With works by H. Smith, C. Williams, Shostakovich, Nixon, and Johnson.

♦ SELECTED RECORDING REVIEW

W19.19　Ditsky, John. "Revelli Years." *Fanfare* 5 (March-April 1982): 330-332. Review of the Golden Crest CRS 4202 (6 discs), 4210 (3 discs), and 4211 (3 discs) recordings. Vol. I includes "Overture and Caccia" from *The Last Savage*, arr. Lang. University of Michigan Band (in vols. I and III) and Marching Band (in vol. II), cond. by William D. Revelli. Includes " . . . the nearly forgotten excerpts from Menotti's third opera . . . These discs are not for everyone . . . but I hope it is . . . clear that many will be pleased with them . . ."

## *W20*　*LA DONNA IMMOBILE* (1972)

Unfinished "Opera buffa" without music.
Dedicated to the memory of Gustav Mahler.
Improvised by Menotti during the summer of 1972.

*W 21*   *DOUBLE BASS CONCERTO* (1983; G. Schirmer; 23 min.)

Double bass; 2+pic.22+bcl.2/4231/timp.perc/hp/str

♦ PREMIERE PERFORMANCE

W21.1   1983 (Oct 20): New York; Lincoln Center; Avery Fisher Hall; James Van Demark, double bass; Zubin Mehta, cond.; New York Philharmonic.

*Reviews:*

W21.1a   "Air on a Bass String: Two Continents to Hear Commissioned Concerto." *Symphony Magazine* 34 (October-November 1983): 63-65. Preview of Van Demark's upcoming performances. Says Van Demark: "It's decidedly up to date and explores things that simply haven't been done by other composers, which I think is good. It certainly has been worth waiting for."

W21.1b   Feder, Susan. "N.Y. Philharmonic: Menotti *Double Bass Concerto.*" *High Fidelity/Musical America* 34 (February 1984): MA23-24.
" . . . once the Concerto got under way it had few surprises in its amiable but innocuous twenty-five minute duration."

*W 22*   *THE EGG* (1976; G. Schirmer; 60 min.)

Opera in one act with libretto (English) by Menotti; "an operatic riddle"
Commissioned by Washington Cathedral through the Edward W. Hazen Foundation.
Cast: high Bar, T, dram S, Bar, B, T, Bar, Mz, silent role, S; SATB chorus
1111/1110/perc/hp.org/vn.va.vc.db

♦ SELECTED PERFORMANCES

W22.1   1976 (Jun 17): Washington, DC; Washington Cathedral; Paul Callaway, cond.; musicians and volunteer members of the Cathedral Festival '76 Chorale; with Matthew Murray (Manuel), Anastasios Vrenios (St. Simeon Stylites), Esther Hinds (Basilissa), Sigmund Cowan (Areobindus), Gimi Beni (Gourmantus), Peter Fish (Priscus), Gene Tucker (Eunich of the Sacred Cubicle), Richard S. Dirksen (Pachomius), Dana Krueger

(Sister of the Basilissa), Frank Phelan (Julian), and Regina McConnell (Beggar Woman) (on a double-bill with *Martin's Lie*)

Reviews:

W22.1a    Sears, L. "Debuts and Premieres at Washington Cathedral." *Music; the A.G.O. and R.C.C.O. Magazine* 10 (October 1976): 48-49.

W22.1b    Timbrell, Charles. "Philadelphia/Washington." *Opera News* 41 (October 1976): 64.
"Though Menotti is reported to have delivered the last forty pages only four days before the premiere, the production was remarkably secure."

W22.1c    Parris, Robert. "Washington Cath.; Menotti Prems." *High Fidelity/Musical America* 26 (November 1976): MA21.
"What little music . . . is very pretty, and derives . . . largely . . . from wisps of Puccini . . . The cast . . . was more than equal to the occasion."

W22.2    1978 (Jan 3): Nottingham, England; Church of St. Mary the Virgin; Nottingham Music Theater (British premiere)

Review:

W22.2a    "Menotti's Epilogue for The Egg." *Times* (London), (September 2, 1977): 7.
Notice that Menotti is writing a new epilogue for the Nottingham Music Theater, a company of young professionals.

W22.3    1978 (Jan 6): Derby Cathedral; Nottingham Music Theatre

W22.4    1978 (May 30): Charleston, SC; Circular Congregational Church; Festival Orchestra; Joseph Flummerfelt, cond.; Princeton High School Choir, cond. by William R. Trego; with Matthew Murray (Manuel), Anastasios Vrenios (Saint Simeon), Esther Hinds (The Basilissa, Pride), Cary Archer Smith (Areobindus, Lust), Carlo Thomas (Gourmantus, Gluttony), Dana Krueger (Basilissa's Sister, Envy), Gene Tucker (Eunuch, Sloth), Mark Blecke (Pachomius, Avarice), Francis Menotti (Julian), Amanda Fulton (Beggar Woman), and Kelley Hollowell (Priscus) (Spoleto Festival U.S.A.; on a double-bill with *Martin's Lie*)

*Reviews:*

W22.4a  Giniger, Ken S. "Menotti's Short Religioso Operas in Lovely Oven-like Church." *Variety* 291 (June 14, 1978): 78.
"Comic elements in 'The Egg' intrude on what is essentially a serious theme."

W22.4b  Porter, Andrew. "Musical Events: Spoleto of the South." *New Yorker* 54 (June 19, 1978): 68.
". . . slight, silly, ethically shallow, and musically worthless."

W22.4c  Jacobson, Robert. "Charleston, S.C." *Opera News* 43 (August 1978): 44.
"Music for *The Egg* is virtually nonexistent, and its message about finding the secret of life by giving it away plummets below the simplistic."

W22.4d  Storrer, William Allin. "Charleston: Menotti and Spoleto U.S.A." *Opera* (England) 29 (Autumn 1978): 116-118.
". . . the dramatic balance is too much shifted from the main character; Menotti's staging had Simeon atop the pillar even as the audience entered the small auditorium."

W22.4e  Mercer, Ruby. "Charleston: Spoleto Festival." *Opera Canada* 19, 3 (1978): 28-29.
"The music, quite operatic at times, is colorful, melodic and altogether charming. I found the characters somewhat silly and disturbingly exaggerated, however."

W22.4f  Cernaz, Bruno. "Spoleto: 21st Festival of Two Worlds." *Opera Canada* 19, 4 (1978): 36-37.
". . . a product of high artistic quality and interesting visual and vocal articulation."

W22.4g  Busnelli, Mariella. "Spoleto's Tragic 'Cenerentola.'" *Opera* (England) 29 (Autumn 1978): 104-105.
"The first night audience was warm in its reception, though I had the distinct impression that it consisted of few critics, many guests and almost no paid-up ticketholders."

W22.5  1980 (Nov 13): Brooklyn; Brooklyn Academy of Music; Brooklyn Philharmonia; members of the Indiana University Opera Theater; Lukas Foss, cond.; with Martin Strother (Manuel), Joseph Levitt (St. Simeon),

Edith Diggory (Basilissa), Steven Nelson (Areobindus), Ted Adkins (Gourmantus), Richard Walker (Eunuch), Jon Fay (Pachomius), Paul Redd (Sister of the Basilissa), Brian Trego (Julian), and Sarah Miller (Beggarwoman) (on a double-bill with John Eaton's *The Cry of Clytaemnestra*)

Reviews:

W22.5a    Henahan, Donal. "Opera: Double Local Debut of One: Actors in Brooklyn." *New York Times*, (November 15, 1980): 13.
"This is simple stuff, but at least Mr. Menotti knows the potential of human voices and how to score for them."

W22.5b    Smith, Patrick J. "New York." *Opera* (England) 32 (March 1981): 274-275.
"The smooth melodic sauce of Menotti's writing causes the simple message to slide down easily . . . and the writing is expertly tailored."

W22.6    1981 (Mar 22): Chicago; Cathedral of St. James; William Ferris Chorale; with John Vorrassi (St. Simeon) (on a double-bill with *The Unicorn, The Gorgon, and the Manticore*)

Review:

W22.6a    Duffie, Bruce. "Chicago: St. James Cathedral." *Opera Canada* 22, 3 (1981): 36.
". . . the soloists, mostly from the Chorale, gave life to their characters, and the text has projected about as clearly as one could have hoped for in the large church."

## *W23*    *THE EMPTY HANDED TRAVELER* (1950; G. Schirmer)

For medium or low voice and piano

## *W24*    *ERRAND INTO THE MAZE* (1947; G. Schirmer; 20 min.)

Modern dance in one act; choreography by Martha Graham.
Title from a poem of Ben Belitt, from his book *Wilderness Stair*.
1111/1000/perc/pf/str

144  Works and Performances

### ♦ ABOUT THE WORK

W24.1  Hodgins, Paul. *Relationships Between Score and Choreography in Twentieth-century Dance: Music, Movement, and Metaphor*. Lewiston, NY: Mellen, 1992.
Identifies characteristics common to both music and dance, introducing a paradigm of choreomusical analysis and applies it, among other works, to *Errand Into the Maze*.

### ♦ SELECTED PERFORMANCES

W24.2  1947 (Feb 27): New York; Ziegfeld Theatre; Louis Horst, cond.; with Martha Graham (The Woman, Ariadne) and Mark Ryder (The Man, Theseus-Minotaur)

W24.3  1974 (Apr 29): New York; Mark Hellinger Theater; Martha Graham Dance Company; with Yuriko Kimura (The Woman) and Tim Wengerd (The Man, Theseus-Minotaur)

*Review:*

W24.3a  Barnes, Clive. "Dance: 'Errand' Revival." *New York Times*, (May 1, 1974): 60.
"Like the dance itself Gian-Carlo Menotti's music is a study in climax, and it effectively reflects the rising fears and tensions of the heroine."

### ♦ DISCOGRAPHY

W24.4  Atlantic Sinfonietta; Andrew Schenck, cond.
Koch International 3-7051-2 H1. digital, compact disc (1991)
Recorded Nov 15, 1990, at Master Sound Astoria Studios, Astoria, NY.
Album title: More Music for Martha Graham.
With works by Hindemith and Schuman.

### ♦ SELECTED RECORDING REVIEWS

W24.5  North, James H. "More Music for Martha Graham." *Fanfare* 15 (September-October 1991): 444-445.
Review of the Koch International Classics 7051 recording. "The first measures announce that this will be unusual Menotti: a neoclassical piano line right from Stravinsky . . . The Koch recording provides the performers with both clarity and warmth."

W24.6    Pincus, Andrew L. "Recordings Reprise Graham Works." *Berkshire Eagle* (Pittsfield, MA), (November 3, 1991)
"It alternates strongly rhythmic sections with freer, more melodic ones in a dramatization of Ariadne's inner torments."

W24.7    Miller, Karl. "Collections — Music for Martha Graham." *American Record Guide* 55 (January-February 1992): 144.
Review of the Koch 7051 recording. "This is the first recording of the Menotti. It is a bit on the austere side for Menotti, but it [is] certainly worth a listen."

W24.8    Dickinson, Peter. "Hindemith. Herodiade — Ballet. Menotti. Errand into the Maze — Ballet. Schuman. Night Journey — Ballet." *Gramophone* 69 (April 1992): 43.
Review of the Koch International Classics recording, 27051 (cassette), 37051-2 (compact disc). "This neat neo-classical score . . . comes from one of Menotti's best periods . . . convincingly played."

## W25    FANFARE FOR CHARLESTON (1976)

Composed for the opening of the first Spoleto U.S.A. Festival, May 25, 1976.

♦ PREMIERE PERFORMANCE

W25.1    1976 (May 25): Charleston, SC; Cistern of the College of Charleston

## W26    FANTASIA FOR VIOLONCELLO AND ORCHESTRA (1975; G. Schirmer; 30 min.)

One-movement work originally entitled *Capriccio*.
Cello; 2+pic.2+ca.2(ebcl)+bcl.2+cbn/4331/timp/4perc/hp/str

♦ SELECTED PERFORMANCES

W26.1    1976 (Jan 16): Turin, Italy; RAI Orchestra; Ferruccio Scaglia, cond.; with Lawrence Lesser, violoncello

*Review:*

W26.1a     Gallarati, Paolo. "A Torino." *Nuova rivista musicale italiana* 10 (January-March 1976): 158-159.

W26.2     1991 (Jun 2): Charleston, SC; Gaillard Auditorium; Mstislav Rostropovich, cond.; with Lawrence Lesser, violoncello


**W27**     *FIVE SONGS FOR VOICE AND PIANO* (1981; G. Schirmer; 12 min.)

Contents: The eternal prisoner — The idle gift — The longest wait — My ghost — The swing.

### ♦ SELECTED PERFORMANCES

W27.1     1981 (Oct 21): New York; Abraham Goodman House; Merkin Concert Hall; with Joseph Porrello (tenor) and Kenneth Merrill (piano) (First four songs only; *see* W27.2)

*Review:*

W27.1a     Krebs, Albin and Robert McG. Thomas. "Menotti Song Cycle to be Performed Tomorrow." *New York Times*, 3 (October 20, 1981): 8.

W27.2     1983 (Dec 12): Palm Beach, FL; Flagler Museum; with Joseph Porrello (tenor) and Kenneth Merrill (piano) (Includes fifth song, which was not written at the time of the premiere mentioned in W27.1)

*Review:*

W27.2a     Hughes, Allen. "Song: Porrello Offers 4 New Menottis." *New York Times*, 3 (October 26, 1981): 21.
"Mr. Porrello's voice is modest, but it was equal to the varying demands of these works, and at his best he sang quite persuasively."

### ♦ DISCOGRAPHY

W27.3     Karan Armstrong, soprano; Alfred Lutz, Mischa Salevic, violins; Stephan Blaumer, viola; Klaus Kühr, violoncello; Helga Storck, harp.
Etcetera KTC 1045, compact disc, digital, stereo. (1988)

With *Nocturne* and *Cantilena e scherzo.*

W27.4 Robin Leggate, tenor; Malcolm Martineau, piano.
Chandos CHAN 9605, digital, stereo., compact disc (1988)
Recorded at St. Paul's Church, Knightsbridge, June 28, 1997.
With *Martin's Lie* and *Canti della lontananza.*

### ♦ SELECTED RECORDING REVIEWS

W27.5 Ardoin, John. "Menotti's Passion Erupts in CD Collection." *Dallas Morning News*, (November 20, 1988)
"Armstrong, however, is not the ideal interpreter . . . Her voice is unsteady and too grainy. At the beginning of her career it was probably an attractive lyric sound."

## *W28* FOR THE DEATH OF ORPHEUS (1990; G. Schirmer; 11 min.)

For tenor, chorus, and orchestra.
Tenor; chorus; 2+pic.2+ca.2(ebcl)+bcl.2/4331/timp.4perc/hp/str

### ♦ SELECTED PERFORMANCES

W28.1 1990 (Nov 8): Atlanta; with Karl Dent (tenor); Robert Shaw, cond.; Atlanta Symphony Orchestra; Atlanta Symphony Chorus (on a program dedicated to the memory of Leonard Bernstein; with works by Bernstein, Dvořák, and Janáćek)

*GIORNO DI NOZZE* See: *The Wedding*

## *W29* GLORIA (1995; G. Schirmer)

Tenor; chorus; 2+pic.2+ca.2(e♭cl)+bcl.2/4331/timp.2perc/hp/str

## *W30* GOYA (1986, rev. 1991; G. Schirmer; evening)

Opera in three acts with libretto by Menotti.
Cast: T, Mz, S, T, Bar, Bar, Mz

2+pic.2+ca.2+bcl.2/4331/timp.perc/pf.hp/str
Offstage: 2tpt

### ♦ PREMIERE PERFORMANCE

W30.1   1986 (Nov 15): Washington, DC; John F. Kennedy Center for the Performing Arts; Washington Opera; Rafael Frühbeck de Burgos, cond.; with Placido Domingo (Goya), Victoria Vergera (Duchess of Alba), Karen Huffstodt (Queen Maria Luisa), Louis Otey (Martin Zapater), Howard Bender (King Charles IV), and Stephen Dupont (Godoy) (The Nov 28 performance was televised nationally as part of PBS's series, "Great Performances")

*Reviews:*

W30.1a   Jarrell, Frank P. "Menotti Says *Goya* Work Will Be His Last Opera." *News and Courier* (Charleston, SC), (June 6, 1982)
"Domingo . . . suggested Goya, I readily accepted. I believe it's the only time I've accepted someone else's idea."

W30.1b   Molotsky, Irvin. "Menotti Plans '86 Premiere in Capital." *New York Times*, 1 (November 3, 1984): 10.
Menotti reveals plans for presenting Goya's premiere in Washington, DC "Two cities love me, Washington and Trieste," Menotti remarked. "In Trieste I can do anything I want. In fact, in Washington I can do anything I want, too."

W30.1c   Snowman, D. "*Goya*." *Montsalvat*, 142 (October 1986): 16-18.

W30.1d   Selch, Frederick R. "Gian Carlo Menotti's *Goya*." *Ovation* 7 (November 1986): 12-14+.
Domingo commented, going on to compliment Menotti on his vocal style. "He writes his music in the melodic way, the only way for a singer — and always for the enjoyment of the audience."

W30.1e   Stearns, David Patrick. "The Man Behind the Artist." *Opera News* 51 (November 1986): 14-18.
Menotti " . . . claims he isn't pinning his hopes on a great success with *Goya*. 'That may be what you want when you're young, but at my age you have to be a fool to be hungry for success.'"

W30.1f   Geracimos, Ann. "Patron Sets Stage for 'Goya.'" *Washington Times*, (November 4, 1986)
Homage to patron and director David Lloyd Kreeger for securing funding for the Washington Opera production.

W30.1g   Molotsky, Irvin. "Music View: Making an Operatic Hero of Goya." *New York Times*, 2 (November 9, 1986): 19.
"It makes a very good libretto — this love triangle," notes Menotti. "Of course, we know by modern scholarship that it did not happen, but it is a good story. As the Italian saying goes, 'It may not be true, but it is well invented.'"

W30.1h   McLellan, Joseph. "Expectations Abound as Washington Prepares for the World Premiere of Gian Carlo Menotti's New Opera." *Washington Post*, (November 9, 1986)
Says Menotti, "Some people may think it is just a love story, but as in all my operas there is a symbolical meaning. The duchess is a symbol of beauty. I think the man struggled all his life in a search for artistic perfection and in the opera at least she symbolizes the perfection of beauty that is unattainable."

W30.1i   Roca, Octavio. "Menotti Trails the True Goya: Search Recalled on Eve of Glitzy Opera Premiere." *Washington Times*, (November 14, 1986)
Remarks Menotti, "And Plácido is a lamb . . . I think that of all the very famous people I have worked with, Placido Domingo and Mirella Freni are the most wonderful, very understanding, very patient, and they accept new ideas so easily."

W30.1j   Wigler, Stephen. "Goya's Spanish Goulash." *Sun* (Baltimore), (November 17, 1986)
"Aria-like passages never interrupt the dramatic flow, and the love duets between Goya and the Duchess have a luscious Pucciniesque plangency. Here the music can bring a catch to the throat."

W30.1k   Jarrell, Frank P. "Premiere of 'Goya' Meant Race to Finish." *News and Courier* (Charleston, SC), (November 16, 1986)
Menotti: "Listen carefully to the libretto. People think I've written an opera about Goya. Not so. It's about the composer . . . I think we artists suffer enough just being artists. We should be forgiven."

W30.1l   Henahan, Donal. "Opera: Menotti's 'Goya' in Washington Premiere." *New York Times*, 3 (November 17, 1986): 15.

*150  Works and Performances*

"This time Mr. Menotti has composed a parody of a Menotti opera."

W30.1m  Gamarekian, Barbara. "For 'Goya' Opening, Capital Becomes a Brilliant Canvas." *New York Times*, 2 (November 17, 1986): 10.
"At the dinner-dance that followed the performance, Placido Domingo . . . was surrounded by admirers. 'It is very emotional for me,' said Mr. Domingo . . . Of the composer, [he] said, 'I hope his words will live — that is the important thing.'"

W30.1n  Goodman, Peter. "Domingo in 'Goya,' a Menotti Premiere." *Newsday* (Long Island, NY), (November 17, 1986)
"The music does not have enough bite or depth for its grand subject. There are many moments of pleasant melody, and some attractive orchestrations, but it's embedded in a mass of 101 strings."

W30.1o  Kimmelman, Michael. "For Menotti's Opera, 'Goya,' a Disappointing Premiere." *Philadelphia Inquirer*, (November 17, 1986)
"'Goya' . . . creates no characters of any depth, no situations of any urgency or importance, no scene at all during the work's nearly three hours in which a viewer might care about what happens to players on stage."

W30.1p  Roca, Octavio. "'Goya': An Unpolished Jewel." *Washington Times*, (November 17, 1986)
"Within the limits of the libretto . . . Mr. Domingo's characterization was as touching as his singing was splendid . . . [but] for every brief outburst of melody there was ages of boring vocal music that recalled 'Chip and His Dog' and the lower slopes of Menottiland."

W30.1q  Fournier, Lou. "Composer Confirms He Aided Menotti." *Washington Times*, (November 21, 1986)
While Menotti wrote every word and note of the opera, composers-arrangers Stephen Douglas Burton and William Brohn allegedly helped with some last-minute orchestrations.

W30.1r  Belt, Byron. "Menotti's 'Goya' Makes Winning Debut in Lavish Staging at the Kennedy Center." *Star-Ledger* (Newark, NJ), (November 21, 1986)
"I find the man [Menotti] a rich contribution to the morality and musicality of our time, and 'Goya' a worthy and meaningful contribution to the aridity dominating the lyric theater today."

W30.1s "Menotti Transforms Goya's Life into a Bland, Predictable Opera." *Courier-Journal* (Louisville, KY), (November 23, 1986)
"'Goya' . . . had everything in its favor except a composer and a librettist capable of dealing in depth with its operatically promising subject. Menotti, functioning as usual in both capacities, has produced a rather stupefying exercise in banality . . ."

W30.1t Allen, Jane Addams. "Menotti's 'Goya': Portrait of the Artist as a Wimp." *Washington Times*, (November 28, 1986)
Chiefly a condemnation of Menotti's concept of what Goya the man was really like. " . . . he created a monumentally dull opera from an intrinsically interesting subject, [and] he has quite unnecessarily turned one of the world's great artists . . . into a sniveling loser whose devotion to art renders him unable to cope with the world."

W30.1u Green, Sara. "Menotti's 'Goya': Not the Traditional Opera." *Washington Times*, (November 28, 1986)
Preview of the Nov 28, 1986 PBS telecast. Said Menotti, "A work of art is never finished, it is just abandoned . . . Some people will say it's reactionary and some people will say 'How nice to hear a melody.'" Includes anecdotal references to Domingo.

W30.1v Ardoin, John. "Menotti's 'Goya.'" *Dallas Morning News*, (November 28, 1986)
Preview of the Nov 30 KERA-13 telecast. Menotti describes his score as "unabashedly melodic and certainly very rooted in the Italian *bel canto* tradition, or whatever you choose to call it. It is obvious that it was an opera commissioned by a tenor written for a tenor."

W30.1w Henahan, Donal. "Music View: the Problems of 'Goya' and the Problem of Menotti." *New York Times*, 2 (November 30, 1986): 21.
"'Goya' showed that Mr. Menotti's instinct for the melodramatic is still reasonably strong, though he no longer seems able to translate his theatrical ideas into interesting music."

W30.1x Walsh, Michael. "A Little Puccini and Water." *Time* 128 (December 1, 1986): 70.
"Menotti has recently confessed that 'I have my doubts about how important my music is.' After *Goya*, he may be the only one who does."

W30.1y Roos, James. "Musical Clichés, Poor Writing Doom Menotti's 'Goya'" *Miami Herald*, (December 1, 1986)

*152 Works and Performances*

          Review of PBS telecast. " . . . a ridiculous story set to Menotti's most nondescript music."

W30.1z    Finn, Robert. "Opera Old-fashioned, its Music Forgettable." *Plain Dealer* (Cleveland), (December 1, 1986)
          Review of PBS telecast. "It is too aggressively old-fashioned, too slavishly imitative of late-romantic Italian models."

W30.1aa    Kerner, Leighton. "Music: Million Dollar Bash (Kennedy Center Opera House)." *Village Voice* 31 (December 2, 1986): 115.

W30.1bb    Brown, Steven. "Televised 'Goya' Is All-Pro, but the Magic Is Missing." *Orlando Sentinel* (Orlando, FL), (December 14, 1986)
          Preview of the WMFE-Channel 24 telecast. "The settings seem truly imposing, though on TV they are largely in shadow, and the cast is always accomplished."

W30.1cc    Porter, Andrew. "Musical Events: Princess and Painter." *New Yorker* 62 (December 22, 1986): 89-93.
          "The only surprises for a listener trying to anticipate what will happen next are provided by measures even more banal than he predicted. The production, directed by Menotti himself . . . looked handsome."

W30.1dd    Rudolf, Bert. "Washington, D.C. (1986-1987 Season)." *Oper und Konzert* 25, 1 (1987): 24-25.

W30.1ee    Dolmetsch, Carl. "Washington Opera." *Opera Canada* 28, 1 (1987): 38.
          "A bagful of labored Menotti-isms, it fails to soar at any point and even its final apotheosis, though stunningly done, failed to move the heart."

W30.1ff    Hamlet-Metz, M. "Estreno mundial de Goya." *Montsalvat*, 145 (January 1987): 46-47.

W30.1gg    Rothstein, Edward. "Sic Transit 'Goya.'" *New Republic* 196 (January 26, 1987): 27-29.
          "Unfortunately, the critical reception was nearly as uniformly negative as the hype and celebration were positive . . . the aesthetic failure combined with the social success probably only increased the sort of brooding that led to the opera in the first place."

W30.1hh    O'Reilly, F. Warren. "Correspondence: Gian Carlo Menotti — an American Composer?" *Ovation* 8 (February 1987): 6.

Reply to Selch's article in the Nov 1986 issue of *Ovation* (*see* W30.1d). In his rebuttal, Selch notes that "... overall, the opera suffered from an unfinished quality ... and from a freshness of its material. This was certainly not Menotti at his inventive best, though the opera did benefit from a splendid production ..."

W30.1ii  Jahant, Charles. "Washington." *Opera* (England) 38 (March 1987): 276-277.
"... outshone anything the Washington Opera has done to date, but the English text was virtually impossible to understand, and I was forced to consult the 'sopra-titles' atop the proscenium."

W30.1jj  Stearns, David Patrick. "Washington, D.C." *Opera News* 51 (March 14, 1987): 38.
"It was not hard to detect some audacity in Menotti's willingness to put a major work onstage without a workshop, provincial tryout or time for revisions. As a result, much of *Goya* seemed the work of last-minute inspiration or no inspiration at all."

W30.1kk  Gregson, David. "Despite Critics, Opera's Menotti Is Busy as Ever." *San Diego Union*, (May 5, 1987)
Interview in San Diego, where *The Medium* and *The Telephone* will open at the Old Globe Theatre. "I really couldn't get too mad at the critics ... because they were really so poisonous, so violent about 'Goya' ... ultimately the reviews had the opposite of a negative result for me because I was immediately commissioned to write an opera for the 1988 Olympics in South Korea, and the Bulgarian government contacted me for a production of 'Goya.'"

W30.1ll  Fabian, Imre. "Washington: die Uraufführung von Menottis 'Goya' mit Placido Domingo." *Opernwelt* 28 (February 1987): 20+.

W30.1mm  McCardell, Charles. "Opera Everywhere: Washington (Washington Opera)." *Musical America* 107 (September 1987): 40-41.
"Unfortunately, it all functions as big-budget window dressing for an opera conspicuously lacking in musical and dramatic content. Since Menotti wears the hats of composer, librettist, and stage director, he must accept all the blame."

W30.1nn  Lipman, Samuel. "A Dissent on Menotti" *in Arguing For Music, Arguing For Culture*, by Samuel Lipman. New York: D.R. Godine in association with American Council for the Arts, 1990.

## ♦ DISCOGRAPHY

W30.2   Penelope Daner, soprano; Suzanna Guzman, mezzo-soprano; César Hernández, Howard Bender, tenors; Boaz Senator, baritone; Andrew Wentzel, bass; Westminster Cathedral Choir; Spoleto Festival Orchestra; Steven Mercurio, cond.
Nuova Era 7060-7061, digital, stereo., 2 compact discs (1992)
Sung in Italian.
Recorded in the Teatro Nuovo, Spoleto, Jun 26-Jul 13, 1991.
Co-production with 34th Festival dei Due Mondi, Spoleto.

## ♦ SELECTED RECORDING REVIEWS

W30.3   Greene, David Mason. "Menotti: *Goya.*" *American Record Guide* 55 (November-December 1992): 160.
Menotti " . . . has long ago assimilated the way the verisimists did it, and he squeezes it out like toothpaste. The result — 'endless melody' — is not unattractive and has its high points (literally) but I have not heard a phrase that rivets the attention and sticks in the memory . . . The cast is satisfactory."

W30.4   Smith, Patrick J. "Goya." *Opera News* 57 (December 19, 1992): 38.
"This recording . . . is immediate, has strong stereo separation and movement and captures what must have been an effective production."


*W31*   *A HAPPY ENDING* (contracted 1947)

Film script for screenplay contracted with MGM in 1947; never produced.
Later reworked and retitled *The Beautiful Snowfall.*


*W32*   *HELP, HELP, THE GLOBOLINKS!* (1968; G. Schirmer; 70 min.)

Opera in one act for children "and those who like children" with libretto (English) by Menotti.
Originally titled "Help, Help, the Astrolix."
Commissioned by the Hamburgische Staatsoper.
Cast: S, S, high Bar, Bar, T, Mz, Bar, B; 12 children, globolinks
2121/2221/timp.perc/pf/str/tape
or 1(pic)11(bcl)0/1101/perc/pf.hp/str/tape or 2pf

## ♦ ABOUT THE WORK

W32.1    Dannenberg, Peter. "Auftragskompositionen für Kinder." *Neue Musikzeitung* 18, 1 (1969): 7.

W32.2    Schonberg, Harold C. "Did Menotti Beat 'The Devils'?" *Opera Journal* 2, no. 4 (1969): 34-35.
"It is the best thing that Menotti has done in years, and some of the stage business is enchanting." Reprinted from *New York Times*, August 24, 1969: 15.

W32.3    Fryer, Judith Anne. "Guide to the Study and Performance of Three Operas of Gian-Carlo Menotti." Ed.D. dissertation, Columbia University Teachers College, 1974.
From the author's abstract: "The purpose of this study is to provide historical information, analytical material, and practical suggestions for the teaching and performance of selected Menotti operas in secondary schools . . . Three operas were chosen for thorough analysis: *The Medium* (1946), *Amahl and the Night Visitors* (1951), and *Help, Help, the Globolinks!*"

## ♦ SELECTED PERFORMANCES

W32.4    1968 (Dec 21): Hamburg; Hamburgische Staatsoper; Matthias Kuntzsch, cond.; with William Workman (Tony), Edith Mathis (Emily), Raymond Wolansky (Dr. Stone), Kurt Marschner (Timothy), Arlene Saunders (Madame Euterpova), Franz Grundheber (Mr. Lavender-Gas), Noël Mangin (Dr. Turtlespit), and Ursula Boese (Penelope Newkirk) (in German; presented on a double-bill with *Amahl and the Night Visitors*)

*Reviews:*

W32.4a   Worbs, Hans Christoph. "Eine neue Kinderoper von Menotti." *Schweizerische Musikzeitung* 109 (January-February 1969): 36.

W32.4b   "Magic and the Globolinks." *Time* 93 (January 3, 1969): 50.
Says Menotti, "Schöffer and Nikolais [lighting and costume designers for the production] are the children of this generation . . . Theirs is the world of mechanized art; mine is still the world of art as dictated by human emotion."

W32.4c   Dannenberg, Peter. "Hamburg: Schöne Bescherung." *Opernwelt* 10 (February 1969): 39-40.

W32.4d   Geitel, Klaus. "Wer hat Angst vor Globolinks?" *Neue Zeitschrift für Musik* 130 (February 1969): 54-55.
Also published in *Orchester* 17 (March 1969):111-112

W32.4e   Wagner, Klaus. "Kaviar fürs Kindervolk: *Hilfe, hilfe, die Globolinks* sind in Hamburg." *Melos* 36 (February 1969): 79-83.

W32.4f   Sutcliffe, James Helme. "Hamburg." *Opera News* 33 (February 8, 1969): 32-33.
Illustrated review. "Menotti's tuneful, traditional music sounded very much like his wonted self and was smoothly coordinated with the electronic passages . . . "

W32.4g   Joachim, Heinz. "Hamburg." *Opera* (England) 20 (March 1969): 236-237.
"Menotti's imaginatively pregnant production, surrealistic costumes . . . and the weightless choreographic visions . . . opened unheard-of new perspectives of fairy-tale fantasy for the visual impact of the modern stage."

W32.4h   Worbs, Hans Christoph. "Menottis neue Kinderoper." *Musica* 23 (March-April 1969): 148-149.

W32.4i   Sutcliffe, James Helme. "Menotti's Globolinks." *High Fidelity/Musical America* 19 (April 1969): MA27-28.
"Cheers for Menotti, whose first venture into electronic music . . . was more dramaturgically meaningful than most dial-twiddling sonics at Hamburg premieres, and a welcome contrast to his tunefully bland 'regular' music."

W32.5    1969 (Aug 1): Santa Fe, NM; Santa Fe Opera; Gustav Meier, cond.; with William Workman (Tony), Judith Blegen (Emily), John Reardon (Dr. Stone), Douglas Perry (Timothy), Marguerite Willauer (Madame Euterpova), Clyde Phillip Walker (Mr. Lavender-Gas), Richard Best (Dr. Turtlespit), and Jean Kraft (Penelope Newkirk) (on a double-bill with Stravinsky's *Le Rossignol*)

W32.5a   Schonberg, Harold C. "Menotti's 'Globolinks' Invades Santa Fe." *Opera Journal* 2, 4 (1969): 33-34.

"Everybody loved it, everybody entered into the spirit of the message. If audience reaction means anything, Menotti has come up with a hit." Reprinted from *New York Times*, August 18, 1969: 28.

W32.5b   Dunning, Bill. "'A Major Opus' Is Verdict after 'Globolinks' Opening." *The New Mexican* (Santa Fe, NM), (August 3, 1969)
"The American premiere . . . propelled the audience into astonished delight, and securely fixed this . . . in orbit as a major opus . . . It is also undoubtedly the finest opera premiered in the Santa Fe Opera's 13 years."

W32.5c   Kolodin, Irving. "Santa Fe's Operatic Oasis." *Saturday Review* 52 (August 30, 1969): 52.
"It has been a long pull for Menotti since his last real success; and that he has asserted again the special theatrical as well as musical instincts that won him fame is a tribute no more to endowment than to perseverance."

W32.5d   Merkling, Frank. "Santa Fe." *Opera News* 34 (September 20, 1969): 23.
". . . most of the guffaws came not from the many children in the audience but from their elders."

W32.5e   Ardoin, John. "Santa Fé — Five Operas in Four Days." *Opera* (England) 20 (November 1969): 977-978.
". . . though the music is not weighty or on a grand scale, I none the less would not like to be part of a musical world which did not have the time to pause and spend a moment of sheer pleasure such as the one offered by the *Globolinks*."

W32.5f   Smith, Patrick J. "Penderecki & Menotti: Pros and Cons." *High Fidelity/Musical America* 19 (November 1969): MA25+.
Because of " . . . the unfailing stage sense of director Menotti in highlighting every trick in the book, the evening provided a modicum of good fun . . . "

W32.5g   Zytowski, Carl B. "Review." *Opera Journal* 3 (Winter 1970): 23-25.
". . . a work which will make the rounds for a time . . . but aside from the 'lesson' it wishes to teach us, it is altogether too old-fashioned to outlive the immediacy of its satirical comment."

*158   Works and Performances*

W32.6    1969 (Nov 21): Cincinnati; College-Conservatory of Music; Corbett Auditorium; with Harlan Jennings/Gerald Phillips (Tony), Kathy Battle/Sara Minton (Emily), Dolores Ivanchich/Fredda Rakusin (Madame Euterpova), Jerry Helton/Clyde Herndon (Dr. Stone), David Bezona/Alan Boyd (Timothy), Harold Custer/Robert Fischer (Dr. Turtlespit), Barbara Daniels/Joyce Farwell (Miss Newkirk), Tom Fox (Mr. Lavender-Gas), Joe Mock (Alister), David Holdgreiwe (Mickey), Jim McKenna (Jerry), Marsie Hall (Sally), Joe Messingschlager (Bobby), Steve Calahan (Tommy), Kathy Messingschlager (Mathilde), Patty Howard (Barbara), Kim Kuethe (Mary-Lou), and Denise Lemon (Tania) ("first collegiate production"; on a double-bill with Gilbert & Sullivan's *Trial By Jury*)

Reviews:

W32.6a   Humphreys, Henry S. "'Globolinks' at Corbett Delights Both Eye and Ear." *Cincinnati Enquirer*, (November 22, 1969): 20.
"I couldn't help but regret that the composer-librettist couldn't have flown here to see and hear it. I doubt whether either of the two earlier 'Globolinks' performances . . . exceeded this one . . ."

W32.6b   Rouse, Jack. "I Believe in 'Globolinks.'" *Music Journal* 28 (April 1970): 30-31.
"I can only hope that future amateur productions are as happy an experience for their groups as the first was for us."

W32.7    1969 (Dec 15): Santa Fe, NM; Santa Fe Opera; presented with same cast as the Aug 1, 1969 performance, but here as part of a double-bill with Penderecki's *Salome*)

W32.8    1969 (Dec 19): New York; New York City Center; Charles Wilson, cond.; with Ellen Faull (Mme. Euterpova), Judith Blegen (Emily), Gene Boucher (Dr. Stone), Raymond Gibbs (Tony), Douglas Perry (Timothy), Clyde Phillip Walker (Mr. Lavender-Gas), Richard Best (Dr. Turtlespit), and Jean Kraft (Miss Penelope Newkirk)  (on a double-bill with *Amahl and the Night Visitors*)

Reviews:

W32.8a   Kupferberg, Herbert. "Bleeps in the Night." *Life* 67 (December 19, 1969): 14.

"With his new opera Menotti will probably not put his critics out of business, but he thumbs his nose at them with an artistry that the merest child can appreciate."

W32.8b   Sargeant, Winthrop. "Musical Events: To the Rescue." *New Yorker* 45 (January 3, 1970): 44.
"The staging has all the features of a mixed-media entertainment, with a light show added to the voices and conventional scenery — and it is lots of fun."

W32.8c   Zimmerman, Paul D. "Operatic Pied Piper." *Newsweek* 75 (January 5, 1970): 61-62.
". . . Madame Euterpova, played with great comic bravura by Ellen Faull, is a figure worthy of fine children's literature — irrepressible, grotesque, self-dramatizing, and, ultimately, a little sad in her ugliness."

W32.8d   Honig, Joel. "New York." *Opera News* 34 (February 7, 1970): 32-33.
"The screams of delight from all ages as Globolinks musically and dramatically disintegrated must have fulfilled the composer-director's dreams."

W32.8e   Weinstock, Herbert. "New York." *Opera* (England) 21 (March 1970): 223-224.
"Very easy to take, often fun to watch, at moments hilarious, the *Globolinks* adds nothing at all to the literature of either opera or music."

W32.8f   Marks, Marcia. "Help, Help, the Globolinks!" *Dance Magazine* 44 (March 1970): 86.
"For the most part, possibilities to achieve the sort of zany foolishness children adore are simply not exploited."

W32.9    1970 (Dec 21): New York; ANTA Theatre; Christopher Keene, cond.; with June Cooper (Emily), Ljuba Tchereskaya (Madame Euterpova), Beverly Evans (Miss Newkirk), Harold van Geldern (Dr. Lavender-Gas), James Fleetwood (Mr. Turtlespit), Douglas Perry (Janitor), John Ostendorf (Tony), and Wayne Turnage (Dr. Stone) (on a double-bill with *Amahl and the Night Visitors*)

*Review:*

W32.9a   Henahan, Donal. "'Amahl' and 'Globolinks' Performed." *New York Times*, (December 24, 1970): 10.
"June Cooper . . . was vocally quite good and convincingly childlike."

W32.10   1971 (Feb 21): Hamburg; Hamburgische Staatsoper; Matthias Kuntzsch, cond.; with Edith Mathis (Emily), Arlene Saunders (Mme. Euterpova), Raymond Wolansky (Dr. Stone), William Workman (Tony), Kurt Marschner (Timothy), Ursula Boese (Newkirk), Franz Grundheber (Dr. Lavender Gas), and Noel Mangin (Turtlespit)

*Review:*

W32.10a  Schneiders, Heinz-Ludwig. "Musikalisches Sacharin." *Opernwelt* 12 (April 1971): 41.

W32.11   1971 (Oct 28): Geneva; Grand Théâtre de Genève; Jean-Pierre Marty, cond.; Orchestre de la Suisse romande; with Catherine Wilson (Mme. Euterpova), Danièle Perriers (Annalie), Donald Bell, Andrew Foldi, and Kerstin Meyer (Students), Jean-Christophe Benoit (schoolmaster), and William Workman (Tony) (translation by Jean-Pierre Marty; on a double-bill with *Amahl and the Night Visitors*)

*Review:*

W32.11a  Bloomfield, Theodore. "Switzerland: Menotti Revival." *Opera* (England) 23 (March 1972): 269.
"A disappointingly small crowd was on hand to greet them. This was too bad, for they offered a welcome relief from the humdrum of daily reality (and occasional operatic banality) . . ."

W32.12   1973 (Jun 16): Birmingham, England; Midlands Art Centre for Young People; Canon Hill Arts Centre; with Sheila Donovan, Fred Sibley, and Jacqueline Blake.

*Reviews:*

W32.12a  Cross, Anthony. "Reports: Birmingham." *Musical Times* 114 (August 1973): 818.
"Production and interpretation were generally efficient but this was hardly enough to redeem a mediocre work."

W32.12b    Bracefield, Hilary. "Birmingham." *Music and Musicians* 22 (October 1973): 80+.
Brief review. "The choruses sounded difficult, but the children were well on top of the material."

W32.13    1978 (Apr 21): New Orleans; University of New Orleans; Performing Arts Center Recital Hall; University of New Orleans Opera Theater; Milton Bush, cond.; with Therese Brassier (Emily), Deborah Matranga (Madame Euterpova), Karl Matherine (Dr. Stone), David Michael Goldstein (Tony), Susan Lincoln Carlson (Penelope Newkirk), Thomas Thomas (Mr. Lavender-Gas), and Mark deVeer (Dr. Turtlespit)

W32.14    1980 (Jun 14): Freiburg, Germany; Hans Urbanek, cond.; with Josephine Cook (Emily), Marilyn Found (Mme. Euterpova), Luis Glocker (Dr. Stone), Morris Morgan (Tony), Willem Verkerk (Schoolmaster), Anita Herrmann (Penelope Newkirk), Paul Winter (Dr. Lavender-Gas), and Jan Alofs (Dr. Turtlespit)

*Reviews:*

W32.14a    Koch, Heinz W. "Zwei Märchen: 'Das Kind und der Zauberspuk' von Ravel und 'Hilfe, Hilfe, die Globolinks' von Menotti in Freiburg." *Opernwelt* 21 (August-September 1980): 39.

W32.14b    Bartenstein, H. "Freiburg: Kinderopern von Ravel und Menotti." *Musik und Bildung* 12 (October 1980): 633-634.

W32.15    1980 (Nov 15): Vienna; Wiener Staatsoper; Wiener Philharmoniker; Reinhard Schwarz, cond.; Gumpoldskirchen Kinderchor; with Renate Holm (Mme. Euterpova), Lesley Manring (Emily), and Gottfried Hornick (Dr. Stone)   (on a double-bill with *Amahl and the Night Visitors*)

*Reviews:*

W32.15a    "Wiener Premieren." *Buehne* 267 (December 1980): 10-11.

W32.15b    Klein, Rudolf. "Wiener Staatsoper für Kinder." *Österreichische Musikzeitschrift* 36 (January 1981): 38.

W32.15c    Klein, Rudolf. "Staatsoper für Kinder." *Opernwelt* 22 (January 1981): 27.

162  Works and Performances

W32.15d  Wechsberg, Joseph. "Austria: Menotti and Verdi for Christmas." *Opera* (England) 32 (March 1981): 283-284.
Menotti " . . . was much cheered and it looks as though his children's operas will be seen and heard by many adults as well — they deserve an adult audience."

W32.15e  Norton-Welsh, Christopher. "Vienna." *Opera News* 45 (March 14, 1981): 38.
"Reinhard Schwarz conducted without great sensitivity, the orchestra delivering ragged entries."

W32.15f  Kutschera, Edda. "Science Fiction nach E.T." *Buehne* 314 (November 1984): 18-19.

W32.15g  Mayer, Gerhard. "Oper anders." *Buehne* 316 (January 1985): 24.

W32.16  1988 (Jun 16): Birmingham, England; Midlands Arts Centre; City of Birmingham Touring Opera; Paul Herbert, cond.; with Eileen Hulse (Mme. Euterpova), Sally Burchell (Penelope Newkirk), Sarah Wright (Emily), Paul Roberts (Tony), Ian Jervis (Dr. Stone), Michael Kennerley (Timothy), Richard Whitehouse (Mr. Lavender-Gas), and Andrew Hammond (Dr. Turtlespit)

*Review:*

W32.16a  Smaczny, Jan. "Help! Help! The Globolinks!" *Opera* (England) 39 (September 1988): 1134.
"While this aging juvenile had an enjoyable time, there remained the nagging worry that children do not really frighten other children, even with costumes and sets as effective as these . . ."

W32.17  1988 (Aug 6): Buxton, England; Paul Herbert, cond.; Buxton Festival Youth Orchestra; with Eileen Hulse (Mme. Euterpova), Sally Burchell (Penelope Newkirk), Sarah Wright (Emily), Paul Roberts (Tony), Ian Jervis (Dr. Stone), Michael Kennerley (Timothy), Richard Whitehouse (Mr. Lavender-Gas), and Andrew Hammond (Dr. Turtlespit) (10th Buxton Festival)

*Review:*

W32.17a  Forbes, Elizabeth. "Buxton Ten Years on." *Opera* (England) 39 (Autumn 1988): 38-40.

"School children and Globolinks were all meticulously rehearsed and the Buxton Festival Youth Orchestra played energetically . . ."

W32.18   1989 (Apr 22): St. Gallen, Switzerland; Eduard Meier, cond.; with Stefanie May-Humes (Emily), Helga Thieme (Mme. Euterpova), Morris Morgan (Dr. Stone), David Geary (Tony), Donna Elizabeth Stone (Penelope Newkirk), Frank Gersthofer (Mr. Lavender-Gas), and Pascal Borer (Dr. Turtlespit)

*Review:*

W32.18a   Fierz, Gerold. "St. Gallen, Luzern: Strawinsky mit Menotti, Ravel." *Opernwelt* 30 (July 1989): 34-35.

W32.19   1994 (Apr 22): New Orleans; University of New Orleans; Performing Arts Center Recital Hall; University of New Orleans Opera Theater; Pamela Legendre, cond.; with Melissa Guillot (Emily), Valerie Ann Jones (Madame Euterpova), Marc Dawson (Dr. Stone), Scott Brush (Tony), Elizabeth Pihl (Miss Penelope Newkirk), Tom Irwin (Mr. Lavender-Gas), and Jay Hall (Mr. Turtlespit)

W32.20   1995 (Dec 2): Arlington, VA; Thomas Jefferson Community Theatre; Opera Theatre of Northern Virginia; John Niles, music director; with Cheri Lynn Reiser (Emily), Joan McFarland (Mme. Euterpova), Wayne King (Tony), and John Boulanger (Dr. Stone)

*Review:*

W32.20a   McLellan, Joseph. "Menotti's 'Globolinks' Makes Opera Child-Friendly." *Washington Post*, Fairfax Weekly (December 7, 1995): 4.
"It is not hard to respond to Menotti's music, which speaks clearly and powerfully in the traditional language of tonal melodies and harmonies, closely linked to the great composers of the past."

W32.21   1996 (Apr 21): Annaberg, Germany; Orchestra of Eduard-von-Winterstein; Ulrich Sprenger, cond.; with Annett Illig (Emily), Maria Maxara (Mme. Euterpova), Knut Weigmann (School director), and Andreas Scholz (Bus driver)

*164 Works and Performances*

Review:

W32.21a   Blumenstein, Gottfried. "Phantasie und Spielwitz." *Opernwelt* 6 (June 1996): 42-43.

W32.22   1996 (Oct 25): Cincinnati; Taft Theatre; Children's Theatre of Cincinnati; with Angela Powell (Mme. Euterpova), David Huffman (Dr. Stone) (a production for Children's Theatre of Cincinnati and Cincinnati Opera Outreach)

Review:

W32.22a   Demaline, Jackie. "'Globolinks' Invasion Grabs Kids' Attention." *Cincinnati Enquirer*, Tempo (October 25, 1996): W37.
"They have a lot of good visual bits of stage business that hold the attention."

## ♦ BRIEFLY NOTED

W32.23   Wiencke, H. E. "Menotti-Oper in Schwerin." *Musik und Gesellschaft* 25 (July 1975): 423-424 ✚ Schuhmann, Claus R. "Innsbruck." *Oper und Konzert* 25, 4 (1987): 10-11. Review of a Mar 6, 1987 performance in Innsbruck.

## ♦ DISCOGRAPHY

### COMPLETE RECORDING

W32.24   Madison Opera; Madison Symphony Orchestra; John DeMain, cond.; with Rachel Joselson (Mme. Euterpova), Erin Windle (Emily), Paul Radulescu (Dr. Stone), David Small (Tony), Mark Schmandt (Timothy), Terry Kiss Frank (Miss Newkirk), Bert Adams (Mr. Lavender-Gas), and Kenneth Church (Dr. Turtlespit)
Newport Classic NPD 86533, compact disc (1998)

### SELECTIONS

W32.25   Philharmonisches Staatsorchester Hamburg; with various soloists, choruses, and conds.
EMI Electrola C 1975-29 107/109 [label on container: Odeon]; Die Stimme seines Herrn 1C195-29 107 — 1C195-29 109, 3 discs, LP, stereo. (1972)

Album title: Musiktheater heute: eine Dokumentation der Hamburgischen Staatsoper.
Selections from contemporary operas performed at the Hamburg Staatsoper, 1959-1973, during the directorship of Rolf Liebermann. With works by Berg, Krenek, Klebe, Werle, Kelemen, and Kagel.

*W33*   *THE HERO* (1952; G. Schirmer; 2 min.)

For medium voice and piano.
Dedicated to Marie Powers, with text by Robert Horan.

*W34*   *THE HERO* (1976; G. Schirmer; evening)

Comic opera in three acts with libretto (English) by Menotti.
Commissioned in 1974 by the Opera Company of Philadelphia.
Cast: S, Mz, Bar, S, T, Mz; Bar, T, Bar, T, B, Bar
2+pic.2+ca.22/4331/perc/hp.cel/str

### ♦ SELECTED PERFORMANCES

W34.1   1976 (Jun 1): Philadelphia; Academy of Music; Opera Company of Philadelphia; Opera Company of Philadelphia Orchestra; Christopher Keene, cond.; with Nancy Shade (Barbara), Dominic Cossa (David Murphy), Diane Curry (Mildred Murphy), David Griffith (Dr. Brainkoff), David Kendall (Mayor), and Richard Shapp (Guide), and also with Fredda Rakusin, Jonathan Reinhold, Hazelita Fauntroy, Paul Adkins, Walter Knetlar, and William Austin.

*Reviews:*

W34.1a   "Philly Funds for Menotti Opera to Mark Bicentennial in '76." *Variety* 277 (November 20, 1974): 60.
Menotti tentatively accepted a commission "by local opera buffs" to compose a Bicentennial opera for Philadelphia's Academy of Music. "Menotti will reportedly get $30,000 (with $10,000 up front) for the English-language opus, for which he will furnish music, libretto and direction."

## 166  Works and Performances

W34.1b  Webster, Daniel. "Philadelphia." *Opera Canada* 17, 3 (1976): 41-42.
". . . an opera as light as thistledown. It is a light, parodistic musical bit, a good Bicentennial laugh, an artifact."

W34.1c  Henahan, Donal. "Premiere of 'Hero' Simple and Funny." *New York Times*, (June 3, 1976): 46.
". . . a mildly diverting bit of theatrical Japeri, but the big targets get away almost untouched . . . a bit threadworn by now, but workable enough."

W34.1d  "Philadelphia is Cradle of Menotti's 17$^{th}$ Opera." *New York Times*, (June 3, 1976): 46.
Regarding the subject of the opera, Menotti notes "Laughter is man's greatest gift. It's what sets him aside from the animals. This opera is a gentle satire on a political theme."

W34.1e  Harris, Harry. "Menotti's 'The Hero' Sleepathon Spoofs U.S. Stunty Bally Hooligans." *Variety* 283 (June 9, 1976): 71+.
"The score is suitably melodic and frolicsome, if not memorable, though there are several showy opportunities for solo and ensemble displays of vocal skill."

W34.1f  Henahan, Donal. "Menotti's 'Hero' — a Comedy That Cannot Be Taken Seriously." *New York Times*, 2 (June 13, 1976): 19.
". . . it fails as satire. But Mr. Menotti's skills and reputation are such by now that any major effort by him is sure to be picked up."

W34.1g  Bender, William. "Opera." *Time* 107 (June 14, 1976): 44.
"It is the kind of morality fable that a Thurber might have conceived. Menotti has dealt with it as though he were writing for Norman Lear."

W34.1h  Jacobson, Robert. "Philadelphia." *Opera News* 41 (August 1976): 36-37.
"The company went the measure in giving Menotti, who directed, a fine cast, conductor, and production . . . Nancy Shade dominated the cast as Barbara with her highly personal, natural acting style and bright, lively voice."

W34.1i  Berglund, Robert. "Philadelphia." *Music Journal* 34 (September 1976): 49.
"The style is one we've come to expect from Menotti — light, bright and witty patter mixed with a few lyrical moments a la Puccini."

W34.1j     Webster, Daniel. "Opera Co.: Menotti Premiere." *High Fidelity/Musical America* 26 (September 1976): MA21-22.
"The text is clever to the extreme of overshadowing the music. Despite the presence of showy duets and ensembles, the score's chief distinction seems to be the deftness with which it provides musical speech."

W34.1k     Baxter, Robert. "Philadelphia and Wilmington." *Opera* (England) 27 (October 1976): 914-916.
"Menotti attempted to disguise his meretricious music with a glib, snappy production . . . too often, however, he tried for effects that were too broad, too coarse."

W34.1l     Porter, Andrew. "Musical Events: Household Tales." *New Yorker* 52 (June 14, 1976): 99-100.
". . . music of such banality that, however sincere Menotti's own feelings may be, the artistic effect is cheap and unworthy."

W34.2      1976 (Apr 25): Brussels; Christian Badea, cond.; with Graeme Matheson-Bruce (Dr. Brainkoff), Ira d'Arès (Mildred), Julian Patrick (David Murphy), Nancy Shade (Barbara), Eric Garrett (Mayor), Geneviève Delavaux and Hartmut Schmiedner (White tourists), Leona Gordon and Jean-Jacques Schreurs (Black tourists), and also with Julien Weisberger.

*Review:*

W34.2a     Fabian, Imre. "Harmlose Satire: Menottis 'The Hero' als europäische Erstaufführung in Brüssel." *Opernwelt* 21 (June 1980): 19+.

W34.3      1980 (May): Liège; La Monnaie; Christian Badea, cond.; with Julian Patrick (David Murphy), Nancy Shade (Barbara), Graeme Matheson-Bruce (Doctor), Eric Garrett (Mayor), and Ira d'Arès (Mildred) (sung in English)

*Review:*

W34.3a     Crichton, Ronald. "Liège: a New Cyrano Opera." *Opera* (England) 31 (Autumn 1980): 63-64.
". . . flimsy but entertaining . . . The composer's own production was typically effective."

W34.4    1980 (Dec 10): New York; Juilliard American Opera Center; Juilliard Theater; Christian Badea, cond.; with Nicholas Karousatos (Hero), Suzanne Hong (virtuous girl), Fredda Rakusin (wife), Michael Austin (doctor), Robert Keefe (mayor), and E. Lynn Nickerson (David)

*Reviews:*

W34.4a   Hughes, Allen. "Juilliard Opera: Menotti's 'The Hero' in a Debut." *New York Times*, 3 (December 11, 1980): 35.
". . . a handsome production that may help gain a public for it here."

W34.4b   Harris, Dale. "New York: American Opera Center." *Opera Canada* 22, 1 (1981): 31.
". . . it struck me as an intolerably crass piece of work, offensively smug in its superiority to American *mores*. Menotti's direction . . . was . . . crude."

W34.4c   Kerner, Leighton. "New York." *Opera* (England) 32 (April 1981): 386.
". . . a load of childish conceits of text and a lot of slick and empty, albeit fluent, composing."

W34.5    1987 (Nov 19): Denton: North Texas State University; North Texas State University School of Music Opera Theater; Serge Zechnacker, cond.; North Texas State University Opera Orchestra; with Susan D'Albergo/Deborah Powell (Barbara), Leah Rizzotto/Todd Taylor (1st Tourist Couple), Sherrie Bay/Jeffery Brockelman (2nd Tourist Couple), Dianna Heldman/Kimberly Livingston (Mildred Murphy), Lee Harris (Jeweller), Richard Hobson/Matthew Smith (David Murphy), and Steven LaCosse/Kenneth Wood (Dr. Brainkoff)

*HILFE, HILFE, DIE GLOBOLINKS!* See: *Help, Help, the Globolinks!*

**W35    *IMPROVISATION* (1931)**

For carillon.
Manuscript held in the Anton Brees Carillon Library, Bok Tower Gardens, Lake Wales, FL.

♦ SELECTED PERFORMANCES

W35.1   1931 (Apr 4): Lake Wales, FL; Bok Singing Tower; Anton Brees, carillonneur (private performance for Mary Louise Curtis Bok, Curtis Bok, Rosario Scalero, and friends)

W35.2   1931 (Jun 4): Lincoln, NE; First Plymouth Church; Anton Brees, carillonneur (first public performance as part of a series of recitals for the dedication of the new carillon for the Church)

W35.3   1933 (Dec 23): Lake Wales, FL; Bok Singing Tower; Anton Brees, carillonneur (Brees also performed this work in Lake Wales on Feb 15, 1934 and Dec 26, 1935)

W35.4   1997 (Jun 5): Lawrence; University of Kansas; William De Turk, carillonneur (on the occasion of the 55th Congress of The Guild of Carillonneurs in North America)


*W36*   *INCIDENTAL MUSIC FOR ANOUILH'S MÉDÉE* (1966)

♦ PREMIERE PERFORMANCES

W36.1   1966 (Dec 20): Rome; Teatro Quirinale; featuring Anna Magnani.


*W37*   *INCIDENTAL MUSIC FOR COCTEAU'S LE POÉTE ET SA MUSE* (1959)

For strings, piano, and percussion.
A "mimodrame" based on "James Deanism."

♦ PREMIERE PERFORMANCE

W37.1   1959 (Jun 12): Spoleto; Teatro Caio Melisso; Carlo Franci, cond.; William Lewis, tenor; with Tomas Milian (Poet), Relda Ridoni (Muse), and Raimonda Orselli, Leo Coleman, and Roberto Pistone (Young People)

*W38*      *INCIDENTAL MUSIC FOR ROMEO AND JULIET* (1968)

Composed for Michael Cacoyannis' production, staged by Théâtre National Populaire.

◆ PREMIERE PERFORMANCE

W38.1      1968 (Apr 19): Paris; Palais de Chaillot, Grande Salle

*W39*      *INTERMEZZO* (1931)

Later renamed "Etude" by Menotti and included as the last movement in *Six Compositions for Carillon*; see W75.

*W40*      *IRENE AND THE GYPSIES* (1949)

Opera with libretto and staging by Menotti.
Commissioned by NBC-TV.
First original opera composed especially for the video medium.

◆ ABOUT THE WORK

W40.1      Taylor, William A. "Radio and Television: Menotti Tells about His Video Opera Commissioned by NBC-TV." *Musical Courier* 139 (May 1, 1949): 8.
Although television has made "... amazing technical strides, [it] is still in the experimental field from a production standpoint. Mr. Menotti believes that an entirely new technique must be evolved for effective TV music productions."

*W41*      *THE ISLAND GOD* (1942)

Tragic opera in one act.
Withdrawn by the composer.

### ♦ PREMIERE PERFORMANCE

W41.1   1942 (Feb 20): New York; Metropolitan Opera House; Ettore Panizza, cond.; with Leonard Warren (Ilo), Astrid Varnay (Telea), Raoul Jobin (Luca), Norman Cordon (Greek God), and John Carter (Voice of a Fisherman) (on a double-bill with *I Pagliacci*)

*Reviews:*

W41.1a  "Two Interludes From the Opera 'The Island God.'" *New York Philharmonic Program Notes* (January 15, 1949)

W41.1b  "Island God. Two Interludes." *San Francisco Symphony Program Notes* (January 3, 1957): 197+.

## W42   *ITALIAN DANCE* (1935)

For string quartet.

### ♦ PREMIERE PERFORMANCE

W42.1   1935 (Jun 30): London; BBC radio concert; with Jascha Brodsky and Charles Jaffe (violins), Max Aronoff (viola), and Orlando Cole (cello) (first known complete performance; a *tarantelle* was given its premiere by the Curtis String Quartet)

## W43   *JACOB'S PRAYER* (1997; G. Schirmer; 14 min.)

For mixed chorus.
Based on verse from the Book of Genesis.
Commissioned by the Endowment Fund of the American Choral Directors Association in memory of Raymond W. Brock.

### ♦ PREMIERE PERFORMANCE

W43.1   1997 (Mar 8): San Diego; Civic Theater; Roger Melone, cond.; San Diego Chamber Orchestra; Oklahoma State University Concert Chorale (Stillwater, OK), University of Wisconsin—Eau Claire Concert Choir, and Texas Christian University Concert Chorale (Ft.

Worth) (1997 National Convention of the American Choral Directors Association (on a double-bill with Howells' *Hymnus Paradisi*)

*Review:*

W43.1a  "Feature Concert." *Choral Journal* 37 (January 1997): 33.
Menotti, who will turn 86 in July, "wanted a text that would depict the struggle of life against absolute darkness."

## W44   *JUANA LA LOCA* (1979; G. Schirmer; evening)

Opera in three acts with libretto (English) by Menotti.
Commissioned by the San Diego Opera to honor Beverly Sills' birthday and retirement, with funding from Cyril Magnin of San Francisco and Lawrence E. Deutsch of the Ledler Foundation.
Cast: S, Bar, T, B, Mz, B-Bar; 4 female, 3 male roles; SATB chorus
2+pic.2+ca.2+bcl.2/4331/timp.2perc/hp.pf/str
Offstage: 2tpt

◆ ABOUT THE WORK

W44.1   Eaton, Quaintance. "Madness Is as Madness Sings." *Music Clubs Magazine* 59, n2 (1979): 10-11.
Reprinted from *Spotlight*, Summer 1979.

W44.2   Grange, Henry Louis de la. "War of Two Worlds." *Music and Musicians* 21 (January 1973): 15-16.
Brief discussion and plot synopsis. "Those who find the subject somewhat sketchy for a full-length opera should recall Menotti's legendary skill, which has often enabled him to bring to theatrical life even the least substantial of libretti."

◆ SELECTED PERFORMANCES

W44.3   1979 (Jun 3): San Diego; Civic Theater; San Diego Opera; Calvin Simmons, cond.; with Susanne Marsee (Doña Manuela), Beverly Sills (Juana), Jane Westbrook (Nurse), Joseph Evans (Miguel de Ferrara), John Bröcheler (Felipe), Vincent Russo (Chaplain), Robert Hale (Ximenes de Cisneros), John Bröcheler (Fernando), Wade Gregg (Carlos V as a Boy), Carlos Chausson (Marqués de Denia), John

Bröcheler (Emperor Carlos V), Marcia Cope and Martha Jane Howe (Ladies in Waiting), and Nancy Coulson (Catalina)

*Reviews:*

W44.3a  "Miss Sills in Premiere of Menotti's 'La Loca.'" *New York Times*, C (June 5, 1979): 7.
"I have never worked so hard on a character in all my life," noted Sills, who was relieved that this was "the last new piece of music I will ever have to learn."

W44.3b  Saal, Hubert. "San Diego Madness." *Newsweek* 93 (June 18, 1979): 90.
"Mixed blessing though the occasion was, one must admire the San Diego Opera for its ambition. The production was staged flawlessly . . ."

W44.3c  Rich, Alan. "No Reign in Spain." *New York* 12 (June 25, 1979): 74-75.
Menotti " . . . has the gift for making gestures count, for bringing together words and music to give each other life, that forms the essence of operatic writing of any style and period."

W44.3d  Ardoin, John. "Menotti's New La Loca, a Triumph for Beverly Sills." *High Fidelity/Musical America* 29 (October 1979): MA38-39.
". . . Miss Sills sang it all with a fervor and a commitment which was riveting. There was no mistaking the fact that the music made a direct and special appeal to her sensibilities and emotions."

W44.4  1979 (Sep 16): New York; New York State Theater; New York City Opera; John Mauceri, cond.; with Susanne Marsee (Doña Manuela), Beverly Sills (Juana), Jane Westbrook (Nurse), Joseph Evans (Miguel de Ferrara), John Bröcheler (Felipe), Vincent Russo (Chaplain), Robert Hale (Ximenes de Cisneros), John Bröcheler (Fernando), Wade Gregg (Carlos V as a Boy), Carlos Chausson (Marqués de Denia), John Bröcheler (Emperor Carlos V), Marcia Cope and Martha Jane Howe (Ladies in Waiting), and Nancy Coulson (Catalina)

*Reviews:*

W44.4a  Harris, Dale. "New York City Opera." *Opera Canada* 20, 4 (1979): 30.
" . . . the work, alas, is irredeemably shallow . . . It is also — notwithstanding Menotti's reputation as a theatrical expert — turgid."

*174  Works and Performances*

W44.4b    Breuer, Robert. "New York." *Oper und Konzert* 17, 11 (1979): 20.

W44.4c    Ardoin, John. "Frantic Nonstop Preparations for a New Menotti Opera." *New York Times*, 2 (September 16, 1979): 1.
The San Diego premiere in June involved last-minute preparations, and the score had not been finished a week before the curtain went up. In the case of the New York premiere, Menotti provided new music for a scene involving sorcerers, even as the opera was in rehearsal.

W44.4d    Schonberg, Harold C. "Opera: 'La Loca' Makes a Debut." *New York Times*, 3 (September 17, 1979): 13.
"Miss Sills brought all of her redoubtable musicianship and acting ability to the role, and at the end was rewarded with cheers."

W44.4e    Kerner, Leighton. "Walk Out Like a Queen (New York City Opera)." *Village Voice* 24 (September 24, 1979): 78.

W44.4f    Hoelterhoff, M. "Beverly Sills Retires from Lustrous Career." *Wall Street Journal*, (September 28, 1979): 23.
Menotti's libretto ". . . turns Juana's interesting conflict into libidinous mush and melodrama."

W44.4g    Eckert, Thor, Jr. "City Opera's Loca: Uninspired Menotti." *Christian Science Monitor*, (October 10, 1979): 18.
The work is ". . . a disjointed pastiche of melodies and ideas that speak more of uninspired Menotti than of any one single musical influence."

W44.4h    Porter, Andrew. "Further Events: Heroine." *New Yorker* 55 (November 19, 1979): 212-215.
The opera ". . . is a decent and accomplished piece of work, and I imagine it will bear revival. Around Miss Sills' incandescent heroine there was an admirable presentation of the piece."

W44.4i    Smith, Patrick J. "New York." *Opera* (England) 30 (December 1979): 1175-1176.
". . . music that is always expertly crafted but that strikes me as devoid of heart and soul."

W44.4j    Jacobson, Robert. "New York." *Opera News* 44 (December 8, 1979): 26.
"Miss Sills played the role for all it is worth, lending it her highly emotional style, often becoming moving . . ."

W44.4k  Oppens, Kurt. "Eine Oper für Beverly Sills: Gian Carlo Menottis 'La Loca,' an der New York City Opera." *Opernwelt* 21 (January 1980): 51.

W44.4l  Smith, Patrick J. "New York: Opera." *Musical Times* 121 (February 1980): 124.
"Menotti's patented music-making seemed written more by rote than through conviction, but the failure of the work lies in its over-reliance on a not very interesting central character."

W44.4m  Heymont, G. "Madness Is its Own Reward — Especially on the Opera Stage." *Fugue* 4 (March 1980): 28-29.

W44.5  1981 (Apr 26): Gießen, Germany; Herbert Gietzen, cond.; with Pamela Myers (Juana), Pertti Lehtinen (Philipp, Fernando, Carlos), Nelson Martilotti (Bishop of Toledo), Melvin Brown (Miguel de Ferrara), Wolfgang Stein (Marquis of Denia), and Pia Arentoft-Nielsen (Doña Manuela) (first European performance; German translation by Herbert Gietzen)

*Reviews:*

W44.5a  Sutcliffe, James Helme. "*Peter Grimes* an der Komischen Oper; Menottis *La Loca* in Gießen; Sängerdarsteller." *Opernwelt* (Yearbook 1981): 115.

W44.5b  Loebe, Bernd. "Beharrlicher Menotti: *La Loca* in Gießen als europäische Erstaufführung." *Opernwelt* 22 (June 1981): 37-38.

W44.5c  Adam, Klaus. "Gießen." *Oper und Konzert* 19, 6 (1981): 9-10.

W44.5d  Sutcliffe, James Helme. "Gießen." *Opera* (England) 32 (October 1981): 1053-1054.
". . . an over-sentimental panaceaic resort to religion that the composer may want to reconsider."

W44.6  1982 (Jul 3): Spoleto; Teatro Nuovo; Herbert Gietzen, cond.; Spoleto Festival Orchestra; Westminster Cathedral Choir; with Pamela Myers (Juana), Brian Schexnayder (Felipe, Ferdinand, and Carlos), Robert Lyon (Miguel de Ferrara), Boris Martinovich (Cardinal of Toledo), Angelo Nosotti (Marqués de Dania), and Petra Malakova (Dona Manuela) (first performance in Italy; Festival of Two Worlds)

176  Works and Performances

*Reviews:*

W44.6a  Bellingardi, Luigi. "Spoleto: a Birthday Season." *Opera* (England) 33 (Autumn 1982): 106-107.
"The audience's approval became progressively warmer, culminating in a triumphant reception at the end of Act 3, after the mad scene."

W44.6b  Bellingardi, Luigi. "Da Spoleto." *Nuova rivista musicale italiana* 16 (October-December 1982): 621-623.

W44.6c  Blumauer, Manfred. "Festival dei due Mondi in Spoleto: Opern von Wagner, Gounod und Menotti." *Opernwelt* 23 (October 1982): 28-29.

W44.6d  Rasponi, Lanfranco. "Spoleto." *Opera News* 47 (October 1982): 42.
"This work stands or falls by its protagonist, and Pamela Myers seemed more preoccupied with the score's problems than with creating a character or with the pathos of the last scenes."

W44.7  1984 (Jun 1): Charleston; Herbert Gietzen, cond.; Spoleto Festival Orchestra U.S.A.; Westminster Cathedral Choir; with Adriana Vanelli (Juana), Louis Otey (Felipe of Burgundy, King Ferdinand II, and Carlos as husband, father, and son), Stephen Dupont (Bishop of Toledo), Jacqueline Venable (Juana's nurse), Philip Bologna (Miguel), and Korby Myrick (Spoleto Festival U.S.A.)

*Reviews:*

W44.7a  Waleson, Heidi. "Gian Carlo Menotti: I'm Taking Stock of What I've Done." *New York Times*, 2 (May 20, 1984): 23.
Remarks concerning the Charleston production, concentrating on certain differences of opinion between Sills, Capobianco, and Menotti.

W44.7b  Page, Tim. "Opera: Menotti's 'Juana' Performed at Festival." *New York Times*, 1 (June 3, 1984): 61.
Menotti " . . . fashioned his own libretto, as has been his custom for the span of his career, and directed as fine a production of his opera as one could have imagined."

W44.7c   Ardoin, John. "Charleston." *Opera News* 49 (September 1984): 61-62.
"One was left with a sense of how artfully created a theater piece it is, how securely its lyrical flights of music and stark drama work together to hold an audience."

W44.7d   Storrer, William Allin. "Spoleto U.S.A.: Variegated Languages." *Opera* (England) 35 (Autumn 1984): 109-110.
". . . unrelievedly dark and negative . . . it is often anti-dramatic; its second-act ending rejects any possibility of crowd-pleasing gesture."

W44.7e   Costanza, Marie Carmen. "Gian Carlo Menotti, Director: an Examination of the Spoleto, U.S.A. Production of 'Juana, La Loca.'" Ph.D. Theater dissertation, New York University, 1991.
Documents Menotti's method of working as an operatic director as shown in the 1984 Spoleto, U.S.A. production of his opera. Includes an examination of his working relationship with his principal performers and his extras and chorus, along with a rehearsal case book.

## *W45*   *LABYRINTH* (1963; G. Schirmer; 45 min.)

Television opera in one act with libretto (English) by Menotti.
Cast: 2 female, 5 male, 1 non-speaking role; chorus
1(pic)1(ca)1(bcl)1/2110/perc/pf/str(1.2.1.1.1)

### ♦ PREMIERE PERFORMANCE

W45.1   1963 (Mar 3): NBC-TV network; NBC Television Opera Company; Herbert Grossman, cond.; with Judith Raskin (Bride), John Reardon (Groom), Elaine Bonazzi (Spy), Robert White (Old Man), Beverly Wolff (Executive Director), Leon Lishner (Desk Clerk), Nikiforos Naneris (Bellboy), Frank Porretta (Astronaut), Leon Lishner (Death), John West (Death's Assistant), Eugene Green (Italian Opera Singer), and Bob Rickner (Executive Director's Secretary)

*Reviews:*

W45.1a   "Menotti's Next Opera." *Times* (London), (November 15, 1960): 16.
Notice that Menotti has been commissioned by the National Broadcasting Company to write another opera for its television service. This will be his fourth opera commissioned by NBC, the other three

*178 Works and Performances*

being *The Old Maid and the Thief* (1937), *Amahl and the Night Visitors* (1951), and *Maria Golovín* (1958).

W45.1b  Prideaux, Tom. "Menotti Opera Runs Riot with a Flood of Tricks." *Life* 54 (March 8, 1963): 46.
Review with photographs. ". . . the first opera to run wild with TV's full bag of electronic tricks: split screens, multiple exposures, and an orgy of out-of-focus hocus-pocus . . . For all this, Menotti has composed some sweet and silvery arias."

W45.1c  "Menotti's Hour." *Time* 81 (March 8, 1963): 46.
"Menotti has not had time within the framework of a television hour to develop either characters or unity of mood, has tailored his libretto to the limitations of the picture tube. But musically, the little opera is somewhat more successful."

W45.1d  Sargeant, Winthrop. "Musical Events: Menotti's New One." *New Yorker* 39 (March 9, 1963): 148-149.
". . . it has moments of weird enchantment, and as a forty-minute television entertainment it holds the onlooker's attention with a sort of theatrical and musical sleight of hand that is entirely peculiar to its composer."

W45.1e  Kolodin, Irving. "Music to My Ears: Szell at the Philharmonic — Menotti's 'Labyrinth.'" *Saturday Review* 46 (March 16, 1963): 94.
"In this creation for the evolving medium of TV, Menotti has worked with purpose and enterprise, and the NBC-TV Opera Company has once again shown its ability to solve well the most challenging problems of electronic dramaturgy."

W45.1f  Ardoin, John. "Menotti's 'Labyrinth.'" *Musical America* 83 (April 1963): 53.
"Borrowing is not an indictment against Menotti, or any composer, for that matter; but his . . . rejuggling of familiar harmonic and melodic clichés in 'Labyrinth' is."

W45.1g  Breuer, Robert. "Menottis Weg ins Freie über den amerikanischen Bildschirn." *Melos* 30 (April 1963): 133-134.

W45.1h  Merkling, Frank. "Menotti and Hindemith." *Opera News* 27 (April 13, 1963): 33.

"The music runs a gamut from grand-opera parody to *da capo* arias to pop euphoria of the Weill variety; *Labyrinth* displays a chastened lyricism, as if Menotti had found new roots."

W45.1i   Reisfeld, Bert. "Menotti's 'Labyrinth.'" *Musica* 17 (May-June 1963): 125.

W45.1j   Sabin, Robert. "New York." *Opera* (England) 14 (June 1963): 393-394.
"The most interesting passage was one imitating the sound of water going down a drain, and one wished that the opera would follow it promptly. The whole thing was like nothing so much as a third-rate Hollywood film."


*W46*   *LANDSCAPES AND REMEMBRANCES* (1976; G. Schirmer; 45 min.)

SATB; soli; chorus; 2+pic.2+ca.2+bcl.2/4331/timp.perc/hp.pf/str.
Cantata in nine movements: Arrival in New York by sea — The abandoned mansion (South Carolina) — Parade in Texas — Nocturne (driving at night through the desert) — A subway ride in Chicago — Picnic by the Brandywine — An imaginary trip through Wisconsin — Farewell at a train station in Vermont — The sky of departure (leaving America by plane at sunset)
Commissioned by the Bel Canto Chorus of Milwaukee for the Bicentennial year and made possible through a grant by Atwood Oceanics, Inc.

♦ SELECTED PERFORMANCES

W46.1   1976 (May 14): Milwaukee; Performing Arts Center; Uihlein Hall; James A. Keeley, cond.; Milwaukee Symphony Orchestra; Bel Canto Chorus of Milwaukee (on a double-bill with *The Telephone*)

*Reviews:*

W46.1a   Joslyn, Jay. "Bel Canto Chorus; Menotti Prem." *High Fidelity/Musical America* 26 (September 1976): MA16-17.
"Menotti breaks no new ground. Nostalgia marks both the music and the autobiographical lyrics."

W46.1b   "Menotti's Rehearsal: Composer in Depth." *News and Courier* (Charleston, SC), (May 28, 1981)

The work is "woven of his memories and impressions of the years he lived in the United States (1928 to 1973) before establishing a permanent residency in Scotland."

W46.2  1981 (May 22): Charleston, SC; Gaillard Auditorium; Joseph Flummerfelt, cond.; with Suzanne Hong (soprano), Tonio di Paolo (tenor), Diane Curry (mezzo-soprano), and Boris Martinovich (bass-baritone); Westminster Cathedral Choir; Charleston Symphony Orchestra Singers Guild; Spoleto Festival Orchestra U.S.A. (Spoleto Festival U.S.A.)

*Reviews:*

W46.2a  Ardoin, John. "Menotti Presents Vibrant Choruses." *Dallas Morning News*, (June 5, 1981)
". . . One of the striking aspects of these highly individual pieces is the wide-ranging imagery of Menotti's free-formed poetry, and the extraordinary way he mirrors his verbal images in sound."

W46.2b  Ardoin, John. "Menotti's *The Last Savage* (Spoleto U.S.A.)." *High Fidelity/Musical America* 31 (September 1981): MA32-33.
". . . one of the strengths of *Landscapes* is the wide-ranging imagery of Menotti's poetry, and the telling way in which he mirrors his verbal images in sound."

W46.3  1996 (Feb 22): New York; Lincoln Center; Alice Tully Hall; Dino Anagnost, cond.; Little Orchestra Society (on a triple-bill with Ballet suite from *Sebastian* and the *Violin Concerto*, in a "Milestone for Menotti" 85th birthday concert)

*Review:*

W46.3a  Dannatt, Adrian. "Classical Milestone for Menotti Alice Tully Hall, New York." *Independent* (London), Review/Arts (February 28, 1996): 5.
". . . made clear what Menotti really lacks is an interpreter of the strictest, 12-tone seriousness to rescue him from his own unstoppable lyricism."

***THE LAST SAVAGE*** *See: Le Dernier Sauvage*

*W47*     *THE LEPER* (1970)

Play in two acts.
Commissioned by Marie Bell.
Premiered as the centerpiece of Florida State University's 1970 Fine Arts Festival and the opening of its Fine Arts Building.

♦ SELECTED PERFORMANCES

W47.1     1970 (Apr 24): Tallahassee; Florida State University; Fine Arts Theater; with Patricia Neway (Queen), Francis Phelan (Alexios), Bruce Pfeffer (Nikitas), Sharon Crowe (Zoe), Jack Sydow (Old Man), Dalton Cathey (Palladius), Bill Shipley (Kosmas), Pamela Bailey (Irene), James Wrynn (Michail), Chuck Rubin (Dimitrios), Bud Ritch (Kirillos), Barbara Manford (Amphissia), Ron Fayad (Potter), Paul Stoakes (Bardas), Rick Alley (Anatellon), Jennifer Meyer (Aglaia), Jerry O'Donnell (Manuel), Charles Bessant (Nilus), Terry McFall (Serphius), Carolyn Werner (Nurse), Chris Meyer (Smith's Apprentice), Elaine Smith (Woman of the Town), Tony Tartaglia (Baker's Errand Boy), Dusty Truran (Ariadne), and Tony Afejusu (Bakur)

*Reviews:*

W47.1a    Taubman, Howard. "Menotti's First Play Presented in Florida." *New York Times*, (April 24, 1970): 40.
          Says Menotti, "The more I thought about the theme, the more subtle and intellectualized it became. Opera is an emotional form. I wanted this work to be philosophical. It just didn't lend itself to music."

W47.1b    Roos, James. "Menotti's 'Leper' Still an Outcast with Audiences." *Miami Herald*, (July 27, 1980)
          Menotti remarks: " . . . the symbol I take for man outside society is homosexuality. But it could be applied to all kinds of 'lepers.'"

W47.2     1982 (May 24): Charleston, SC; College of Charleston; Albert Simons Center for the Arts (Spoleto Festival U.S.A.)

*Reviews:*

W47.2a    "'Leper' — Maestro's Blind Spot?" *News and Courier* (Charleston, SC), (May 26, 1982)

"I'm afraid Menotti's friends were right to have been offended after the first [1970] production, and whatever the changes Menotti has made in the intervening dozen years, the thing still doesn't fly."

W47.2b　　Jarrell, Frank P. "Menotti Defends Play." *News and Courier* (Charleston, SC), (May 26, 1982)
Interview with Menotti. "*The Leper* . . . can be anybody who takes revenge on society — rather than contributing. It happens with so many minorities. Once they don't receive the kiss of brotherhood, they turn into a malignant force."

*W48*　　*LEWISOHN STADIUM FANFARE* (1965; G. Schirmer; 5 min.)

For brass, timpani, and percussion.
Written for the Metropolitan Opera's inaugural summer concert.
0000/4331/timp.perc/str

♦ PREMIERE PERFORMANCE

W48.1　　1965 (Jun 21): New York; Lewisohn Stadium; Fausto Cleva, cond.; Metropolitan Opera Orchestra

*W49*　　*A LITTLE CANCRIZAN FOR MARY* (1951)

For three singers.
Humorous setting of "Happy Birthday to You," with one of the parts "to be sung standing on one's head." Conceived and compiled by Samuel Barber in 1951, twenty-four other composers contributed to this gift to Mary Louise Zimbalist for her 75th birthday.

*W50*　　*LLAMA DE AMOR VIVA* (1991; G. Schirmer; 10 min.)

Cantata.
For baritone; mixed chorus; 2+pic.2+ca.2+bcl.2/4331/timp.2perc/hp.pf/str

♦ PREMIERE PERFORMANCE

W50.1    1991 (Apr 28): Washington, DC; Catholic University; Randall Craig Fleischer, cond.; with Christopher Trakis, baritone (Kennedy Center benefit concert)


*LA LOCA* See: *Juana La Loca*


**W51    LULLABY FOR ALEXANDER** (1978)

For piano.
Written for, and performed at, the christening of Menotti's godson, Alexander, marquess of Douglas and Clydesdale.

♦ PREMIERE PERFORMANCE

W51.1    1978 (Jul 29): Lennoxlove, Haddington, Scotland


**W52    MARIA GOLOVÍN** (1958; Belwin Mills)

Opera in three acts.

♦ ABOUT THE WORK

W52.1    Zottos, Ion. "G. C. Menotti: *Maria Golovin*." *Moussikologia* 1, 1 (1985): 77-93.
"The work is assessed and an analysis of part of the opera is attempted. The subject of jealousy — the theme of the opera — and its expression in musical and dramatic terms is given particular emphasis." In Greek.

♦ SELECTED PERFORMANCES

W52.2    1958 (Aug 20): Brussels; Brussels World Exposition; U.S. Pavilion; American Theater; NBC Opera Company; Peter Herman Adler, cond.; Antwerp Philharmonic Orchestra; with Richard Cross (Donato), Ruth Kobart (Agata), Patricia Neway (Donato's Mother), Herbert Handt (Dr. Zuckertanz), Franca Duval (Maria), Lorenzo Muti (Trottolò), William Chapman (Prisoner), and John Wheeler (Servant)

*184 Works and Performances*

Reviews:

W52.2a "Bob Sarnoff's 'You Can Thank Our Westerns for Our Menotti Operas.'" *Variety* 209 (February 19, 1958): 20.
Bob Sarnoff, NBC President, announces the Brussels premiere. Says Sarnoff, "If the networks were to program only for members of TV's critical minority . . . we would lose our mass audience and with it the economic supports that permit us to continue non-profitable programs of more limited appeal."

W52.2b "Premiere of Maria Golovin." *Times* (London), (August 21, 1958): 12.
"There is not much memorable or striking melodic line to heighten the salient verbal phrases. But as an evening in the theatre it certainly holds the attention."

W52.2c Rosen, George. "Fancy Brussels Premiere but Menotti's 'Maria Golovin' Not Grade-A Opera." *Variety* 211 (August 27, 1958): 2+.
The opera " . . . suffers chiefly from being an opera of recitatives solely for story progression rather than libretto on which to hang Menotti's musical creations."

W52.2d Taubman, Howard. "Operatic Fusion." *New York Times*, 2 (August 31, 1958): 7.
"There is no one in sight who can compare with Mr. Menotti when it comes to using the varied resources of the lyric theatre. He does not entirely scale the heights, but he knows his craft thoroughly."

W52.2e Klein, Rudolf. "'Maria Golovin' in Brüssel Weltauraufgeführt." *Österreichische Musikzeitschrift* 13 (September 1958): 391-392.

W52.2f "Menotti's Latest." *Time* 72 (September 1, 1958): 40.
"The audience applauded mightily, but the work had moments rather than momentum. The music consisted of only a few themes linked by weak chains."

W52.2g "Opera in a Frenzy." *Newsweek* 52 (September 1, 1958): 54.
"In Brussels, Menotti found the climate much friendlier . . . [the work was] applauded warmly by a distinguished audience, including Queen Mother Elisabeth of Belgium."

W52.2h Peltz, Mary Ellis. "Menotti in Brussels." *Opera News* 23 (September 29, 1958): 4.

"... many tricks of Menotti's familiar trade showed through the slightly worn texture of the work ... even the musings of his rich imagination ... are not enough to rouse an audience to the sense of catharsis ..."

W52.2i   Mellen, Constance. "Brussels." *Musical Courier* 158 (October 1958): 33.
"The total impression was of an evening of engrossing theatre, but none of the music greatly enkindled the heart, perhaps because it did not seem to come from the hearts of the characters."

W52.2j   Briner, Andres. "Gian-Carlo Menottis neue Oper 'Maria Golovin.'" *Schweizerische Musikzeitung* 98 (October 1958): 379-380.

W52.2k   Koegler, Horst. "Ein neuer Menotti." *Musica* 12 (October 1958): 611.

W52.2l   Mousset, Edouard. "New Menotti Opera Receives Premiere at Brussels Fair." *Musical America* 78 (October 1958): 17.
"The opera met with warm success and the composer, who attended the performance, was loudly applauded."

W52.2m   Warrack, Jack. "Brussels." *Opera* (England) 9 (November 1958): 712+.
"Menotti the composer is no match for Menotti the thriller-writer. I should have enjoyed *Maria Golovin* more without the music."

W52.2n   "I've Been Broke." *Newsweek* 52 (November 17, 1958): 75.
"Some of Menotti's calculated effects proved a heavy burden for a fragile story. But his music collaborated quite effectively to produce real emotional impact."

W52.3   1958 (Nov 5): New York; Martin Beck Theatre; with Richard Cross (Donato), Ruth Kobart (Agata), Patricia Neway (Mother), Norman Kelley (Dr. Zuckertanz), Franca Duval (Maria), Lorenzo Muti (Trottolò), William Chapman (Prisoner), and John Kuhn (Servant) (produced on television Mar 8, 1959)

*Reviews:*

W52.3a   Gelb, Arthur. "Theatrical Suspense in a Composer's World." *New York Times*, 2 (November 2, 1958): 1+.

"Often characterized as being more theatrical than operatic, Mr. Menotti concedes that in his latest work . . . the dramatic values take precedence over the music."

W52.3b  "Maria Golovin." *Variety* 212 (November 12, 1958): 58+.
"As in many of his prior efforts, Menotti the composer and Menotti the dramatist are unevenly matched. But the daring and creativity in both functions remain clear."

W52.3c  Eyer, Ronald. "Menotti's Latest Opera Brought to Broadway." *Musical America* 78 (November 15, 1958): 18.
"Without exception, the principals realized their roles with naturalness and conviction of a stripe that is rare at any time in the operatic realm."

W52.3d  Sargeant, Winthrop. "Musical Events: Menotti Again." *New Yorker* 34 (November 15, 1958): 189.
"The production . . . could not have been more adroit. A superb cast of singing actors . . . strove valiantly to bring the work to life."

W52.3e  "Blind, Burning & Bland." *Time* 72 (November 17, 1958): 54+.
"At its worst, the . . . score is not only too sweet but too facile . . . At its best, the score is hauntingly tender and compelling . . ."

W52.3f  Evett, Robert. "Menotti Melodrama." *New Republic* 139 (November 17, 1958): 22-23.
". . . the production was sumptuous and expert in the highest degree . . . and it would be a pity if all the time and talent that went into producing it were lost."

W52.3g  Kolodin, Irving. "Menotti's 'Maria' — New and Old Met Standards." *Saturday Review* 41 (November 22, 1958): 43.
"As casting director and stage manager, Menotti brought together a believable group of performers who were well schooled to achieve the desired end."

W52.3h  Trimble, Lester. "Music." *Nation* 187 (November 22, 1958): 395-396.
"Certainly, he has never given a better sign of being potentially the great opera composer so many people feel he is already."

W52.3i  Taubman, Howard. "Don't Say 'Opera.'" *New York Times*, 2 (November 30, 1958): 11.

"Was it that bad? Not at all . . . It is a pity that today's mad imperatives on Broadway demand immediate success or total failure. It would be a greater pity if original work in the lyric theatre had to depend entirely on the opera house. Broadway and the lyric theatre have been enriched by their occasional union."

W52.3j  Krokover, Rosalyn. "Martin Beck Theatre." *Musical Courier* 158 (December 1958): 14.
". . . a slender plot, developed in episodic scenes, and music that did not on the whole equal in richness or inventiveness other operas by this versatile composer-librettist."

W52.3k  Fitzgerald, Gerald. "Menotti in New York." *Opera News* 23 (December 15, 1958): 14-15.
"The uninterrupted series of theatrical 'moments' supplied by the composer fails to compensate for a lack of real musical and dramatic substance . . ."

W52.3l  "Novo Menottijevo delo." *Zvuk: jugoslovenska muzicka revija*, 24-25 (1959): 191-192.

W52.3m  Severi, G. G. "'Maria Golovin' ovvero Il Caso Menotti." *Musica d'oggi* 2 (January 1959): 14-16.

W52.3n  Coleman, Emily. "Menotti, Very Momentarily." *Theatre Arts* 43 (January 1959): 68.
"The score is quite the thinnest he has produced in recent years, for it has neither the set pieces of an opera nor the symphonic surge of music drama . . . excellent singing actors who met Menottian melodrama in full embrace and with no embarrassment whatsoever."

W52.3o  "Maria Golovin (by NBC Opera Co.)" *Variety* 214 (March 11, 1959): 37.
Review of the NBC Opera Company's "tintcast." ". . . its reduced size projection made much more acceptable the melodramatic story and more understandable the neurotic development of the blind, love-torn youth."

W52.3p  Bernstein, B. "TV 'Golovin' Can Spark LP Sales." *Billboard* 71 (March 23, 1959): 24.

*188   Works and Performances*

W52.4    1959 (Mar 30): New York; City Center; New York City Opera; Herbert Grossman, cond.; with Richard Cross (Donato), Ilona Kombrink (Maria), Patricia Neway (Donato's Mother), Regina Sarfaty (Servant), Norman Kelley (Tutor), Chester Ludgin (Prisoner), and Craig Sechler (Trottolò).

**Reviews:**

W52.4a   "Maria Golovin." *Variety* 214 (April 8, 1959): 72.
". . . musically the work has unfailing operatic quality. There are pages of great beauty in the score . . . [and the] Production was an excellent one."

W52.5    1965 (Jan 22): Washington DC; Opera Society of Washington; Paul Callaway, cond.; National Symphony Orchestra; with Joan Marie Moynagh (Maria), John Reardon (Donato), Elaine Bonazzi (Agata), Patricia Neway (Donato's Mother), Herbert Handt (Dr. Zuckertanz), Adid Fazah (Prisoner), and Ritchie Preston (Trottolò) (revised version)

**Reviews:**

W52.5a   Schauensee, Max de. "Baltimore/Washington." *Opera* (England) 16 (April 1965): 279.
Menotti " . . . had made minute and extensive adjustments rather than any introduction of new themes and ideas. He had also completely re-orchestrated the score . . . the entire cast were given an ovation at the final curtain."

W52.5b   Smith, French Crawford. "Twin Capitals." *Opera News* 29 (April 3, 1965): 31.
"The work still seems tame and is brightened only occasionally . . . by touches of the composer's genius."

W52.6    1971 (Jan 29): Marseille; Opéra de Marseille; Reynald Giovaninetti, cond.; with Richard Stilwell (Donato), Suzanne Sarroca (Maria), Denise Scharley (Donato's Mother), Danièle Grima (Agatha), Francis Dresse (Dr. Zuckertanz) (revised version)

**Reviews:**

W52.6a   Chedorge, A. "Opera de Marseille, le theatre moderne et Louis Ducreaux." *Opera* (France) 11, 93 (1971): 10-12.

W52.6b  Rizzo, Francis. "Diary of Two Deadlines." *Opera News* 35 (March 13, 1971): 26-28.
The production only two months away, " . . . only the composer himself can say how much of it has been completed, and he is notably reluctant to discuss the matter."

W52.6c  Mayer, Tony. "Marseilles." *Opera* (England) 22 (June 1971): 529-530.
"It would be difficult to imagine a better cast . . . Stilwell, as Donato, acted and sang with prodigious mastery."

W52.7  1972 (Dec 7): Paris; Opéra de Paris Orchestre; Reynald Giovaninetti, cond.; with Richard Stilwell (Donato), Suzanne Sarroca (Maria), Rita Gorr (Donato's Mother), Danièle Grima (Agata) (Paris premiere; performed in translation by André Burgaud)

*Reviews:*

W52.7a  Barichella, Monique. "Paris." *Opera Canada* 13, 1 (1972): 25.
"Performances were superb, with Rita Gorr, Suzanne Sarroca (who gave a moving interpretation of the title role), and Richard Stilwell, who was exceptional. The orchestra . . . has never sounded better; nor has it played with such precision."

W52.7b  Pitt, Charles. "Paris." *Opera* (England) 23 (April 1972): 347.
"The finest thing about this production were the sets . . . but the work would probably have benefitted by having been produced in the confines of a smaller house such as the Opéra-Comique."

W52.8  1976 (Mar 19): London; Collegiate Theatre; Park Lane Opera; Nicholas Braithwaite, cond.; Park Lane Players; with Alison Hargan (Maria), Richard Jackson (Donato), Maureen Morelle (Donato's Mother), Bernard Dickerson (Dr. Zuckertanz), Rosalind Plowright (Agata), Ian Caddy (Prisoner), and James Dening (Trottolò) (Camden Festival)

*Reviews:*

W52.8a  Barker, Frank Granville. "Camden Festival: Maria Golovin." *Music and Musicians* 24 (May 1976): 41-42.
". . . the sad truth is that his melodies are just not memorable. He tries very hard, for which I respect him, but . . . the music never got off the ground."

W52.8b  Lavender, E. W. "Editorial Notes." *Strad* 87 (May 1976): 3+.
"Very, very stagey, and yet unredeemed, with the exception of some most telling concerted numbers, by music of any real substance or originality."

W52.8c  Taylor, Peter. "Opera and Ballet in London." *Musical Opinion* 99 (May 1976): 363.
"There were some effective scenes and strong moments which impressed but which in the final instance never for one moment touched the heart."

W52.8d  Dean, Winton. "Maria Golovin." *Musical Times* 117 (May 1976): 419.
The production " . . . was thoroughly professional . . . it was not his [Jackson] fault that our withers remained unwrung."

W52.8e  Rosenthal, Harold D. "Maria Golovin: Park Lane Opera at the Collegiate Theatre, Camden Festival." *Opera* (England) 27 (May 1976): 481.
"What made this sorry evening doubly distressing was the excellence of Menotti's own production . . . of such worthless stuff."

W52.9  1977 (Jun 29): Spoleto; Teatro Nuovo; Christian Badea, cond.; Spoleto Festival Orchestra U.S.A.; with Fiorella Carmen Forti (Magda), Charles Long (Donato), Maureen Morelle (Donato's Mother), Giovanna Fioroni (Agata), Andreas Kouloumbis (Prisoner), Florindo Andreolli (Dr. Zuckertanz), and Marco Biscardini (Trottolò) (performed in translation by Alearco Ghigi)

*Reviews:*

W52.9a  Kessler, Giovanna. "Begegnungen mit jungen Künstlern: 'Das Festival zweier Weltern' in Spoleto." *Opernwelt* 18 (1977): 13-14.

W52.9b  Rinaldi, M. "Spoleto 1977." *Rassegna musicale Curci* 30, 2 (1977): 60-62.

W52.9c  Weaver, William. "Spoleto." *Opera News* 42 (September 1977): 50-51.
" . . . you could almost breathe the dusty air of the run-down villa, feel the heat on the arbored terrace."

W52.9d   Eckert, Carola. "Spoleto: Wie geht's weiter?" *Buehne*, 228 (September 1977): 23.

W52.9e   Bellingardi, Luigi. "Da Spoleto." *Nuova rivista musicale italiana* 11 (July-September 1977): 423.

W52.9f   Cernaz, Bruno. "Spoleto: Festival of Two Worlds." *Opera Canada* 18, 4 (1977): 44.
"We can consider Maria Golovin as the most successful and most forceful of Menotti's works, for musical structure and stage craftsmanship."

W52.9g   Gould, Susan. "Spoleto in the Doldrums." *Opera* (England) 28 (December 1977): 1140-1143.
". . . literate, singable, and thanks to the careful union with the music and the superb diction of the performers, almost totally comprehensible."

W52.10   1978 (Jan 25): The Hague, Netherlands; Forum; Gustav Fülleborn, cond.; Forumorkest; with Richard Jackson (Donato), Nancy Henninger (Maria), Maureen Morelle (Donato's Mother), and also with Rita Noel, Bernard Dickerson, and Allan Evan.

*Review:*

W52.10a   Mayer, Harry. "Maria Golovin' van Menotti." *Mens en melodie* 33 (April 1978): 118.

W52.11   1985 (Apr 20): Denton; North Texas State University; School of Music; North Texas State University Opera Theatre; Marc Mourier, cond.; Pamela O'Briant and Rebecca Turner, pianists; with William Sinclair/Ronald Earl (Donato), Carol Attmore/Catherine McManus (Donato's Mother), Cathy Geary/Bessie Johnson (Agata), and Roberta Arendt/Kim Kronenberg (Maria)

W52.12   1986 (Apr 27): Gießen, Germany; Stadttheater Gießen; Herbert Gietzen, cond.; with Penelope Thorn (Maria), Paul Yoder (Donato), Rodica Mitrica (Donato's Mother), Roman Gonzales (Dr. Zuckertanz), and Wolfgang Stein (Prisoner) (performed in translation by Herbert Gietzen)

*192    Works and Performances*

Reviews:

W52.12a   Zimmermann, Christoph. "Gießen." *Oper und Konzert* 24, 6 (1986): 8-9.

W52.12b   Ludwig, Heinz. "Elegische Blicke auf die Vergangenheit." *Opernwelt* 22 (July 1986): 46.

W52.12c   Zondergeld, Rein A. "Germany: Menotti's New Home, Gießen." *Opera* (England) 37 (July 1986): 828-829.
"The masterly performance . . . completely refuted the customary accusation that he [Menotti] writes dramatic film music . . . At the end the residents of Giessen quite rightly acclaimed *their* Menotti."

W52.12d   Thaler, Lotte. "Mit Blindheit geschlagen: Deutsche Erstaufführung von Menottis 'Maria Golovin' in Gießen." *Orchester* 34 (July-August 1986): 826.

W52.13   1991 (May 23): Charleston, SC; Sottile Theater; Spiros Argiris, cond.; Spoleto Festival Orchestra U.S.A.; with Louis Otey (Donato), Stella Zambalis (Maria), Edna Garabedián (Agata), James Alexander Mims (Prisoner), Rebecca Russell (Donato's Mother), and Adolfo Llorca (Dr. Zuckertanz) (Spoleto Festival U.S.A.)

Reviews:

W52.13a   Holland, Bernard. "Where Life and Opera Are about the Same." *New York Times*, C (May 28, 1991): 11.
"Mr. Menotti is a composer one wants to admire, for his lyrical gift, for the directness of expression and the acute feel for everything theatrical. His operas get into trouble when they give way to emotional opportunism."

W52.13b   Smith, Jeffrey C. "Charleston: Spoleto Festival." *Opera Canada* 32, 3 (1991): 37.
"The music, which is well constructed, and has some lush, melodramatic moments, serves the drama well but it is old-fashioned and less interesting, finally, than the story."

W52.13c   Halperin, Carl J. "Charleston, S.C." *Opera News* 56 (October 1991): 46-47.

"As the guilty heroine, newcomer Stella Zambalis articulated Maria's longing and unfulfilled desires with a plangently beautiful soprano, drawing one into the intensity of her characterization."

W52.14   1991 (Jun 2): Charleston, SC; Gaillard Auditorium; Spiros Argiris, cond.; Spoleto Festival Orchestra U.S.A.; with Stella Zambalis (Maria), Louis Otey (Donato), Rebecca Russell (Donato's Mother), and Edna Garabedian (Agata) (performed Maria's aria from Act I and quartet from Act II; Birthday Gala concert honoring Menotti)

*Review:*

W52.14a   Gudger, William D. "Birthday Treat: Gala Concert Honors Founder of the Festival." *Post-Courier* (Charleston, SC), June 3, 1991: 5A. "The radiant soprano sound of Stella Zambalis would be a great birthday present for anyone."

♦ DISCOGRAPHY

W52.15   Franca Duval (Maria), Richard Cross (Donato), Patricia Neway (Donato's Mother), Genia Las (Agata), William Chapman (Prisoner), Herbert Handt (Dr. Zuckertanz), Lorenzo Muti (Trottolò); Peter Herman Adler, cond.
RCA Victor LM 6142, 3 discs, LP, mono, LP (1958)
Sung in English; recorded in Rome.

*THE MARRIAGE* See: *The Wedding*

**W53**   ***MARTIN'S LIE*** (1964; G. Schirmer; 50 min.)

Opera in one act with libretto (English) by Menotti.
Commissioned for the Canterbury Festival at Canterbury Cathedral.
Cast: Mz, Tr, T, 2 Tr, Bar, B; treble chorus
1111/1210/timp.3perc/hp/va.vc.db
*Pierpont Morgan Library* has "piano-vocal score. With numerous letters, telegrams, programs, newspaper and periodical clippings, and other documents relating to the commissioning and early performances of the opera. The gift of John Davis Skilton, Jr., and Ernest Hillman." 81 p., 34 x 26.5 cm.

194   Works and Performances

♦ SELECTED PERFORMANCES

W53.1    1964 (Jun 3): Bristol, England; Bristol Cathedral; produced at the Bath Festival Society in association with the Labyrinth Corporation of America and the Columbia Broadcasting System; Lawrence Leonard, cond.; English Chamber Orchestra and Chorus of St. Mary Redcliffe Secondary School; with William McAlpine (Father Cornelius), Noreen Berry (Naninga), Donald McIntyre (Stranger), Otakar Kraus (Sheriff), Michael Wennink (Martin), Keith Collins (Christopher), and Roger Nicholas (Timothy) (Bath Festival)

*Reviews:*

W53.1a   Maciejewski, B. M. "List z Londynu." *Ruch muzyczny* 8, 19 (1964): 11.

W53.1b   Loveland, K. "Menottiho 'Martin lhar' v Bristolu." *Hudebni rozhledy* 17, 14 (1964): 620.

W53.1c   "Menotti Premiere at Bath for U.S. TV." *Times* (London), (February 8, 1964): 5.
"The Columbia Broadcasting System plans to record the world premiere . . . in Bath, Somerset, and show it on television in the United States next autumn."

W53.1d   "Controversial Morality Opera by Menotti." *Times* (London), (June 4, 1964): 20.
". . . the performance tonight was distinguished by some expert singing . . . We wish that his music were as strong as his techniques of production."

W53.1e   Baro, Gene. "Boy Befriends a Heretic." *New York Times*, 2 (June 14, 1964): 11.
". . . a chamber opera does not belong in Bristol Cathedral . . . The opera's mixed reception in the British press is, I believe, a matter of its still not having been heard properly."

W53.1f   "Menotti in the Cathedral." *Newsweek* 63 (June 15, 1964): 93.
"What is intended by Menotti to be a pattern of simplicity becomes instead simple-minded; and instead of the complications of art, Menotti provides only an easy artlessness."

W53.1g   Cairns, David. "Bath Festival." *Musical Times* 105 (July 1964): 526.
"The music is skilfully arranged, with appropriately modal sounds . . . The drama is not disturbed by anything so unmannerly as musical invention."

W53.1h   Barnes, Clive. "Mendacious Menotti." *Music and Musicians* 12 (August 1964): 22.

W53.1i   Jacobs, Arthur. "Bath." *Opera* (England) 15 (Autumn 1964): 34-35.
"It seems to me that the whole work is worth very little. I must report, however, that colleagues observed some of the audience moved to tears."

W53.1j   Aprahamian, Felix. "Notes From Our Correspondents: London." *High Fidelity* 14 (September 1964): 12.
". . . unlike so many of his avant-garde confreres, Menotti successfully pulls the heart-strings of the many rather than the legs of the few."

W53.2   1964 (Sep 26): Perugia, Italy; San Michele Arcangelo; Carlo Franci, cond.; with Michael Wennink (Martin), Giovanna Fioroni (mezzo-soprano), Herbert Handt (tenor), Alberto Rinaldi (baritone), and Lorenzo Gaetani (bass) (19th Sagra Musicale Umbra; performed in Italian translation by Menotti)

*Reviews:*

W53.2a   Guglielmi, E. "La 19 Sacra Musicale Umbra." *Musica d'oggi* 7, 8 (1964): 235-236.

W53.2b   Weaver, William. "Perugia." *Opera* (England) 15 (December 1964): 817-818.
" . . . exploited ably the beauty of the little, round church . . . [The opera] was an almost unanimous success."

W53.3   1965 (Jan 24): American premiere canceled by CBS-TV due to death of Winston Churchill.

*Review:*

W53.3a   Menotti, Gian Carlo. "'Martin's Lie': a New Opera." *Show* 4 (December 1964): 44-45+.

196  Works and Performances

                Complete libretto of the opera, anticipating the CBS television premiere, which was ultimately canceled due to the death of Winston Churchill.

W53.4      1965 (May 30): CBS-TV; same cast as that given above for the Bristol production.

W53.5      1976 (Jun 17): Washington, DC; Washington Cathedral; Paul Callaway, cond.; with Gene Tucker (Father Cornelius), Simon Jackson (Martin), Richard Dirksen (Fugitive), Dana Krueger (Housekeeper), and Gimi Beni (Sheriff) (on a double-bill with *The Egg*)

            *Reviews:*

W53.5a    Sears, L. "Debut and Premieres at Washington Cathedral." *Music; the A.G.O. and R.C.C.O. Magazine* 10 (October 1976): 48-49.

W53.5b    Timbrell, Charles. "Philadelphia/Washington." *Opera News* 41 (October 1976): 64.
            "The performance was on a high level, the rich, focused singing of tenor Gene Tucker . . . well matched by the communicative singing and acting of boy soprano Simon Jackson as Martin."

W53.5c    Parris, Robert. "Washington Cath.; Menotti Prems." *High Fidelity/Musical America* 26 (November 1976): MA21.
            "There was neither a dull moment, nor, I believe, a moist eye."

W53.6      1978 (May 30): Charleston, SC; Circular Congregational Church; Joseph Flummerfelt, cond.; Spoleto Festival Orchestra U.S.A.; Porter-Gaud School Boy Choristers dir. by W. Benjamin Hutto; with Sean Coogan (Martin), Gene Tucker (Father Cornelius), Dana Krueger (Naninga), Cary Archer Smith (Fugitive), Carlo Thomas (Sheriff), Andre Hardmon (Christopher), Timothy Cartwell (Patrick), Sammy Backer (Timmy), and Lonnie Ladsen (Executioner) (Spoleto Festival U.S.A.; on a double-bill with *The Egg*)

            *Reviews:*

W53.6a    Giniger, Ken S. "Menotti's Short Religioso Operas in Lovely Oven-Like Church." *Variety* 291 (June 14, 1978): 78.
            "Performances are first rate, 12-year old Sean Coogan as Martin achieving outstanding results."

W53.6b    Porter, Andrew. "Musical Events: Spoleto of the South." *New Yorker* 54 (June 19, 1978): 68.
"... commissioned for Canterbury Cathedral but denied performance there as being theologically shaky — which it is. But at least it is an efficient tearjerker."

W53.6c    Jacobson, Robert. "Charleston, S.C." *Opera News* 43 (August 1978): 44.
"... at least offers effective theater, if not distinguished music, with its naive style of telling a medieval morality play."

W53.6d    Mercer, Ruby. "Charleston: Spoleto Festival." *Opera Canada* 19, 3 (1978): 28-29.
"There were fine characterizations and some excellent singing..."

W53.6e    Busnelli, Mariella. "Spoleto's Tragic 'Cenerentola.'" *Opera* (England) 29 (Autumn 1978): 104-105.
"... with Menotti's always effective and dignified music it could not fail to grip the audience already moved by the precocious bravura of the 12-year-old protagonist Sean Coogan."

W53.6f    Storrer, William Allin. "Charleston: Menotti and Spoleto, U.S.A." *Opera* (England) 29 (Autumn 1978): 116-118.
"... had moments of searing drama, beautifully realized in Menotti's music."

♦ DISCOGRAPHY

W53.7    Connor Burrowes, treble; Pamela Helen Stephen, mezzo-soprano; Robin Leggate, tenor; Alan Opie, baritone; Matthew Best, bass; Tees Valley Boys' Choir; Northern Sinfonia Orchestra; Richard Hickox, cond.
Chandos CHAN 9605, digital, stereo., compact disc (1998)
Recorded in Jubilee Theatre, St. Nichola's Hospital, Gosforth, Newcastle Upon Tyne, Nov 22-23, 1996.
With *Five Songs* and *Canti della lontananza*.

## *W54*    *MARY'S MASS* (1984)

For choir and congregation according to the new English liturgy.

Commissioned by the Maryland Catholic Conference in celebration of the 350th anniversary of the founding of Maryland.

### ♦ PREMIERE PERFORMANCE

W54.1   1984 (Jun 10): Baltimore; Basilica of the Assumption of the Blessed Virgin Mary; Larry Vote, choral director; Chapman Gonzalez, organ; Members of the Church of the Archdiocese of Baltimore.

*W55*   **MASS FOR THE CONTEMPORARY ENGLISH LITURGY** (1985; G. Schirmer; 9 min.)

For congregation, SATB chorus, and organ.

*W56*   **THE MEDIUM** (1946, rev. 1947; G. Schirmer; 80 min.)

Tragic opera in two acts with libretto (English) by Menotti.
Commissioned by the Alice M. Ditson Fund of Columbia University.
Cast: A, S, S, Bar, Mz; dancer
1111/1100/perc/pf 4 hands(cel)/str
*The Stanford University Libraries*, Memorial Library of Music (MLM) has an inscribed copy of the G. Schirmer 1947 vocal score (French version by Léon Kochnitzky), Pl. no. 41701, inscribed for the collection by Menotti. The inscription includes two bars of music from the score.
*Pierpont Morgan Library* has "full score of the opera. Dated at the end: 'April 20, 1946.' With the piano-vocal score. 79 p. 34.5 x 27 cm." Description of the full score: 225 p. 34.5 x 27 cm.

### ♦ ABOUT THE WORK

W56.1   "Notes and Comments." *New Yorker* 23 (June 7, 1947): 23-24.
General article on Menotti's operas, with emphasis on the then-current *The Medium* and *The Telephone*. Says Menotti, "Skepticism is a barren thing compared to faith. I try to show this in the opera. I was shocked to see it labelled a killer-diller. It's meant to be a philosophical play."

W56.2   Menotti, Gian Carlo. "Medium in Four Mediums." *Saturday Review of Literature* 31 (February 28, 1948): 43-44.
Discusses the four manifestations of his opera: recently presented on Broadway, broadcast on the radio, recorded on Columbia, and now to

be filmed. ". . . as long as I am alive I find it exciting and challenging to adapt it to all modern mediums."

W56.3   Fryer, Judith Anne. "Guide to the Study and Performance of Three Operas of Gian-Carlo Menotti." Ed.D. dissertation, Columbia University Teachers College, 1974.
From the author's abstract: "The purpose of this study is to provide historical information, analytical material, and practical suggestions for the teaching and performance of selected Menotti operas in secondary schools . . . Three operas were chosen for thorough analysis: *The Medium* (1946), *Amahl and the Night Visitors* (1951), and *Help, Help, the Globolinks!*"

W56.4   Marriott, Richard John. "Gian-Carlo Menotti, Total Musical Theatre: a Study of His Operas." Ph.D. dissertation, University of Illinois, 1975.
From the author's abstract: "Menotti is most successful in his chamber operas: *The Medium*, *The Consul*, and *Amahl and the Night Visitors*. In the successful chamber operas, Menotti's goal of effective theatre is realized; they have complete integration of libretto, music, staging, and above all theatricality — they have the qualities of a consciously dramatic stage play."

W56.5   Ardoin, John. "The Menotti Magic." *Dallas Morning News*, (May 22, 1983)
Includes remarks made during Menotti's judging for the revamped C.B. Dealey Awards for Young Artists. "I wanted to prove that opera, if presented with the care and love for detail with which a play is presented, could find a new audience and even pay for itself, and no longer depend on subsidization. All of this I think I proved with *The Medium* and *The Consul* . . ."

W56.6   Beckwith, Nina. "40 Years Later . . . Menotti Reflects on *The Medium*." *San Francisco Opera* 4 (Summer 1986): 48-51.

W56.7   Witzke, Ronald. "The Duality of Faith and Skepticism in the Operas of Gian Carlo Menotti: A Dramaturgical Study of *The Medium* and *Amahl and the Night Visitors*." D.M.A. performance dissertation, Indiana University, 1997.

## ◆ PREMIERE PERFORMANCES

W56.8    1946 (May 8): New York; Columbia University; Brander Matthews Theater; Otto Luening, cond.; with Evelyn Keller (Monica), Leo Coleman (Toby), Claramae Turner (Flora), Beverly Dame (Mrs. Gobineau), Jacques La Rochelle (Mr. Gobineau), and Virginia Beeler (Mrs. Nolan) (produced by Columbia Theater Associates in cooperation with the Columbia University Department of Music)

*Reviews:*

W56.8a   Simon, Robert A. "Uptown." *New Yorker* 22 (May 18, 1946): 96.
"... the opera is an expert venture in musical theatre, in spite of some awkward prosody in the early scenes ... The performance ... was first rate, and there were notable performances in the two principal singing roles ..."

W56.8b   Barlow, S. L. M. "In the Theatre." *Modern Music* 23 (July 1946): 223.
"Almost every note is like a dry powder in a trail leading to the catastrophe. *The Medium* has real significance as departure."

W56.9    1947 (February 18): New York; Heckscher Theater; Ballet Society; Leon Barzin, cond.; musicians from the Ballet Society Orchestra; with Evelyn Keller (Monica), Leo Coleman (Toby), Marie Powers (Flora), Beverly Dame (Mrs. Gobineau), Paul Kwartin (Mr. Gobineau), and Virginia Beeler (Mrs. Nolan) ("revised version"; on a double-bill with *The Telephone*)

*Reviews:*

W56.9a   "Opera in Embryo." *Newsweek* 29 (March 3, 1947): 76.
"The cast was extraordinary. And if it could not be said that Menotti always sustained the continuity between his melodramatic high points, he did show a sense of theater all too rare in most contemporary opera."

W56.9b   Phelan, Kappo. "Stage & Screen: *The Medium*." *Commonweal* 45 (March 7, 1947): 518.
"In the title rôle, I thought Marie Powers vocally, emotionally, pictorially ... superb. And her trio of customers ... as studiously chosen and executed."

W56.9c    Smith, Cecil. "Rights of Privacy." *New Republic* 116 (March 10, 1947): 40.
"The music has many good moments; on the whole, however, it lacks the sharp rhythmic definition and cumulative intensity of structure which are important means of reinforcing dramatic situations in opera."

W56.9d    Smith, Cecil. "Ventures in Lyric Theatre." *Theatre Arts* 31 (May 1947): 60.
"The result is a well-told story festooned with music, rather than a translation of the drama into continuous and apposite musical expression."

W56.9e    Wyatt, Euphemia Van Rensselaer. "Drama: National Catholic Theater Conference." *Catholic World* 165 (June 1947): 265-266.
"Leo Coleman . . . gives more than speech to Toby in his fluid pantomime."

W56.9f    Thomson, Virgil. "Farce and Melodrama." in *The Art of Judging Music*, by Virgil Thomson. p. 127-129. New York: A. A. Knopf, 1948.
Reprint of Thomson's Feb 19, 1947 review in the *New York Herald Tribune*. "The visual production . . . was one of unusual distinction. The casting . . . was excellent. Particularly notable for both singing and acting were Marie Powers . . . and Evelyn Keller. . ."

W56.10    1947 (May 1): New York; Ethel Barrymore Theatre; Emanuel Balaban, cond.; with Evelyn Keller (Monica), Leo Coleman (Toby), Marie Powers (Flora), Beverly Dame (Mrs. Gobineau), Frank Rogier (Mr. Gobineau), and Virginia Beeler (Mrs. Nolan) (produced by Chandler Cowles and Efrem Zimbalist, Jr., in association with Edith Lutyens; presented on a double bill with *The Telephone*)

*Reviews:*

W56.10a    Lardner, John. "Low Crimes and Singing Plays." *New Yorker* 23 (May 10, 1947): 50+.
"It is doubtful . . . that Mr. Menotti could have recruited a finer troupe for the execution of his special form."

W56.10b    Krutch, Joseph Wood. "Drama Note." *Nation* 164 (May 24, 1947): 637.
"The conception of the text is better than its rather fumbling development, but I gladly joined the audience in hearty applause."

W56.10c   Brown, John Mason. "Seeing Things." *Saturday Review of Literature* 30 (May 31, 1947): 22-24.
Concerning Marie Powers, "From the moment she emerged . . . it was apparent that a player who is mistress of her craft had entered."

W56.10d   Sargeant, Winthrop. "American Opera on Broadway." *Life* 22 (June 9, 1947): 95-96.
Menotti's " . . . remarkable feat is causing critics to wonder . . . whether America can actually create first-class opera, which up to now it has not done." Includes four photographs from the production.

W56.10e   Beyer, William. "The State of the Theater: Drama and Music-drama." *School and Society* 66 (July 26, 1947): 66.
Marie Powers " . . . is immersed in the character and plays it as a singing actress of authority and distinction, making the opera an unforgettable experience."

W56.10f   Nathan, George Jean. *The Theatre Book of the Year, 1947-1948: A Record and an Interpretation.* p. 3-5. New York: A. A. Knopf, 1948.
"The voices are acceptable enough, though Marie Powers' . . . suffers from what seems to be a slight lisp, and Evelyn Keller's . . . from a periodic tendency to shrillness."

W56.11    1951 (Sep 5): New York; Sutton Theater; released by Transfilm; Thomas Schippers, cond.; Orchestra of Rome della Radio-televisione Italiana; with Marie Powers (Flora), Anna Maria Alberghetti (Monica), Leo Coleman (Toby), Belva Kibler (Mrs. Nolan), Beverly Dame (Mrs. Gobineau), and Donald Morgan (Mr. Gobineau) (80-minute motion picture filmed in Rome)

*Reviews:*

W56.11a   Downes, Olin. "Menotti, Pioneer: His Movie Adaptation of 'The Medium' Heralds Way Toward Screen Opera." *New York Times*, 2 (September 16, 1951): 9.
". . . the opera, which fits the stage like a glove, feels like a badly cut suit of clothes when transferred to the cinema."

W56.11b   Bauer, Leda. "Menotti Films *The Medium*: One-man Show." *Theatre Arts* 35 (October 1951): 32-33+.

"... dancer Leo Coleman proves himself again an expert pantomimist, giving here a brilliant performance, heartbreaking in its mingled savagery and pathos."

W56.11c   Rigault, Jean de. "A Menotti rien d'impossible." *Revue musicale* 211 (March 1952): 33-35.

W56.11d   Sabin, Robert. "Film Version of *The Medium* Directed by Menotti in Rome." *Musical America* 71 (April 15, 1951): 21.
"... this powerful work (gratefully free from the pretentious settings and extraneous effects) should act as an inspiration to other producers, as well as winning Menotti new friends."

W56.11e   Menotti, Gian Carlo. "Trials and Tribulations of 'The Medium.'" *New York Times*, 2 (August 26, 1951): 5.
"I am often asked whether I liked the filming of 'The Medium.' I feel that that is like asking a surgeon whether or not he liked a certain operation. All I can say is that the patient is still alive, and even looks a little better than before."

W56.11f   Deke, R. F. "The Medium." *Film Music* 11 (September-October 1951): 13-15.
"The primary purpose of this piece is to assess the value of Menotti's work on two levels, the purely musical and the theatrical-screen. By theatrical-screen, I refer to the ways in which Mr. Menotti makes his music serve the stage or screen."

W56.11g   Knight, Arthur. "Menotti and the Movie Medium." *Saturday Review of Literature* 34 (September 8, 1951): 36+.
"All the violence latent in the stage work emerges with gruesome explicitness on the screen... Perhaps it would be best to regard 'The Medium' as an experiment that produces as well as promises a new and thrilling art experience for its audience."

W56.11h   "'The Medium': Film of Menotti's Opera." *Times* (London), (March 30, 1953): 9.
This "... is first and foremost a film, and, what is more, a film of macabre power, shaking at the folds of the curtains of supernatural mysteries."

W56.11i   Keller, Hans. "Film Music and Beyond: the Civilization of Musical Refuse Through 'The Medium' of Menotti." *Music Review* 14 (May 1953): 141-143.
"There is nothing to be acknowledged in 'The Medium' whose success is, for an artist, the end of a culture, though for the uninvolved historian, it may be the culture of an end."

W56.11j   Thomas, Christopher J. "Gian Carlo Menotti." *Opera Quarterly* 3 (Summer 1985): 133-134.
Review of the videotape of the original 1950 film version. "This film reminds us, and will prove to future generations, that his [Menotti's] genius as a stage director equals his genius as a musician."

### ♦ OTHER SELECTED PERFORMANCES

W56.12   1949 (Apr 7): New York; New York City Opera; Joseph Rosenstock, cond.; with Evelyn Keller (Monica), Leo Coleman (Toby), Marie Powers (Flora), Leona Scheunemann (Mrs. Gobineau), Edwin Dunning (Mr. Gobineau), and Frances Bible (Mrs. Nolan) (on a double-bill with *The Old Maid and the Thief*)

Review:

W56.12a   "Contralto on Broadway." *Time* 49 (June 30, 1947): 69.
Largely concerns Marie Powers. "Marie's portrayal of the opera's title character has had a lot to do with The Medium's success. She is by no means the world's greatest contralto, but she has what better contraltos often lack, a superb dramatic skill."

W56.13   1949 (Dec 9): Cleveland; Karamu Lyric Theatre; Zelma George (Flora) (revival productions with Ms. George followed Nov 11-Dec 15, 1951 and Oct 23-Nov 17, 1962)

W56.14   1950 (Jul 19): New York; Arena Theatre, formerly a ballroom of the Hotel Edison; with Zelma George (Flora), Derna de Lys/Evelyn Keller (Monica), Edith Gordon/Dorothy Staiger (Mrs. Gobineau), Doria Avila (Mrs. Nolan), Paul King (Mr. Gobineau), and Leo Coleman (Toby) (on a double-bill with *The Telephone*)

*Reviews:*

W56.14a   Smith, Cecil. "Menotti Double Bill Returns in Arena-Style Production." *Musical America* 70 (August 1950): 17.
"... Mrs. George is a novel and interesting personality, deserving of the enthusiasm which has led Mr. Menotti to declare informally that he would like to write an opera especially for her."

W56.14b   Wyatt, Euphemia Van Rensselaer. "Theater." *Catholic World* 171 (September 1950): 469.
"After the shooting, she [Zelma George] heaves herself out of the chair and flops herself like a seal over Toby's body when her hollow cackles of hysterical laughs make the spine tingle. The audience rose as a man to hail a great performance."

W56.14c   Atkinson, Brooks. "Medium Revisited: Menotti Opera Effective in Arena Presentation." *New York Times*, 2 (September 3, 1950): 1.
"Mr. Menotti's miniature opera trembles all over when Mrs. [Zelma] George rolls into the midst of it."

W56.15   1959 (Apr 16): New York; New York City Opera; Werner Torkanowsky, cond.; with Claramae Turner (Flora), Joy Clements (Monica), José Perez (Toby), Mary Le Sawyer (Mrs. Gobineau), Arthur Newman (Mr. Gobineau), and Regina Sarfaty (Mrs. Nolan) (on a double-bill with Dello Joio's *The Triumph of St. Joan*)

*Review:*

W56.15a   Ericson, Raymond. "Triumph of St. Joan, The Medium." *Musical America* 79 (May 1959): 8.
"... Claramae Turner's harrowing portrait of Madame Flora once again chilled the spectator."

W56.16   1962 (Oct 23): Cleveland; Karamu Lyric Theatre; with Barbara Knighton (Monica), Sidney Smart (Toby), Dolores McCann (Flora), Maxine Titus (Mrs. Gobineau), Illinois Wilson (Mr. Gobineau), and Betty Appling (Mrs. Nolan) (on a double-bill with Gluck's *The Betrayed Betrayer*)

W56.17   1963 (May 5): New York; New York City Center; New York City Opera; Robert La Marchina, cond.; with Lili Chookasian (Flora), Lee Venora (Monica), Nikiforos Naneris (Toby), Bonnie Heller (Mrs.

Gobineau), David Smith (Mr. Gobineau), and Marlena Kleinman (Mrs. Nolan) (on a double-bill with *Amelia al ballo*)

Review:

W56.17a    Sargeant, Winthrop. "Musical Events: Origin of a Species." *New Yorker* 39 (May 18, 1963): 96.
"Chookasian " . . . held the center of the stage and did a bang-up job in the part of that distraught spiritualist."

W56.18    1964 (Sep 26): Kansas City; Lyric Opera of Kansas City; Russell Patterson, cond.; with June Card (Monica), Jim Assad (Toby), Dorothy Cole (Flora), Joanne Highley (Mrs. Gobineau), Ronald Highley (Mr. Gobineau), and Marlene Wesemann (Mrs. Nolan) (on a double-bill with Puccini's *Gianni Schicchi*)

Review:

W56.18a    "Lively Opera Duo Offered by Lyric." *Kansas City Star*, (September 27, 1964)
"Jim Assad's Toby was impressive. Unable to utter a sound, he had to communicate his longing for Monica, his fear of Baba, and his lack of understanding of the mystical forces that were using him through his face and body. No note came from his mouth, but his movements were melody enough."

W56.19    1968 (Mar 30: Paris; Opéra-Comique; Richard Blareau, cond.; with Denise Scharley (Flora), Eliane Lublin (Monica), Frank Phelan (Toby), Solange Michel (Mrs. Nolan), Georgette Rispal (Mrs. Gobineau), and Claude Genty (Mr. Gobineau) (on a double-bill with *The Telephone*)

Review:

W56.19a    Howe, Richard. "Paris." *Opera* (England) 19 (June 1968): 486.
". . . under Menotti's tutelage emerged as the most valid drama offered by Paris opera houses in years . . . The tears were real, the whiplashes strung and the blood at least looked real."

W56.20    1969 (Jul 8): Spoleto; Teatro Caio Melisso; Bruno Campanella, cond.; with Muriel Greenspon (Flora), Joanna Bruno (Monica), Frank Phelan (Toby) (Festival of Two Worlds; in Italian; on a double-bill with Falla's *El retablo de Maese Pedro*)

*Reviews:*

W56.20a  Weaver, William. "Menotti and Rossini at Spoleto." *Opera* (England) 20 (Autumn 1969): 112-113.
Greenspon ". . . took Menotti's protagonist and made her into a kind of Medea, towering, tormented, in turn odious and pathetic."

W56.20b  Weaver, William. "Spoleto: Scandal over Rossini." *High Fidelity/Musical America* 19 (October 1969): MA30-31.
". . . this outstanding Spoleto production — in a theater better suited to the work than most Italian opera houses — should give Menotti's opera new Italian lease on life."

W56.20c  Geitel, Klaus. "69,- DM für eine Woche Musik." *Opernwelt* 11 (September 1970): 37.

W56.21  1974 (May 30): Munich; Gärtnerplatztheater; Peter Falk, cond.; with Sona Cervena (Flora), Gisela Ehrensperger (Monica), Frank Phelan (Toby), Marion Briner (Mrs. Gobineau), Eva Maria Görgen (Mrs. Nolan), and Richard Kogel (Mr. Gobineau)

*Reviews:*

W56.21a  Huber, Hans. "München." *Oper und Konzert* 12, 7 (1974): 14-15.

W56.21b  Schmidt-Garre, Helmut. "'Das Medium' und 'Der Zar läßt sich photographieren.'" *Neue Zeitschrift für Musik* 135 (July 1974): 436-438.

W56.21c  "Menotti und Weill in Gärtnerplatztheater." *Orchester* 22 (July-August 1974): 444-445.

W56.21d  Schmidt, Dietmar N. "Viele viele Späßchen — Münchner Premieren." *Opernwelt*, 7 (July 1974): 30-32.

W56.22  1974 (Jul 11): Stratford, Ont.; Third Stage; Raffi Armenian, cond.; Stratford Festival Orchestra; with Sebastien Dhavemas (Toby), Maureen Forrester (Flora), Janis Orenstein (Monica), *Sister* Barbara Ianni (Mrs. Nolan), Dan Lichti (Mr. Gobineau), and Lynda Neufeld (Mrs. Gobineau)

*208  Works and Performances*

Reviews:

W56.22a  Nau, Tim. "Stratford's Experimental Theatre Moves into the Main Stream." *Performing Arts in Canada* 11, 3 (1974): 19-21.
"The casting of Maureen Forrester as Madame Flora was perfect. She thoroughly understood the role and executed it flawlessly."

W56.22b  Jacobs, Arthur. "Stratford: Wilson's 'Everyman.'" *Opera (England)* 25 (Autumn 1974): 110.
"Never in several hearings have I felt so strongly the emptiness of Menotti's score (save for Monica's waltz-song)."

W56.22c  Jacobson, Robert. "Stratford, Ont." *Opera News* 39 (October 1974): 53.
Forrester " . . . affected a full range of vocal color, from whispers to sounds of immense force at both extremes of the range . . . She was riveting, a great incarnation of a great role."

W56.23  1975 (Apr 4): Munich; Gärtnerplatztheater; Peter Falk, cond.; with Gretel Hartung (Flora), Gisela Ehrensperger (Monica), Richard Kogel (Mr. Gobineau), Barbara Blanchard (Mrs. Gobineau), Eva Maria Görgen (Mrs. Nolan), and Marian Jagust (Toby)

Review:

W56.23a  Huber, Helga. "München." *Oper und Konzert* 13, 5 (1975): 22-23.

W56.24  1976 (May 13): New York; Universalist Center for the Arts; New York Lyric Opera Company; Arthur Lief, cond.; with Stephanie Low (Flora), Marcia Parks (Monica), Rick Ebeling (Toby), Eva de la O (Mrs. Nolan), Gloria Lerner (Mrs. Gobineau), Wayne Sherwood (Mr. Gobineau) (on a double-bill with Dennis Arlan's *Meanwhile, Back at Cinderella's*)

Review:

W56.24a  Ericson, Raymond. "Opera: Cinderella Spoof." *New York Times*, (May 15, 1976): 15.
". . . admirably directed . . . from the point of view of the fine characterizations he got from his singers . . ."

W56.25  1976 (May 29): Augusta, GA; Augusta Opera; Robert Austin, cond.; with Carolyne James (Flora), Jeanette Jung (Monica), Barbara Dean

(Mrs. Gobineau), Joseph Amaya (Mr. Gobineau), Ron Colton (Toby), and Brenda Boozer (Mrs. Nolan) (on a double-bill with Barber's *A Hand of Bridge*)

*Review:*

W56.25a    Fleming, Shirley. "Augusta Opera: The Medium." *High Fidelity/Musical America* 26 (October 1976): MA17.
"The roles were all handled with a high degree of professionalism and dramatic persuasiveness. The mute part of Toby . . . was touchingly projected by Ron Colton who . . . had a dancer's understanding of the power of mime."

W56.26    1978 (Sep 26): Kansas City; Lyric Opera of Kansas City; Byron Dean Ryan, cond.; with Carolyne James (Mme. Flora), Dorothy Setian (Monica), Samuel Hernandez (Toby), Joanne Highley (Mrs. Gobineau), Ronald Highley (Mr. Gobineau), and Margaret Donnell (Mrs. Nolan)

W56.27    1980 (Nov 22): Little Rock; Arkansas Opera Theatre; A. Clyde Roller, cond.; members of the Arkansas Symphony; with Lili Chookasian (Flora), Sherry Henderson (Monica), Mark Hudson (Toby), Fred Fox (Mr. Gobineau), Therese Brown (Mrs. Gobineau), and Theresa McRee (Mrs. Nolan)

*Review:*

W56.27a    Feldman, M. A. "Little Rock." *Opera News* 45 (March 7, 1981): 24.
"As Flora, Miss Chookasian portrayed a tormented woman who was both violent and vulnerable, a crafty charlatan as well as a tender mother. Every word was comprehensible, and her voice had both power and beauty."

W56.28    1981 (Mar 13): West Palm Beach, FL; Palm Beach Civic Opera; with Beverly Evans (Flora), Francis Menotti (Toby), Cheryl Cavendish (Monica) (on a double-bill with *Amelia al ballo*)

*Review:*

W56.28a    De Marcellus, Juliette. "West Palm Beach." *Opera News* 45 (June 1981): 40.
Evans' " . . . depiction of a disintegrating mind and personality caught an eerie quality of horror and reality; she moved her voice effortlessly

*210    Works and Performances*

in and out of the half-speech and the rather dry vocal projection this music requires."

W56.29     1981 (Jun 26): Spoleto; Caio Melisso; Christian Badea, cond.; with Beverly Evans (Flora), Hey Kyung-Hong (Monica), Francis Menotti (Toby) (performed in Italian translation by Fedele D'Amico)

*Review:*

W56.29a     Bellingardi, Luigi. "Spoleto: From Gluck to Lehár." *Opera* (England) 32 (Autumn 1981): 106.
". . . there was general admiration for the fresh invention of the music and in particular for the effectiveness of the composer's striking production."

W56.30     1982 (May 5): Nantes, France; Nantes Opera; Guy Condette, cond.; with Maria Murano (Flora), Monique Baudoin (Monica), and René Bazinet (Toby) (on a double-bill with *Amahl and the Night Visitors*)

*Review:*

W56.30a     Pitt, Charles. "Nantes." *Opera* (England) 34 (September 1983): 1002-1003.
Murano " . . . gave a touching impersonation of a vulnerable woman, a sort of Edith Piaf rather than the usual *monstre sacrée*."

W56.31     1983 (Nov 13): Gießen, Germany; Herbert Gietzen, cond.; with Carol Smith (Flora), Rosanne Duncombe (Monica), Thomas Seel (Toby), Hildegard Berkenhoff (Mrs. Gobineau), Bernhard Adler (Mr. Gobineau), and Helen Bolton-Nüsse (Mrs. Nolan)

*Review:*

W56.31a     Loebe, Bernd. "Menottis Filiale: 'Das Medium' in Gießen." *Opernwelt* 25 (February 1984): 43.

W56.32     1983 (December 2): Reykjavik; National Theatre; Icelandic Opera; Marc Tardue, cond.; with Elín Sigurvinsdóttir (Monica), Thurídur Pálsdóttir (Flora), Viðar Eggertsson (Toby) (performed in an Icelandic translation by Magnús Ásgeirsson; on a double-bill with *The Telephone*)

*Review:*

W56.32a   Símonarson, Baldur. "Reykjavik." *Opera* (England) 35 (March 1984): 317.
"... the use of a clapped-out toy pistol almost turned the end of *The Medium* into an anti-climax."

W56.33   1983 (Dec 19): Washington, DC; John F. Kennedy Center for the Performing Arts; Terrace Theater; Washington Opera; Lorenzo Muti, cond.; with Beverly Evans (Flora), Elizabeth Carron (Mrs. Gobineau), Judith Weyman (Mrs. Nolan), John Fiorito (Mr. Gobineau), Francis Menotti (Toby), and Nadia Pelle (Monica) (on a double-bill with *The Telephone*)

W56.34   1984 (Apr 12): Edinburgh; King's Theatre; Washington Opera; Cal Stewart Kellogg, cond.; Scottish Chamber Orchestra; with Nadia Pelle (Monica), Beverly Evans (Flora), Elizabeth Carron (Mrs. Gobineau), Judith Weyman (Mrs. Nolan), Francis Menotti (Toby), and John Fiorito (Mr. Gobineau) (Edinburgh Festival; on a double-bill with *The Telephone*)

W56.35   1984 (Apr 13): Dallas; Majestic Theatre; Dallas Opera; Nicola Rescigno, cond.; with Carolyne James (Flora), Jeanne Ommerlé (Monica), Malcolm Arnold (Mr. Gobineau), Francis Menotti (Toby), Deidra Palmour (Mrs. Gobineau), and Judith Christin (Mrs. Nolan) (on a double-bill with *Amelia al ballo*)

*Reviews:*

W56.35a   Ardoin, John. "Opera Reachers New Heights." *Dallas Morning News*, (April 16, 1984)
"... Carolyne James was riveting not only in the power of her singing, but in the strength of her portrayal ... the impact of her acting and her dominating presence was out of the ordinary."

W56.35b   Chism, Olin. "Dallas Opera Goes it Alone with Fine Twin Bill." *Dallas Times Herald*, (April 16, 1984)
"A virtuoso performance by mezzo Carolyne James made this one of the most gripping presentations the Dallas Opera has come up with in several years."

212    Works and Performances

W56.36    1985 (Jan 6): Washington, DC; John F. Kennedy Center for the Performing Arts; Terrace Theater; Washington Opera; Cal Stewart Kellogg, cond.; with Beverly Evans (Flora), Nadia Pelle (Monica), Francis Menotti (Toby) (Note: Jan 6 was the date of the closing performance)

*Review:*

W56.36a    Crutchfield, Will. "Washington Opera's Menotti." *New York Times*, 3 (January 8, 1985): 20.
"It aims at melodramatic thrill, and hits. It also has some of Mr. Menotti's more successful music in it, and his direction is mostly apt and effective."

W56.37    1985 (Jan 25): Boston; Boston Conservatory Theater; Opera Theater of Boston; John Moriarty, cond.; Jacqueline Marx (Flora), Amy Cochrane (Monica), John Noseworthy (Toby) (on a double-bill with Ravel's *L'Heure Espagnole*)

*Review:*

W56.37a    Pfeifer, Ellen. "Opera Theatre of Boston Presents Keen Musical, Dramatic Ensemble." *Boston Herald*, (January 28, 1985)
"Menotti shamelessly manipulates the viewer with wrenching and, occasionally, grotesque theatrical situations and effects. And his music is wallpaper in a garish print — intended to make an effect, but undistinguished nevertheless."

W56.38    1986 (Jan 27): Philadelphia; Academy of Music; Opera Company of Philadelphia; Gianfranco Masini, cond.; with Régine Crespin (Flora), Nadia Pelle (Monica), and Jean-Louis Loca (Toby) (on a double-bill with Puccini's *Suor Angelica*)

*Reviews:*

W56.38a    Crutchfield, Will. "Opera: Menotti's 'Medium.'" *New York Times*, 3 (January 29, 1986): 24.
Crespin's "voice is rich and powerful in its new mezzo-soprano habitat, and she is still, grandly, a master of the stage."

W56.38b    Webster, Daniel. "Opera: Menotti, Puccini Share Bill." *Philadelphia Inquirer*, (January 29, 1986)

Crespin " . . . is a presence now, not the monumental soprano of her great days, and her portrayal here was pure star turn."

W56.38c  Baxter, Robert. "Philadelphia." *Opera* (England) 37 (July 1986): 813.
"At the centre of the drama stood Crespin, still magnetic, still colossal, still one of the great artists on the opera stage."

W56.39  1986 (Jun 19): San Francisco; War Memorial Opera House; San Francisco Opera; Jérôme Kaltenbach, cond.; with Régine Crespin (Flora), Li-Chan Chen (Monica), Jean-Louis Loca (Toby), Susan Patterson (Mrs. Gobineau), Monte Pederson (Mr. Gobineau), and Kathryn Cowdrick (Mrs. Nolan) (on a double bill with Poulenc's *La Voix Humaine*)

*Reviews:*

W56.39a  Commanday, Robert. "Double Bill Needs More than Divas." *San Francisco Chronicle*, (June 21, 1986)
"Régine Crespin was a more potent Madame Flora than any I've seen, because she did not play a witchy old harridan . . . She was thereby more believable when she is frightened into reform and renouncing her swindle-trade."

W56.39b  Green, Judith. "'La Vox Humaine,' 'The Medium' Team up for a Top-Notch Show." *San Jose Mercury News*, (June 21, 1986)
The opera "was given in a film noir production borrowed from the Théâtre Musical de Paris. Everything from the junky Soho loft interior [to] expressionist lighting points up the spooky, haunted libretto."

W56.39c  Ross, Janice. "Opera Doubles Pleasure with its Offbeat Twin Bill." *Oakland Tribune*, (June 25, 1986)
"Crespin plays Crespin, neatly side stepping the opera's intended air of fear and fantasy in favor of a more broadly eccentric portrayal of the medium as a dotty aunt, an aging woman losing her grip on reality."

W56.39d  "Voix Humaine/The Medium." *San Francisco Opera*, 4 (Summer 1986): entire issue.

W56.39e  Bloomfield, Arthur. "San Francisco." *Opera* (England) 37 (October 1986): 1144.
"Régine Crespin was sympathetic, perhaps too sympathetic . . . an exotic rather than earthy deceiver. . ."

214  *Works and Performances*

W56.40    1986 (Sep 8): Syracuse, NY; Syracuse University; Carrier Theater; Syracuse Opera; with Patti Thompson (Flora), Julie Newell (Monica), and Eileen Clark, Kristine Bregenzer, and Patrick J. Denniston (two-piano reduction on a double-bill with Argento's *A Water Bird Talk*)

*Review:*

W56.40a   Holland, Bernard. "Opera: 'Water Bird Talk' and 'Medium' in Syracuse." *New York Times*, 3 (February 11, 1986): 17.
"Flora's blatant bottle-waving and swigging establishes her drunkenness with a . . . heavy hand. The singing, which was generally good, deserved to be better served."

W56.41    1986 (Sep 25): Linz, Austria; Landestheater Linz; Ernst Dunshirn, cond.; with Althea Bridges (Flora), Cheryl Lichter (Monica), Paula Swepston (Mrs. Gobineau), Leopold Köppl (Mr. Gobineau), Virgil Stanciu (Toby), and Birgit Greiner (Mrs. Nolan) (on a double-bill with *The Old Maid and the Thief*)

*Reviews:*

W56.41a   Rudolf, Bert. "Linz." *Oper und Konzert* 24, 11 (1986): 12.

W56.41b   Cossé, Peter. "Verlust mit Gewinn." *Opernwelt* 27, 11 (1986): 36-37.

W56.42    1987 (May 7): Buenos Aires; Teatro Colón; Mario Perusso, cond.; with Régine Crespin (Flora), Mariana Altamira (Monica), Jean-Louis Loca (Toby), Africa de Retes (Mrs. Gobineau), Ricardo Ortale (Mr. Gobineau), and Marta Blanco (Mrs. Nolan) (sung in English; on a double-bill with Pompeyo Camps' *La Hacienda*)

W56.43    1987 (May 9): San Diego; Old Globe Theater; with Beverly Evans (Flora), Nadia Pelle (Monica), Francis Menotti (Toby), Harlan Foss (Mr. Gobineau), Barbara Hocher (Mrs. Gobineau), and Nancy Carol Moore (Mrs. Nolan) (on a double-bill with *The Telephone*)

*Review:*

W56.43a   Dierks, Donald. "Globe's Intimacy Adds Greatly to Superb Menotti Productions." *San Diego Union*, (May 11, 1987)
Evans was " . . . entirely convincing in her moods of supreme self-confidence, uncontrolled rage and tortured fear."

W56.44    1987 (Feb 13): Reno; Nevada Opera; with Willene Gunn (Flora), Monica Puffer (Monica), and Paul Williams (Toby) (on a double-bill with Mascagni's *Cavalleria rusticana*)

W56.45    1987 (Nov 5): Philadelphia; Curtis Institute of Music; Herbert Gietzen, cond.; Curtis Student Orchestra; with Francis Menotti (Toby), Laura Mashburn (Flora), Olive Lynch (Monica), Marian Johnson-Healy (Mrs. Gobineau), John Kramar (Mr. Gobineau), and Jennifer Jones (Mrs. Nolan) (on a double-bill with *Amelia al ballo*)

*Review:*

W56.45a    Webster, Daniel. "Menotti Directs His 'Amelia' and 'The Medium.'" *Philadelphia Inquirer*, (November 7, 1987)
"The entire work played with an intensity that made the music seem a part of speech, the action seem instrumental. The piece removes itself from discussions of its modernity or its nostalgic basis; its music and drama are as inseparable as body and skin."

W56.46    1988 (Apr 15): New Orleans; Performing Arts Center Recital Hall; University of New Orleans Opera Theater; David Nelson, cond.; with Penny Rubinfield (Monica), John Aleman (Toby), Kathryn Barnes-Burroughs (Flora), Deanna Dugas (Mrs. Gobineau), Alexander Todd (Mr. Gobineau), and Michelle Kemp (Mrs. Nolan) (performed also, with the same cast, opening Nov 4 as part of a Menotti Festival, produced by The University of New Orleans and Hispanidad)

W56.47    1988 (Nov 25): Croydon, England; Croydon College; Peter Jackson Studio Theatre; Helen Leaf, cond.; with Josephine Morgan (Flora), Regina Nathan (Monica), and Lyndon George (Toby)

W56.48    1990 (May 19): Glassboro, NJ: Wilson Hall; Donald Portnoy, cond.; with Beverly Evans (Flora), Deborah Golembiski (Monica), Tao Ruspoli (Toby), Barbara Hocher (Mrs. Nolan), Judith Weyman (Mrs. Gobineau), and William Parcher (Mr. Gobineau) (Hollybush Festival; on a double-bill with *The Telephone*)

*Reviews:*

W56.48a    Webster, Daniel. "Menotti Operas 'The Telephone' and 'The Medium.'" *Philadelphia Inquirer*, (May 21, 1990)

*216    Works and Performances*

"Evans not only created this furtive, howling, gasping woman, but she sang with admirable care in projecting the text and in presenting her role as music."

W56.48b    Baxter, Robert. "Glassboro, New Jersey (Hollybush Festival)." *Opera* (England) 41 (October 1990): 1199.
"Evans seized every melodramatic moment and made it her own, from her frightening entrance right up [to] the final catastrophe."

W56.49    1990 (Jun 11): Pittsburgh; Pittsburgh Opera Center; Metropol; Danielle Orlando, piano; with Dani Raphael (Flora), Laura Knoop (Monica), Barton Green (Toby), Lisa Actor (Mrs. Nolan), Manuel Lanza (Mr. Gobineau), and Heidi Skok (Mrs. Gobineau)

*Review:*

W56.49a    Croan, Robert. "Menotti Opera Gripping at Metropol." *Pittsburgh Post Gazette*, (June 12, 1990)
Raphael " . . . is a young singer to watch for, who uses her opulent mezzo-soprano sound to meaningful dramatic effect, and establishes her character before she has sung a single note."

W56.50    1990 (Oct 2): Tel Aviv; New Israeli Opera; Asher Fisch, cond.; Rishon Letzion Symphony; with Mira Zakai (Flora), Efrat Bin-Nun (Monica), Kobi Hagoel (Toby), Robin Weisel-Capsouto (Mrs. Gobineau), Sorin Semilian (Mrs. Gobineau), and Tzvia Litevsky (Mrs. Nolan) (sung in Hebrew)

*Reviews:*

W56.50a    Springer, Morris. "Tel Aviv: New Israeli Opera." *Opera Canada* 32, 1 (1991): 41.
". . . the opera worked best where orchestration was light and the Hebrew text came through . . . Heading the cast was Mira Zakai's wrenchingly effective portrayal of the unhinged Flora."

W56.50b    Springer, Morris. "Tel Aviv." *Opera News* 55 (March 16, 1991): 45.
"Mira Zakai's wrenchingly effective portrayal of the unhinged, self-deluding Flora matched memories of Marie Powers, who created the role."

W56.51   1992 (Feb 8): Richmond; Virginia Opera Association; Michael Ching, cond.; with Edna Garabedian (Flora), Victoria Castle (Monica), David Norris (Toby), Christine Akre (Mrs. Gobineau), Michael Caldwell (Mr. Gobineau), and Leslie Valentine (Mrs. Nolan) (on a double-bill with Ching's *Cue 67*)

*Reviews:*

W56.51a   Dolmetsch, Carl. "Virginia Opera." *Opera Canada* 33, 2 (1992): 35.
". . . Garabedian's Flora was vocally and dramatically top class. So was young Davis [sic] Norris' mute gypsy boy . . ."

W56.51b   Modi, Sorab. "Richmond." *Opera News* 56 (April 11, 1992): 48.
"In Edna Garabedian, VOA found a stunning singing actress who made an overpowering, wrenchingly effective Mme. Flora."

W56.52   1992 (Feb 14): Augusta, GA; Augusta Opera; Ted Taylor, cond.; with Penny Johnson (Monica), John Lescault (Toby), Cynthia Munzer (Flora), Charles Huddleston (Mr. Gobineau), Sarah Colburn (Mrs. Gobineau), and Zanice Muckler (Mrs. Nolan) (on a double-bill with *The Telephone*)

*Review:*

W56.52a   Crook, John. "Augusta." *Opera News* 56 (May 1992): 56.
". . . what was harrowing forty years ago now seems hackneyed . . . The Augusta production was as solid as the piece is likely to receive these days."

W56.53   1992 (Jun 12): Chicago; Chicago Opera Theater; Kurt Klippstatter, cond.; with Mignon Dunn (Flora), Robert Orth (Mr. Gobineau), Diane Ragains (Mrs. Gobineau), Claudia Kerski-Nienow (Mrs. Nolan), Patrice Michaels Bedi (Monica), and John Schroeder (Toby) (on a double-bill with Argento's *A Water Bird Talk*)

*Review:*

W56.53a   Rhein, John von. "Chicago." *Opera News* 57 (November 1992): 52-53. Dunn " . . . commanded the stage. Her cynical, cruel, finally pathetic Mme. Flora was a memorable character study, whether preying on her gullible clients . . . or falling apart when the spirit world turned frighteningly real."

*218 Works and Performances*

W56.54     1994 (Aug 20): Houston; Miller Outdoor Theater; Ebony Opera Guild; with Rubye Hebert (Flora), Kimla Beasley (Monica), Gwendolyn Dorsey (Mrs. Gobineau), and Fanchon Angela Moore (Mrs. Nolan)

*Review:*

W56.54a     Ward, Charles. "Classic Operas Display Ebony Guild Strengths." *Houston Chronicle*, (August 22, 1994)
"Hebert gave Flora an imperious bearing that slowly slid into fragility as her fears mounted . . . "

W56.55     1997 (Apr 4): Carmichael, CA; Voice Fitness Institute of Sacramento; La Piccola Scala; Gerald Rheault, musical director and pianist; with Elaine Benoit (Flora), Adrienne Fortini (Monica), Shawn Marie Williams (Mrs. Nolan), Lanny Malfar (Mr. Gobineau), Hannah Mitchell (Mrs. Gobineau), and Fred Wilson (Toby) (on a double-bill with *The Telephone*)

*Review:*

W56.55a     Glackin, William. "The Memorable Menotti." *Sacramento Bee*, Scene (March 18, 1997): E8.
"Elaine Benoit plays Flora powerfully well, singing the role in a strong voice that she's not afraid to roughen to make her feelings felt, and getting across the toughness and suspicion in her treatment of the young people."

W56.56     1997 (Jun 6): Brookville, NY; New York Institute of Technology; Salten Center; Yelena Polezhayev, musical director and pianist; with April Lindevald (Flora), Penelope Grover (Monica), Scott Jarvis (Toby), Alan Czak (Mr. Gobineau), Gina Marie Mazzara (Mrs. Gobineau), and Anne Jacobs (Mrs. Nolan) (A Small Company in America's production)

*Review:*

W56.56a     Parks, Steve. "A Medium Has a Message." *Newsday*, 2, Weekend (June 6, 1997): B20.
"April Lindevald . . . has enough of the wild-eyed diva in her to project her character's descent into madness and carry the day for this challenging production."

W56.57    1997 (Oct 8): Dallas; Deep Ellum Opera Theatre; Gleni Tai, cond.; ensemble of piano, synthesizer and trumpet; with Jodi Crawford (Flora), Dara Whitehead (Flora), Brian Gonzales (Toby), Kathryn Allen (Mrs. Gobineau), Laurie Rickard (Mrs. Nolan), and Eugene LeBeaux (Mr. Gobineau) (preview given on Oct 8, with official opening on Oct 9)

*Review:*

W56.57a    Chism, Olin. "Production Is a Happy 'Medium': DEOT's Faker Scares the Ectoplasm out of Herself." *Dallas Morning News*, Overnight (October 9, 1997): 41A.
"Deep Ellum is fortunate in having a singer with a real sense of theater in soprano Jodi Crawford, whose intense performance dominates the evening."

### ♦ DISCOGRAPHY

COMPLETE RECORDINGS

W56.58    Joyce Castle (Flora), Patrice Michaels Bedi (Monica), Diane Ragains (Mrs. Gobineau), Peter Van De Graaff (Mr. Gobineau), Barbara Landis (Mrs. Nolan), Joanna Lind (Girl's voice); Ensemble of Chicago Opera Theater; Lawrence Rapchak, cond.
Cedille CDR 90000 034 (CD) (1997)
Recorded November 12, 16, 17, and 23, 1996, in Bennett-Gordon Hall, Ravinia, Highland Park, Illinois.

W56.59    Marie Powers (Flora), Evelyn Keller (Monica), Beverly Dame (Mrs. Gobineau), Catherine Mastice (Mrs. Nolan), Frank Rogier (Mr. Gobineau); Ballet Society Orchestra; Emanuel Balaban, cond.
Columbia SL 54 (ML 4174-4175), ML 4174-4175, OSL-154 (OL 4174-4175), LP; Columbia/Odyssey Y2 35239, Y 35979; CBS M2P 39532; on 3 sides of 2 discs, LP. mono. (1949)
Original 1947 performance.
With *The Telephone*.

W56.60    Regina Resnik (Flora), Judith Blegen (Monica), Emily Derr (Mrs. Gobineau), Julian Patrick (Mr. Gobineau), Claudine Carlson (Mrs. Nolan); Opera Society of Washington; Jorge Mester, cond.
Columbia Masterworks MS 7387, LP, analog, stereo.

W56.61   Denise Scharley (Flora), Eliane Lublin (Monica), Nicole Menut (Mrs. Gobineau), Claude Genty (Mr. Gobineau), Solange Michel (Mrs. Nolan); Richard Blareau, cond.
RCA France 640.006/7, LP. In French.
With *The Telephone*.

SELECTIONS

*Monica's Aria*

W56.62   Jennifer Poffenberger, soprano; Lori Piitz, piano.
Enharmonic ENCD93-012. digital, compact disc (1993)
Album title: Mostly Americana.
With songs by Hundley, Rorem, D. Baker, Lehman, and Turina.

*Toby, What Are You Doing?*

W56.63   Betty Jane Grimm, contralto; Roy Johnson, piano.
Century 33527, LP, mono. (1968)
Album title: Betty Jane Grimm in Concert.
Recorded by KFSU-FM, Tallahassee, Florida.

FILM

W56.64   Beverly Dame (Mrs. Gobineau), Belva Kibler (Mrs. Nolan), Anna Maria Alberghetti (Monica), Leo Coleman (Toby), Marie Powers (Flora), Donald Morgan (Mr. Gobineau); Orchestra of Rome della Radio-televisione Italiana; Thomas Schippers, cond.
Mercury MGL 7 (MG 10095-MG 10096), 2 discs, mono., LP (1951)
Recorded at studios of Radio italiana.

### ♦ SELECTED RECORDING REVIEWS

W56.65   Kolodin, Irving. "Murder and Mirth." *Saturday Review of Literature* 31 (January 31, 1948): 44.
Review of the Columbia M726 recording. ". . . it is the evidence of the recordings (the first of an American conceived opera to be presented complete) that the music, if anything, is better than it sounds in the theatre."

W56.66   Todd, Arthur. "Theatre on the Disc." *Theatre Arts* 36 (June 1952): 6-7.

Brief reviews of then-recent recordings of *Amahl*, *The Medium*, *The Telephone*, *The Consul*, *Sebastian*, *Amelia al ballo*, and *The Old Maid and the Thief.*

W56.67  Ellsworth, Ray. "Americans on Microgroove: A Discography, Part II." *High Fidelity* 6 (August 1956): 62.
Brief review of the Columbia OSL 154 and Mercury MGL 7 recordings. "If his operas do have certain shortcomings . . . they nevertheless throb with life on the stage, the television screen, or records."

W56.68  Goodman, John. "I Hear Wagner Singing." *New Leader* 53 (August 17, 1970): 25-26.
Review of the Columbia Records MS7387 recording. ". . . it is impossible to be serious about a work that presents one inflated, sensational cliché after another in a straight, naturalistic manner . . . all didactic content, irrational plot and realistic language — none of it very memorable except for the composer's gaffes."

W56.69  Simmons, Walter. "Menotti: *The Medium; The Telephone.*" *Fanfare* 3 (May-June 1980): 107-108.
Review of the Odyssey Y2 35239 (2 discs) recording. "The least attractive aspect of the production is the raucous little orchestra, whose puny contribution detracts at times from the power of the work."

W56.70  Waleson, Heidi. "Classical Keeping Score." *Billboard* (November 8, 1997)
Review of the Cedille recording. "Cedille . . . has filled a significant catalog gap with its new recording . . . a dramatic, well-paced performance."

W56.71  Zakariasen, Bill. "Menotti: The Medium." *Opera News* 62 (January 3, 1998): 40.
Review of the Cedille recording. ". . . captures the quirky dramatics of the piece, thanks in no small part to conductor Lawrence Rapchak, his crack instrumental ensemble and a recording that puts everything (including sound effects) into perfect perspective . . . A first-rate recording of a durable classic."

*222   Works and Performances*

## W57   MIRACLES (1979)

Eight musical miniatures based on poetry written by children between the ages of five and thirteen; twelve songs were originally planned.

### ♦ PREMIERE PERFORMANCE

W57.1   1979 (Apr 22): Fort Worth; Tarrant County Convention Center Theater; John Giordano, cond.


## W58   MISSA O PULCHRITUDO IN HONOREM SACRATISSIMI CORDIS JESUS (1979; G. Schirmer; 45 min.)

Composed for the Bel Canto Chorus of Milwaukee.
"The text . . . uses the Roman Catholic text for the Mass except for the Credo, which is replaced by a motet based on the words of St. Augustine."
SMSTB; soli; chorus; 2+pic.22+bcl.2/4331/timp.2perc/hp/str

### ♦ ABOUT THE WORK

W58.1   Robinson, Ray. "Gian Carlo Menotti's New Mass." *Choral Journal* 20 (January 1980): 5-8.
Analysis, with musical examples, of the first setting, by which time the 'Credo' had not yet been composed.

W58.2   "Menotti's Rehearsal: Composer in Depth." *News and Courier* (Charleston, SC), (May 28, 1981).
The work represents "a resolution of the long-standing conflict between Menotti's own deeply ingrained religious beliefs and his rejection of organized religion." Says Menotti: "I do not believe entirely in the text of the Credo . . . and so I thought it would be dishonest of me to set it. Instead, I substituted words of St. Augustine, which says, in effect, 'I search for beauty outside myself, without realizing that the only true beauty is the beauty within us.'"

### ♦ SELECTED PERFORMANCES

W58.3   1979 (May 11): Milwaukee; Performing Arts Center; Uihlein Hall; James A. Keeley, cond.; Milwaukee Symphony Orchestra and Bel Canto Chorus of Milwaukee; with Brenda Quilling (soprano), Cynthia

Munzer (mezzo-soprano), David Bender (tenor), and David Berger (baritone) (first setting; the "Credo" had not yet been composed)

W58.4   1979 (Jul 15): Spoleto; Christian Badea, cond.; Westminster Cathedral Choir; Bel Canto Chorus of Milwaukee; with Beniamino Prior (tenor), and Ferruccio Furlanetto (bass) (Italian premiere)

W58.5   1981 (May 22): Charleston, SC; Gaillard Auditorium; Joseph Flummerfelt, cond.; Westminster Cathedral Choir; Singers Guild of the Charleston Symphony Orchestra; Spoleto Festival Orchestra U.S.A.; with Suzanne Hong (soprano), Tonio di Paolo (tenor), Diane Curry (mezzo-soprano), and Boris Martinovich (bass-baritone) (Spoleto Festival U.S.A.; on a double-bill with *Le Dernier Sauvage*)

*Reviews:*

W58.5a  Ardoin, John. "Menotti Presents Vibrant Choruses." *Dallas Morning News*, (June 5, 1981)
"Here he is creating not only on a highly expressive level, one in which rich melodic ideas pour forth with almost embarrassing generosity, but one as individual as at any stage in his career."

W58.5b  "Menotti Choral Circuit." *Variety* 303 (June 10, 1981): 58.
". . . it is an impressive musical contribution which nevertheless fails to achieve that searing expression of faith characteristic of the great achievements in liturgical music."

W58.5c  Ardoin, John. "Menotti's *The Last Savage* (Spoleto U.S.A.)." *High Fidelity/Musical America* 31 (September 1981): MA32-33.
Menotti " . . . is creating not only on a highly expressive plane — one in which melodies pour forth with almost embarrassing generosity — but in a style as individual as at any other stage in his career."

### ♦ DISCOGRAPHY

W58.6   Renata Baldisseri, soprano; Wilma Borelli, mezzo-soprano; Beniamino Prior, tenor; Ferruccio Furlanetto, bass; Westminster Cathedral Choir; Bel Canto Chorus of Milwaukee; Spoleto Festival Orchestra; Christian Badea, cond.
Fonit Cetra FDM 0001, LP, analog, stereo. (1981)
Recorded in the Piazza del Duomo, Spoleto, July 1979, at the closing concert of the Festival of Two Worlds, 1979.

*224  Works and Performances*

    *Review:*

W58.6a    Ellis, Stephen W. "Menotti: Mass 'O Pulchritudo.'" *Fanfare* 7 (November-December 1983): 265-266.
    Review of the Fonit Cetra FDM 001 recording (distributed by IBR). "If I were Menotti, I would be very upset to see this particular recording of his *Mass* issued. The work needs all the help it can get — and forces here work against it."

W58.7    Suzanne Hong, soprano; Diane Curry, mezzo-soprano; Tonio di Paolo, tenor; Boris Martinovich, bass; Westminster Cathedral Choir; Spoleto Festival Orchestra; Joseph Flummerfelt, cond.
    Westminster Choir WC-5, LP, analog, stereo. (1981); Westminster Choir WC-5 L3RS 4087, LP, stereo. (1981)
    Recorded in Jun 1981 at the Spoleto Festival U.S.A.

    *Review:*

W58.7a    Ardoin, John. "Menotti's Mass Recorded for First Time." *Dallas Morning News*, (October 17, 1982)
    ". . . an expansive canvas of sound, one harmonically fresh (with strong key centers and only quick brush strokes of dissonance) and one continually resourceful in its use of imitation and other weapons from the contrapuntal arsenal. This spontaneous piece belongs first and foremost to the chorus and a quartet of soloists."

*W59*    *MOANS, GROANS, CRIES, AND SIGHS* (1981; G. Schirmer; 6 min.)

"A composer at work."
Madrigal for six voice *a capella* chorus.

    ♦ **PREMIERE PERFORMANCE**

W59.1    1981 (Aug 31): Edinburgh; Usher Hall; The King's Singers (Jeremy Jackman and Alastair Hume, countertenors, Bill Ives, tenor, Anthony Holt and Simon Carrington, baritones, and Brian Kay, bass)

*W60*    *THE MOST IMPORTANT MAN* (1971; G. Schirmer; evening)

Opera in three acts with libretto (English) by Menotti.
Cast: dram Bar, dram T, Mz, lyr S, dram S; Bar, 2 T, Bar, B, buffo B
2+pic.2+ca.2+bcl.2+cbn/4331/timp.2perc/hp.pf.org/str

### ♦ SELECTED PERFORMANCES

W60.1    1971 (Mar 7): New York; Lincoln Center; New York State Theater; New York City Opera; Christopher Keene, cond.; with Eugene Holmes (Toimé Ukamba), Harry Theyard (Dr. Otto Arnek), Beverly Wolff (Leona Arnek), Richard Stilwell (Eric Rupert), Joanna Bruno (Cora Arnek), John Lankston (Prof. Clement), Joaquin Romaguera (Prof. Risselberg), Thomas Jamerson (Prof. Bolental), William Ledbetter (Prof. Hisselman), Don Yule (Prof. Grippel), Jack Bittner (Under Secretary of State), and Delores Jones (Mrs. Agebda Akawasi)

*Reviews:*

W60.1a    "Dokumentation." *Opernwelt* (Yearbook (1971): 100.

W60.1b    "First Performances." *World of Music* 13, 2 (1971): 75.

W60.1c    "The Most Important Man." *Variety* 262 (March 17, 1971): 74.
"... it's a dull job by composer-librettist-director Gian Carlo Menotti, unlikely to survive in repertory or get much production around the world."

W60.1d    "Musical Events: Sci-Fi in the Veldt." *New Yorker* 47 (March 20, 1971): 132.
"... I found it one of the most impressive of all his works for the stage ... it is a highly effective piece of musical theatre, and at its close the other night the audience could scarcely contain its emotion."

W60.1e    Barnes, Clive. "The Conundrum of Film-Making." *Times* (London), (March 20, 1971): 21.
"The difficulty with Menotti is quite simply that his florid lyricism sounds false in relation to contemporary music. It lacks the energy of anything but pastiche ... [Nevertheless] the opera was well performed, and the conductor ... is a young man we are going to hear much of."

W60.1f  Bender, William. "Living Children." *Time* 97 (March 22, 1971): 59.
"Strains of Richard Strauss float from the pit during one interlude. By the final duet . . . Menotti is unashamedly into the heart-throbbing lyricism of Puccini . . ."

W60.1g  Kastendieck, Miles and Louis Snyder. "Menotti Premiere and Two 'Louise' Revivals." *Christian Science Monitor*, (March 22, 1971): 5.
"Neither the death of the hero nor his tragic pronouncement that the world did not deserve his formula mattered. Without this impact, the final curtain fell inconsequentially. Incidentally, the audience applauded politely."

W60.1h  Kolodin, Irving. "Music to My Ears: an Opera to Forget and a Tenor to Remember." *Saturday Review* 54 (March 27, 1971): 16+.
"By much the most expert achievement of the evening was [the] . . . evocation of the scene, followed closely by Menotti's staging of his own work and young Christopher Keene's productive music direction. Too bad they were not all involved with a less unhappy problem."

W60.1i  Freeman, John W. "New York." *Opera News* 35 (April 17, 1971): 29.
". . . there are snatches of billowing melody often enough to lift the audience's spirits above the mechanics of situation. Confronted with their roles at the last moment, the singers did an admirable job . . ."

W60.1j  Freeman, John W. "Da New York." *Nuova rivista musicale italiana* 5 (May-June 1971): 507-508.

W60.1k  Trebor, Emil. "New York State Theatre." *Music Journal* 29 (May 1971): 69-70.
"The first act was a total success for those who don't sneer at Menotti's Pucciniesque (therefore unabashedly beautiful) line."

W60.1l  Weinstock, Herbert. "New York." *Opera* (England) 22 (June 1971): 507-508.
"If an opera were to be judged by its social intentions, this one would earn high marks. But, alas, [this] . . . must be judged as an opera, by qualities entirely apart from its 'message': as such it struck me as a disaster."

W60.1m  Oppens, Kurt. "New York: Crime and Sex." *Opernwelt* 12 (June 1971): 33-34.

W60.1n   Movshon, George. "New York City Opera." *High Fidelity/Musical America* 21 (June 1971): MA16.

". . . this music is rather a sort of dilute Cilea, with all the good melodies left out. A faded wall-paper that never intrudes."

W60.2    1972 (Jan 18): Trieste, Italy; Christopher Keene, cond.; with Renato Cioni (Prof. Otto Arnek), Maria Luisa Bordin Nave (Leona), Giovanna Bruno (Cora), Allan Evans (Toimé Ukamba), Maria Helenita Olivares (Mme. Akawasi), Dario Zerial (Erik), Oslavio Di Credio (Prof. Klement), Benedetto Salvemini (Prof. Rüsselberg), Lucio Rolli (Prof. Bohlental), Paolo Cesari (Prof. Hisselmann), Carlo Padoan (Prof. Grüppel), and Vito Susca (Under Secretary)

*Review:*

W60.2a   Kessler, Giovanna. "Menottis Engagement." *Opernwelt* (March 1972): 20.

## *W61*   *MUERO PORQUÉ NO MUERO* (1982; G. Schirmer; 15 min.)

Cantata for soprano, chorus, and orchestra; "Cantata for St. Teresa"
Soprano; chorus; 2222/4331/timp.perc/hp/str

### ♦ PREMIERE PERFORMANCE

W61.1    1982 (Oct 15): Washington, DC; Cathedral of St. Matthew the Apostle; Orchestra and Chorus of the Catholic University of America; Robert Ricks, cond.; with Marvis Martin, soprano.

## *W62*   *MY CHRISTMAS* (1987; G. Schirmer; 15 min.)

For male chorus; fl, ob, cl, hn, hp, db

## *W63*   *NOCTURNE* (1982; G. Schirmer; 6 min.)

For high voice, harp, and string quartet.

### ♦ SELECTED PERFORMANCES

W63.1   1982 (Oct 24): New York; Lincoln Center; Alice Tully Hall; with Marvis Martin (soprano), Karen Lindquist (harp), James Buswell (violin), Lynn Chang (violin), Walter Trampler (viola), and Leslie Parnas (cello).

W63.2   1986 (Dec 13): Brooklyn; Brooklyn Academy of Music; with Marvis Martin (soprano), Barbara Allen (harp), and the Ridge Quartet.

*Review:*

W63.2a   Crutchfield, Will. "Music: Menotti Program." *New York Times*, 3 (December 15, 1986): 22.
Menotti's "chamber music, though not questing or gripping, has been sensitively conceived, and skillfully and affectionately carried out. . ."

### ♦ DISCOGRAPHY

W63.3   Karan Armstrong, soprano; Alfred Lutz, Mischa Salevic, violins; Stephan Blaumer, viola; Klaus Kühr, violoncello; Helga Storck, harp. Etcetera KTC 1045, compact disc, digital, stereo. (1988)
With *Canti della lontananza* and *Five songs* (1981)

### ♦ SELECTED RECORDING REVIEWS

W63.4   Miller, Philip L. "Menotti: Songs." *American Record Guide* 51 (November-December 1988): 61.
Review of the Etcetera 1045 CD (Qualiton) recording. Armstrong's " . . . voice is a round and healthy soprano and she sings Menotti's songs with full conviction. The assisting artists are all first rate."

W63.5   Ardoin, John. "Menotti's Passion Erupts in CD Collection." *Dallas Morning News*, (November 20, 1988)
"Armstrong, however, is not the ideal interpreter . . . Her voice is unsteady and too grainy. At the beginning of her career it was probably an attractive lyric sound."

*W64*   *THE OLD MAID AND THE THIEF* (1939; G. Ricordi)

*See also: Ricercare and Toccata on a Theme from the Old Maid and the Thief*

Opera buffa in 14 scenes; "A Grotesque Comedy."
Commissioned by the National Broadcasting Corporation.

♦ ABOUT THE WORK

W64.1   Wilson, J. Kenneth. "Ricecare [sic] and Toccata on a Theme From *The Old Maid and the Thief.*" *Musical Courier* 150 (September 1954): 43. Review of the Ricordi score. "Rarely does the composer go outside the limits of a diatonic seven-note scale, except to embellish a modulation, and the harmonies produced by the passing of lines in this narrow framework are both sensitive and satisfying."

W64.2   Sternfeld, Frederick W. "Irwin Bazelon: Sonata for Piano . . . Gian-Carlo Menotti: Ricercare and Toccata, on a Theme from 'The Old Maid and the Thief' . . . William Schuman: Voyage . . . Virgil Thomson: Nine Etudes. . . " *Notes (Music Library Association)* 12 (March 1955): 329.
Review of the G. Schirmer score (1953, 11 p.) "Why take a perfectly serviceable operatic theme and subject it to the instrumental vicissitudes of a ricercare and toccata? . . . Menotti should not waste his well-known dramatic and lyrical talents on what seems, at least to this reviewer, a barren extravaganza."

W64.3   Ryan, Sylvia Watkins. "Solo Piano Music of Gian-Carlo Menotti: A Pedagogical and Performance Analysis." D.M.A. dissertation, University of Oklahoma, 1993.
Discusses *Poemetti* (1937), *Ricercare and Toccata on a Theme from The Old Maid and the Thief* (1953), and the piano version of *Amahl and the Night Visitors* (1951). This study is intended to serve as a reference work for teachers of contemporary piano literature.

♦ SELECTED PERFORMANCES

W64.4   1939 (Apr 22): New York; National Broadcasting Company Blue Network (WJZ); NBC Symphony Orchestra; Alberto Erede, cond.; with Joseph Curtin (Narrator), Mary Hopple (Miss Todd), Robert Weede (Bob), Margaret Daum (Laetitia), and Dorothy Sarnoff (Miss Pinkerton)

*Review:*

W64.4a  Downes, Olin. "New Radio Opera of Menotti Given." *New York Times*, (April 23, 1939): sect. III, p. 6.
"The opera shows again how skillful and adroit Mr. Menotti becomes when he approaches the stage. He has lost nothing of his native wit and his easy, plentiful invention."

W64.5  1948 (Apr 8): New York; New York City Opera; Thomas P. Martin, cond.; with Marie Powers (Miss Todd), Virginia MacWatters (Laetitia), Norman Young (Bob), and Ellen Faull (Miss Pinkerton) (on a double-bill with *Amelia al ballo*)

*Reviews:*

W64.5a  "Opera Can Be Fun." *Time* 51 (April 19, 1948): 50.
"The audience loved every minute of it, right down to the final clinch . . ."

W64.5b  Smith, Cecil. "Operatic Gagster." *New Republic* 118 (April 26, 1948): 36-37.
"The performances of the principals . . . refuted the notion that the same people can never both sing and act well."

W64.6  1948 (Oct 9): New York; New York City Opera; Thomas P. Martin, cond.; with Virginia MacWatters (Laetitia), Muriel O'Malley (Miss Todd), Ellen Faull (Miss Pinkerton), and Norman Young (Bob) (on a double-bill with *Amelia al ballo*)

W64.7  1952 (Apr 9): New York; New York City Center; New York City Opera; Thomas Schippers, cond.; with Mary Kreste (Miss Todd), Adelaide Bishop (Laetitia), Ellen Faull (Miss Pinkerton), and Andrew Gainey (Bob) (on a double-bill with *Amahl and the Night Visitors*)

*Reviews:*

W64.7a  Eaton, Quaintance. "Menotti's Amahl and the Night Visitors is Second Novelty of the Spring Season." *Musical America* 72 (April 15, 1952): 5.
"The performance . . . was excellent. All the singers were in vein and acted smoothly as a team . . . general high-spirits of a performance that also had real vocal quality."

W64.7b  Watt, Douglas. "Musical Events: Large and Small." *New Yorker* 28 (April 19, 1952): 91.
". . . it's a sort of interminable joke set to music — mildly entertaining in the telling, but without much punch."

W64.8  1952 (Sep 19): New York; New York City Opera; Thomas Schippers, cond.; with Adelaide Bishop (Laetitia), Mary Kreste (Miss Todd), Ellen Faull (Miss Pinkerton), and Thomas Tipton (Bob) (on a double-bill with *Amahl and the Night Visitors*)

Review:

W64.8a  "Actor's Ensemble." *Counterpoint* 18 (February 1953): 32-33.

W64.9  1954 (May 6): BBC Radio; Third Programme broadcast; Nicholas Goldschmidt, cond.; with Marjorie Westbury, Gwen Catley, Catherine Lawson, and Frederick Sharp.

Review:

W64.9a  "Menotti Opera." *Times (London)*, (May 7, 1954): 10.
"The score breathes real dramatic life, the vocal parts . . . are eminently singable, and the orchestra is transparent enough to allow the singers' words to come through with clarity — one of the chief prerequisites of radio opera."

W64.10  1968 (Nov 6): Hattiesburg; University of Southern Mississippi; School of Fine Arts; Department of Music; Jerrald D. McCollum, musical director and accompanist; with Nancy Hullum/Rachel Stanley (Miss Todd), Sandra White/Cheryl Wilgar (Laetitia), Linda Burke/Mildred Hong (Miss Pinkerton), and Jimmy Cutrell/Tim Davis (Bob) (on a double-bill with *The Telephone*) (played Nov 11 at East Central Junior College, Decator, MS, and Nov 12 at University Military School, Mobile, AL)

W64.11  1972 (Mar 22): New York; 92nd St. Y.M. & Y.W.H.A.; Mannes College of Music; student orchestra; Paul Berl, cond.; with James Hooper (Bob), Lynn Brackens (Laetitia), Stephanie Low (Miss Todd), and Denise Movroson (Miss Pinkerton)

*232  Works and Performances*

Review:

W64.11a   Ericson, Raymond. "2 Comic Works Given by Mannes Group." *New York Times*, (March 24, 1972): 30.
"The music remains skillful, unpretentious and entertaining, unlike some of his later works."

W64.12   1975 (Jul 5): Spoleto; Teatro Caio Melisso; David Agler, cond.; with Karen Hunt (Letitia), Sigmund Cowan (Bob), Muriel Greenspon (Miss Todd), and Margaret Baker (Miss Pinkerton) (sung in Italian; on a triple-bill with *The Telephone* and Bizet's *Le Docteur Miracle*)

Review:

W64.12a   Blyth, Alan. "Menotti and Spoleto." *Opera (England)* 26 (Autumn 1975): 10-19.
" . . . one of Menotti's happiest scores, economic, well-timed, unassuming, consistently constructed in his most fluent vein."

W64.13   1978 (Apr 22): Stockton, CA: University of the Pacific; Conservatory of Music; Conservatory Auditorium; John Ballerino and Bernadette Hoke, pianists; with Anne Watson/Leslie Maslow (Miss Todd), Tina Toone/Melissa Spotts (Laetitia), Debra Mather/Denise Mallery (Miss Pinkerton), and James Meade (Bob) (on a program of "100 Years of Music, 1878-1978")

W64.14   1981 (Dec 17): New York; Chamber Opera Theatre of New York; Ainslee Cox, cond.; with Chris Santy (Announcer), Sally Mitchell Motyka (Laetitia) and Diane Armistead (Miss Todd), Molly Stark (Miss Pinkerton), and Michael Scarborough (Bob) (on a double-bill with Mollicone's *The Face on the Barroom Floor*)

Reviews:

W64.14a   Holland, Bernard. "Music: Chamber Opera." *New York Times*, (December 20, 1981): 73.
The music " . . . was joyful and energetic, and Sally Mitchell Motyka's extended aria as the lovelorn Laetitia was appealingly lyrical. . ."

W64.14b   "The Face on the Barroom Floor (Mollicone) and The Old Maid and the Thief (Menotti)." *Variety* 305 (January 6, 1982): 76.

"... took the opera back to its roots by setting it in a radio studio at a rehearsal. The resulting situation, in which the actors are viewed both as actors and as characters in the opera, is tricky, yet ultimately rewarding."

W64.15   1985 (Dec 8): Marseille; Opéra de Marseille; with Rita Gorr (Miss Todd), Françoise Garner (Miss Pinkerton), Danielle Chlostawa (Laetitia), René Franc (Bob) (on a triple-bill with Dallapiccola's *Volo di notte* and Massenet's *La Navarraise*)

*Review:*

W64.15a   Mayer, Tony. "Marseilles." *Opera (England)* 37 (March 1986): 320-322.
Regarding Gorr, "The passing of the years do not seem to have taken toll of her voice, as powerful and lyrical as ever..."

W64.16   1986 (Mar 21): Hof, Germany; Erich Waglechner, cond.; with Eligia Klosowska (Miss Todd), Christine Leyser (Laetitia), and Alois Walchshofer (Bob)

*Review:*

W64.16a   Stöckl, Rudolf. "Gar nichts gesehen: Opern-Einaker Menottis in Hof." *Opernwelt* 27 (July 1986): 46-47.

W64.17   1986 (Sep 25): Linz, Austria; Landestheater Linz; Ernst Dunshirn, cond.; with Althea Bridges (Miss Todd), Cheryl Lichter (Laetitia), Paula Swepston (Miss Pinkerton), and Leopold Köppl (Bob) (on a double-bill with *The Medium*)

*Reviews:*

W64.17a   Cossé, Peter. "Verlust mit Gewinn." *Opernwelt* 27 (November 1986): 36-37.

W64.17b   Rudolf, Bert. "Linz." *Oper und Konzert* 24, 11 (1986): 12.

W64.18   1993 (Apr 30): Fort Worth; Scott Theatre; Fort Worth Opera; John Balme, cond.; with Donna Stephenson (Miss Todd), Susanna Buratto (Miss Pinkerton), Belinda Thayer Oswald (Laetitia), and William Swain

(Bob) (Fort Worth Opera's Menotti Festival; on a triple bill with *Triplo Concerto* and *The Telephone*)

*Review:*

W64.18a    Maurin, Gaston C. "Fort Worth." *Opera News* 58 (October 1993): 43.
"... John Balme paid careful attention to balances while conducting a fine ensemble with genuine comic flair. Though words were not always audible, visual cues and a cast of accomplished actors clarified matters."

### ♦ DISCOGRAPHY

COMPLETE RECORDING

W64.19    Judith Blegen (Laetitia), Margaret Baker (Miss Pinkerton), Anna Reynolds (Miss Todd), John Reardon (Bob); Teatro comunale "Giuseppe Verdi"; Jorge Mester, cond.
Mercury SR 90521, (1970), LP, mono.; Vox CT-2256, cassette; Turnabout TV 34745 (1979), LP, stereo.

W64.20    Mary Hopple, Margaret Daum, Dorothy Sarnoff, Robert Weede, soloists; Orchestra; Alberto Erede, cond.
Unique Opera Records UORC 141, analog, mono, LP (1972)
Recorded Apr 22, 1939.
"World premiere broadcast."
"Private record, not for sale."

SELECTIONS

*Overture*

W64.21    Radio-Torino Orchestra; Alfredo Simonetti, cond.
P. CB 20502.

*What a Curse for a Women Is a Timid Man*

W64.22    Dawn Upshaw, soprano; Orchestra of St. Luke's; David Zinman, cond.
Elektra/Asylum/Nonesuch 79187, 9 79187, analog, digital, LP; 79187-2, 9 79187-2, digital, stereo., compact disc (1989)
Recorded Aug 1988 at Manhattan Center Studios, New York City.
With works by Barber, Harbison, and Stravinsky.

♦ SELECTED RECORDING REVIEWS

W64.23   Todd, Arthur. "Theatre on the Disc." *Theatre Arts* 36 (June 1952): 6-7.
Brief review of then-recent recordings of *Amahl and the Night Visitors, The Medium, The Telephone, The Consul, Sebastian, Amelia al ballo,* and *The Old Maid and the Thief.*

W64.24   Kolodin, Irving. "Recordings in Review: Menotti's 'Old Maid.'" *Saturday Review* 53 (December 26, 1970): 42-43.
Review of the Mercury stereo SR 90521 recording. "The articulation of the text is particularly good, and eloquent evidence of the skill with which words and music are joined."

W64.25   Miller, Karl. "Barber: Knoxville: Summer of 1915." *American Record Guide* 52 (November-December 1989): 32-33.
Review of the Nonesuch 79187 (WEA) recording. "The Stravinsky and Menotti arias further demonstrate the versatility and intelligence of this remarkable performer. She [Dawn Upshaw] brings power and depth to her interpretations."

W64.26   Simmons, Walter. "Barber: Knoxville — Summer of 1915. Harbison: Mirabai Songs. Stravinsky: The Rake's Progress: Excerpts. Menotti: The Old Maid and the Thief: Excerpt." *Fanfare* 14 (March-April 1991): 445.
Review of the Elektra Nonesuch 9 79187-2 [DDD] recording. " . . . a thoroughly delightful yet uncompromisingly artistic assemblage of twentieth-century American vocal music . . . deserves to be more widely known, as it represents the composer at his most gorgeously lyrical and romantic."

*W65*   **PASTORALE AND DANCE FOR STRINGS AND PIANO**
(1933; G. Schirmer; 8 min.)

pf/str

♦ SELECTED PERFORMANCES

W65.1   1934 (Jan 4): Vienna; Menotti's and Samuel Barber's studio; Edith Evans Braun, piano; Samuel Barber, cond. (private performance)

236  Works and Performances

W65.2   1934: Vienna; Menotti's and Samuel Barber's studio; Edith Evans Braun, piano; Carl Bamberger, cond. (first public performance)

W65.3   1935 (Mar 20): Philadelphia; Menotti, piano; Fabien Sevitzky, cond.; Philadelphia Chamber String Sinfonietta.

**W66**   *PIANO CONCERTO IN F MAJOR* (1945; G. Ricordi; 30 min.)
In three movements.

### ♦ ABOUT THE WORK

W66.1   Bales, Richard. "Gian Carlo Menotti's Concerto in Fa per Pianoforte e Orchestra." *Notes* (Music Library Association) 10 (September 1953): 676.
Review of the Ricordi two-piano score. ". . . one hopes that its value as a highly enjoyable display piece might give some of its older relatives in this form a well-deserved grazing period in that part of the field reserved for 'war horse' concertos!"

W66.2   Hanson, John Robert. "Macroform in Selected Twentieth-century Piano Concertos." Ph.D. dissertation, Eastman School of Music, University of Rochester, 1969.
Analyses in diagram form of 33 piano concertos, including that of Menotti.

### ♦ SELECTED PERFORMANCES

W66.3   1945 (Nov 2): Boston; Rudolf Firkušný, piano; Richard Burgin, cond.; Boston Symphony Orchestra.

W66.4   1949 (Jan 20): New York; Rudolf Firkušný, piano; Leopold Stokowski, cond.; New York Philharmonic

*Review:*

W66.4a   "Menotti Concerto Premiered." *Musical Courier* 139 (February 15, 1949): 35.
"Firkušný's playing, with its elegance and *brio*, its technical freedom and its singing tone, showed the music in the best possible light."

W66.5 1955 (Mar 13): New York; Carnegie Hall; Leonid Hambro, piano; Leon Barzin, cond.; Symphony of the Air.

*Reviews:*

W66.5a Downes, Olin. "Music: Series is Ended: Symphony of the Air Conducted by Barzin." *New York Times*, (March 14, 1955): 29.
"It is never dull; the composer is never at a loss as to what to do next; but it would gain, particularly in the first movement, by pruning."

W66.5b Barter, Christie. "Barzin Conducts Final Pulitzer Prize Concert." *Musical America* 75 (April 1955): 15.
". . . while it struck this listener as being somewhat overextended, particularly in the opening movement, it radiates throughout the same charm that we associate with the composer's lighter stage works."

W66.6 1997 (Aug): Belfast; Ulster Hall; Philip Martin, piano; Niklas Willen, cond.; Ulster Orchestra (BBC Invitation Concert; on a triple-bill with Puccini's *Preludio sinfonico* and Sibelius' *Lemminkainen Suite)*

*Review:*

W66.6a Gault, Dermot. "Ulster Orchestra/Niklas Willen." *Irish Times*, Arts (August 19, 1997): 6.
"The lush slow movement is worth rescuing from the repetitive allegros that surround it, but Philip Martin played it all with perfect fluency and fine shading."

### ♦ DISCOGRAPHY

W66.7 Yuri Boukoff, piano; Société des concerts du Conservatoire Orchestre; André Cluytens, cond.
La Voce del Padrone QALP 176, analog, mono, LP (195-?)
Recorded at the Théâtre des Champs-Elysées, Paris.

W66.8 Earl Wild, piano; Symphony of the Air; Jorge Mester, cond.
Vanguard VRS-1070, LP, mono; Vanguard VSD 2094 (1961), LP, stereo. ; Vanguard SVC-3 (1995), CD; Vanguard Classics OVC 4029 (1991), CD.
Recorded in 1961.
Series: Landmarks of America series; Vanguard Recordings for the Connoisseur.

"A west projects release."
With Copland's *Concerto for Piano and Orchestra.*

♦ SELECTED RECORDING REVIEWS

W66.9    March, Ivan. "Earl Wild Plays Copland and Menotti." *Gramophone* 69 (February 1992): 98.
Review of the Vanguard 08 4029 reissue. ". . . this is surely a collector's item for those who enjoy second-rate piano concertos . . . The CD transfer is extremely vivid and if the piano is balanced well forward . . . one hardly minds with such brilliant solo playing."

W66.10   Lehman, Mark L. "Copland: Piano Concerto; Menotti: Piano Concerto." *American Record Guide* 58 (July-August 1995): 103.
Review of the Vanguard 3 (Koch) recording, a release in stereo of the 1961 LP. "The music is grand, the recording stunning, and Earl Wild . . . 'terrific.'"

*W67*    *PIANO CONCERTO NO. 2*

Despite the mention of this Concerto in a very few reference sources, apparently the work does not exist. Menotti was commissioned by Miami's New World Festival of the Arts to write his *Second Piano Concerto.* He had been paid $10,000 to composer the concerto, but he subsequently said that he was unable to complete it in time for the June, 1982 performance at the Festival. Therefore, he "regretfully returned the money." *See* Gerald Clarke's article, as reported by Marilyn Alva, entitled "Sweating it Out in Miami," in *Time* 119 (June 28, 1982): 69.

*W68*    *POEMETTI* (1937; G. Ricordi)

Twelve pieces for piano solo dedicated to the memory of Maria Rosa Menotti, Menotti's youngest sister.
Contents: Giga — *Ninna-Nanna* (Lullaby) — Bells at dawn (Alba festiva) — The spinner (La filatrice) — The bagpipers (I zampognari) — The brook (Il ruscello) — The shepherd (Il pastore) — Nocturne (Notturne) — The stranger's dance (Danza dello straniero) — Winter wind (Vento invernale) — The manger (Il presepis) — War song (Canzone guerresca).

### ♦ ABOUT THE WORK

W68.1    Ryan, Sylvia Watkins. "Solo Piano Music of Gian-Carlo Menotti: A Pedagogical and Performance Analysis." D.M.A. dissertation, University of Oklahoma, 1993.
Discusses *Poemetti* (1937), Ricercare and Toccata on a Theme from '*The Old Maid and the Thief*' (1953), and the piano version of *Amahl and the Night Visitors* (1951). This study is intended to serve as a reference work for teachers of contemporary piano literature.

### *W69*    *RICERCARE* (1984; G. Schirmer; 15 min.)

For organ.
Commissioned for the 1984 annual convention of the American Guild of Organists.

### ♦ ABOUT THE WORK

W69.1    Covington, Kate. "Ned Rorem . . . Gian Carl Menotti: *Ricercare for organ* (1984) . . ." *Notes* (Music Library Association) 48 (March 1992): 1102-1104.
Review of the 1990 G. Schirmer (Hal Leonard) score (16 p., Ed. 3803). "Menotti's work as a director, librettist, and composer of operas has established his dramatic skills, and the contrasts in this sectional piece must be thought of as changing scenes with a variety of characters on stage."

### ♦ PREMIERE PERFORMANCE

W69.2    1984 (Jun 28): San Francisco; Grace Cathedral; John Weaver (organ)

*Review:*

W69.2a   Gustafson, Bruce. "AGO San Francisco — Some Perspectives." *Diapason* 75 (October 1984): 6.
". . . successful in translating the composer's lyrical gift to organ without sounding trite."

### *W70*    *RICERCARE AND TOCCATA ON A THEME FROM THE OLD MAID AND THE THIEF* (1951; G. Ricordi)

Piano solo.

Dedicated to Ania Dorfmann.

♦ **PREMIERE PERFORMANCE**

W70.1   1951 (Nov 1): New York; Town Hall; Ania Dorfmann, piano.

*Review:*

W70.1a   Ryan, Sylvia Watkins. "Solo Piano Music of Gian-Carlo Menotti: a Pedagogical and Performance Analysis." D.M.A. dissertation, University of Oklahoma, 1993.
Discusses *Poemetti* (1937), *Ricercare and Toccata on a Theme from 'The Old Maid and the Thief'* (1953), and the piano version of *Amahl and the Night Visitors* (1951). This study is intended to serve as a reference work for teachers of contemporary piano literature.

♦ **DISCOGRAPHY**

W70.2   Michael Boriskin, piano.
New World Records 80402-2. digital, stereo., compact disc (1991)
Recorded at the American Academy and Institute of Arts and Letters Auditorium, New York, Jul 10-12, 1991.
Album title: Works by Irving Fine . . . [et al.]
With works by Shapero, Fine, and Ruggles.

W70.3   Silva Costanzo, piano.
Nuova Era Records 7122. digital, stereo., compact disc (1992)
Series: Icarus
Recorded at Teatro S. Marco, Cologno Monzese and Chiesa Protoromantica di S. Martino in Palazzo Pignano, Cremonia, Mar 18, 19, and 30, 1992.
With *The Telephone* and *Canti della lontananza*.

W70.4   Ania Dorfmann, piano.
RCA Victor LM 1758 (49-4118 — 49-4121), LP, mono. (n.d.)
Album title: An Ania Dorfmann Recital.
With works by Schumann, Mendelssohn, Chopin, Liszt, and Ravel.

W70.5   Raymond Lewenthal, piano.
Westminster XWN 18362 (XTV 25742-25743), LP, mono. (1956)
With works by Schumann, Alkan, Czerny, Della Ciaia, Bach, Prokofiev, Debussy, Ravel, Jelobinsky, and Lewenthal.

W70.6        Ralph Votapek, piano.
             EDUL ED-008, mono, LP (between 1966 and 1969?)
             With works by Haydn and Bartók.

   ♦ SELECTED RECORDING REVIEWS

W70.7        Burwasser, Peter. "Shapero: Piano Sonatas: No. 1; No. 2; No. 3. Fine: Music for Piano. Ruggles: Evocations — Four Chants for Piano. Menotti: Ricercare and Toccata on a Theme from 'The Old Maid and the Thief.'" *Fanfare* 15 (March-April 1992): 405.
             Review of the New World Records 80402-2 recording. ". . . Menotti's characteristically sappy piece . . . Boriskin's playing is essentially faultless."

W70.8        Pincus, Andrew L. "New CDs Offer Short Course in 20th-Century Music." *Berkshire Eagle* (Pittsfield, MA), (April 26, 1992)
             Short review of the New World 80402-2 recording. ". . . Menotti's neo-baroque *Ricercare and Toccata* on a theme from his opera . . . round out an imaginative, satisfying release."


*W71*        *RICERCARE SU NOVE TONI* (1956)

For piano.
Written for mezzo-soprano Marya Freund for her 80th birthday.


*W72*        *THE SAINT OF BLEECKER STREET* (1954; G. Schirmer; evening)

Music drama in three acts with libretto (English) by Menotti; Italian translation by Fedele D'Amico.
Awarded the Pulitzer Prize and the New York Drama Critics Award in 1955.
Cast: S, Mz, Mz, Bar, B; Mz, S, Mz, Bar; SSAATTBB chorus
2+pic.2+ca.2+bcl.2+cbn/4331/timp.3perc/hp.pf/str
Stage music: pic/3tpt.tbn.tba/2perc
*Pierpont Morgan Library* has "full score; the vocal lines and the text (in English and Italian) are in the hand of a copyist. With: the piano-vocal score. 264 p. 34.5 x 27 cm. Incomplete: the last 56 measures of Act I, Scene I, and all of Act II are lacking. Purchased as the gift of Frederick R. Koch." Pagination of the full score: 787 leaves. 51 x 33 cm.

*242  Works and Performances*

## ♦ ABOUT THE WORK

W72.1   Blitzstein, Marc. "Gian-Carlo Menotti: The Saint of Bleecker Street." *Notes* (Music Library Association) 13 (June 1956): 521-523.
Review of the G. Schirmer vocal score. "Menotti is a fiendishly talented music-theater man. But he rarely, if ever, writes about themes which have been his long-time convictions; the convictions grow with the actual working, and may quite possibly fade with a work's completion."

W72.2   Kirstein, Lincoln. "The Future of American Opera." *Atlantic* 199 (March 1957): 50-55.
"The story is more complex than in most successful operas, with meanings on many levels . . . This may indicate how great a range of sentiment exists for operatic use when sentiment is sufficiently invested with passionate vocalism."

W72.3   Barber, Samuel. "On Waiting for a Libretto." *Opera News* 22 (January 27, 1958): 4-6.
Says Barber, ". . . I could immediately understand and appreciate the economy of Menotti's use of words, so necessary for the singing stage; their utter simplicity . . . and his sense of theatrical timing, which seems to me indeed unique."

W72.4   "Menotti Plans for Spoleto." *Times* (London), (February 8, 1968): 7.
Until now, Menotti " . . . had kept his own work out of the Spoleto Festival in order to avoid accusations of using it to sell his own wares. But now that he was no longer artistic director he had agreed to direct two operas — his *The Saint of Bleecker Street* and Wagner's *Tristan and Isolde.*"

W72.5   Gruen, John. "'Saint' — An Opera That Mirrors Menotti's Soul." New York Times, 2 (April 16, 1978): 17.
Adaptation of Chapter 12 of Gruen's then-forthcoming biography of Menotti. "Looking back on 'The Saint,' Mr. Menotti maintained that the work somehow pinpointed the psychological and religious ambiguities that had always dwelled within him." Menotti remarks: "The opera symbolizes my own inner conflict — the split in my personality. . ."

W72.6   Kerman, Joseph. *Opera as Drama.* Berkeley: University of California Press, 1988.

"Menotti is a sensationalist in the old style, and in fact a weak one, diluting the faults of Strauss and Puccini with none of their fugitive virtues." (p. 264)

### ◆ SELECTED PERFORMANCES

W72.7   1954 (Dec 27): New York; Broadway Theatre; Thomas Schippers, cond.; Equinox Symphony; with Catherine Akos (Assunta), Maria di Gerlando (Carmela), Maria Marlo (Maria Corona), Ernesto Gonzales (Maria Corona's Son), Leon Lishner (Don Marco), Virginia Copeland/Gabriella Ruggiero (Annina), David Poleri/Davis Cunningham (Michele), Gloria Lane (Desideria), David Aiken (Salvatore), and Lucy Becque (Concettina)

*Reviews:*

W72.7a   "New Menotti Opera Nears Completion." Symphony 8 (June 1954): 6.

W72.7b   Kirstein, Lincoln. "Menotti: The Giants in Bleecker Street." *Center, a Magazine of the Performing Arts* 1 (December 1954): 3-8.

W72.7c   "Saint's Song." *Vogue* 124 (December 1954): 114-115.

W72.7d   "Saint of Bleecker Street." *Variety* 197 (December 29, 1954): 48.
"Although some stray ends dangle in the libretto . . . Menotti has successfully married dramatic music to dramatic action. To the solid merits of score and script he has added sheer loving care in production."

W72.7e   "Mr. Menotti's New Opera." *Times* (London), (December 30, 1954): 3.
". . . the whole company, trained under the composer's direction, sings and acts . . . with something of his acute awareness of the life and problems, above all the humanity, of his fellow beings."

W72.7f   Cowles, Chandler. "Broadway Bailiwick for Opera." *Theatre Arts* 39 (January 1955): 72-73.
"The most significant contribution in reviving popular interest in opera has come from the N.B.C. 'Television Opera Theatre' . . . I believe this venture has done more for the cause in five years than all of the American repertory companies have been able to do in fifty."

*244   Works and Performances*

W72.7g    Atkinson, Brooks. "'Bleecker Street': Menotti's Opera About a Neighborhood Saint." *New York Times*, 2 (January 2, 1955): 1.
". . . Nothing put on the Broadway stage this year approaches it for passion and beauty. Mr. Menotti is interested in people, and he writes about them as an accredited member of the human race."

W72.7h    Kolodin, Irving. "Menotti's 'The Saint of Bleecker Street.'" *Saturday Review* 38 (January 8, 1955): 28.
"Whatever may be the eventual judgment . . . it may be endorsed at once as his most ambitious theatrical undertaking to date, and musically his most impressive one."

W72.7i    Sargeant, Winthrop. "Menotti's New Opera." *New Yorker* 30 (January 8, 1955): 74-76.
"Gloria Lane stopped the show in the second act, not only because she is obviously a young singer who has extraordinary dramatic and vocal gifts but also because the role had this earthy reality."

W72.7j    "Saint of Bleecker Street." *Newsweek* 45 (January 10, 1955): 62.
"As a librettist, Menotti is a man of many pedestrian words and very little genuine poetry. Like Tennessee Williams, he is not ashamed to use any device that sacrifices logic in favor of theatrical impact."

W72.7k    "Successful *Saint*." *Time* 65 (January 10, 1955): 42.
The opera " . . . has everything, in fact, except perhaps the ability to make its hearers identify themselves with its characters. It is not so much moving as effective."

W72.7l    Levinger, Henry W. "New York Concert and Opera Beat: Broadway Theatre." *Musical Courier* 151 (January 15, 1955): 13-14.
". . . the initial doubts concerning certain aspects of the new opera were stilled, and things which seemed disturbing at first hearing fell into their right place."

W72.7m   Sabin, Robert. "Menotti's Latest Opera Given Broadway Premiere." *Musical America* 75 (January 15, 1955): 3.
". . . an experience that no one should miss. It is a pastiche, but a pastiche of enormous talent and theatrical magic."

W72.7n    Lewis, Theophilus. "Theatre: The Saint of Bleecker Street." *America* 92 (January 22, 1955): 434.

"While Mr. Menotti seems to hog more than his share of credits in the playbill, it must be conceded that he is a sound craftsman in each of the functions he has assumed."

W72.7o   Clurman, Harold. "Theater." *Nation* 180 (January 22, 1955): 83.
"The music generally is easy to listen to: it is (much) lesser Puccini with a sprinkling of other pleasant tidbits in a facile Italianate vein. The voices are admirable and the production is superior."

W72.7p   "Saint of Bleecker Street." *Opera News* 19 (January 24, 1955): 15.
"He has treated his theme with sensitive reverence, contrasted jukebox and plain-song with skillful perception . . ."

W72.7q   Kolodin, Irving. "From 'Amelia' to 'The Saint.'" *Saturday Review* 38 (January 29, 1955): 37.
"Some commentary from the dramatic side has suggested that, whatever Menotti's musical accomplishment, the literary value of the text is undistinguished. Who, it might be asked, quotes Wagner's 'Tristan' text in English II at Radcliffe?"

W72.7r   Zoff, Otto. "'Die Heilige aus der Bleecker Street' in New York uraufgeführt." *Melos* 22 (February 1955): 57-58.

W72.7s   "Heilige von der Bleecker Street." *Musikleben* 8 (February 1955): 59.

W72.7t   S., H. E. "Saint, but No Sinner." *International Musician* 53 (February 1955): 11.
"Even in this opera the birth pangs are apparent. There lacks only one element to bring it to being. Is there, perchance, in this emergency, a librettist in the audience?"

W72.7u   Wyatt, Euphemia Van Rensselaer. "Theater." *Catholic World* 180 (February 1955): 385.
"The whole cast is young and very vital . . . Menotti has breathed life into operatic formalism and lit it with faith."

W72.7v   Hayes, Richard. "Stage: The Saint of Bleecker Street." *Commonweal* 61 (February 4, 1955): 476-477.
" . . . a contemporary document of much energy and some power, imposing itself — in a production of great brilliance and *éclat* — as one of the season's more decisive experiences."

246    Works and Performances

W72.7w    "Saint of Bleecker Street." *Down Beat* 22 (February 9, 1955): 8.
"...opened to the most glowing set of press notices received by any work presented on Broadway this season, and seems certain to take a key place in the frequently performed Menotti repertoire..."

W72.7x    "Saint Sings in Menotti's Best." *Life* 38 (February 14, 1955): 62-63.
"...Menotti has topped his previous successes. Its clashing drama and soaring melodies mark it as the best new opera to be heard in the U.S. since Gershwin's *Porgy and Bess*."

W72.7y    Hijman, Julius. "Menotti's nieuwe opera." *Mens en melodie* 10 (March 1955): 77-79.

W72.7z    "On Broadway: The Saint of Bleecker Street." *Theatre Arts* 39 (March 1955): 17.
Cast, plot synopsis, and photograph from the Broadway Theatre production. "The conflict [is] between a saintly girl and her agnostic brother, which is the principal theme of Menotti's new opera..."

W72.7aa   Mannes, Marya. "Broadway Speculations: II. The Saint and Fry." *Reporter* 12 (April 7, 1955): 40.
"'The Saint' disturbs many of us, not because it makes us think but because it tries to make us feel what we cannot believe... Whatever the reason, a major work of contemporary theater is dying in its feet."

W72.7bb   "New York Drama Critics' Awards." *Times* (London), (April 22, 1955): 17.
On Apr 12, 1955, *The Saint of Bleecker Street* was voted the best musical play of the season.

W72.7cc   "1955 Pulitzer Prizes." *Times* (London), (May 3, 1955): 10.
*The Saint of Bleecker Street* was selected for the music award.

W72.7dd   "New York Award for Agatha Christie." *Times* (London), (May 17, 1955): 3.
On May 15, 1955, Menotti received the New York Drama Critics Circle award for *The Saint of Bleecker Street*, selected as the best musical.

W72.8     1955 (May 8): Milan; La Scala; Thomas Schippers, cond.; with Gabriella Ruggiero (Assunta) and David Poleri (Michele)

Reviews:

W72.8a  Selden-Goth, Gisella. "Italy." *Musical Courier* 151 (June 1955): 25.
". . . bringing finally to the Italo-American composer the overwhelming success which up to now had never been accorded to his previously presented works."

W72.8b  Malipiero, Riccardo. "Milan." *Opera* (England) 6 (July 1955): 451-452.
"It is an ugly score . . . Music for an evening, like newspapers or flashy books which after one reading are of no more interest! . . . The production was good . . . The principal singers . . . sang splendidly."

W72.8c  Seelmann-Eggebert, U. "New Italy in Vecchia Italia (La Scala)." *Musikleben* 8 (September 1955): 325.

W72.9  1956 (Oct 4): BBC telecast; Thomas Schippers, cond.; London Symphony Orchestra; with Virginia Copeland (Annina), Raymond Nilsson (Michele), Rosalind Elias (Desideria), Jess Walters (Don Marco), June Bronhill (Carmela), and also with Janet Howe and Rita McKerrow (first performance in Britain)

Reviews:

W72.9a  "Menotti's Premiere on Television." *Times* (London), (September 21, 1956): 3.
"Although described as a music drama . . . [it] is perhaps rather an opera in the Italian tradition, full of melodious arias and duets, but written in Menotti's vein of realism."

W72.9b  Warrack, Jack. "Television: The Saint of Bleecker Street." *Opera* (England) 7 (November 1956): 703-704.
". . . very soon Menotti's always dominant sense of theatre . . . took charge, and one found oneself caught up in the drama without worrying about the music's eclecticism . . . the opera is a powerful piece of theatre, old fashioned in its ingredients, modern in setting."

W72.10  1962 (Jul 27): Orpington, England; Civic Hall; Kentish Opera Group; Audrey Langford, cond.; with Mary Wells (Annina), John Brooks (Don Marco), Malcolm Robertson (Michele), Moyna Cope (Desideria), and Gillian Verrier (Assunta)

*248  Works and Performances*

Review:

W72.10a  Dunlop, Lionel. "Kentish Opera Group Season." *Opera* (England) 13 (September 1962): 634-636.
"As the protagonist Mary Wells . . . was in splendidly rich voice, and took full advantage of the soaring *cantilena* with thrilling effect. Virtue may be its own reward, but it is rarely rewarding to act."

W72.11  1965 (Mar 18): New York; New York City Opera; Vincent La Selva, cond.; with Muriel Greenspon (Assunta), Joan Sena (Annina), Mary Jennings (Carmela), Anita Darian (Maria Corona), Clyde Ventura (Maria Corona's Son), Beverly Wolff (Desideria), Enrico Di Giuseppe (Michele), and Thomas Paul (Don Marco)

Reviews:

W72.11a  Sargeant, Winthrop. "Musical Events: Callas!" *New Yorker* 41 (March 27, 1965): 171-174.
". . . the music is melodious and gripping, generated by a mind that has shown great courage, in a period of gimmickry, by sticking firmly to an expressive idiom that audiences can understand."

W72.11b  Osborne, Conrad L. "Spring Comes to City Center." *High Fidelity/Musical America* 15 (June 1965): 116-117+.
". . . a taut, propulsive reading, and the principals . . . turned in work of great intensity and impact."

W72.12  1965 (Sep 29): New York; New York City Opera; Vincent La Selva, cond.; with Muriel Greenspon (Assunta), Mary Jennings (Carmela), Anita Darian (Maria Corona), Clyde Ventura (Maria Corona's Son), Malcolm Smith (Don Marco), Julia Migenes (Annina), Harry Theyard (Michele), and Beverly Wolff (Desideria)

W72.13  1969 (Dec 6): Trieste; Maurizio Arena, cond.; with Ana Maria Miranda (Annina), Franco Bonisolli (Michele), Gloria Lane (Desideria), Anna Assandri (Carmela), and Pierre Filippi (Don Marco)

Review:

W72.13a  Bremini, Ireneo. "Trieste." *Opera* (England) 21 (February 1970): 123.
"The production was in the hands of the composer himself who earned rapturous applause."

W72.14   1972 (Sep 22): Kansas City; Lyric Opera of Kansas City; Russell Patterson, cond.; with Joan Patenaude (Annina), Harry Denner (Michele), Karen Altman (Carmela), Eugene Green (Don Marco), Jocelyn Wilkes (Assunta), Joan Caplan (Maria Corona), Dorothy Krabill (Desideria), and Walter Hook (Salvatore).

*Review:*

W72.14a   Haskins, John. "Music in Mid-America." *Kansas City Times* (Kansas City, MO), (September 23, 1972)
". . . musically right and at all times arresting theater."

W72.15   1973 (Feb 22): Baltimore; Baltimore Opera Company; Charles Wendelken-Wilson, cond.; Baltimore Symphony Orchestra; with Patricia Craig (Annina), Nicholas Di Virgilio (Michele), and Ara Berberian (Don Marco)

*Review:*

W72.15a   Galkin, Elliott W. "Baltimore." *Opera News* 37 (April 21, 1973): 27.
"Frequently considered Menotti's most significant accomplishment, *The Saint* received a poignant and powerful production . . ."

W72.16   1976 (Nov 5): New York; Lincoln Center; State Theater; Cal Stewart, cond.; with Catherine Malfitano (Annina), Jeanne Piland (Desideria), Diana Soviero (Carmela), Jane Shaulis (Assunta), Judith De Rosa (Maria Corona), Diana Kehrig (Young woman), Enrico Di Giuseppe (Michele), Irwin Densen (Don Marco), William Ledbetter (Salvatore), Howard Hensel (Young man), Jerold Siena (First Guest), and Alan Baker (Second Guest)

*Reviews:*

W72.16a   Blau, Eleanor. "'Saint' is Back in a New Life." *New York Times*, 3 (November 5, 1976): 5.
Regarding recent tendencies of critics to downgrade his works, Menotti responds: "Only the future will say who is right or wrong . . . My 'Saint' so far . . . enjoys good health and I have a suspicion that it will survive me and my critics."

W72.16b   Hughes, Allen. "Opera: 'Saint of Bleecker Street.'" *New York Times*, (November 6, 1976): 10.

Because Menotti was so faithful to the *verismo* style, the work "has not dated at all, and it seems unlikely that it ever will. As a matter of fact, the older it gets, the less anachronistic it will seem."

W72.16c  Calder, Ethan and Kurt Moses. "Opera Season: Back to Work." *American Record Guide* 40 (December 1976): 57-58.
The opera "virtually made a star of Catherine Malfitano. At all times she sang beautifully — the voice is rich and strong — and she acted with enormous conviction."

W72.17  1976 (Dec 3): San Diego; San Diego Opera; Theo Alcantara, cond.; with Lorna Haywood (Annina), Enrico Di Giuseppe (Michele), Beverly Wolff (Desideria), and Richard Torigi (Don Marco)

*Review:*

W72.17a  Bernheimer, Martin. "San Diego." *Opera* (England) 28 (April 1977): 372.
" . . . singers worked valiantly to lend credibility to the simplistic platitudes imposed upon them."

W72.18  1981 (Oct 24): Providence, RI; Ocean State Performing Arts Center; Providence Opera Theater; Lorenzo Muti, cond.; with Michael Harrison (Michele), Gloria Capone (Annina), Barbara Meistre (Friend), Mary Ann Martini (Desideria), J. Scott Brumit (Don Marco), and Alicia O'Neill (Neighbor Woman)

*Review:*

W72.18a  Safford, Edwin. "Providence." *Opera News* 46 (January 16, 1982): 34.
"On the whole, singers had difficulty projecting the text, a notable exception being Michael Harrison's anguished Michele . . ."

W72.19  1982 (Apr 30): Bristol, England; Victoria Rooms; Bristol Opera Company; David Selwyn, cond.; with Sylvia Griffin (Annina), Clive Watts (Michele), Malcolm Daw (Don Marco), Susan Weaver (Carmela), Daphne Brand (Assunta), and Meirion Ashton (Maria Corona) (first fully-staged performance in Britain)

Review:

W72.19a   Still, Barry. "Saint of Bleecker Street." *Opera* (England) 33 (July 1982): 770-771.
"This was a further milestone in the valued work of the BOC, whose policy is to offer quality productions of works outside the normal professional repertoire."

W72.20   1982 (Nov 10): Bridgeport; Connecticut Grand Opera; Lorenzo Muti, cond.; with Elizabeth Volkman (Annina), Melvyn Poll (Michele), and Rose Marie Freni (Desideria)

Review:

W72.20a   Mott, Gilbert. "Bridgeport." *Opera News* 47 (January 29, 1983): 36.
Menotti's ". . . hand was evident throughout, detailing character, pointing out individuals in the many crowd scenes. Occasionally, however, directorial inventiveness became distracting. The constant passersby drew attention away from the main singers in the San Gennaro scene."

W72.21   1986 (May 23): Charleston, SC; Gaillard Auditorium; Christian Badea, cond.; Spoleto Festival Orchestra U.S.A.; Westminster Cathedral Choir; with Gail Dobish (Annina), Franco Farina (Michele), Leslie Richards (Desideria), Margaret Haggart (Maria Corona), Julien Robbins (Don Marco), Anna Maria Silvestri (Assunta) (Spoleto Festival U.S.A.)

Reviews:

W72.21a   Page, Tim. "Opera: U.S. Spoleto Festival Opens." *New York Times*, 1 (May 25, 1986): 60.
". . . despite its vulgarities, [the opera] remains a convincing opera, written in a manner that is organic, individual, accessible and idiomatic for the voice."

W72.21b   "Passion and Sincerity Shine Through in Opera about the Saint Next Door." *News and Courier* (Charleston, SC), (May 25, 1986)
". . .what gives 'Saint' its real power is the inescapable aura of passion and sincerity, unsullied by any feeling that the composer is cynically striving just for *effect*. . ."

*252 Works and Performances*

W72.21c Starr, William W. "'Saint of Bleecker Street' Delights Spoleto Audience." *State* (Columbia, SC), (May 25, 1986)
"As presented at Spoleto, it is a major 20$^{th}$ century operatic composition, and this production seems likely to be long remembered as the maestro's word on the work."

W72.21d Storrer, William Allin. "Charleston: Spoleto U.S.A., Menotti's Birthday Present." *Opera* (England) 37 (Autumn 1986): 114-115.
"The set appeared too shallow and undifferentiated in level. Though this allowed for quick changes of scene in the first and last acts, the crowding of the chorus was unfortunate."

W72.22 1986 (Jul 7): Spoleto; Tzimon Barto, cond.; Spoleto Festival Orchestra; Westminster Cathedral Choir; with Adriana Morelli (Annina), Richard Burke (Michele), Antonia Brown (Carmela), Graziella Bondini (Assunta), Margaret Haggart (Maria Corona), Gabriele Monici (Don Marco), Giorgio Gatti (Salvatore), and Adriana Cicogna (Desideria) (performed in Italian translation by Fedele D'Amico; 29$^{th}$ Festival of Two Worlds)

*Review:*

W72.22a Bellingardi, Luigi. "Birthday 'Saint.'" *Opera* (England) 37 (Autumn 1986): 105-106.
"There were stirring ovations, and all the later performances, not only the first night, earned a clear-cut success from both public and critics."

W72.23 1989 (Jun 29): New York; New York University; NYU University Theatre; Kurt P. Reimann Opera Studio; Robert Wallace, cond.; with Susan Warren (Annina), Carol Andrews (Desideria), Brannon Hall-Garcia (Don Marco), and Ernesto Zuccarelli (Michele)

*Reviews:*

W72.23a Elliott, Susan. "Stunning Moments in 'The Saint.'" *New York Post*, (July 1, 1989)
Warren was "A committed and highly effective actress, [and] her tone was consistently open and generous, with enough vocal freedom to express any mood, from pensive to frenzied."

W72.23b Pniewski, Tom. "Menotti's 'Saint' Revived in NYU Production." *New York Tribune*, (July 12, 1989)

"Although billed as an 'opera studio,' this was a full and successful presentation, professional in its casting and direction, and an achievement to be proud of . . ."

W72.24   1989 (Nov 20): Philadelphia; Academy of Music; Opera Company of Philadelphia; Steven Mercurio, cond.; with Adriana Vanelli (Annina), Franco Fabrina (Michele), Jody Kidwell (Desideria, replacing Victoria Vergera), Joseph Rouleau (Don Marco), Randi Marrazzo (Carmela), and Susan Shafer (Maria Corona) (co-produced with Spoleto Festival U.S.A.)

Reviews:

W72.24a  Valdes, Lesley. "OCP Pulls out Stops in Menotti's 'Saint.'" *Philadelphia Inquirer,* (November 22, 1989)
"Although the ensemble is not without its flaws — vocal refinement being the primary lack — it functions more often than not as a unit, which is much to its credit."

W72.24b  Baxter, Robert. "Philadelphia." *Opera News* 54 (February 17, 1990): 46-47.
"Steven Mercurio shaped a powerful musical performance, his incisive baton drawing disciplined playing from the orchestra and impassioned singing from principals and chorus."

W72.24c  Baxter, Robert. "Philadelphia." *Opera* (England) 41 (March 1990): 308-309.
"The production . . . carried the stamp of authenticity through the composer's gritty, gutsy staging."

W72.25   1991 (Jan 19): Washington, DC; John F. Kennedy Center for the Performing Arts; Washington Opera; Stephen Crout Chorus; Steven Mercurio, cond.; with Maryanne Telese (Annina), Michael Myers/Don Bernardini (Michele), Gail Dobish (Carmela), Leslie Richards (Desideria), John Stephens (Don Marco), and Daniel Narducci (Salvatore)

Reviews:

W72.25a  Holland, Bernard. "Honoring the Two M's (Mozart and Menotti)." *New York Times*, (January 22, 1991): C16.
"The music is unremarkable but it suits the voice. It knows just when climaxes will work, and every time we drop our guard, its sentimentality bores in."

254  Works and Performances

W72.25b  Dolmetsch, Carl. "Washington Opera." *Opera Canada* 32, 2 (1991): 40-41.
"As for one who saw the 1954 Broadway premiere of this undeservedly neglected work, arguably Menotti's best score to date, I found the Washington revival every bit as good as the original . . . and . . . somewhat better."

W72.25c  Jahant, Charles. "Washington, D.C." *Opera News* 55 (June 1991): 45.
The opera ". . . is difficult to stage convincingly, but . . . emerged as the well-thought-through piece it is. The best characterization . . . came from Leslie Richards as Desideria . . ."

W72.26  1991 (Sep 21): Fort Lauderdale, FL; Broward Center for the Performing Arts; Fort Lauderdale Opera; Steven Mercurio, cond.; Florida Philharmonic; with Maryanne Telese (Annina), Allan Glassman (Michele), John Stephens (Don Marco), Suzanna Guzman (Desideria), Eugenie Grunewald (Assunta), Susan Shafer (Maria Corona), Marie Caruso (Carmela), and Virginia Browning (Young Woman)

*Reviews:*

W72.26a  Roos, James. "*Saint* Hits All the Right Notes: Both Opera and House Outstanding." *Miami Herald*, (September 23, 1991)
". . . the production was so outstanding that, in the best of all possible worlds, it would have settled down for a long and lustrous run."

W72.26b  Smith, Tim. "Fort Lauderdale." *Opera News* 56 (December 7, 1991): 64.
". . . the young company can take credit for one of the most satisfying, enriching opera experiences in south Florida in the past ten years."

### ♦ DISCOGRAPHY

W72.27  Gabriella Ruggiero (Annina), Maria di Gerlando (Carmela), Maria Marlo (Maria Corona), Lucy Becque, Elizabeth Carron, Gloria Lane (Desideria), Catherine Akos (Assunta), David Poleri (Michele), David Aiken (Salvatore), Russell Goodwin, John Reardon, Leon Lishner (Don Marco), and also with Ernesto Gonzales, Keith Kaldenberg, R. Cassilly; Orchestra and chorus conducted by Thomas Schippers.
RCA Victor LM 6032, 2 discs, LP, analog, stereo. (1955); RCA Red Seal CBM 2-2714, 2 discs, LP, mono. (1978)
Recorded under the direction of the composer.

### ♦ SELECTED RECORDING REVIEWS

W72.28 Watt, Douglas. "Musical Events: Concert Records." *New Yorker* 31 (June 4, 1955): 100.
Review of the Victor recording, " . . . which was made under the composer's supervision, is excellently conducted by Thomas Schippers and is sung with great conviction . . ."

W72.29 Kresh, Paul. "The Saint of Bleecker Street." *Stereo Review* 41 (September 1978): 105.
Review of the RCA CBM2-2741 (2 discs) recording, a reissue of the original 1954 recording. "The production, an exceptionally impassioned one, brings out every bit of choral and orchestral color in the score . . . more than welcome in this long-overdue return to the catalog."

W72.30 Harris, Kenn. "Menotti: The Saint of Bleecker Street." *Fanfare* 2 (November-December 1978): 87.
Review of the RCA Victor Red Seal CBM2-2714 (2 discs, mono.) recording. ". . . the members of the original Broadway company performed the thinnish music and weepy drama with great conviction and a high degree of musical style . . . RCA's mono sound is quite decent, although today's techniques might have made Ms. Ruggiero's singing sound smoother."

## *W73  SEBASTIAN* (1944; G. Ricordi)

Ballet in one act and three scenes.

### ♦ SELECTED PERFORMANCES

W73.1  1944 (Oct 31): New York; International Theatre; Alexander Smallens, cond.; with Viola Essen (Courtesan), Kari Karnakoski (Prince), Lisa Maslova (Flora), Yvonne Patterson (Maddalena), Francisco Moncion (Sebastian), Nina Golovina (Fortune Teller), and Jacquelyn Cezanne (Countess)

W73.2  1945 (Aug 8): New York; Lewisohn Stadium; Alexander Smallens, cond.; New York Philharmonic ("Suite" including *Introduzione, Barcarola, Baruffa, Cortège,* and *Pavane*)

*256   Works and Performances*

W73.3   1981 (Dec 13): Philadelphia; Academy of Music; Lorenzo Muti, cond.; Curtis Student Orchestra.

*Review:*

W73.3a   Felton, James. "His Alma Mater Serves up a Weekend-long Menotti Feast." *Evening Bulletin* (Philadelphia), (December 14, 1981)
"The music is unusually robust for Menotti, though it retains his lyrical stamp throughout."

W73.4   1991 (Jun 2): Charleston, SC; Gaillard Auditorium; Spiros Argiris, cond.; Spoleto Festival Orchestra U.S.A. ("Sebastian Suite"; Birthday Gala concert honoring Menotti)

*Review:*

W73.4a   Gudger, William D. "Birthday Treat: Gala Concert Honors Founder of the Festival." *Post-Courier* (Charleston, SC), June 3, 1991: 5A.
"Argiris had prepared a spotless performance."

W73.5   1996 (Feb 22): New York; Lincoln Center; Alice Tully Hall; Dino Anagnost, cond.; Little Orchestra Society ("Ballet Suite" performed on a triple-bill with the *Violin Concerto* and *Landscapes and Remembrances*, in a "Milestone for Menotti" 85th birthday concert)

*Review:*

W73.5a   Dannatt, Adrian. "Classical Milestone for Menotti: Alice Tully Hall, New York." *Independent* (London), Review/Arts (February 28, 1996): 5.
". . . clear kitsch, low-grade film-scoring heavy on the glissandi, but frankly, if the likes of Corigliano or Taverner can garner serious critical attention . . . poor old Menotti's comeback must surely lurk in the wings."

◆ DISCOGRAPHY

*Ballet Suite*

W73.6   London Symphony Orchestra; José Serebrier, cond.
Desto DC 6432, LP, stereo. (1969); Peerless PRCM 202, LP, stereo. (1975); Desto (CMS Records) X46432, 1 cassette, analog, stereo., Dolby (1979?); ASV CD DCA 741, CD, digital, stereo. (1990); Phoenix PHCD 101, CD, digital, analog recording (AAD) (1988)

W73.7   NBC Symphony Orchestra (members); Leopold Stokowski, cond.
RCA Victor LM 1858, mono, LP (1955); CCS-29, 1 sound tape reel, analog, 7½ ips, 4 track, stereo., 7 in. (1955); RCA Victor Red Seal ARL1-2715, stereo., LP (1978); ARK1-2715, 1 cassette, stereo. (1978)
With selections from Prokofiev's *Romeo and Juliet*.

W73.8   New Zealand Symphony Orchestra; Andrew Schenck, cond.
Koch International Classics 2-7005-4, cassette, analog (1990); Koch International Classics 3-7005-2, compact disc, digital, stereo. (1990)
Recorded at Symphony House, Wellington, New Zealand, October 1989.
With selections from *Amahl and the Night Visitors* and *Souvenirs* by Barber.

W73.9   Orchestre symphonique de la R.T.B.F.; Spiros Argiris, cond.
EMS SBCD 6600, compact disc, digital, stereo. (1988)
Recorded at the studios of R.T.B.F. in 1988.
With *Apocalypse*.

W73.10  Robin Hood Dell Orchestra of Philadelphia; Dimitri Mitropoulos, cond.
Columbia MX 278, 2 discs, 78 rpm, mono, 12 in. (1948); Columbia ML 2053, LP, mono (1949)

W73.11  University of Houston Concert Band; James T. Matthews, cond.
F. Colombo BP 107, analog, stereo., LP (1968)
Series: Educational Record Reference Library. Band Program, 7.
With works by H. Smith, W. Benson, N. Long, and Bartók.

W73.12  University of Houston Symphonic Wind Ensemble; James T. Matthews, cond.
Oliver W. Perry [label number unspecified], analog, stereo. (1968)
With work by A. Reed.

*Barcarolle*

W73.13  Boston Pops Orchestra; Arthur Fiedler, cond.
RCA LM 1726.
CBS Records Masterworks MLK 45660, analog, digital, stereo., compact disc.
Album title: Greatest Hits, the Ballet, vol. 3.
Consists of material previously released in 1972 and 1976.
With works by Glazunov, Tchaikovsky, Chopin, Delibes, and Falla.

### ♦ SELECTED RECORDING REVIEWS

W73.14 Todd, Arthur. "Theatre on the Disc." *Theatre Arts* 36 (June 1952): 6-7.
Brief reviews of then-recent recordings of *Amahl and the Night Visitors, The Medium, The Telephone, The Consul, Sebastian, Amelia al ballo,* and *The Old Maid and the Thief.*

W73.15 Ditsky, John. "Menotti: Sebastian — Ballet; Luening: Lyric Scene for Flute and Strings; Legend, for Oboe and Strings." *Fanfare* 13 (November-December 1989): 281.
Brief review of the Phoenix PHCD 101 recording; distributed by Allegro; CD transfer of the earlier Desto LP) ". . . whatever its merits as a ballet, [*Sebastian*] is a lovely score that reminds one of Menotti's buddy Barber's *Medea* but for the latter's darkness."

W73.16 Vroon, Donald R. "Menotti: Sebastian Suite." *American Record Guide* 53 (July-August 1990): 71.
Review of the Koch 7005 recording. Sebastian " . . . may have been a fine ballet, but like so many ballets its music doesn't hold up well without the dancing. You probably don't want it complete."

W73.17 Seckerson, Edward. "Barber. Souvenirs, Op. 28 — Ballet Suite. Menotti: Sebastian — Ballet Suite. Amahl and the Night Visitors — Introduction; March; Shepherds' Dance." *Gramophone* 68 (September 1990): 507.
Review of the Koch International Classics 27005-4 (cassette), 37005-2 (compact disc) recording. "It's a slight but useful (meaning versatile) score, blessed with a sweet lyric lilt that simply cries out for body language . . . Decent recording, big-boned and open."

W73.18 North, James H. "Barber: Souvenirs, op. 28. Menotti: Sebastian. Amahl and the Night Visitors: Introduction; March; Shepherd's Dance." *Fanfare* 14 (September-October 1990): 162-163.
Review of the Koch International Classics CD 7005 recording. "At one hearing his [Menotti's] music seems revoltingly saccharine, at another perfectly charming; so it is with his 1944 ballet *Sebastian*."

W73.19 Bookspan, Martin. "The Checkered Life of 'Sebastian.'" *New York Times*, (November 18, 1990): H32.
Review of recording with Andrew Schenck conducting the New Zealand Symphony Orchestra. "The complete score contains stretches of padding that are meaningless without the accompanying stage action . . . It is nevertheless an honest and forthright account of the music."

W73.20 Rothweiler, Kyle. "Menotti: Sebastian." *American Record Guide* 53 (November-December 1990): 80.
Review of the Phoenix 101 (Koch International) recording. ". . . it is a real pleasure to listen to and, as one might expect from this composer, highly dramatic . . . provided you're not itching for meatier musical fare."

W73.21 Saltzman, Eric. "Barber: Souvenirs . . . Menotti: Sebastian, Ballet Suite. Amahl and the Night Visitors. Introduction, March, and Shepherd's Dance." *Stereo Review* 56 (January 1991): 98.
Brief mention of the Koch International Classics 3-7005-2 recording.

W73.22 Grueninger, Walter F. "Barber: Souvenirs and Menotti: Sebastian; Amahl and the Night Visitors." *Consumers' Research Magazine* 74 (February 1991): 43.
Review of recording with the New Zealand Symphony Orchestra under Andrew Schenck. "Totally idiomatic, never over dramatized, delightful playing. Well recorded in Wellington."

W73.23 Dickinson, Peter. "Luening. Legend (1951). Lyric Scene (1958). Menotti. Sebastian — Ballet (1944)." *Gramophone* 68 (May 1991): 2009-2010.
Review of the ASV ZCDCA741, CDDCA741 recording. "The performance is effective and well recorded . . . The gentle lyricism of the 'Barcarolle' and especially the final 'Pavane' shows Menotti at his best — no histrionics, no sentimentality, just natural melody."

W73.24 Herman, Justin. "Menotti: Sebastian." *American Record Guide* 54 (July-August 1991): 88.
Review of the Harmonia Mundi USA ASV 741 recording. This is a reissue of a reissue from Desto/CRI LP; the same tapes were released and are still available on Phoenix 101. "The suite contains almost half the complete score, but is missing some vintage romantic Menotti . . . highly enjoyable and recommendable."

W73.25 Matthews-Walker, Robert. "Menotti: Sebastian — Complete Ballet. Luening: Lyric Scene." *Musical Opinion* 114 (August 1991): 300.
Review of the ASV CD DCA 741 recording. "This is an album for those who enjoy investigating the byways of music: if it appeals to you I can virtually guarantee you will not be disappointed . . ."

*W74   THE SINGING CHILD* (1993; G. Schirmer; 30 min.)

Opera in one act with libretto (English) by Menotti.
Cast: 2 boy S, S, S, Bar, Mz, T
1111/1100/perc/pf/str

◆ SELECTED PERFORMANCES

W74.1   1993 (May 31): Charleston, SC; College of Charleston; Albert Simons Center for the Arts; Federico Cortese, cond. New Jersey's American Boychoir; with William Cole (Jeremy), Harold Haughton (Singing child), Ana Maria Martinez (Mother), Eric McClusky (Father), Maria Fenty (Miss Plotts), and Alan Fischer (Doctor) (on a double-bill with Zemlinsky's *The Birthday of the Infanta;* Spoleto Festival U.S.A.)

*Reviews:*

W74.1a  Storrer, William Allin. "Spoleto U.S.A.: Gentrified." *Opera* (England), Festival issue (1993): 25-26.
"In melodic invention it is Puccini-esque Menotti at his best, and evidence that age has only ripened the master's touch."

W74.1b  "Menotti's Opera House in the Stables." *World Monitor* 6, 3 (March 1993): 8.
Discusses how Menotti is planning to convert a 19th-century stable block into a $14.2 million opera house on his 18-acre estate outside of Edinburgh and how he wrote the new children's opera *The Singing Child* for a premiere at the Spoleto Festival U.S.A. in Charleston.

W74.1c  Rossi, Nick. "Charleston, SC — Spoleto U.S.A.: Menotti, *The Singing Child.* Zemlinsky, *The Birthday of the Infanta.*" *American Record Guide* 56 (September-October 1993): 54-55.
"The boys who sang these parts, William Cole as Jeremy and Harold Haughton . . . as the singing child . . . were outstanding, their voices beautiful of timbre . . . their intonation near-perfect, their acting professional and convincing in every way."

W74.1d  Rossi, Nick. "World Report: Charleston." *Opera Canada* 34 (Fall 1993): 27.
"The two boys . . . were outstanding, their voices beautiful of timbre (especially Haughton's), their intonation near-perfect and their acting both professional and convincing."

W74.1e Halperin, Carl J. "Charleston, South Carolina." *Opera News* 58 (November 1993): 50-51.
"Menotti staged his piece at the College of Charleston from the child's point of view that all adults are caricatures of themselves."

## W75   *SIX COMPOSITIONS FOR CARILLON* (1931-32; G. Schirmer)

Composed 1931-32 at Mountain Lake, Florida, while Menotti was studying the carillon with Anton Brees, carillonneur at Mountain Lake Singing Tower.
Movements: Preludio — Arabesque — Dialogue — Pastorale — Canzone — Etude (this last movement was originally called "Intermezzo"; *see W39*)
*Curtis Institute of Music* has holograph in ink of "Intermezzo" ([2] p. of music ; 35 cm.)

### ♦ SELECTED PERFORMANCES

W75.1   1932 (Oct 16-Nov 8): Richmond; Virginia War Memorial; Anton Brees, carillonneur (Brees performed "Etude" on Oct 16, "Preludio" on Oct 23, "Canzone" on Nov 1, "Dialogue" on Nov 6, and "Pastorale" on Nov 8, 1932; there is no evidence that Brees performed "Arabesque")

W75.2   1954 (Aug 5): Ann Arbor; University of Michigan; Percival Price, University Carillonneur (earliest known performance of all six pieces on one recital)

W75.3   1931 (Apr 4): Lake Wales, FL; Bok Singing Tower; Anton Brees, carillonneur (private performance for Mary Louise Curtis Bok, Curtis Bok, Rosario Scalero, and friends) (only "Intermezzo," later renamed "Etude")

W75.4   1934 (Jan 27): Lake Wales, FL; Bok Singing Tower; Anton Brees, carillonneur (Brees performed this 88 times from 1934-66) ("Etude" only)

W75.5   1997 (Feb 21): Lake Wales, FL; Bok Singing Tower; William De Turk, carillonneur (on the occasion of the Bok Tower Gardens' 12th International Carillon Festival)

W75.6   1997 (Jun 5): Lawrence; University of Kansas; William De Turk, carillonneur (on the occasion of the 55th Congress of The Guild of Carillonneurs in North America)

**W76   A SONG OF HOPE (AN OLD MAN'S SOLILOQUY)** (1980; G. Schirmer; 10 min.)

For baritone, chorus, and orchestra.
Baritone; chorus; 2+pic.2+ca.2+bcl.2/4331/timp.perc.xyl/hp.pf/str

♦ PREMIERE PERFORMANCE

W76.1   1980 (Apr 25): Ann Arbor; University of Michigan; Hill Auditorium; Stanisław Skrowaczewski, cond.; Philadelphia Orchestra and University of Michigan Choral Union; with Leslie Guinn (baritone)

**W77   SUITE FOR TWO VIOLONCELLOS AND PIANO** (1973; G. Schirmer; 20 min.)

♦ SELECTED PERFORMANCES

W77.1   1973 (May 20): New York; Lincoln Center; Alice Tully Hall; with Gregor Piatigorsky and Leslie Parnas (violoncellos), and Charles Wadsworth (piano)

*Review:*

W77.1a   Hiemenz, Jack. "CMS: Piatigorsky Gala." *High Fidelity/Musical America* 23 (August 1973): MA14-15.
The work " . . . kept within conventional tonal bounds. This twenty-minute piece involved its unusual instrumental combinations with cunning variety . . ."

W77.2   1986 (Dec 13): Brooklyn; Brooklyn Academy of Music; Carter Brey (violoncello) and Jean-Yves Thibaudet (piano)

*Review:*

W77.2a   Crutchfield, Will. "Music: Menotti Program." *New York Times*, 3 (December 15, 1986): 22.
Menotti's " . . . chamber music, though not questing or gripping, has been sensitively conceived, and skillfully and affectionately carried out . . ."

♦ DISCOGRAPHY

W77.3   Denis Brott and Evan Drachman, violoncellos; Samuel Sanders, piano. Mastersound DFCDI 013, digital, stereo., compact disc, 1990.
Album title: Homage to Piatigorsky.
With works by Piatigorsky, Beglarian, and Haydn.

**W78   *SYMPHONY NO. 1 IN A MINOR ("THE HALCYON")*** (1976; G. Schirmer; 30 min.)

Commissioned by the Saratoga Performing Arts Center Board of Trustees.
2+pic.2+ca.2+bcl.2/4231/timp.perc/hp.pf/str

♦ PREMIERE PERFORMANCE

W78.1   1976 (Aug 4): Saratoga, NY; Saratoga Spa State Park; Saratoga Performing Arts Center; Eugene Ormandy, cond.; Philadelphia Orchestra (Saratoga Springs Festival)

*Review:*

W78.1a   Fleming, Shirley. "Notes: a Summer of Premieres for Menotti." *New York Times*, sect. 2 (May 9, 1976): 17.
Says Menotti, "Why has it taken me so long to write a symphony? Well, everyone kept commissioning operas, and I had a lot to get off my chest. Now my theatrical obsessions are gone. After one more work I'm through with the theater."

W78.1b   Malitz, Nancy. "Phila. Orch.: Menotti Premiere." *High Fidelity/Musical America* 26 (November 1976): MA26-27.
"The Philadelphia Orchestra gave its finest support to the argument, but for stimulating vocabulary, progressive syntax, and dramatic thrust, *The Halcyon* lost its case . . ."

**W79   *TAMU-TAMU (THE GUESTS)*** (1973; G. Schirmer; 75 min.)

Chamber opera in two acts for nine singers and two nonsingers with libretto (English and Indonesian) by Menotti.
Commissioned by the Ninth International Congress on Anthropological and Ethnological Sciences, for their Chicago conference on the subject of "Man, One Species, Many Cultures."

Cast: high Bar, 2 S, Mz, Bar, child S, T, 7 silent roles
1010/1100/timp.2perc/pf.hp/3vn.3vc.db

### ♦ ABOUT THE WORK

W79.1 "Menotti Composes for the Sciences." *New York Times*, (August 3, 1973): 17.
Menotti believes that "music should be taken out of the connoisseurs' hothouses and brought back into the open air."

### ♦ SELECTED PERFORMANCES

W79.2 1973 (Sep 5): Chicago; Studebaker Theater; Christopher Keene, cond.; with Robert J. Manzari (Husband), Sylvia Davis (Wife), Sung Sook Lee (Radna), Theresa Teng Chen (Nenek), Sung Kil Kim (Anonto), Sumiko Murashima (Indra), Ferlina Newyanti Darmodihardjo (Solema), Joseph Hutagalung (Kakek), Horas Hutagalung (Djoko), Douglas Perry (Doctor), Samuel Terry (Priest), and Michael Takada and Damon Ho (Soldiers and Assistant Priests)

*Reviews:*

W79.2a "Menotti's 'Tamu-Tamu' is Cheered in Chicago." *New York Times*, (September 7, 1973): 43.
"The performance brought the opening night audience of about 1,000 people to its feet to cheer the composer and the cast, but it was less enthusiastically received by local music critics."

W79.2b Jacobi, Peter P. "Menotti's . . . 'Tamu-Tamu' — Not 'Aida,' But . . ." *Christian Science Monitor*, (September 8, 1973): 16.
"Menotti obviously feels for the have-nots. His Eastern characters — singing in Indonesian — are warm and gentle and grateful for small things. They are the life of the opera. Menotti's Americans are banal, plastic, even embarrassing to look upon."

W79.2c Davis, Peter G. "Menotti's Hard Blow to the Gut." *New York Times*, 2 (September 16, 1973): 17.
" . . . it is a vulnerable piece, easily dismissed by those who dislike having their emotions manipulated so flagrantly. Still, it does 'work,' one is engaged after a fashion, and audiences are going to love it."

W79.2d Kroll, Jack. "Anthroperalogy." *Newsweek* 82 (September 17, 1973): 90.
"The anthropologists delighted in the opera. Margaret Mead called it 'a beautiful, magnificent thing' and added, 'What's really important is that this opera was commissioned by scientists.'"

W79.2e "Menotti's 'Tamu-Tamu' Jarring to Scientists Who Commissioned It." *Variety* 272 (September 19, 1973): 42.
" . . . not Menotti's finest operatic hour . . . but it is undeniably a compelling work that deserves to survive its tepid premiere reception."

W79.2f Monson, Karen. "Opera Circuit: Chicago Menotti Premiere." *High Fidelity/Musical America* 23 (December 1973): MA16+.
"The score holds a few attractive melodies, but the strength of *Tamu-Tamu* rests in the shock value of a series of ultra-theatrical tableaux. Between these moments of effect, Menotti has allowed mundane silliness to undermine his essential seriousness . . ."

W79.2g Covello, Richard. "Chicago." *Opera Canada* 14, 4 (1973): 27-28.
"Ironically, the one effective moment of *Tamu-Tamu* comes at the very end when the husband and wife exchange exactly one line of spoken dialogue, and the curtain falls."

W79.2h Freeman, John W. "Dagli Stati Uniti." *Nuova rivista musicale italiana* 7 (July-December 1974): 472-474.

W79.2i "'Tamu-Tamu': Gian Carlo Menotti." *Pan Pipes of Sigma Alpha Iota* 66 (March 1974): 6.
"The chamber opera is sung part in Indonesian, and Menotti had to learn to master a completely alien language within a single year. The cast proved to be excellent singing actors."

W79.2j Dettmer, Roger. "Chicago." *Opera* (England) 25 (January 1974): 35-38.
" . . . forced one finally to conclude that scientists are innocent of art in their time; at best, backward-looking and label-seeking."

W79.2k McDaniel, Charles-Gene. "An Opera for Today." *Progressive* 38 (January 1974): 52-53.
"The music is neither *avant garde* nor strictly traditional. Menotti has woven Oriental themes into the music, melding the score and the libretto in a way the two cultures could not be . . . it's not an opera one wants to forget."

W79.21 "Opera from Coast to Coast." *International Musician* 72 (February 1974): 13.

W79.3 1974 (Jun 29): Spoleto; Teatro Caio Melisso; John Mauceri, cond.; with Sylvia Davis (Wife), Sung Sook Lee (Radna), Sung Kil Kim (Anonto), Sumiko Murashima (Indra), and Theresa Teng Chen (Nenek) (first European performance)

*Reviews:*

W79.3a Bellingardi, Luigi. "Da Spoleto." *Nuova rivista musicale italiana* 8 (July-September 1974): 406-410.

W79.3b Weaver, William. "Spoleto: Polanski's 'Lulu.'" *Opera* (England) 25 (Autumn 1974): 96-97.
" . . . all the singers were good. In fact, the opera could hardly have been more favourably presented . . . The music itself was the only problem: sometimes touching, but, more often, rhetorical."

W79.3c Kessler, Giovanna. "Nicht nur für die Elite: Puccini, Menotti- und Salieri-Premieren in Spoleto." *Opernwelt* (October 1974): 20-21.

W79.3d Weaver, William. "Spoleto." *Opera News* 39 (October 1974): 58-59.
" . . . all of them singing and acting well . . . As in the U.S., the opera received mixed notices."

W79.4 1987 (Apr 14): New York; Juilliard American Opera Center; Mark Stringer, cond.; with Stephen Biggers (Mr. Hudson), and also with Renee Fleming, Young Ok Shin, Peiwen Chao, Kewei Wang, and Mi-Hae Park (on a double-bill with *Amelia al ballo*)

*Reviews:*

W79.4a Waleson, Heidi. "Contemporary Political Opera." *Newsday* (Long Island, NY), (April 19, 1987)
Says Menotti, "They wanted me to write a big pageant, about how all races are getting together . . . Well, I don't believe they are . . . It would be better to teach people to be aware of what our neighbors go through, and make them realize how indifferent we really are to the human condition."

W79.4b   Davis, Peter G. "Trivial Pursuits." *New York* 20 (May 11, 1987): 64+.
"... has the artificial heart, mind, and soul of a ... TV sitcom ... an audience has been ill-used and had its time wasted."

W79.4c   Porter, Andrew. "Big and Small in New York." *Opera* (England) 38 (August 1987): 864.
"Menotti's generous heart was in the right place, but his words and his notes are cheap, wretched."

## W80   *THE TELEPHONE, OR L'AMOUR À TROIS* (1947; G. Schirmer; 20 min.)

Opera buffa in one act with libretto (English) by Menotti.
Cast: S, Bar
1111/1100/perc/pf/str
*The Stanford University Libraries*, Memorial Library of Music (MLM) has an inscribed copy of the G. Schirmer 1947 vocal score (French version by Léon Kochnitzky), Pl. no. 41735 C, first edition, inscribed for the collection by Menotti. The inscription includes one bar of music from the score.

### ♦ ABOUT THE WORK

W80.1   Brasch, Alfred. "Musik für Zuschauer." *Neue Zeitschrift für Musik* 129 (December 1968): 524.

W80.2   Holden, Randall LeConte, Jr. "Seattle Production of 'The Telephone' by Gian Carlo Menotti." D.M.A. dissertation, University of Washington, 1970.
The first part of the author's work, documenting a production of *The Telephone* prepared under his direction. Includes biographical material, summary analyses of Menotti's style, a catalogue of his operas, and a discussion of directorial challenges and solutions.

W80.3   Peterson, Daniel A. "Reading Bodily Action from the Operatic Score: A New Approach to Operatic Criticism Demonstrated with Reference to Gian-Carlo Menotti's 'The Telephone.'" Ph.D. dissertation, Music, New York University, 1986.
From the author's abstract: "The several plots, themes, and characters of *The Telephone* are enumerated and described, showing many of the complexities of its structure. Eight passages are ... examined for the way the three elements interact in affecting dramatic tension."

W80.4  Kerner, Leighton. "That Was Then." *Opera News* 61 (December 1996): 10-12.

Historical sketch considering the fate of 17 new operas composed in the year beginning July 1946, including *The Telephone*.

W80.5  Honig, Joel. "Is It Curtains For American Chamber Opera?" *Opera News* 62 (August 1997): 10+.

Notes several reasons for the flourishing of chamber opera in America during the 1940s through 1960s when many of the mainstays of this repertoire were composed, including *The Telephone*.

### ♦ SELECTED PERFORMANCES

W80.6  1947 (Feb 18): New York; Heckscher Theater; Ballet Society; Leon Barzin, cond.; with Marilyn Cotlow (Lucy) and Frank Rogier (Ben) (on a double-bill with *The Medium*)

*Reviews:*

W80.6a  "Opera in Small Packages." *Time* 49 (March 3, 1947): 65.

" . . . the music is a briskly running satirical commentary . . . College and small-town music groups could tackle it easily — musically or financially."

W80.6b  "Opera in Embryo." *Newsweek* 29 (March 3, 1947): 76.

" . . . and that's 'The Telephone,' an adequate curtain raiser for 'The Medium' which followed."

W80.6c  Phelan, Kappo. "Stage & Screen: The Medium." *Commonweal* 45 (March 7, 1947): 518.

" . . . a light, fairly amusing satirical stuff . . . on the acting (not singing) end, it seemed stilted . . ."

W80.6d  Smith, Cecil. "Rights of Privacy." *New Republic* 116 (March 10, 1947): 40.

"The music ripples along gayly . . . but in general the score, while good fun, does not appear to be the product of much thought."

W80.6e  Smith, Cecil. "Ventures in Lyric Theatre." *Theatre Arts* 31 (May 1947): 60.

"Despite its outward neatness of form and the spice of the orchestration, the music does not wear an air of importance, for it does not show the considered workmanship which alone can turn a good initial conception into a substantial and durable masterpiece."

W80.6f  Thomson, Virgil. "Farce and Melodrama" *in The Art of Judging Music*, by Virgil Thomson. p. 127-129. New York: A. A. Knopf, 1948.
Reprint of Thomson's Feb 19, 1947 review in the *New York Herald Tribune*. "It is gay and funny and completely humane . . . infused with a straightforward humanity that is a welcome note of sincerity in contemporary operatic composition."

W80.7  1947 (May 1): New York; Ethel Barrymore Theatre; Leon Barzin, cond.; with Marilyn Cotlow (Lucy) and Frank Rogier (Ben)

*Reviews:*

W80.7a  Lardner, John. "Low Crimes and Singing Plays." *New Yorker* 23 (May 10, 1947): 50+.
"In a way, Mr. Menotti may have done himself a poor turn by writing 'The Telephone,' for you cannot miss the thin, pedestrian quality of the talk beneath the trimmings of his music . . ."

W80.7b  Krutch, Joseph Wood. "Drama Note." *Nation* 164 (May 24, 1947): 637.
" . . . merely a curtain-raiser which is hardly more than a superior sort of revue sketch . . ."

W80.7c  Brown, John Mason. "Seeing Things." *Saturday Review of Literature* 30 (May 31, 1947): 22-24.
"In a revue it would have exhausted itself in from three to five minutes . . . This was precisely what it did in opera form, too, only I discovered it also exhausted me."

W80.7d  Wyatt, Euphemia Van Rensselaer. "Drama: National Catholic Theater Conference." *Catholic World* 165 (June 1947): 265-266.
"The music is gay and satirical and adds substance to the joke but it seems to lack a lilting melody which would bind it together."

W80.7e  Beyer, William. "The State of the Theater: Drama and Music-Drama." *School and Society* 66 (July 26, 1947): 66.
"The result is an engaging musical apéritif which spreads geniality and whets the appetite, as befits any self-respecting curtain-raiser."

270  *Works and Performances*

W80.7f  Nathan, George Jean. *The Theatre Book of the Year, 1947-1948: a Record and an Interpretation.* p. 3-5. New York: A. A. Knopf, 1948.
" . . . intermittently ingenious in a musical direction . . . but in the aggregate forced, much too long, overdone, and tiresome."

W80.8  1950 (Jul 19): New York; Arena Theatre, formerly a ballroom of the Hotel Edison; with Edith Gordon (Lucy) and Paul King (Ben) (produced by Chandler Cowles and Efrem Zimbalist, Jr., in association with Edith Lutyens; on a double-bill with *The Medium*)

*Reviews:*

W80.8a  Smith, Cecil. "Menotti Double Bill Returns in Arena-Style Production." *Musical America* 70 (August 1950): 17.
" . . . a piece, goodness knows, that is slight enought [sic] under the best of circumstances — was even more pallid because it was poorly sung."

W80.8b  Wyatt, Euphemia Van Rensselaer. "Theater." *Catholic World* 171 (September 1950): 469.
"The musical score has always seemed to me to lack lyrical gaiety or spontaneity, especially in the closing duet but Edith Gordon sings it gracefully."

W80.9  1968 (Nov 6): Hattiesburg; University of Southern Mississippi; School of Fine Arts; Department of Music; Margaret Peden, musical director and accompanist; with Susan McClintock (Lucy) and Robert Moody (Ben) (on a double-bill with *The Old Maid and the Thief*)

W80.10  1971 (Jan 13): Vienna; Wiener Kammeroper; Michael Dittmann, cond.; with Susan Wold (Lucy) and Hans Gunter Regger (Ben) (in a translation by Marcel Prawy; on a double-bill with Poulenc's *La voix humaine*, here *Die menschliche Stimme*)

*Review:*

W80.10a  Heller, Elisabeth. "Telephongespräche in der Wiener Kammeroper." *Österreichische Musikzeitschrift* 26 (February 1971): 97-98.

W80.11  1975 (Jul 15): Spoleto; Teatro Caio Melisso; Maurizio Rinaldi, cond.; with Mariella Devia (Lucy) and Giorgio Gatti (Ben) (in Italian; on a triple-bill with *The Old Maid and the Thief* and Bizet's *Le Docteur Miracle*)

*Review:*

W80.11a  Blyth, Alan. "Menotti and Spoleto." *Opera* (England) 26 (Autumn 1975): 10-19.
" . . . uncertain treatment from Mariella Devia's thoroughly unsympathetic, vocally and dramatically, Lucy, and Giorgio Gatti's pale Ben."

W80.12  1976 (May 14): Milwaukee; Performing Arts Center; Uihlein Hall; James A. Keeley, cond.; Milwaukee Symphony Orchestra; with Judith Blegen (Lucy) and Gary Kendall (Ben) (on a double-bill with *Landscapes and Remembrances*)

W80.13  1983 (Dec 2): Reykjavik; National Theatre; Icelandic Opera; Marc Tardue, cond.; with Elín Sigurvinsdóttir (Lucy) and John Speight (Ben) (in English; on a double-bill with *The Medium*)

*Review:*

W80.13a  Símonarson, Baldur. "Reykjavik." *Opera* (England) 35 (March 1984): 317.
"The gaudy costumes . . . reflected European preconceptions about Americans in an amusing way."

W80.14  1983 (Dec 19): Washington, DC; John F. Kennedy Center for the Performing Arts; Terrace Theater; Washington Opera; Lorenzo Muti, cond.; with Sheryl Woods (Lucy) and Wayne Turnage (Ben)

W80.15  1984 (Apr 12): Edinburgh; King's Theatre; Washington Opera; Cal Stewart Kellogg, cond.; Scottish Chamber Orchestra; with Sheryl Woods (Lucy) and Wayne Turnage (Ben) (Edinburgh Festival; on a double-bill with *The Medium*)

*Review:*

W80.15a  Monelle, Raymond. "Edinburgh: A Temporary Lull." *Opera* (England) 35 (Autumn 1984): 34-36.
" . . . Turnage . . . was the complete comic, gasping and glowering . . . and Sheryl Woods as the telephone addict was brainless and bewitching . . ."

W80.16    1984 (Nov 18): New York; St. Michael's Church; American Chamber Opera; Douglas Anderson, cond.; with Holly Hall (Lucy) and Michael Kutner (Ben) (Nov 18 was the closing date of the run; on a double-bill with Jack Beeson's *Hello Out There*)

*Review:*

W80.16a   Holland, Bernard. "Opera: New Chamber Group in an American Double Bill." *New York Times*, sect. 3 (November 20, 1984): 16.
" . . . modest production values, some shaky orchestra playing and singing which was usually healthy but sometimes misdirected."

W80.17    1985 (Jan 6): Washington, DC; John F. Kennedy Center Terrace Theater; Washington Opera; with Sheryl Woods (Lucy) and Wayne Turnage (Ben) (Jan 6 was the closing night of the run; on a double-bill with *The Medium*)

*Review:*

W80.17a   Crutchfield, Will. "Washington Opera's Menotti." *New York Times*, 3 (January 8, 1985): 20.
" . . . a period farce that can't be saved because there is nothing funny in it beyond the fact that people now have telephones, and they can interrupt conversations and stave off human contact."

W80.18    1987 (May 9): San Diego; Old Globe Theater; with Amy Burton (Lucy) and Wayne Turnage (Ben) (on a double bill with *The Medium*)

*Review:*

W80.18a   Dierks, Donald. "Globe's Intimacy Adds Greatly to Superb Menotti Productions." *San Diego Union*, (May 11, 1987)
"It seems doubtful that Menotti . . . needed to spend much energy coaching these seasoned pros."

W80.19    1989 (Jan 28): Koblenz, Germany; Eberhard Friedrich, cond.; with Takako Masuda (Lucy) and Michael Hamlett (Bill)

*Review:*

W80.19a   Norquet, Matthias. "Koblenz: Kurzopern." *Opernwelt* 30 (April 1989): 40.

W80.20    1990 (May 19): Glassboro, NJ: Wilson Hall; Donald Portnoy, cond.; with Sandra Ruggles (Lucy) and William Parcher (Ben) (Hollybush Festival; on a double-bill with *The Medium*)

*Review:*

W80.20a   Webster, Daniel. "Menotti Operas 'The Telephone' and 'The Medium.'" *Philadelphia Inquirer*, (May 21, 1990)
"The writing is near-perfect in its concision, and Menotti awarded each of the characters substantial arias."

W80.21    1990 (Dec 4): Florence; Teatro Puccini; Giuseppe Mega, cond.; Maggio Musicale Fiorentino Orchestra; with Alessandra Ruffini (Lucy) and Armando Ariostini (Ben) (in an Italian trans. by Fedele D'Amico)

*Review:*

W80.21a   Budden, Julian. "Florence." *Opera* (England) 42 (March 1991): 337.
". . . mild-flavoured Poulencquerie with Wolf-Ferrari seasoning, all in direct descent from Pergolesi's *La serva padrona* . . ."

W80.22    1991 (Feb 22): Köln, Germany; Musikhochschule; Francis Sippy, cond.; with Sibylle Wolf (Lucy) and Bernd Valentin (Ben)

*Review:*

W80.22a   Hiller, Carl H. "Köln (Musikhochschule): Menotti, 'Das Telefon' und Milhaud 'Der arme Matrose.'" *Opernwelt* 32 (April 1991): 52.

W80.23    1991 (May 29): New York; Bryant Park; Stephen Rogers Radcliffe, cond.; New York Chamber Ensemble; with Jeanne Ommerlé (Lucy) and Richard Holmes (Ben)

*Review:*

W80.23a   Holland, Bernard. "Chamber Ensemble vs. Noise: Music Wins." *New York Times*, (May 31, 1993): 15.
". . . whether it was the weekend slowdown or the placing of the small stage at the east rather than the west end of the park, music held its own against city noise more effectively than I can remember it ever doing so."

*274   Works and Performances*

W80.24   1991 (Nov 7): Sutton, England; Charles Cryer Theatre; Regency Opera; with Lorna Gyton (Lucy) and Fenton Gray (Ben)

*Review:*

W80.24a   Hick, Bryan. :"Recordings and Regency." *Musical Opinion* 115 (February 1992): 75.
" . . . worked admirably in this relaxed setting and Lorna Gyton has both the vocal fluency and subtlety of manner to convey every nuance."

W80.25   1992 (Feb 14): Augusta, GA; Augusta Opera; Ted Taylor, cond.; with Penny Johnson (Lucy) and Charles Huddleston (Ben) (on a double-bill with *The Medium*)

*Review:*

W80.25a   Crook, John. "Telephone." *Opera News* 56 (May 1992): 56.
" . . . this piece is dated and lightweight, even for a curtain-raiser, and ready to be retired to opera workshops."

W80.26   1993 (Apr 30): Fort Worth; Scott Theatre; Fort Worth Opera; John Balme, cond.; with Belinda Thayer Oswald (Lucy) and William Swain (Ben) (on a triple-bill with *Triplo Concerto* and *The Old Maid and the Thief*) (Fort Worth Opera's Menotti Festival)

*Review:*

W80.26a   Maurin, Gaston C. "Fort Worth." *Opera News* 58 (October 1993): 43.
"Sadly, their fine diction was sometimes obscured by an acoustic that favored the orchestra, even in the appropriately intimate Scott Theatre."

W80.27   1996 (Feb 3): Sarasota, FL; David Cohen Hall; with Sarita Roche (Lucy) and Munroe Nelson (Ben) (presented by the Sarasota Music Archive)

W80.28   1996 (Mar 17): Dayton; Dayton Art Institute; Renaissance Auditorium; with Jennifer Layman (Lucy) and Mark Walters (Ben) (Afternoon Musicale series)

W80.29   1996 (Oct 6): Cleveland; Cleveland State University; Drinko Recital Hall, Greg Upton, pianist; with Diane Julin Menges (Lucy) and David Hoffman (Ben)

W80.30   1997 (Mar 2): Penn Hills, PA; Mount Hope Church; Robert Shoup, music director and pianist; with Melanie Vaccarri (Lucy) and Robert Fire (Ben) ("Opera for Opera Haters," the Celebration Series of the Arts program)

Review:

W80.30a   Carlin, Karen. "Audience Comes to Have Fun at 'Opera for Opera Haters.'" *Pittsburgh Post-Gazette*, Metro (March 2, 1997): EW-5.
"Shoup concedes opera can be a hard sell — people can be turned off by the mere mention of an aria . . . The MTV generation, which I'm a part of, is trained to respond to the sound bite, the quick hit . . . We can't pay attention to anything longer than three or four minutes."

W80.31   1997 (Apr 4): Carmichael, CA; La Piccola Scala; Voice Fitness Institute of Sacramento; Gerald Rheault, musical director and pianist; with Linda Stevens/Suzanne Thomas (Lucy) and Bob Raymond/Michael Walker (Ben) (on a double-bill with *The Medium*)

Review:

W80.31a   Glackin, William. "The Memorable Menotti." *Sacramento Bee*, Scene (March 18, 1997): E8.
"Linda Stevens played with a deft sense of humor and sang the role in a strong soprano, extending it a couple of times to shrieks of laugher."

W80.32   1997 (May 13): Wichita; Opera Kansas; Vernon Yenne, cond.; with Karla Hughes (Lucy) and Tracy Herron (Ben) (Wichita River Festival; on a double-bill with Douglas Moore's *Gallantry*)

♦ BRIEFLY NOTED

W80.33   Werker, Gerard. "Utrechtse opera-belevenissen." *Mens en melodie* 7 (January 1952): 7-8. Review of a Utrecht performance ✚ Razboynikov, S. "Tri ednoaktni operi na Sofiyska stsena." *Bulgarska Muzika* 19, 4 (1968): 50-53 ✚ Howe, Richard. "Paris." *Opera* (England) 19 (June 1968): 486. Review of the 1968 Paris production. "Some shouting on the first night indicated that much of the audience had come for more serious purposes. But that's their problem." ✚ Pitt, Charles. "Paris." *Opera* (England) 23 (April 1972): 347. Very brief review of the Paris production. " . . . charmingly sung . . ." ✚ Trilling, Ossia. "Turku: Estonian Visitors." *Opera* (England) 32 (Autumn 1981): 66-67. Brief

review of a Turku performance. " . . . a stylish production . . . [with] an ingenious modernistic interior, dominated by a huge, round mirror-frame downstage, though which the lovers were espied by turns."
✢ Gevisser, Mark. "Music Theater." *Opera News* 53 (August **1988**): 41. The Fifth Annual New Works Festival of T.W.E.E.D. (Theatre-Works: Emerging and Experimental Directions) in New York City included performances of Tom Judson's 'Connor O'John and The Cardinals Confront a Modern Musical Epidemic,' Lynn Standford and Sarah Neece's 'Stations of the Crossed,' and Menotti's 'The Telephone.'

### ♦ DISCOGRAPHY

W80.34    Anne Victoria Banks (Lucy), Gian Luca Ricci (Ben); Orchestra da camera di Milano conducted by Paolo Vaglieri.
Nuova Era Records 7122, CD (1992)
Recorded at Teatro S. Marco, Cologno Monzese (Mi) and Chiesa Protoromanica di S. Martino in Palazzo Pignano, Cremona, Mar 18, 19, 20, 1992.
Series: Icarus.
With *Ricercare and Toccata* and *Canti della lontananza*.

W80.35    Liliane Berton (Lucy), Jean-Christophe Benoit (Ben); Richard Blareau, cond.
RCA France 640.006/7, LP. In French.
With *The Medium*.

W80.36    Marilyn Cotlow (Lucy), Frank Rogier (Ben); Orchestra conducted by Emanuel Balaban.
Columbia SL 154 (ML 4174-4175), ML 4174-4175, OSL-154 (OL 4174-4175); Columbia/Odyssey Y2 35239, Y 35979; CBS M2P 39532; on 3 sides of 2 discs, LP, mono (1949)
Original 1947 performances.
With *The Medium*.

W80.37    Paula Seibel (Lucy), Robert Orth (Ben); Louisville Orchestra; Jorge Mester, cond.
Louisville Orchestra LS-767, LP, stereo. (1979)
With Themmen's *Shelter this Candle from the Wind*.

W80.38    Jeanne Ommerlé (Lucy) and Richard Holmes (Ben); New York Chamber Ensemble; Stephen Rogers Radcliffe, cond.
Albany Records TROY 173, CD (1995)

Album title: Happy Endings.
Recorded May 30-31, 1994, LeFrak Concert Hall, Queens College, Flushing, New York.
With Douglas Moore's *Gallantry* and Hindemith's *Hin und Zuruck*.

### ♦ SELECTED RECORDING REVIEWS

W80.39   Kolodin, Irving. :Murder and Mirth." *Saturday Review of Literature* 31 (January 31, 1948): 44.
Review of the Columbia M726 recording. "Miss Cotlow delivers the music with airy perfection, and with almost total intelligibility. If there is more to ask, I can't imagine what."

W80.40   Todd, Arthur. "Theatre on the Disc." *Theatre Arts* 36 (June 1952): 6-7.
Brief reviews of then-recent recordings of *Amahl, The Medium, The Telephone, The Consul, Sebastian, Amelia al ballo,* and *The Old Maid and the Thief.*

W80.41   Simmons, Walter. "Menotti: *The Medium; The Telephone.*" *Fanfare* 3 (May-June 1980): 107-108.
Review of the Odyssey Y2 35239 (2 discs) recording. " . . . inflated witlessly, and whose stereotyped depiction of a woman would amuse only a restricted group today."

W80.42   Simmons, Walter. "Menotti: The Telephone. Themmen: Shelter This Candle From the Wind." *Fanfare* 3 (May-June 1980): 107-108.
Review of the Louisville LS-767 recording. "The orchestra phrases the twerpy melodies with the most extraordinary finesse, and the soloists, though a bit hammy, sing very nicely."

W80.43   Greene, David Mason. "Menotti: *The Telephone, Ricercare and Toccata on a Theme from The Old Maid and the Thief; Canti della lontananza.*" *American Record Guide* 56 (March-April 1993): 111-112.
Review of the Nuova Era 7122 (Koch) recording. Ricci " . . . alone cannot save the day for this quite mirthless performance. The final chord is cut off in mid-reverberation."

W80.44   McLellan, Joseph. "New Releases: Classical." *Washington Post*, G (January 21, 1996): 11.
Review of the Albany TROY 173 disc. " . . . charming disc . . . and performed in sparkling style by a cast of American singers . . ."

*278 Works and Performances*

**W81    THE TRIAL OF THE GYPSY** (1978; G. Schirmer; 25 min.)

Dramatic cantata in one act with text (English) by Menotti.
Commissioned by the Newark Boys' Chorus.
4 soli (1 major, 3 minor roles); boys' choir; perc[opt]/pf.

### ♦ PREMIERE PERFORMANCE

W81.1    1978 (May 24): New York; Lincoln Center; Alice Tully Hall; Newark Boys' Chorus; Terence Shook, cond.; Barbara J. Chernichowski; piano; with Andre Hardmon (Gypsy) and Ivan Bonilla, James Byrd, and Sean Sirmans (Judges)

*Reviews:*

W81.1a   Hughes, Allen. "Newark Boys Choir Sings New Menotti Opera." *New York Times*, 3 (May 25, 1978): 21.
" . . . an unpretentious and deftly written work that children can perform with ease and understanding and that should delight young audiences who see and hear it."

W81.1b   Porter, Andrew. "Musical Events: Master of All Music." *New Yorker* 54 (June 12, 1978): 103.
"The four anonymous soloists . . . and the chorus were firm and clear. They deserved something better to exercise their talents on."

W81.1c   Jacobs, Arthur. "New York." *Opera* (England) 29 (August 1978): 784+.
" . . . it seems a pale echo of Menotti's real self, a parade of facility and not of inspiration."

W81.1d   "Newark Boys' Chorus: Menotti Prem." *High Fidelity/Musical America* 28 (September 1978): MA18.
"The Newark boys attacked the score with relish and accomplishment, though with no outstanding soloist."


**W82    TRIO FOR A HOUSEWARMING PARTY** (1936)

For piano, cello, and flute.
Written to celebrate Eric Gugler's renovation of the New York City house of Mrs. John Bitter.

♦ PREMIERE PERFORMANCE

W82.1    1936 (Spring): with Menotti, piano, Rohini Coomara, violoncello, and John Bitter, flute.

## W83    TRIO FOR VIOLIN, CLARINET, AND PIANO (1996; G. Schirmer)

♦ SELECTED PERFORMANCES

W83.1    1996 (Jul 17): Spoleto; Verdehr Trio (only the first two movements completed; the third movement was completed in Sep 1996)

*Review:*

W83.1a   McLellan, Joseph. "Verdehr Trio's Rich Rewards." *Washington Post*, Style, C (January 14, 1997): 2.
"Those who know Gian Carlo Menotti's track record on deadlines will not be surprised that he completed only the first and second movements . . . in time for his 85th birthday concert at the Spoleto Festival on July 17. The third movement was not completed until September, and it sounds as though the composer was in a hurry."

W83.2    1996 (Sep 28): East Lansing; Michigan State University; Verdehr Trio (Menotti's 85th birthday celebration)

W83.3    1997 (Jan 12): Washington, DC; National Gallery of Art; Verdehr Trio (performed with Kramer's *Serbelloni Serenade* and Bolcom's *Trio*, as well as arrangements of a Mozart *Sonata for Piano, Four Hands*, and three short pieces by Bruch)

## W84    TRIPLO CONCERTO A TRE (1968; G. Schirmer; 20 min.)

Triple concerto for three concertato groups of solo instruments and orchestra, in three movements.
Commissioned by the Samuel Rubin Foundation.
I: Pf.Hp/Perc II: Ob.Cl.Bn III: Vn.Va.Vc; 2222/2231/timp.perc/hp.pf/str

*280  Works and Performances*

## ♦ SELECTED PERFORMANCES

W84.1   1970 (Oct 6): New York; Carnegie Hall; Leopold Stokowski, cond.; American Symphony Orchestra; with Arthur Krilov (oboe), Joseph Rabbai (clarinet), William Scribner (bassoon), Mary Blankstein (violin), Maxine Johnson (viola), Jascha Silberstein (violoncello), Rex Cooper (piano), Lise Nadeau (harp), and Lawrence Jacobs and Alan Silverman (percussion).

*Reviews:*

W84.1a   Schonberg, Harold C. "Stokowski Conducts Tribute." *New York Times*, (October 8, 1970): 60.
"Nothing here to strain the intellect, and one can make a safe prophecy that the work will soon be in the repertory of symphony orchestras all over the country."

W84.1b   Kolodin, Irving. "Music to My Ears: Cossotto in 'Norma'; Berio, Menotti Revisited." *Saturday Review* 53 (October 24, 1970): 58.
"As often as not, one had to guess at the whole character of the work, for balances were none too good . . . Of course, that is Menotti's penalty for writing music where one may notice such deviations, but he sowed better than he reaped."

W84.1c   Phraner, Leighton. "Carnegie Hall." *Music Journal* 28 (December 1970): 89.
"A welcome and important addition to the ever-narrowing mainstream of palatable new music."

W84.1d   DeRhen, Andrew. "American Symphony: Menotti Premiere." *High Fidelity/Musical America* 21 (January 1971): MA12.
"The intricate scoring . . . suggests the unlikely influence of Elliott Carter, but the music itself . . . is no more harmonically advanced than Prokofiev's *Classical* Symphony."

## ♦ DISCOGRAPHY

W84.2   London Symphony Orchestra; David Amos, cond.
Harmonia Mundi France HMU 906010, CD (1990)
Album title: Modern masters I.
Recorded July 1990, Angel Recording Studios, London.
With works by Rózsa, Gould, and Lavry.

♦ SELECTED RECORDING REVIEWS

W84.3   Seckerson, Edward. "Modern Masters, Volume I." *Gramophone* 69 (July 1991): 74.
Review of the Harmonia Mundi HMU40 6010, HMU90 6010 recording. "Menotti's admirers should make straight for the slow movement . . . where they'll find a very enticing example of his fragrant melodic style . . . I've been moved to repeat the experience several times already."


*L'ULTIMO SELVAGGIO; L'ULTIMO SUPERUOMO* See: Le Dernier Sauvage


W85   THE UNICORN, THE GORGON AND THE MANTICORE (THE THREE SUNDAYS OF A POET) (1956; G. Ricordi)

Madrigal fable for 24-voice chorus, ten dancers, and nine instruments.
The chorus is for SSAATTBB, principally unaccompanied. The orchestration, used principally as interludes to the choral sections, is for flute, oboe, clarinet, bassoon, trumpet, violoncello, double-bass, percussion, and harp.
Commissioned by the Elizabeth Sprague Coolidge Foundation in the Library of Congress.
The *Library of Congress Quarterly Journal of Current Acquisitions*, vol. 15, no. 1 (November, 1957) remarks that this work " . . . is only represented so far by two of the *a cappella* madrigals. The inevitable changes involved in a dramatic presentation have deferred the arrival of the finished autograph until later." Vol. 16, no. 1 (November, 1958) of the same publication mentions the holograph of the "score, chiefly pencil, with the instrumental passages set for piano — a veritable working copy."

♦ ABOUT THE WORK

W85.1   Lowens, Irving. "Current Chronicle: Washington." *Musical Quarterly* 43 (January 1957): 94-97.
General discussion including poetic and textual considerations. "It is a stimulating, attention-gripping work completely free from any suggestion of *Kitsch*. And it is, I believe, an earnest of finer things yet to come from the fertile imagination and keen intelligence of its composer."

W85.2   Levine, Joseph. "Gian Carlo Menotti: The Unicorn, the Gorgon, and the Manticore." *Notes* (Music Library Association) 15 (December 1957): 144-145.
Review of the G. Ricordi piano-vocal score. "Admirers of Gian Carlo Menotti will recognize here the finesse, craftsmanship, and gaiety of his style. One can enjoy his evident delight in compounding note against note to produce a freshly modern counterpart of the renaissance sound-fabric called a madrigal."

W85.3   Bilanchone, Victor, Jr. "'Unicorn, the Gorgon, and the Manticore' by Gian Carlo Menotti: A Study of Twentieth-century Madrigal Fable." D.M.A. dissertation, University of Miami, 1977.
Consideration of the development, stylistic characteristics, and composers of the 16th-century Italian madrigal comedy and its relation to the Menotti work. Rehearsal techniques used by the author are also included.

W85.4   Hopkins, John. "Menotti's Medieval Menagerie . . . Producing the Unicorn, the Gorgon, and the Manticore." *Choral Journal* 26 (December 1985): 21-26.
"The unique combination of the choral and dance mediums, which gives it its charm and freshness, may be the stumbling block for conductors wishing to mount a production. The conductor is given few instructions in the score."

W85.5   Reinthaler, Joan. "A Magical 'Unicorn.'" *Washington Post*, (May 20, 1997): E:.3.

### ♦ PREMIERE PERFORMANCES

W85.6   1956 (Oct 19): Washington, DC; Library of Congress; Coolidge Auditorium; Paul Callaway, cond.; Chamber Chorus of Washington; with Talley Beatty (Unicorn), John Renn (Gorgon), Dorothy Ethridge (Manticore), Swen Swenson (Poet), Loren Hightower (Count), Gemze de Lappe (Countess), John Foster (Doctor), Ethel Martin (Doctor's Wife), Jack Leigh (Mayor), and Lee Becker (Mayor's Wife) (Callaway replaced the previously-announced Thomas Schippers at the last moment; 12th Festival of Chamber Music)

*Reviews:*

W85.6a  "Menotti's Latest Opera." *Times* (London), (May 10, 1956): 3.
Announcement that Menotti's new work, then still unnamed, would have a Washington premiere in October.

W85.6b  Evett, Robert. "Nail Is 'It on the 'Ead, Alors." *New Republic* 135 (October 29, 1956): 23.
" . . . whatever its antecedents, the new work is as original in its conception as it is expert in its execution."

W85.6c  "So Menotti Beguiles." *Newsweek* 48 (November 5, 1956): 79.
" . . . a distinct change of pace, forsaking modern melodrama for a format which the composer compares with a combination of sixteenth-century Italian madrigal and the Japanese Kabuki."

W85.6d  "Madrigal & Mine." *Time* 68 (November 5, 1956): 61.
"As the last note died away, the tough audience . . . leaped to their feet and called for one curtain call after another . . . One critic predicted that the madrigal . . . might be in for a revival."

W85.6e  Schaefer, Theodore. "Menotti's New Chamber Opera Given at Library of Congress." *Musical America* 76 (November 15, 1956): 6.
" . . . the clarity of diction was remarkable, especially considering the brevity of rehearsal time permitted by the composer in his tardy, piecemeal delivery of the score."

W85.6f  Nordlinger, Gerson. "Washington, D.C." *Musical Courier* 154 (November 15, 1956): 21.
"Much of the credit for the great critical and popular success of the work lies with Paul Callaway, who . . . stepped in at the last moment and conducted the performance . . ."

W85.6g  Mellen, Constance. "Beastes Among the Books." *Opera News* 21 (December 3, 1956): 14.
" . . . it is certain that Menotti's lovable bestiary will fast become a popular favorite."

W85.6h  "Twelfth Festival of Chamber Music, Library of Congress. "*Pan Pipes of Sigma Alpha Iota* 49 (January 1957): 15.
" . . . using a small chorus and nine instrumentalists in the pit with the action suggested in the libretto mimed and danced on the stage. For his inspiration Menotti went back to the late 16th century Italian composer Orazio Vecchi."

*284  Works and Performances*

W85.6i  Manville, Stewart R. "Washington." *Opera* (England) 8 (January 1957): 36-37.
"The score captures the essence of the traditional madrigal in a wonderful way. Yet it is somehow thoroughly contemporary, especially in the 'modern' sound of the instrumentation."

W85.7  1957 (Jan 15): New York; City Center; New York City Ballet; Thomas Schippers, cond.; Ballet Society; with Arthur Mitchell (Unicorn), Eugene Tanner (Gorgon), Richard Thomas (Manticore), Nicholas Magallenes (Poet), Roy Tobias (Count), Janet Reed (Countess), Jonathan Watts (Doctor), Lee Becker (Doctor's Wife), John Mandia (Mayor), and Wilma Curley (Mayor's Wife) (preceded by works by Balanchine)

*Reviews:*

W85.7a  Krokover, Rosalyn. "Dance." *Musical Courier* 155 (February 1957): 47.
"The work was superbly produced and performed . . . and the whole thing had a medieval air about it."

W85.7b  Sabin, Robert. "New York City Ballet Gives Menotti Premiere." *Musical America* 77 (February 1957): 218.
" . . . the performance of this curious work was superb in every department. The small chorus . . . sang the difficult music a capella with remarkable clarity, purity of intonation, and expressive resourcefulness."

W85.7c  Kolodin, Irving. "Menotti's Madrigal, Wagner's 'Rheingold.'" *Saturday Review* 40 (February 2, 1957): 27.
"Could it be that Menotti has reached a point where the creation of an entertaining, fanciful trifle isn't enough, that 'significance' must evolve? Better a wholehearted trifle than disjointed symbolism, in this view."

W85.7d  Coleman, Emily. "Prokofieff, Perichole and a Center City Pact: Messrs. Menotti and Rudel to the Fore: The Unicorn, the Gorgon, and the Manticore." *Theatre Arts* 41 (March 1957): 82-83.
"Creations of this sort seldom make engrossing theatre, but *The Unicorn* is superbly and tastefully integrated."

W85.7e  Holde, A. "Randbemerkungen zum New-Yorker Musikleben." *Neue Zeitschrift für Musik* 118 (May 1957): 295.

W85.7f   Glock, W. "Musical Survey." *London Music* 13 (September 1958): 24-25.

### ♦ OTHER SELECTED PERFORMANCES

W85.8    1972 (Apr 29): Cincinnati; Music Hall Auditorium; Thomas Schippers, cond.; Cincinnati Ballet; University of Cincinnati Chamber Choir; Cincinnati Symphony Orchestra; with Sharon Cole (Countess) and Orrin Kayan (Poet) [other roles unspecified in cited reviews]

*Reviews:*

W85.8a   Terry, Walter. "World of Dance." *Saturday Review* 55 (May 27, 1972): 62.
" . . . how marvelous to see total lyric theater in which dance, song, poetry, instruments, acting, staging are one, for 'all remains intact within the poet's heart.'"

W85.9    1981 (Mar 22): Chicago; Cathedral of St. James; William Ferris Chorale (on a double-bill with *The Egg*)

*Review:*

W85.9a   Duffie, Bruce. "Chicago: St. James Cathedral." *Opera Canada* 22, 3 (1981): 36.
" . . . the audience followed the progress and laughed and cried with the composer as he led them through the foibles of life."

W85.10   1983 (Jun 3): Charleston, SC; Dock Street Theater; North Carolina Dance Theater; Joseph Flummerfelt, cond.; Westminster Cathedral Choir; with Richard Prewitt (Man in the Castle) and Edward Campbell (Countess)

*Review:*

W85.10a  "'Unicorn' is 55 Bubbling Minutes." *News and Courier* (Charleston, SC), (June 4, 1983)
"The effect is one of gentle mockery, but the mockery soon sprouts genuine thorns, and the little piece takes on a prickly vitality all its own."

W85.11   1996 (Feb 2): La Jolla; University of California, San Diego; Mandeville Auditorium; California Ballet; David Chase, cond.; La Jolla

*286   Works and Performances*

Civic/University Symphony Orchestra and Chorus; with Manuel Alcantara (Poet), Denise Dabrowski (Unicorn), Yvonne Montelius (Gorgon), and Andrew Manzo (Manticore) (on a program called "Dance, Magic and Madrigal Fables," with Orff's *Carmina Catulli*)

*Reviews:*

W85.11a   Welsh, Anne Marie. "Of Unicorns and Fables Choirs, Symphony to Help Dancers Tell Tales of Love, Woe." *San Diego Union-Tribune*, Night & Day (February 1, 1996): 32.
"Musically, its prototypes are late Renaissance; theatrically, it is hard to pigeonhole . . . it's very challenging, remind me of some Stravinsky like *Histoire du Soldat*."

W85.11b   Welsh, Anne Marie. "They Need a Little More Magic." *San Diego Union-Tribune*, Lifestyle (February 6, 1996): E4.
" . . . the production felt vaguely provincial, a good idea executed by semi-professionals who need to go farther imaginatively."

W85.12   1997 (May 18): Washington, DC; Bradley Hills Presbyterian Church; Sondra Proctor, cond.; University Circle Singers; with Robert Sidney, Alison Crosby, Jennifer Olin, and Matthew J. Gayton.

*Review:*

W85.12a   Reinthaler, Joan. "A Magical 'Unicorn.'" *Washington Post*, Style, E (May 20, 1997): 3.
" . . . the audience response, in laughter at absurdity and in silence at the touching conclusion, spoke to the quality."

### ♦ DISCOGRAPHY

W85.13   University of Colorado University Singers; Charles Byers, cond.
Century Records 31544, LP, stereo. (1968)
Recorded in concert May 6, 1968.

W85.14   Colgate University Chorus; Marietta Cheng, cond.
Redwood Records ES-15, LP, stereo. (1970-80?)

W85.15   University of Michigan Chamber Choir, with instrumental ensemble; Thomas Hilbish, cond.
University of Michigan Records SM0012, LP, stereo. (1979)

Recorded at Hill Auditorium, the University of Michigan, Ann Arbor. "A centennial year production of the University of Michigan School of Music."

W85.16  Paul Hill Chorale and Orchestra; Paul Hill, cond.
Golden Crest CRS 4180, LP, stereo. (1978)
Series: Golden Crest laboratory series.

W85.17  Chorus (SSAATTBB) and instrumental ensemble (flute, oboe, clarinet, bassoon, trumpet, violoncello, double-bass, percussion, harp); Thomas Schippers, cond.
Angel Records 35437, LP, mono (1957)
"Recorded in Europe, in cooperation with the New York City Ballet."

W85.18  Cecilia Society of Boston; Donald Teeters, cond.
Newport Classic NPD 85621, CD (1996)
With Thomson's *Parson Weems & the Cherry Tree.*

W85.19  Margaret Howell, soprano; Polly Detels, mezzo-soprano; Roxanne Frederickson, contralto; Carleton College Chamber Singers with instrumentalists; William Wells, cond.
Record manufacturer unidentified, LPS-3031, LP, stereo. (1970)
"Recorded during live performances in Skinner Chapel, April 17-18, 1970."
With choral works by Monteverdi and Morley.

♦ SELECTED RECORDING REVIEWS

W85.20  Ditsky, John. "Menotti: The Unicorn, the Gorgon, and the Manticore." *Fanfare* 2 (May-June 1979): 62-63.
Review of the Golden Crest 4180 recording. " . . . for the new purchaser — or even the veteran wishing to upgrade the sound of his *Unicorn* — the new version is certainly adequate, and can be recommended without fear of much contradiction."

W85.21  Ditsky, John. "Menotti: The Unicorn, the Gorgon, and the Manticore." *Fanfare* 3 (July-August 1980): 111.
Review of the University of Michigan Records SM0012 recording, produced by Abe Torchinsky. "All things considered . . . this is a very fine disc, recommendable on all counts . . ."

*288   Works and Performances*

W85.22   Ditsky, John. "Menotti: The Unicorn, the Gorgon, and the Manticore." *Fanfare* 4 (January-February 1981): 150.
Review of the Redwood Records ES-15 recording. ". . . this is a good *Unicorn*, and Colgate can be proud of the results of this annual check-up."

W85.23   Dyer, Richard. "Boston Cecilia; Donald Teeters, conductor; Menotti: The Unicorn, the Gorgon and the Manticore." *Boston Globe*, Calendar (October 2, 1997): 30.
Review of the Newport Classics recording. "The Boston Cecilia has mastered the English style of choral singing, which is how most of us, probably including Menotti, learned to hear Renaissance Italian choral music for the first time."

## *W86*   *VARIATIONS AND FUGUE FOR STRING QUARTET* (1932)

Based on an unpublished theme of Antonio Caldara.

### ♦ PREMIERE PERFORMANCE

W86.1   1932 (May 12): Philadelphia; Curtis Institute of Music; with James Bloom and Frances Wiener (violins), Arthur Granick (viola), and Samuel Geschichter (cello) (on a double-bill with Barber's *Dover Beach*)

## *W87*   *VARIATIONS ON A THEME OF SCHUMANN* (1930)

For piano solo.
A set of eleven variations on Schumann's "Zum Schluss," op. 25, no. 26.
Awarded the 1931 Carl F. Lauber Composition Prize.

### ♦ PREMIERE PERFORMANCE

W87.1   1930 (May 5): Philadelphia; Curtis Institute of Music; with Jeanne Behrend, piano (performed as an in-house recital)

## *W88*   *VIOLIN CONCERTO IN A MINOR* (1952; G. Schirmer; 24 min.)

In three movements.

Violin; 2+pic.222/2200/timp.perc/hp/str

♦ SELECTED PERFORMANCES

W88.1   1952 (Dec 5): Philadelphia; Academy of Music; Efrem Zimbalist, violin; Eugene Ormandy, cond.; Philadelphia Orchestra

*Reviews:*

W88.1a  "Wordless Menotti." *Time* 60 (December 15, 1952): 49.
" . . . its easygoing expression was well suited to Zimbalist's delicate tone and refined phrasing. For Philadelphians it was pleasant listening: the audience gave a rousing round of applause . . ."

W88.1b  Kolodin, Irving. "Met's 'Carmen' on Theatre TV — Menotti, Bartok & Cantelli." *Saturday Review* 35 (December 27, 1952): 29.
"The inventive quality of much of the material suggested that it could mean more under other circumstances, though the conventional treatment of the solo instrument didn't encourage hopes of a really strong work . . ."

W88.1c  Singer, Samuel L. "New Scores Aired by Philadelphians." *Musical Courier* 147 (January 15, 1953): 17.
" . . . the work is the most engaging new concerto heard here in many seasons. Lyric elements are almost always foremost, and there is a quality of directness in Menotti's writing, here as elsewhere."

W88.2   1981 (Dec 13): Philadelphia; Academy of Music; Joseph Silverstein, violin; Lorenzo Muti, cond.; Curtis Student Orchestra

*Review:*

W88.2a  Felton, James. "His Alma Mater Serves up a Weekend-long Menotti Feast." *Evening Bulletin* (Philadelphia), (December 14, 1981)
"This substantial contribution to string literature isn't known well enough by the general public. A large audience last night had a chance to enjoy its structural beauties and its felicitous writing for the violin."

W88.3   1996 (Feb 22): New York; Lincoln Center; Alice Tully Hall; Dino Anagnost, cond.; Little Orchestra Society (on a triple-bill with ballet suite from *Sebastian* and *Landscapes and Remembrances*, in a "Milestone for Menotti" 85th birthday concert)

Review:

W88.3a  Dannatt, Adrian. Classical Milestone for Menotti; Alice Tully Hall, New York." *Independent* (London), Review/Arts (February 28, 1996): 5.
" . . . had not been heard in New York since 1952, and sounded like it."

♦ BRIEFLY NOTED

W88.4  Rinaldi, M. "Roma." *Musica d'oggi* 3 (January 1960): 25 ✢ Graeser, L. "Zum ersten Male in Europa; Aufführung des Violinkonzertes von Menotti in Gelsenkirchen." *Orchester* 10 (September 1962): 289 ✢ Graeser, L. "Europäische Erstauffuhrung: Gian Carlo Menotti's Violinkonzert in Gelsenkirchen." *Orchester* 10 (November 1962): 372.

♦ DISCOGRAPHY

W88.5  Ruggiero Ricci, violin; Pacific Symphony Orchestra; Keith Clark, cond.
Varese Sarabande VCD 47239, CD (1985); Reference Recordings RR-45CD, CD (1991)
Recorded Oct 16, 1983, Santa Ana, CA High School Auditorium.
"A Prof. Johnson digital master recording."
Album title of the 1985 recording: Menotti and Barber Violin Concertos; of the 1991 recording: Violin Concertos.
With Barber's *Violin Concerto.*

W88.6  Tossy Spivakovsky, violin; Boston Symphony Orchestra; Charles Munch, cond.
RCA Victor LM 1868, LP (1955)
With Honegger's *Symphony No. 2 for String Orchestra.*

♦ SELECTED RECORDING REVIEW

W88.7  Brown, Royal S. "Menotti: Concerto in A Minor for Violin and Orchestra. Barber: Concerto for Violin and Orchestra, Op. 14." *Fanfare* 10 (September-October 1986): 186.
Review of the Varèse Sarabande VCD 47239 compact disc. " . . . absolutely top-flight performances and beautifully detailed, although slightly hard, sound . . . The folks at Varèse Sarabande continue to serve the cause of music with their imaginative and sensitive approach to repertoire."

*W89* *THE WEDDING* (*GIORNO DI NOZZE, THE MARRIAGE*)
(1988; G. Schirmer; evening)

Comic opera in two acts with libretto (Italian) by Menotti.
Largely ignored by the press.

♦ PREMIERE PERFORMANCE

W89.1   1988 (Sep 16): Seoul, South Korea; with Jee Hyun Lim (soprano) (performed in conjunction with the XXIV Olympiad's Arts Festival)

ARRANGEMENT

*W90*   *BACH, JOHANN SEBASTIAN. HARPSICHORD MUSIC* (1931?)

Polonaise; Little prelude; Minuet.
For carillon.
Arranged from BWV Anh. 119 (no. 7 in 2. Notenbuch für Anna Magdalena, BWV 939), no. 1 of 5 Kleine Präludien, and minuets from BWV 822 (Suite in G minor, mvts. 5-7)
*Curtis Institute of Music* has holograph in pencil ([3] p. of music; 35 cm.)

# Appendix A: Chronological List of Works

1922          *The Death of Pierrot* (W17)

1930          *Variations on a Theme of Schumann* (W87)

1931          *Arrangement of Bach's Works for Carillon* (W90)
                  *Improvisation* (W35)
                  *Intermezzo* (W39)

1932          *Variations And Fugue For String Quartet* (W86)

1932-33      *Six Compositions For Carillon* (W75)

1933          *Pastorale and Dance for Strings and Piano* (W65)

1935          *Italian Dance* (W42)

1936          *Trio For a Housewarming Party* (W82)

1937          *Amelia al ballo* (W4)
                  *Poemetti* (W68)

1939          *The Old Maid and the Thief* (W64)

1942          *The Island God* (W41)

1943          *The Catalogue* (W11)

1944          *Sebastian* (W73)

294   Appendix A: Chronological List

1945            Piano Concerto in F Major (W66)

1946            The Medium (W56)

1947            Á l'ombre des jeunes filles en fleurs (W1)
                The Bridge (W8)
                A Copy of Madame Aupic (W15)
                Errand Into the Maze (W24)
                A Happy Ending (W31)
                The Medium (rev.) (W56)
                The Telephone (W80)

1949            Irene and the Gypsies (W40)

1950            The Consul (W14)
                The Empty Handed Traveler (W23)

1951            Amahl and the Night Visitors (W3)
                Apocalypse (W5)
                A Little Cancrizan for Mary (W49)
                Ricercare and Toccata on a Theme from the Old Maid and the Thief (W70)

1952            The Hero (songs) (W33)
                Violin Concerto in A Minor (W88)

1954            The Saint of Bleecker Street (W72)

1956            Ricercare su nove toni (W71)
                The Unicorn, The Gorgon And The Manticore (W85)

1958            Maria Golovín (W52)

1959            Incidental Music For Cocteau's Le Poéte et sa muse (W37)

1959-62         Album Leaves (W2)

1961            Canti della lontananza (W9)
                A Chance for Aleko (W12)

1963            The Death of the Bishop of Brindisi (W18)
                Le Dernier Sauvage (W19)

Labyrinth (W45)

1964      Martin's Lie (W53)

1965      Lewisohn Stadium Fanfare (W48)

1966      Incidental Music for Anouilh's Médée (W36)

1968      Help, Help, the Globolinks! (W32)
Incidental Music for Romeo and Juliet (W38)
Triplo Concerto a Tre (W84)

1970      The Leper (W47)

1971      The Most Important Man (W60)

1972      La Donna immobile (W20)

1973      Suite for Two Violoncellos and Piano (W77)
Tamu-Tamu (W79)

1974      The Days of the Shepherd (W16)

1975      Fantasia for Violoncello and Orchestra (W26)

1976      The Egg (W22)
Fanfare For Charleston (W25)
The Hero (opera) (W34)
Landscapes and Remembrances (W46)
Symphony No. 1 in A Minor (W78)

1977      Cantilena and Scherzo (W10)

1978      Chip and His Dog (W13)
Lullaby For Alexander (W51)
The Trial of the Gypsy (W81)

1979      Missa O Pulchritudo in Honorem Sacratissimi Cordis Jesus (W58)
Juana La Loca (W44)
Miracles (W57)

1980           *A Song of Hope (An Old Man's Soliloquy)* (W76)

1981           *Five Songs for Voice and Piano* (W27)
                     *Moans, Groans, Cries, and Sighs* (W59)

1982           *The Boy Who Grew Too Fast* (W6)
                     *A Bride From Pluto* (W7)
                     *Muero Porqué No Muero* (W61)
                     *Nocturne* (W63)
                     *Piano Concerto No. 2* (W67)

1983           *Double Bass Concerto* (W21)

1984           *Mary's Mass* (W54)
                     *Ricercare* (W69)

1985           *Mass for the Contemporary English Liturgy* (W55)

1986           *Goya* (W30)

1987           *My Christmas* (W62)

1988           *The Wedding* (W89)

1990           *For the Death of Orpheus* (W28)

1991           *Goya* (rev.) (W30)
                     *Llama de Amor Viva* (W50)

1993           *The Singing Child* (W74)

1995           *Gloria* (W29)

1996           *Trio for Violin, Clarinet, and Piano* (W82)

1997           *Jacob's Prayer* (W43)

# Appendix B: Genre List of Works

**VOCAL WORKS**

OPERAS

*Amahl and the Night Visitors* (W3)
*Amelia al ballo* (W4)
*The Boy Who Grew Too Fast* (W6)
*A Bride From Pluto* (W7)
*Chip and His Dog* (W13)
*The Consul* (W14)
*The Death of Pierrot* (W17)
*Le Dernier Sauvage* (W19)
*La Donna Immobile* (W20)
*The Egg* (W22)
*Goya* (W30)
*Help, Help, the Globolinks!* (W32)
*The Hero* (W34)
*Irene and the Gypsies* (W40)
*The Island God* (W41)
*Juana La Loca* (W44)
*Labyrinth* (W45)
*Maria Golovín* (W52)
*Martin's Lie* (W53)
*The Medium* (W56)
*The Most Important Man* (W60)
*The Old Maid and the Thief* (W64)
*The Saint of Bleecker Street* (W72)
*The Singing Child* (W74)

*Tamu-Tamu* (W79)
*The Telephone* (W80)
*The Wedding* (W89)

CHORAL

*Canti della lontananza* (W9)
*The Catalogue* (W11)
*The Death of the Bishop of Brindisi* (W18)
*The Empty Handed Traveler* (W23)
*Five Songs for Voice and Piano* (W27)
*For the Death of Orpheus* (W28)
*Gloria* (W29)
*The Hero* (W33)
*Jacob's Prayer* (W43)
*Landscapes and Remembrances* (W46)
*A Little Cancrizan for Mary* (W49)
*Llama de Amor Viva* (W50)
*Mary's Mass* (W54)
*Mass for the Contemporary English Liturgy* (W55)
*Miracles* (W57)
*Missa o Pulchritudo in Honorem Sacratissimi Cordis Jesus* (W58)
*Moans, Groans, Cries, and Sighs* (W59)
*Muero Porqué No Muero* (W61)
*My Christmas* (W62)
*Nocturne* (W63)
*A Song of Hope* (W76)
*The Trial of the Gypsy* (W81)
*The Unicorn, the Gorgon, and the Manticore* (W85)

## *INSTRUMENTAL WORKS*

ORCHESTRAL

*Apocalypse* (W5)
*Double Bass Concerto* (W21)
*Fantasia for Violoncello and Orchestra* (W26)
*Piano Concerto in F Major* (W66)
*Piano Concerto No. 2* (W67)
*Symphony No. 1 in A Minor* (W78)
*Triplo Concerto a Tre* (W84)
*Violin Concerto in A Minor* (W88)

Appendix B: Genre List    299

BALLET/DANCE

    *Á l'ombre des jeunes filles en fleurs* (W1)
    *The Days of the Shepherd* (W16)
    *The Errand Into the Maze* (W24)
    *Sebastian* (W73)

CHAMBER MUSIC

    *Cantilena and Scherzo* (W10)
    *Italian Dance* (W42)
    *Lewisohn Stadium Fanfare* (W48)
    *Pastorale and Dance for Strings and Piano* (W65)
    *Suite for Two Violoncellos and Piano* (W77)
    *Trio for a Housewarming Party* (W82)
    *Trio for Violin, Clarinet, and Piano* (W82)
    *Variations and Fugue for String Quartet* (W86)

SOLO INSTRUMENTAL

    *Fanfare for Charleston* (W25)
    *Improvisation* (W35)
    *Intermezzo* (W39)
    *Lullaby for Alexander* (W51)
    *Poemetti* (W68)
    *Ricercare* (W69)
    *Ricercare and Toccata on a Theme from The Old Maid and the Thief* (W70)
    *Ricercare su nove toni* (W71)
    Six Compositions for Carillon (W75)
    *Variations on a Theme of Schumann* (W87)

INCIDENTAL MUSIC

    *Incidental Music for Anouilh's Médée* (W36)
    *Incidental Music for Cocteau's Poéte et sa muse* (W37)
    *Incidental Music for Romeo and Juliet* (W38)

MISCELLANEOUS WORKS

    *Album Leaves* (W2)
    *Arrangement of Bach Works for Carillon* (W90)

*The Bridge* (W8)
*A Chance for Aleko* (W12)
*A Copy of Madame Aupic* (W15)
*A Happy Ending* (W31)
*The Leper* (W47)

# Author Index

A., P., W14.18b, W14.19a
Ackart, Robert, G28
Adam, Klaus, G88; W44.5c
Adler, Peter Herman, W3.10n
Aguiar, William, Jr., W19.10b
Allen, Jane Addams, W30.1t
Alva, Marilyn, W67
Amico, Fedele d', W14.13
Andersen, Jane Lee, W3.38a
Anthony, Michael, W3.59a
Apone, Carl, G139
Aprahamian, Felix, W53.1j
Ardoin, John G130, G132, G141,
    G143, G144, G145, G157, G196;
    W4.11a, W9.8, W14.14,
    W14.26a, W19.11d, W27.6,
    W30.1v, W32.5e, W44.3d,
    W44.4c, W44.7c, W45.1f,
    W46.2a, W46.2b, W56.35a,
    W56.5, W58.5a, W58.5c,
    W58.7a, W63.5
Asche, Gerhart, W3.25a, W14.55a
Ashley, Dottie, G215, G220
Atkinson, Brooks, W56.14c, W72.7g
Atterfors, G., W14.67
Aulicino, Armand, G20

Baldini, G., W14.67
Bales, Richard, W66.1
Barber, Samuel, W72.3
Barichella, Monique, W52.7a

Barker, Frank Granville, W14.40e,
    W52.8a
Barlow, S. L. M., W56.8b
Barnes, Clive, W24.3a, W53.1h,
    W60.1e
Barnes, J., G186
Baro, Gene, W53.1e
Bartenstein, H., W32.14b
Barter, Christie, W66.5b
Bauer, Leda, W56.11b
Baxter, Robert, G160; W34.1k,
    W56.38c, W56.48b, W72.24b,
    W72.24c
Beard, H., G23
Beckwith, Nina, G103, G107; W56.6
Bell, Eleanor, W18.1b
Bellingardi, Luigi, W4.9a, W19.13a,
    W44.6a, W44.6b, W52.9e,
    W56.29a, W72.22a, W79.3a
Belt, Byron, W30.1r
Bender, William, W34.1g, W60.1f
Benesch, G., W14.67
Benjamin, Arthur, W14.5
Berger, Melvin, G86
Berglund, Robert, W34.1i
Berio, Luciano, G77
Bernheimer, Martin, W19.9b,
    W72.17a
Bernstein, B., W52.3p
Beyer, William, W14.16s, W56.10e,
    W80.7e

## Author Index

Bilanchone, Victor, Jr., W85.3
Bing, Rudolf, G20
Blau, Eleanor, W72.16a
Blitzstein, Marc, W72.1
Bloomfield, Arthur, W56.39e
Bloomfield, Theodore, W3.23a, W32.11a
Blum, Michael I., W14.12
Blumauer, Manfred, W44.6c
Blumenstein, Gottfried, W32.21a
Blyth, Alan, W14.40b, W64.12a, W80.11a
Bond, David, W10.8
Bookspan, Martin, W73.19
Bowen, J., W19.8m
Boyden, Matthew, G223
Bracefield, Hilary, W32.12b
Bradley, Jeff, W14.62a
Brasch, Alfred, W80.1
Bremini, Ireneo, W72.13a
Breuer, Robert, W19.8p, W44.4b, W45.1g
Bridges, John, G136
Briggs, John, G45; W4.24
Brindle, Reginald Smith, W4.7a
Briner, Andres, W52.2j
Brohn, William, W30.1q
Brooks, Gene, G222, G225
Brown, John Mason, W14.16n, W56.10c, W80.7c
Brown, Rebecca, W3.39b
Brown, Royal S., W88.7
Brown, Steven, G178; W3.39a, W30.1bb
Brownlow, Art, G147
Brozan, Nadine, G193
Brozen, Michael, W19.8a
Budden, Julian, W80.21a
Burton, Stephen Douglas, W30.1q
Burwasser, Peter, W70.7
Busnelli, Mariella, W22.4g, W53.6e
Butler, Henry, G57
Byrne, Kevin, G100

Cairns, David, W53.1g
Calder, Ethan, W72.16c
Campbell, Mary, G212
Cantrell, Scott, W3.48a
Carlin, Karen, W80.30a
Casmus, Mary Irene, G46
Cernaz, Bruno, W22.4f, W52.9f
Chacon, Victor, G165
Chapman, Frank, G40
Chase, Gilbert, G62
Chedorge, A., W52.6a
Chism, Olin, W4.11b, W56.35b, W56.57a
Clarke, Gerald, W67
Clurman, Harold, W14.16m, W72.7o
Coco, David, W3.58a
Coggi, Anthony D., W3.75
Coleman, Emily, W52.3n, W85.7d
Colurso, Mary, W3.46a
Commanday, Robert, W56.39a
Cossé, Peter, W56.41b, W64.17a
Costanza, Marie Carmen, W44.7e
Courir, Duilio, G77
Covello, Richard, W79.2g
Covington, Kate, W69.1
Cowell, Henry, W3.10k, W14.1
Cowles, Chandler, W72.7f
Credle, Melanie, W3.62b
Crichton, Ronald, W34.3a
Croan, Robert, W56.49a
Crook, John, W56.52a, W80.25a
Cross, Anthony, W32.12a
Crowe, Jerry, W3.83
Crutchfield, Will, W9.2a, W10.3a, W13.5a, W56.36a, W56.38a, W63.2a, W77.2a, W80.17a
Cunningham, Eloise, G101

Dannatt, Adrian, W46.3a, W73.5a, W88.3a
Dannenberg, Peter, W3.20a, W32.1, W32.4c
Danzuso, D., W14.67
Davis, Peter, W18.2c
Davis, Peter G., W4.12a, W79.2c, W79.4b
De Marcellus, Juliette, W4.10a, W56.28a

## Author Index  303

Dean, Winton, W52.8d
Deke, R. F., W56.11f
Dekom, Otto, W6.1a
Delacoma, Wynne, W14.63a
Demaline, Jackie, W32.22a
DeRhen, Andrew, W84.1d
Derrickson, Jay, W6.1d
Dettmer, Roger, W79.2j
Diamonstein, Barbara Lee, G99
Dickinson, Peter, W5.6, W24.8, W73.23
Dierks, Donald, W56.43a, W80.18a
Ditsky, John, W19.19, W73.15, W85.20, W85.21, W85.22
Dolmetsch, Carl, W19.11f, W30.1ee, W56.51a, W72.25b
Downes, Olin, W3.10c, W56.11a, W64.4a, W66.5a
Duck, Leonard, W14.49a
Duffie, Bruce, W22.6a, W85.9a
Dunlop, Lionel, W72.10a
Dunning, Bill, W32.5b
Dyer, Richard, W85.23

Eaton, Quaintance, W3.10e, W3.12a, W4.6a, W44.1, W64.7a
Eckert, Carola, W52.9d
Eckert, Thor, Jr., W44.4g
Eckertsen, Dean, G31
Edwards, S., G64
Elliott, Susan, W3.40a, W72.23a
Ellis, Stephen W., W58.6a
Ellsworth, Ray, W56.67
Ericson, Raymond, G91, G104, G109, G117; W56.15a, W56.24a, W64.11a
Evett, Robert, W52.3f, W85.6b
Eyer, Ronald, W52.3c

Fabian, Imre, G124; W30.1ll, W34.2a
Fahy, Joe, W3.34b
Feder, Susan, W21.1b
Feldman, M. A., W56.27a
Felten, Eric, G182
Felton, James, W73.3a, W88.2a
Fierz, Gerold, W32.18a

Finn, Robert, G138; W30.1z
Fitzgerald, Gerald, W19.8k, W52.3k
Fix, Sybil, G197
Fleming, John, G218
Fleming, Shirley, G111; W14.39d, W56.25a, W78.1a
Floyd, Jerry, W6.1c, W7.1b
Fogel, Henry, G187; W10.6
Folk, Lucia, G224
Forbes, Elizabeth, W14.38a, W14.40a, W32.17a
Fossum, Knut, W14.46a
Fournier, Lou, W30.1q
Fowler, Jimmy, W3.60b
Frankenstein, Alfred, W14.32a
Fratani, A., G154
Freeman, John W., W19.8j, W60.1i, W60.1j, W79.2h
Fryer, Judith Anne, G96; W3.5, W32.3, W56.3
Funke, Phyllis, W3.24a

Gagnard, Frank, G156
Galatopoulos, Stelios, W14.7
Galkin, Elliott W., W72.15a
Gallarati, Paolo, W26.1a
Gamarekian, Barbara, W30.1m
Garde, C. O., W14.67
Gault, Dermot, W66.6a
Geitel, Klaus, W3.20b, W32.4d, W56.20c
Gelatt, Roland, G110
Gelb, Arthur, W52.3a
Genêt, W19.7b
Geracimos, Ann, W30.1f
Gevisser, Mark, W80.33
Gibbons, Andrew, G168
Giffin, Glenn, W3.36a
Giniger, Ken S., W22.4a, W53.6a
Glackin, William, W56.55a, W80.31a
Glock, W., W85.7f
Glueck, Grace, G114
Goléa, Antoine, G80; W19.7d, W19.7f
Goodman, John, W56.68
Goodman, Peter, W30.1n

Goodwin, Noel, W14.40c
Gould, Susan, W52.9g
Goury, J., W14.67
Gradenwitz, Peter, W14.30b
Graeser, L., W88.4
Grange, Henry Louis de la, W44.2
Green, Judith, W3.34a, W56.39b
Green, Sara, W30.1u
Greene, David Mason, W9.9, W30.3, W80.43
Greenwood, Don, W3.55b
Gregson, David, W30.1kk
Greinus, Jochen, W14.33a, W14.67
Grieb, Lyndal, G97, G105, G106, G108
Groth, H., G42
Gruen, John, G98, G113, G115, G116, G119, G120, G121, G122, G123, G126; W72.5
Grueninger, Walter F., W3.82, W73.22
Gudger, William D., W52.14a, W73.4a
Guglielmi, E., W53.2a
Gustafson, Bruce, W69.2a
Gutman, John, G20

Haggin, B. H., W14.16r
Halperin, Carl J., W52.13c, W74.1e
Hamburger, Philip, W3.10g
Hamlet-Metz, M., W30.1ff
Handelman, Jay, W3.61a
Hanson, John Robert, W66.2
Harris, Dale, W34.4b, W44.4a
Harris, Harry, W34.1e
Harris, Kenn, W72.30
Harrison, Jay S., W19.8e
Haskins, John, W72.14a
Hawkins, Robert F., G37
Hawley, David, W3.28a
Hayes, Richard, W72.7v
Heinz, Joachim, W14.68
Hell, Henri, W14.67
Heller, Elisabeth, W80.10a
Helm, Everett, W19.8s
Hemming, Roy, W3.26d

Henahan, Donal, W3.22a, W10.1a, W14.9, W22.5a, W30.1l, W30.1w, W32.9a, W34.1c, W34.1f
Herman, Justin, W73.24
Hertelendy, Paul, W3.30a
Hess, John L., G92
Heyman, Barbara B., G196
Heymont, G., W44.4m
Hick, Bryan, W80.24a
Hiemenz, Jack, W77.1a
Higgins, Tom, G216
Hijman, Julius, W3.10m, W72.7y
Hiller, Carl H., W80.22a
Hirsch, N., G50
Hodgins, Paul, W24.1
Hoelterhoff, M., W44.4f
Holde, A., W3.2, W85.7e
Holden, Randall LeConte, Jr., W80.2
Holland, Bernard, G177; W14.58a, W52.13a, W56.40a, W64.14a, W72.25a, W80.16a, W80.23a
Honan, William H., G181
Honig, Joel, G119, G176, G204; W3.21a, W32.8d, W80.5
Hopkins, John, W85.4
Howard, John Tasker, W4.1
Howe, Richard, W56.19a, W80.33
Huber, Hans, W56.21a
Huber, Helga, W56.23a
Hughes, Allen, W14.35a, W27.2a, W34.4a, W72.16b, W81.1a
Humphreys, Henry S., W32.6a
Hyman, Ann, G203

Jacobi, Peter P., W79.2b
Jacobs, Arthur, W3.19a, W6.4c, W14.17f, W14.31a, W19.7g, W53.1i, W56.22b, W81.1c
Jacobson, Robert, W3.26c, W14.39c, W19.11g, W22.4c, W34.1h, W44.4j, W53.6c, W56.22c
Jahant, Charles, W14.51b, W14.51c, W30.1ii, W72.25c
Jalon, Allan, G153
Jarrell, Frank P. G142, G158, G164,

## Author Index  305

G171, G174, G185; W30.1a,
W30.1k, W47.2b
Joachim, Heinz, W3.20c, W14.67,
W32.4g
Johnson, David, W14.48b
Jolly, Cynthia, G38, G41
Jones, Robert, G143
Jones, Tina P., W3.53a
Joslyn, Jay, W46.1a
Jurik, M., W14.67

Kaczynski, T., W14.33b
Kanski, J., G89; W3.7, W14.67
Kastendieck, Miles, W60.1g
Kaufman, Wolfe, W19.7c
Kay, N., G67
Keller, Hans, W56.11i
Keller, James M., G196
Kennedy, Michael, W14.49b
Kennicott, Philip, G179; W3.85
Kerman, Joseph, W72.6
Kerner, Leighton, W30.1aa, W34.4c,
W44.4e, W80.4
Kessler, Giovanna, W14.6, W52.9a,
W60.2a, W79.3c
Kessler, H., G70
Khadzhimishev, M., G150
Killingsworth, Kay, G78
Kimmelman, Michael, W30.1o
Kinkaid, Frank, W14.37a
Kirchberg, Klaus, W14.56a
Kirstein, Lincoln, W3.10l, W14.17c,
W72.2, W72.7b
Klein, Rudolf, W3.27b, W3.27c,
W32.15b, W32.15c, W52.2e
Knight, Arthur, W56.11g
Koch, Gerhard R., W14.33c
Koch, Heinz W., W32.14a
Koegler, Horst, W52.2k
Kolodin, Irving, G16, G102; W3.10i,
W3.12c, W4.25, W14.16d,
W14.73, W18.2b, W19.8h,
W32.5c, W45.1e, W52.3g,
W56.65, W60.1h, W64.24,
W72.7h, W72.7q, W80.39,
W84.1b, W85.7c, W88.1b

Königsberg, A., G72
Kornick, Rebecca Hodell, G167
Kozinn, Allan, G163, G172, G184,
G192, G198, G214; W3.49a
Krakauer, P. M., W14.67
Krause, Manfred, W14.41b
Krebs, Albin, G134; W27.1a
Kresh, Paul, W72.29
Krokover, Rosalyn, W52.3j, W85.7a
Kroll, Jack, W79.2d
Krutch, Joseph Wood, W14.16i,
W56.10b, W80.7b
Kubly, Herbert, G4
Kupferberg, Herbert, W32.8a
Kutschera, Edda, W32.15f

L., J., W3.14a
Lane, John Francis, G137
Lansdale, Nelson, G17
Lardner, John, W56.10a, W80.7a
Lavender, E. W., W52.8b
Lehman, Mark L., W66.10
Levine, Joseph, W85.2
Levinger, Henry W., W3.10f,
W14.16h, W72.7l
Lewis, Theophilus, W72.7n
Lipman, Samuel, W30.1nn
Loebe, Bernd, W14.41a, W44.5b,
W56.31a
Loomis, George W., W3.77
Loskill, Jörg, W19.12a
Loveland, K., W53.1b
Lowens, Irving, W7.1c, W85.1
Ludwig, Heinz, W52.12b
Luten, C. J., W18.6
Luys, Thomas, W14.56c

M., W. S., W14.23a
Maciejewski, B. M., W53.1a
Mail, Jens, W14.56b
Malipiero, Riccardo, W72.8b
Malitz, Nancy, W78.1b
Manishen, James, W14.64b
Mannes, Marya, W72.7aa
Manning, Gerald, W13.1a
Manville, Stewart R., W85.6i

March, Ivan, W66.9
Marks, Marcia, W32.8f
Markwardt, Ross A., G164, G171, G173
Marriott, Richard John, W3.6, W14.10, W56.4
Martin, George, G145
Martynov, Ivan, G95
Marx, H., G10; W14.16q
Matthews-Walker, Robert, W73.25
Matz, Charles A., G61
Maurin, Gaston C., W64.18a, W80.26a
Mayer, Gerhard, W32.15g
Mayer, Harry, W52.10a
Mayer, Martin, W19.9c
Mayer, Tony, W52.6c, W64.15a
McCardell, Charles, W30.1mm
McDaniel, Charles-Gene, W79.2k
McDowell, Elsa F., G133, G190
McKinnon, Arlo, Jr., W14.58b
McLellan, Joseph, G191, G210; W18.3a, W30.1h, W32.20a, W80.44, W82.1a
McPhail, Claire, W6.3a
Mead, Margaret, W79.2d
Mellen, Constance, W52.2i, W85.6g
Mellers, W., G30
Mendel, Arthur, W4.1
Menotti, Francis, G168
Menotti, Gian Carlo (as author), G5, G8, G9, G17, G18, G25, G34, G39, G53, G56, G60, G76, G77, G78, G83, G84, G85, G87, G88, G93, G94, G98, G99, G100, G115, G118, G131, G135, G138, G139, G148, G152, G153, G158, G159, G160, G161, G169, G170, G178, G183, G193, G212, G217, G225; W3.34b, W6.1a, W14.14, W14.48a, W17, W18.1a, W19.8a, W19.8b, W30.1a, W30.1b, W30.1e, W30.1g, W30.1h, W30.1i, W30.1k, W30.1kk, W30.1u, W30.1x, W32.4b, W34.1d, W44.7a, W47.1a, W47.1b, W47.2b, W53.3a, W56.1, W56.2, W56.11e, W56.5, W58.2, W72.16a, W72.5, W78.1a, W79.1, W79.4a
Mercer, Ruby, G105; W13.2a, W14.39a, W22.4e, W53.6d
Merkling, Frank, G29; W14.25b, W32.5d, W45.1h
Michaels, Connie, W14.44a
Miller, Karl, W5.7, W24.7, W64.25
Miller, Philip L., W3.73, W3.74, W63.4
Modi, Sorab, W7.1a, W56.51b
Molotsky, Irvin, G140; W30.1b, W30.1g
Monelle, Raymond, W3.43a, W14.48a, W80.15a
Monson, Karen, W79.2f
Montsalvatge, X., G149
Morse, Bob, W14.18a
Moses, Kurt, W72.16c
Mott, Gilbert, W72.20a
Mott, Michael, W7.1d
Mousset, Edouard, W52.2l
Movshon, George, W9.1a, W60.1n
Mueller, L., G124

Nathan, George Jean, W14.16a, W56.10f, W80.7f
Nau, Tim, W56.22a
Neufert, Kurt, W6.2b, W6.2c, W13.4a, W13.4b, W14.52a
Nordlinger, Gerson, W85.6f
Norquet, Matthias, W80.19a
North, James H., W3.80, W24.5, W73.18
Norton-Welsh, Christopher, W3.27e, W32.15e

O'Connor, John J., W3.26b
Oestreich, James R., G205, G206
Oliver, Michael, W10.7
Onnen, Frank, W19.7h
Oppens, Kurt, W44.4k, W60.1m
O'Reilly, F. Warren, W30.1hh
Osborne, Conrad L., W19.8q,

W72.11b

Paap, Wouter, W14.67
Page, Tim G169, G213; W44.7b, W72.21a
Paller, Rebecca, W14.75
Parinaud, A., G55; W19.4
Parks, Steve, W56.56a
Parmenter, Ross, G33; W19.2
Parouty, Michel, W14.50a, W14.50c
Parris, Robert, W22.1c, W53.5c
Parsons, Charles, W14.60b
Pataki, Ladislaus, W14.30a
Peltz, Mary Ellis, W52.2h
Peterson, Daniel A., W80.3
Pfeifer, Ellen, G125; W56.37a
Phelan, Kappo, W14.16k, W56.9b, W80.6c
Phraner, Leighton, W84.1c
Piccoli, Sean, G226; W3.84
Pincherle, Marc, W19.5
Pincus, Andrew L., W24.6, W70.8
Pines, Roger G., W3.26e
Pinzauti, Leonardo, G85
Pitt, Charles, W3.33a, W14.50b, W52.7b, W56.30a, W80.33
Plussain, Michel, W19.8n
Pniewski, Tom, W72.23b
Popoff, Wilf, W3.32a, W13.3a
Porter, Andrew, W22.4b, W30.1cc, W34.1l, W44.4h, W53.6b, W79.4c, W81.1b
Pound, Ezra, G61
Prideaux, Tom, W45.1b
Prokopiou, Stavros, G71
Proust, Marcel, W1

Rasponi, Lanfranco, W44.6d
Razboynikov, S., W80.33
Redmond, Michael, G202
Redvall, Eva, W14.42a
Reese, Catherine, W3.44a
Reich, Willi, W14.67
Reinthaler, Joan, W85.12a, W85.5
Reisfeld, Bert, W45.1i
Reynolds, M., W19.6

Rhein, John von, W14.47a, W14.47b, W14.47d, W14.63b, W14.63d, W56.53a
Rich, Alan, W44.3c
Richter, Arnd, W14.56d
Riedlbauer, Jörg, W14.50a
Rigault, Jean de, W56.11c
Rinaldi, M., W52.9b, W88.4
Ringham, Wynne, W14.63c
Rizzo, Eugene, G81
Rizzo, Francis, W52.6b
Robertshaw, N., W6.2a
Robertson, Nan, G148
Robinson, Ray, W58.1
Roca, Octavio, W3.42a, W30.1i, W30.1p
Roepke, Gabriela, W14.11
Roewade, Svend A. K., W13.1c
Rogers, Harold, G93; W18.2d
Rohde, Gerhard, W14.61a
Rohrbaugh, Anne, G108
Roos, James, G183; W30.1y, W47.1b, W72.26a
Rorem, Ned, G180
Rosen, George, W52.2c
Rosenberg, Donald, W14.57a
Rosenthal, Harold D., W14.22a, W52.8e
Rosenwald, H., G14
Ross, Janice, W56.39c
Rossi, Nick, W74.1c, W74.1d
Rostirolla, Giancarlo, W14.13
Rothstein, Edward, W19.11b, W30.1gg
Rothweiler, Kyle, W73.20
Rouse, Jack, W32.6b
Routte Gomez, Eneid, W3.47a
Rudolf, Bert, W14.45a, W30.1dd, W56.41a, W64.17b
Ryan, Sylvia Watkins, W3.8, W64.3, W68.1, W70.2

S., H., W14.16g
S., H. E., W72.7t
Saal, Hubert, W44.3b
Sabin, Robert, W5.3a, W14.16b,

W19.8r, W45.1j, W56.11d,
W72.7m, W85.7b
Sadie, Stanley, W6.4a
Safford, Edwin, W72.18a
Saltzman, Eric, W3.81, W73.21
Samachson, Dorothy, W14.47c
Samson, Charley, W3.35a
Sandberg, Ingrid, W14.20a
Sargeant, Winthrop, G2, G12, G44,
G54; W14.25a, W18.2a, W19.8f,
W32.8b, W45.1d, W52.3d,
W56.10d, W56.17a, W72.11a,
W72.7i
Sarnette, E., W19.8u
Sbisà, Nicola, G208
Schaefer, Theodore, W85.6e
Schauensee, Max de, W52.5a
Schmidt, Dietmar N., W56.21d
Schmidt-Garre, Helmut, W56.21b
Schneiders, Heinz-Ludwig, W32.10a
Schoenegger, H., W14.45b
Schonberg, Harold C., W14.39b,
W32.2, W32.5a, W44.4d,
W84.1a
Schuhmann, Claus R., W32.23
Schulman, Michael, W13.1b
Sears, L., W22.1a, W53.5a
Seckerson, Edward, W3.79, W73.17,
W84.3
Seelmann-Eggebert, U., W72.8c
Selch, Frederick R., W30.1d,
W30.1hh
Selden-Goth, Gisella, W72.8a
Severi, G. G., W52.3m
Shanet, H., W3.3
Shepard, Richard F., W3.26a
Sime, Tom, W3.50a
Simmons, Walter, W4.26, W56.69,
W64.26, W80.41, W80.42
Simon, John, G221
Simon, Robert A., W56.8a
Símonarson, Baldur, W56.32a,
W80.13a
Singer, Samuel L., W14.15a, W88.1c
Skowron, Zbigniew, G209
Smaczny, Jan, W4.14a, W32.16a

Smith, Cecil, W3.10j, W4.4b,
W14.3, W14.4, W56.14a,
W56.9c, W56.9d, W64.5b,
W80.6d, W80.6e, W80.8a
Smith, French Crawford, W52.5b
Smith, Helen C., G173
Smith, Jeffrey C., W52.13b
Smith, Patrick J., G121; W22.5b,
W30.4, W32.5f, W44.4i, W44.4l
Smith, Susan Lampert, W3.55a
Smith, Tim, W72.26b
Snowman, D., W30.1c
Snyder, Louis, G94; W60.1g
Sokol, Martin L., G127
Sommerich, Phillip, W3.45a
Soria, Dorle J., G84, G90, G118;
W19.7i
Springer, Morris, W56.50a, W56.50b
Stadem, Catherine, W3.56a
Starr, William W., W72.21c
Stearns, David Patrick, W5.8,
W30.1e, W30.1jj
Stefanovic, Pavle, G146
Stein, Elliott, W19.7k
Stern, W. H., G51
Sternfeld, Frederick W., W64.2
Stevens, D., G52
Still, Barry, W72.19a
Stöckl, Rudolf, W14.54a, W64.16a
Storrer, William Allin, W3.18a,
W19.11e, W22.4d, W44.7d,
W53.6f, W72.21d, W74.1a
Stowe, Dorothy, W3.29a, W3.44b
Stravinsky, Igor, W19.8o
Strini, Tim, W14.60a
Sutcliffe, James Helme, W32.4f,
W32.4i, W44.5a, W44.5d

Taitte, Lawson, W3.60a
Taubman, Howard, G1, G6, G15,
G82; W47.1a, W52.2d, W52.3i
Taylor, Peter, W6.4b. W14.40d,
W52.8c
Taylor, William A., W40.1
Teachout, Terry, W3.76
Ter-Simonyan, M., W14.67

Terry, Walter, G135; W85.8a
Thaler, Lotte, W52.12d
Thomas, Christopher J., W56.11j
Thomas, Robert McG., G134; W27.1a
Thomson, Virgil, W14.16t, W56.9f,
   W80.6f
Timbrell, Charles W22.1b, W53.5b
Todd, Arthur, W3.72, W4.23,
   W14.74, W56.66, W64.23,
   W73.14, W80.40
Tomasi, Gioacchino Lanza, G77
Tompkins, Jimmy, G73
Tonkonogy, Alwin, W3.62a
Trebor, Emil, W60.1k
Tricoire, Robert, G63
Trilling, Ossia, W80.33
Trimble, Lester, W52.3h
Trucco, Terry, G152

Übel, Ruth, W19.8t

Valdes, Lesley, W72.24a
Villion, François, G61
Vroon, Donald R., W3.78, W73.16

Wagner, Klaus, W32.4e
Waleson, Heidi, W44.7a, W56.70,
   W79.4a
Walsh, Michael, W30.1x
Ward, Charles, W56.54a
Warrack, Jack, W52.2m, W72.9b
Watmough, David, W14.27a
Watt, Douglas, W3.12b, W14.16e,
   W14.21a, W64.7b, W72.28
Weaver, William, W14.34a, W52.9c,
   W53.2b, W56.20a, W56.20b,
   W79.3b, W79.3d
Webster, Daniel, G161; W4.13a,
   W34.1b, W34.1j, W56.38b,
   W56.45a, W56.48a, W80.20a
Wechsberg, Joseph, W3.27d,
   W32.15d
Wechsler, Bert, G122
Weinraub, Judith, G199
Weinstock, Herbert, W32.8e, W60.1l
Welsh, Anne Marie, W85.11a,
   W85.11b
Werker, Gerard, W80.33
White, Michael, G219
Wiencke, H. E., W32.23
Wigler, Stephen, W30.1j
Williams, Barbara S., G129
Wilson, J. Kenneth, W64.1
Wimbush, Roger, G79
Winters, Lee, W19.10a
Witzke, Ronald, W3.9, W56.7
Wolz, Larry, G112
Worbs, Hans Christoph, G65, G66;
   W32.4a, W32.4h
Wyatt, Euphemia Van Rensselaer,
   W3.12e, W14.16p, W56.14b,
   W56.9e, W72.7u, W80.7d,
   W80.8b

Yarustovsky, Boris, G47
Yohalem, John, G120
Young, Allen, W3.36b

Zakariasen, Bill, W56.71
Zijlstra, Miep, G106
Zimmerman, Paul D., W32.8c
Zimmermann, Christoph, W52.12a
Zoff, Otto, W72.7r
Zondergeld, Rein A., W52.12c
Zottos, Ion, W52.1
Zytowski, Carl B., W32.5g

# Performer Index

Aceto, Raymond, W14.58
Actor, Lisa, W56.49
Adams, Bert, W32.24
Adkins, Paul, W34.1
Adkins, Ted W22.5
Adler, Bernhard, W56.31
Adler, Peter Herman, W52.15, W52.2
Afejusu, Tony, W47.1
Agler, David, W64.12
Aiken, David, W3.10, W3.14, W3.28, W3.28a, W3.57, W3.57a, W3.64, W72.27, W72.7
Akos, Catherine, W72.27, W72.7
Akre, Christine, W56.51
Alberghetti, Anna Maria, W56.11, W56.64
Alcantara, Manuel, W85.11
Alcantara, Mireille, W14.52
Alcantara, Theo, W72.17
Aleman, John, W56.46
Alexander, John, W19.9
Allen, Barbara, W10.3, W63.2
Allen, Chet, W3.10, W3.10b, W3.10d, W3.10i, W3.12, W3.12a, W3.64, W3.71
Allen, Jayson, W3.50
Allen, Kathryn, W56.57
Alley, Rick, W47.1
Alofs, Jan, W32.14
Altamira, Mariana, W56.42

Altman, Karen, W72.14
Alvary, Lorenzo, W4.3
Amadini, Maria, W4.15
Amaya, Joseph, W56.25
Ambrosian Singers, W3.26
American Ballet Theatre School of Classical Ballet, W3.40
American Chamber Opera, W80.16
American Symphony Orchestra, W84.1
Amos, David, W84.2
Anagnost, Dino, W3.40, W46.3, W73.5, W88.3
Anchorage Concert Chorus, W3.56
Anderson, Douglas, W80.16
Andreassi, Maria, W14.15, W14.69
Andreolli, Florindo, W52.9
Andresen, Robert, W14.65
Andrews, Carol, W72.23
Andries, Eric, W3.58
Antwerp Philharmonic Orchestra, W52.2
Appelgren, Richard, W3.46
Appling, Betty, W56.16
Archdiocese of Baltimore, W54.1
Arena, Maurizio, W72.13
Arendt, Roberta, W52.11
Arentoft-Nielsen, Pia, W44.5
Argiris, Spiros, G199; W5.4, W14.61, W52.13, W52.14, W73.4,

W73.4a, W73.9
Ariostini, Armando, W80.21
Arkansas Opera Theatre, W56.27
Arkansas Symphony, W56.27
Armenian, Raffi, W56.22
Armistead, Diane, W64.14
Armitage, Walter, W15.1
Armstrong, Karan, W9.4, W9.8, W9.9, W27.3, W27.5, W63.3, W63.4, W63.5
Arnold, Dave, W3.29, W3.44
Arnold, Malcolm, W4.11, W56.35
Aronoff, Max, W42.1
Ashton, Meirion, W72.19
Assad, Jim, W56.18, W56.18a
Assaf, Nancy, W9.3
Assandri, Anna, W72.13
Atlanta Civic Opera, W14.43
Atlanta Opera Orchestra, W14.43
Atlanta Symphony Chorus, W28.1
Atlanta Symphony Orchestra, W28.1
Atlantic Sinfonietta, W24.4
Attmore, Carol, W52.11
Auburtin, Christophe, W6.2
Augusta Opera, W56.25, W56.52, W80.25
Austin, Michael, W34.4
Austin, Robert, W56.25
Austin, William, W34.1
Aver, Phyllis, W3.37
Avila, Doria, W56.14
Ayres, Tony, W3.41, W4.14
Azova, Ludmilla, W14.28

Backer, Sammy, W53.6
Baclanova, Olga, W15.1
Bacquier, Gabriel, W19.7
Badea, Christian, W19.11, W34.2, W34.3, W34.4, W52.9, W56.29, W58.4, W58.6, W72.21
Bahny, Nathan, W14.58
Bailey, Pamela, W47.1
Bainbridge, Elizabeth, W6.4, W6.5
Baker, Alan, W72.16
Baker, Margaret, W64.12, W64.19
Balaban, Emanuel, W56.10, W56.59,
W80.36
Baldisseri, Renata, W58.6
Ballerino, John, W64.13
Ballet Society, W56.9, W80.6, W85.7
Ballet Society Orchestra, W56.59, W56.9
Balme, John, W64.18, W64.18a, W80.26
Baltimore Opera Company, W72.15
Baltimore Symphony Orchestra, W72.15
Bamberger, Carl, W65.2
Banaszczyk, Eugeniusz, W14.33
Bankl, Wolfgang, W14.55
Banks, Anne Victoria, W9.5, W9.9, W80.34
Barber, Meredith, W14.65
Barber, Samuel, W65.1
Barnes-Burroughs, Kathryn, W56.46
Barr, Bruce, W3.48
Barra, Donald, W10.4
Bartelloni, Anne, W14.50
Barto, Tzimon, W72.22
Bartoletti, Bruno, W4.9
Barzin, Leon, W56.9, W66.5, W66.5a, W66.5b, W80.6, W80.7
Bate, Derek, W3.31
Baton Rouge Little Theatre, W3.58, W3.58a
Battle, Kathy, W32.6
Baudo, Serge, W19.7, W19.7g
Baudoin, Monique, W56.30
Bay, Sherrie, W34.5
Bazile, Bridget A., W14.66
Beasley, Kimla, W56.54
Beattie, Herbert, W3.18, W14.28
Beattie, Mark, W3.18
Beatty, Talley, W85.6
Beck, Thomas, W15.1
Becker, Don, W3.44
Becker, Lee, W85.6, W85.7
Becque, Lucy, W72.7, W72.27
Bedi, Patrice Michaels, W56.53, W56.58
Beeken, Julia, W3.17
Beekman, Will, W3.38, W3.38a

Beeler, Virginia, W56.10, W56.8, W56.9
Behrend, Jeanne, W87.1
Bel Canto Chorus of Milwaukee, W46.1, W46.1a, W58, W58.3, W58.4, W58.6
Bell, Donald, W32.11
Bell, Michel Warren, W3.48
Bender, David, W58.3
Bender, Howard, W3.34, W30.1, W30.2
Bender, Philippe, W6.2, W6.6
Beni, Gimi, W22.1, W53.5
Bennett, Miriam, W6.1
Benoit, Elaine, W56.55, W56.55a
Benoit, Jean-Christophe, W32.11, W80.35
Berberian, Ara, W72.15
Berger, David, W58.3
Bergeron, Jean-Clément, W14.64
Berkenhoff, Hildegard, W14.41, W56.31
Berkshire Opera Company, W14.68, W14.75
Berl, Paul, W64.11
Bernardi, Mario, W14.27, W14.27a
Bernardini, Don, W72.25
Berry, Noreen, W53.1
Bertini, Gary, W14.30, W14.32
Berton, Liliane, W80.35
Bertram, Claire, W4.14
Bessant, Charles, W47.1
Best, Matthew, W53.7
Best, Richard, W32.5, W32.8
Bezona, David, W32.6
Bible, Frances, W56.12
Biggers, Stephen, W79.4
Bihler-Shah, Rose, W14.54
Bin-Nun, Efrat, W56.50
Bingaman, Roger, W14.65
Biscardini, Marco, W52.9
Bishop, Adelaide, W64.7, W64.8
Bisson, Yves, W14.50
Bitter, John, W82.1
Bittner, Jack, W14.28, W14.29, W60.1

Björker, Leon, W14.20, W14.71
Björling, Bette, W14.71
Blackburn, Harold, W14.23
Blackey, Donald, W14.15
Blake, Jacqueline, W32.12
Blanchard, Barbara, W56.23
Blanco, Marta, W56.42
Blankstein, Mary, W84.1
Blanzat, Anne-Marie, W14.52
Blareau, Richard, W56.19, W56.61, W80.35
Blaumer, Stephan, W9.4, W10.5, W27.3, W63.3
Blecke, Mark, W22.4
Bleeke, Steve, W3.63
Blegen, Judith, W32.5, W32.8, W56.60, W64.19, W80.12
Blieck, Marilyn de, W3.43
Bloom, James, W86.1
Boese, Ursula, W32.10, W32.4
Boldt, Marjorie, W3.32
Bolgan, Maria, W19.13
Bologna, Philip, W44.7
Bolthouse, Colleen, W3.50
Bolton-Nüsse, Helen, W56.31
Bonazzi, Elaine, W14.27, W45.1, W52.5
Bondini, Graziella, W72.22
Bone, Matthew, W3.63
Bonilla, Ivan, W81.1
Bonini, Peggy, W14.19
Bonisolli, Franco, W72.13
Boozer, Brenda, W56.25
Bordino, Ruggero, W4.9
Borelli, Wilma, W58.6
Borer, Pascal, W32.18
Boriskin, Michael, W70.2, W70.8
Borkh, Inge, W14.70
Boston Cecilia, W85.23
Boston Pops Orchestra, W73.13
Boston Symphony Orchestra, W18.2, W18.5, W66.3, W88.6
Botkin, Ernst, W19.12
Boucher, Gene, W32.8
Boucher, Paul, W3.19
Boukoff, Yuri, W66.7

## Performer Index

Boulanger, John, W32.20
Bowen Park Opera Company, W14.65
Bower, Beverly, W4.8
Boyd, Alan, W32.6
Brackens, Lynn, W64.11
Braithwaite, Nicholas, W52.8
Bramwell, Raymond, W3.43
Brand, Daphne, W72.19
Brassier, Therese, W32.13
Braun, Edith Evans, W65.1, W65.2
Braun, Mel, W14.64
Brees, Anton, W35.1, W35.2, W35.3, W75.1, W75.3, W75.4
Bregenzer, Kristine, W56.40
Bresowar, Mary, W3.58
Brey, Carter, W77.2
Bridges, Althea, W14.45, W56.41, W64.17
Briner, Marion, W56.21
Brisbon, Perry, W4.13
Bristol Opera Company, W72.19, W72.19a
Brobyn, Virginia, W14.35
Bröcheler, Caspar, W3.25
Bröcheler, John, W44.3, W44.4
Brockelman, Jeffery, W34.5
Brockmann, Dora F., W14.56
Brodsky, Jascha, W42.1
Bronhill, June, W72.9
Brooklyn Philharmonia, W22.5
Brooks, Dorothy Howard, W3.32
Brooks, John, W72.10
Brothers, Ronald, W9.3
Brott, Denis, W77.3
Brown, Antonia, W72.22
Brown, Jonathan Willis, W6.3
Brown, Melvin, W14.41, W44.5
Brown, Teresa, W58.27
Brown, Warren, W3.30
Browning, Virginia, W72.26
Bruckmann, Ilana, W14.32
Bruckner-Orchester, W14.45
Brüggemann, Doris, W14.56
Brumit, J. Scot, W72.18
Brun-Baranska, Bozena, W14.33
Bruno, Giovanna, W60.2

Bruno, Joanna, W19.10, W56.20, W60.1
Bruschi, Aldo, W3.24a
Brush, Scott, W32.19
Bryn-Julson, Phyllis, W18.3
Buckley, Richard, W14.63
Bullard, Gene, W14.28, W14.29
Buratto, Susanna, W64.18
Burchell, Sally, W32.16, W32.17
Burgess, Sally, W14.40
Burgin, Richard, W66.3
Burke, Linda, W64.10
Burke, Richard, W72.22
Burke, Veronica, W14.58
Burney, Harry L., III, W3.39
Burns, Christian, W3.59
Burrowes, Connor, W53.7
Burton, Amy, W80.18
Busch, Hans, W3.11b
Bush, Milton, W32.13
Buswell, James, W10.1, W63.1
Butler, James, W3.49
Butler, Kathleen, W14.47, W14.48
Butschek, Maria, W14.41
Buxton Festival Youth Orchestra, W32.17, W32.17a
Bybee, Ariel, W14.51
Byers, Charles, W85.13
Byrd, James, W81.1

Caddy, Ian, W52.8
Cadoul, Christiane, W3.33, W3.33a
Cakveyri, Martine, W6.2
Calahan, Steve, W32.6
Caldwell, Michael, W56.51
Caldwell, William, W3.63
California Ballet, W85.11
Callaway, Paul, W22.1, W52.5, W53.5, W85.6, W85.6f
Camerata New York Orchestra, W14.68
Cameron, Christopher, W3.31, W4.11
Campanella, Bruno, W56.20
Campbell, Edward, W85.10
Campi, Enrico, W4.15

Canadian Children's Opera Chorus,
  W3.31, W13.1, W13.2, W13.2a,
  W13.3, W13.7, W3.31
Canadian Opera Chorus, W13
Canadian Opera Company, W13.1
Canadian Opera Company Ensemble,
  W3.31
Cangelosi, David, W14.68
Cantelo, April, W3.19
Capetillo, Charlene Vernelle, W14.44
Caplan, Joan, W72.14
Capobianco, Tito, W44.7a
Capone, Gloria, W72.18
Caproni, Bruno, W14.49
Card, June, W56.18
Cardozo, Cathy, W3.45
Cariaga, Marvellée, W14.37,
  W14.37a, W14.39, W14.39d,
  W14.43
Carleton College Chamber Singers,
  W85.19
Carlsen, Svein, W14.46
Carlson, Ben, W13.1
Carlson, Benjamin, W3.31
Carlson, Claudine, W56.60
Carlson, Susan Lincoln, W32.13
Carosio, Margherita, W4.7, W4.15
Carr, Howard, W14.57
Carrington, Simon, W59.1
Carron, Elizabeth, W14.28, W56.33,
  W56.34, W72.27
Carter, John, W41.1
Cartwell, Timothy, W53.6
Caruso, Marie, W72.26
Casarini, Gianfranco, W14.34
Casas, Rubin, W3.46
Cassel, Walter, W4.4, W4.5
Cassilly, R., W72.27
Castel, Nico, W3.26, W14.34,
  W14.35
Castle, Joyce, W14.68, W56.58
Castle, Victoria, W56.51
Cathedral Festival '76 Chorale, W22.1
Cathey, Dalton, W47.1
Catholic Memorial, W18.2, W18.5
Catholic University of America
  Orchestra and Chorus, W61.1
Catley, Gwen, W64.9
Cavendish, Cheryl, W56.28
Cecilia Society of Boston, W85.18
Cervena, Sona, W56.21
Cesari, Paolo, W60.2
Cezanne, Jacquelyn, W73.1
Chaiken, Joel, W3.40, W3.40b,
  W3.42
Chalfoun, Leila, W14.61
Chamber Chorus of Washington,
  W85.6
Chamber Opera Theatre of New York,
  W64.14
Chamberlain, William, W14.65
Chang, Lynn, W63.1
Chao, Peiwen, W79.4
Chapman, William, W14.26, W52.15,
  W52.2, W52.3
Chard, Geoffrey, W14.40
Charleston Opera Company, W6.3
Charleston Symphony Orchestra
  Singers Guild, W46.2, W58.5
Chase, David, W85.11
Chausson, Carlos, W44.3, W44.4
Cheek, John, W14.68
Chen, Li-Chan, W56.39
Chen, Theresa Teng, W79.2, W79.3
Cheng, Marietta, W85.14
Chernichowski, Barbara J., W81.1
Chicago Opera Theater, W14.47,
  W56.53, W56.58
Children's Chorus of the Catholic
  Memorial, W18.2
Children's Theatre of Cincinnati,
  W32.22
Chiles, Torin, W14.64
Ching, Michael, W56.51
Chioldi, Michael, W14.68
Chlostawa, Danielle, W64.15
Cho, Grace, W14.66
Chookasian, Lili, W18.2, W18.2d,
  W18.5, W18.6, W19.8, W19.8k,
  W19.9, W56.17, W56.17a,
  W56.27, W56.27a
Choral Arts Society, W18.3, W18.3a

## 316   Performer Index

Christin, Judith, W4.11, W56.35
Church, Kenneth, W32.24
Cicogna, Adriana, W72.22
Ciesinski, Katherine, W9.2
Cincinnati Ballet, W85.8
Cincinnati Opera Outreach, W32.22
Cincinnati Symphony Orchestra, W85.8
Cioni, Renato, W60.2
City of Birmingham Touring Opera, W32.16
Clark, Eileen, W56.40
Clark, Keith, W88.5
Clark, Kelly, W3.46
Clark, Thomas, W14.44
Clarkson, Stanley, W14.22
Clatworthy, David, W3.22, W14.29, W14.39, W19.10, W19.11
Clavensy, Charles, W19.7
Clements, Joy, W56.15
Cleva, Fausto, W48.1
Cleveland Pops Orchestra, W3.67
Clink, Robert, W3.56
Cluytens, André, W66.7
Cochran, Grant, W3.56
Cochrane, Amy, W56.37
Coffey, Denise, W6.1
Cohen, David, W3.30
Cohen, Jedidiah, W3.40, W3.40a
Colburn, Sarah, W56.52
Cole, Dorothy, W14.27, W56.18
Cole, Orlando, W42.1
Cole, Sharon, W85.8
Cole, William, W74.1, W74.1c
Coleman, Leo, W37.1, W56.8, W56.9, W56.9e, W56.10, W56.11, W56.11b, W56.12, W56.14, W56.64
Colgate University Chorus, W85.14, W85.22
Collins, Keith, W53.1
Collins, Peter, W9.3
Collins, Sandra, W3.39, W3.39b
Colorado Lyric Theatre, W14.62
Colton, Ron, W56.25, W56.25a
Columbia Symphony Orchestra, W4.16, W4.17
Concert Singers of Cary, W3.62
Condette, Guy, W3.33, W56.30
Connecticut Grand Opera, W14.48, W72.20
Coogan, Sean, W53.6, W53.6a, W53.6e
Cook, Josephine, W32.14
Coomara, Rohini, W82.1
Cooper, June, W32.9, W32.9a
Cooper, Rex, W84.1
Cope, Marcia, W44.3, W44.4
Cope, Moyna, W72.10
Copeland, Virginia, W72.7, W72.9
Coppola, Anton, W3.49
Cordon, Norman, W41.1
Cordova, Vincent de, W3.34
Corretto, Anthony, W3.24
Cortese, Federico, W74.1
Cossa, Dominic, W34.1
Costa-Greenspon, Muriel, W14.36
Costanzo, Anthony Roth, W3.62
Costanzo, Silva W9.5, W70.3
Cotlow, Marilyn, W80.6, W80.7, W80.36, W80.39
Coulson, Nancy, W44.3, W44.4
Coulter, David, W13.1, W13.2, W13.2a, W13.7
Cowan, Richard, W14.63
Cowan, Sigmund, W22.1, W64.12
Cowdrick, Kathryn, W56.39
Cox, Ainslee, W64.14
Crader, Jeannine, W14.31
Craft, Barry, W3.39
Crafts, Edward, W3.42, W14.43, W14.61
Craig, Patricia, W72.15
Crawford, Jodi, W56.57, W56.57a
Crawford, Shelley, W3.60
Crespin, Régine, W56.38, W56.38a, W56.38b, W56.38c, W56.39, W56.39a, W56.39c, W56.39e, W56.42
Crofoot, Alan, W14.27
Crook, Paul, W6.4, W6.5
Crosby, Alison, W85.12

Cross, Richard, W3.66, W18.1,
    W52.2, W52.3, W52.4, W52.15
Crowe, Sharon, W47.1
Cunningham, Davis, W72.7
Curley, Wilma, W85.7
Curry, Diane, W34.1, W46.2,
    W58.5, W58.7
Curtin, Joseph, W64.4
Curtis String Quartet, W42.1
Curtis Student Orchestra, W4.2,
    W4.13, W56.45, W73.3, W88.2
Custer, Harold, W32.6
Cutrell, Jimmy, W64.10
Czak, Alan, W56.56
Czerwenka, Oskar, W3.27

Dabrowski, Denise, W85.11
Dabrowski, Marek, W14.33
Dahl, Ingolf, W14.19
Dairs, Sylvia, W14.39
Dale Warland Chamber Singers,
    W3.28
Dallas Opera, W4.11, W4.11b,
    W56.35, W56.35b
Dame, Beverly, W56.10, W56.11,
    W56.59, W56.64, W56.8, W56.9
Dancuo, Mirjana, W14.46
Daner, Penelope, W30.2
Daniels, Barbara, W14.63, W14.63b,
    W32.6
Daniels, Charlotte, W4.2
Darian, Anita, W72.11, W72.12
Darmodihardjo, Ferlina Newyanti,
    W79.2
Darrenkamp, John, W14.35, W14.36
Daum, Margaret, W4.2, W64.4,
    W64.20
Davidge, Ric, W3.56
Davidson, Joy, W3.21, W14.31,
    W14.34
Davies, John, W14.68
Davis, Sylvia, W79.2, W79.3
Davis, Tim, W64.10
Davrath, Netania, W14.30, W14.32
Daw, Malcolm, W72.19
Dawson, Marc, W32.19

De la O, Eva, W56.24
De Lappe, Gemze, W85.6
De Lys, Derna, W56.14
De Retes, Africa, W56.42
De Rosa, Judith, W14.35, W14.36,
    W72.16
De Rugeriis, Joseph, W14.47
De Sabata, Victor, W5.1, W5.2,
    W5.3, W5.3a
De Turk, William, W35.4, W75.5,
    W75.6
Dean, Barbara, W56.25
Deas, Kevin, W3.62
Deaton, Anthony, W6.3
Deep Ellum Opera Theatre, W3.50,
    W3.60, W3.60a, W56.57,
    W56.57a
Del Vivo, Graziano, W14.34
Delavaux, Geneviève, W34.2
Deletré, Bernard, W14.50
DeLon, Jack, W3.11
DeMain, John, W32.24
Dening, James, W52.8
Denis, Fabien, W3.33, W3.33a
Denner, Harry, W72.14
Denniston, Patrick J., W56.40
DeNoon, Debra, W14.65
Densen, Irwin, W72.16
Dent, Karl, W28.1
Denver Chamber Orchestra, W3.35,
    W3.36
Depraz, Xavier, W19.7
DePreist, James, W5.5, W5.6, W5.7
Dernesch, Helga, W3.27
Derr, Emily, W56.60
Detels, Polly, W85.19
Dettmers, Christian, W3.25
DeVeer, Mark, W32.13
Devia, Mariella, W80.11, W80.11a
Dhavemas, Sebastien, W56.22
Di Credio, Oslavio, W60.2
Di Gerlando, Maria, W14.25, W72.7,
    W72.27
Di Giuseppe, Enrico, W72.11,
    W72.16, W72.17
Di Paolo, Tonio, W19.11, W46.2,

W58.5, W58.7
Di Virgilio, Nicholas, W72.15
Dickerson, Bernard, W52.8, W52.10
Diggory, Edith, W22.5
Dihel, Viorel, W3.31
Dirksen, Richard, W53.5
Dirksen, Richard S., W22.1
Dishtchekenian, Ameen, W19.12
DiSimone, Lorraine, W14.58
Dittmann, Michael, W80.10
Dixon, Kevin, W3.34
Dobish, Gail, W72.21, W72.25
Dobreva, Blagovesta Karnobatlova, W9.6
Dobson, John, W3.37, W3.65
Dods, Marcus, W14.38
Dodson, Elizabeth, W3.46
Domingo, Placido, W30.1, W30.1a, W30.1d, W30.1i, W30.1ll, W30.1m, W30.1n, W30.1p, W30.1u
Don Ana Lyric Opera Company, W3.54
Donnell, Margaret, W56.26
Donner, Franz, W14.45
Donovan, Sheila, W32.12
Dorfmann, Ania, W70.1, W70.4
Dorka, Marianne, W14.56
Dorsey, Gwendolyn, W56.54
Dowling, Denis, W14.22
Downing, David, W14.44
Drachman, Evan, W77.3
Dresse, Francis, W52.6
Dubarry, Chantal, W14.52
Dübbers, Marita, W14.55
Dublin, Stephen, W14.44
Dubre, Bette, W4.4
Dudley, Geoffrey, W3.17, W3.17a
Dudley, Jennifer, W14.63
Dudley, Robert, W3.38
Dufour, Marc, W13.4
Dugas, Deanna, W56.46
Dumas, Aline, W13.4
Duncombe, Rosanne, W56.31
Dunn, Mignon, W56.53, W56.53a
Dunning, Edwin, W56.12

Dunshirn, Ernst, W56.41, W64.17
Dupont, Stephen, W30.1, W44.7
Duval, Franca, W52.2, W52.3, W52.15
Duyn, James, W14.18
D'Albergo, Susan, W34.5
D'Arès, Ira, W34.2, W34.3

Earl, Ronald, W52.11
Earle, Roderick, W3.37
Easthope, Roderick, W4.14
Ebeling, Rick, W56.24
Ebony Opera Guild, W56.54
Eckhoff, Herbert, W3.62
Eddolls, Ronald, W14.22
Edwards, Alan, W3.29
Edwards, Sian, W14.49
Eggertsson, Viðar, W56.32
Ehrensperger, Gisela, W56.21, W56.23
Ehrling, Sixten, W14.20, W14.71
Einsel, Richard, W3.52
Elias, Rosalind, W14.23, W18.1, W72.9
Ellis, Osian, W10.1
Engel, Lehman, W14.15, W14.69, W14.72
English Chamber Orchestra, W53.1
English National Opera, W14.40
Equinox Symphony, W72.7
Erede, Alberto, W64.4, W64.20
Ericson, Barbro, W14.42
Eriksen, Arild, W14.46
Errante, Valerie, W14.55
Espirita, Arthur, W14.66
Essen, Viola, W73.1
Ethridge, Dorothy, W85.6
Etienne, Patricia, W3.57
Etzion, Adi, W14.32
Eustis, Edwina, W4.2
Evan, Allan, W52.10, W60.2
Evans, Beverly, W14.28, W14.29, W14.48, W32.9, W56.28, W56.28a, W56.29, W56.33, W56.34, W56.36, W56.43, W56.43a, W56.48, W56.48a,

## Performer Index  319

W56.48b
Evans, Edith, W14.21
Evans, Joseph, W44.3, W44.4

Fabrina, Franco, W72.24
Fair, Joseph, W14.29
Falk, Peter, W56.21, W56.23
Falkman, Carl Johan, W14.42
Falletta, JoAnn, W3.36
Farina, Franco, W72.21
Farmer, Elisabeth, W14.28
Farnham Grammar School, W3.17
Farrell, Eileen, W3.36
Farris, Judith, W14.47
Farwell, Joyce, W32.6
Faull, Ellen, W32.8, W34.8c, W64.5, W64.6, W64.7, W64.8
Fauntroy, Hazelita, W34.1
Fay, Jon, W22.5
Fayad, Ron, W47.1
Fazah, Adid, W52.5
Feiner, Mitch, W3.55
Fenty, Maria, W74.1
Fernandez, Matt, W3.56
Festival Orchestra, W22.4
Fiedler, Arthur, W73.13
Filippi, Pierre, W72.13
Fink, Ben, W3.52
Fiorito, John, W56.33, W56.34
Fioroni, Giovanna, W14.34, W52.9, W53.2
Fire, Robert, W80.30
Firkušný, Rudolf, W66.3, W66.4, W66.4a
Fisch, Asher, W56.50
Fischer, Alan, W74.1
Fischer, Robert, W32.6
Fish, Peter, W22.1
Flagello, Ezio, W19.8, W19.8k
Fleck, William, W19.10
Fleetwood, James, W32.9
Fleischer, Randall Craig, W50.1
Fleming, Renee, W79.4
Florentine Opera, W14.60
Florida Philharmonic, W72.26
Florida Symphony Orchestra, W3.39

Fluck, Alan, W3.17
Flummerfelt, Joseph, W19.11, W22.4, W46.2, W53.6, W58.5, W58.7, W85.10
Foldi, Andrew, W32.11
Fordyce, Nancy Hitch, W4.3
Forrester, Maureen, W56.22, W56.22a, W56.22c
Fort Lauderdale Opera, W72.26
Fort Worth Opera, W64.18, W80.26
Forti, Fiorella Carmen, W52.9
Fortini, Adrienne, W56.55
Fortuna, Maria, W4.13, W4.13a
Forumorkest, W52.10
Foss, Harlan, W56.43
Foss, Lukas, W22.5
Foster, John, W85.6
Foster, Mark, W13.4
Found, Marilyn, W32.14
Fountain Street Choir, W3.70
Fox, Fred, W58.27
Fox, Tom, W32.6
Franc, René, W64.15
Franci, Carlo, W37.1, W53.2
Frank, Terry Kiss, W32.24
Franks, Russell, W14.57
Frederickson, Roxanne, W85.19
Fredricks, Richard, W14.26
Freeh, Penelope, W3.59
Freni, Mirella, W30.1i
Freni, Rose Marie, W72.20
Friedrich, Eberhard, W80.19
Friedrich, Roland, W14.54
Friesen, Arthur, W14.56
Frizzell, Todd, W3.35
Frühbeck de Burgos, Rafael, W30.1
Fülleborn, Gustav, W52.10
Fulton, Amanda, W22.4
Furlanetto, Ferruccio, W58.4, W58.6
Furman, John, W14.57

Gabriel, Marilyn, W14.44
Gadd, Stephen, W14.49
Gaetani, Lorenzo, W53.2
Gainey, Andrew, W64.7
Galiano, Joseph, W3.22

## 320  Performer Index

Galinas, Paul, W3.49
Gao, Ding, W3.46
Garabedian, Edna, W52.13, W52.14, W56.51, W56.51a, W56.51b
Garen, David, W4.6
Garff, Laura, W3.29
Gari, Giulio, W4.3
Garner, Françoise, W64.15
Garrard, Don, W3.19
Garrett, Eric, W6.4, W6.5, W34.2, W34.3
Garrett, Lesley, W14.38
Garrott, Alice, W14.39
Gates, Darin, W3.29, W3.29a
Gatti, Giorgio, W72.22, W80.11, W80.11a
Gauthier, Gregory, W3.58
Gayer, Josepha, W14.60, W14.61, W14.63
Gaynes, George, W14.21, W14.26
Gayton, Matthew J., W85.12
Geary, Cathy, W52.11
Geary, David, W32.18
Gedda, Nicolai, W19.8, W19.8k
Gee, Paul, W6.3
Gemert, Theo van, W14.56
Genty, Claude, W56.19, W56.61
George, Lyndon, W56.47
George, Zelma, W14.24, W56.13, W56.14, W56.14a, W56.14b, W56.14c
Georgiou, Vilma, W14.21
Gersthofer, Frank, W32.18
Geschichter, Samuel, W86.1
Giancola, Barbara, W3.24
Gibbs, John, W14.40
Gibbs, Raymond, W32.8
Gibson, Alexander, W14.22, W14.23
Gibson, Sian Wyn, W14.49
Giebel, Matt, W3.57
Giesl, Erica, W13.7
Gietzen, Herbert, W4.13, W14.41, W44.5, W44.6, W44.7, W52.12, W56.31, W56.45
Giffey, Nancy, W3.55
Gilbert, Jane, W3.48

Gilgore, Lawrence, W14.48
Gill, Brian, W14.62
Gilmore, Gail, W14.41
Giordano, John, W57.1
Giorgetti, Giorgio W14.34
Giovaninetti, Reynald, W52.6, W52.7
Glass, Audrey, W14.27
Glassman, Allan, W72.26
Glaze, Gary, W19.10
Glocker, Luis, W32.14
Godfrey, Graham, W6.4, W6.4b, W6.5
Goeglein, William, W3.44
Golden, Emily, W14.43, W14.51, W14.61, W14.63, W14.68
Goldenthal, Bibiana, W14.32, W14.39, W14.48, W14.51, W14.61
Goldschmidt, Nicholas, W64.9
Goldstein, David Michael, W32.13
Golembiski, Deborah, W56.48
Golmagro, Gianluigi, W14.34
Golovina, Nina, W73.1
Gonzales, Brian, W56.57
Gonzales, Ernesto, W72.7, W72.27
Gonzales, Roman, W52.12
Gonzalez, Chapman, W54.1
Goodman, Jonathan, W3.58
Goodwin, Russell, W72.27
Gordon, Edith, W56.14, W80.8, W80.8b
Gordon, Leona, W34.2
Görgen, Eva Maria, W56.21, W56.23
Górny, Waclawa, W19.12
Gorr, Rita, W14.50, W52.7, W52.7a, W64.15, W64.15a
Graham, Martha, G179; W10.2, W24, W24.2, W24.5, W24.7
Gramm, Donald, W19.9
Granick, Arthur, W86.1
Gray, Badiene, W14.51, W14.51c, W14.58, W14.58a, W14.58b
Gray, Fenton, W80.24
Graybill, Nancy, W14.44
Green, Barton, W56.49
Green, Eugene, W45.1, W72.14

Green, Paul Lamont, W3.49
Greenspon, Muriel, W14.35, W56.20, W56.20a, W64.12, W72.11, W72.12
Greenwell, Gean, W4.4
Greenwood, Ben, W3.55
Gregg, Wade, W44.3, W44.4
Greiner, Birgit, W14.45, W56.41
Griffin, Sylvia, W72.19
Griffith, David, W34.1
Griffiths, Greg, W3.44
Grima, Danièle, W52.6, W52.7
Grimm, Betty Jane, W56.63
Grossman, Herbert, W3.66, W45.1, W52.4
Groth, David, W14.51, W14.60
Grover, Penelope, W56.56
Gruett, Jon David, W14.47
Grundheber, Franz, W32.4, W32.10
Grunewald, Eugenie, W72.26
Gudas, Paul, W3.42, W14.53
Guigue, Paul, W14.52
Guillot, Melissa, W32.19
Guimares, Leila, W14.61
Guinn, Leslie, W76.1
Gumpoldskirchen Kinderchor, W32.15
Gunder, Gregory, W14.58
Gunn, Willene, W14.37, W56.44
Guzman, Suzanna, W3.42, W30.2, W72.26
Gyton, Lorna, W80.24, W80.24a

Habermann, Roswitha, W3.25
Hacker, John, W14.65
Haeems, David, W3.37
Hafermann, Gene, W3.55
Hafermann, Holly, W3.55
Hagan, Peter, W14.66
Hagen-William, Louis, W3.23
Haggart, Margaret, W72.21, W72.22
Hagoel, Kobi, W56.50
Hagopian, Sara, W6.1
Halasz, Laszlo, W4.3
Hale, Robert, W44.3, W44.4
Hall, Holly, W80.16
Hall, Jay, W32.19

Hall, Jay V., Jr., W14.66
Hall, Marsie, W32.6
Hall, Van Anthony, W3.50
Hall-Garcia, Brannon, W72.23
Hallman, Bjørn, W14.42, W14.46
Halverson, Peter, W3.59
Hambro, Leonid, W66.5
Hamburgische Staatsoper, W3.20, W32.4, W32.10, W32.25
Hamlett, Michael, W80.19
Hammel, Bonita, W3.59
Hammel, Jesse, W3.59
Hammond, Andrew, W32.16, W32.17
Handt, Herbert, W52.2, W52.5, W52.15, W53.2
Handzlik, Jean, W14.18
Hanslowe, Theodora, W14.57
Haparnas, Willy, W14.30, W14.32
Hardie, Sheila, W14.23
Harding, Cynthia, W14.57
Hardmon, Andre, W53.6, W81.1
Hargan, Alison, W52.8
Harkness Ballet, W16
Harper, Joe Don, W3.50
Harper, Timothy, W14.38
Harris, Lee, W34.5
Harrison, Michael, W72.18, W72.18a
Harrold, Jack, W14.25
Hartmann, Donald, W3.34
Hartung, Gretel, W56.23
Hasslo, Hugo, W14.20
Hastings, Elizabeth, W14.58
Haughton, Harold, W74.1, W74.1c, W74.1d
Havranek, Roger, W3.57, W19.11
Hawaii Opera Theater, W19.10
Hays, Marian Rian, W10.4
Haywood, Lorna, W3.37, W3.40, W3.40a, W3.40b, W3.65, W72.17
Hebert, Rubye, W56.54, W56.54a
Hecht, Joshua, W14.25, W14.32
Hedlund, Ronald, W14.47, W14.48
Heffernan, Priscilla, W13.1, W13.7
Hegierski, Kathleen, W14.60, W14.64
Heimann, Keith, W4.12

## 322  Performer Index

Heininger, Cynthia, W3.61, W3.61a
Helbig, Avril, W13.1
Heldman, Dianna, W34.5
Heller, Barbara, W13.5
Heller, Bonnie, W56.17
Helm, Alicia, W3.51
Helton, Jerry, W32.6
Henderson, Robert, W3.29
Henderson, Sherry, W56.27
Hendriksen, Arne, W14.20, W14.71
Heninger-Potter, Joseph, W3.44, W3.44b
Henninger, Nancy, W14.41, W52.10
Henriksen, Daryl, W3.49
Hensel, Howard, W72.16
Heppner, Ben, W3.31
Herbert, Paul, W32.16, W32.17
Hermalyn, Joy, W14.58
Hermann, Thomas, W14.54
Hernández, César, W30.2
Hernandez, Samuel, W56.26
Herndon, Clyde, W32.6
Herrero, Ana, W3.47
Herrmann, Anita, W32.14
Herron, Tracy, W80.32
Hersh, Sarah, W14.65
Hertzberg, Brita, W14.20, W14.20a, W14.71
Hickox, Richard, W53.7
Hicks, Pamela, W19.12
Highley, Joanne, W56.18, W56.26
Highley, Ronald, W56.18, W56.26
Hightower, Loren, W85.6
Hilbish, Thomas, W85.15
Hilgenberg, Katherine, W14.19
Hill, Don, W3.58
Hill, Paul, W85.16
Hillier, Helen, W14.22
Hinchman, Pamela, W7.1, W7.1b
Hinds, Esther, W22.1, W22.4
Hinshaw, Susan, W14.47, W14.47d, W14.48, W14.48a
Ho, Damon, W79.2
Hobday, Heidi, W13.1, W13.7
Hobson, Richard, W34.5
Hocher, Barbara, W14.36, W14.51, W56.43, W56.48
Hoffman, David, W80.29
Hoffman, Ernst, W3.11
Hoke, Bernadette, W64.13
Holdgreiwe, David, W32.6
Holley, David, W3.53
Hollowell, Kelley, W22.4
Holm, Renate, W32.15
Holman, Derek, W13.7
Holmes, Eugene, W60.1
Holmes, Justin, W3.49
Holmes, Richard, W80.23, W80.38
Holt, Anthony, W59.1
Hong, Mildred, W64.10
Hong, Suzanne, W19.11, W19.11g, W34.4, W46.2, W58.5, W58.7
Hook, Walter, W72.14
Hooper, James, W64.11
Hoops, Frances, W14.18
Hopple, Mary, W64.4, W64.20
Horn, Wilburta, W4.2
Horne, Marilyn, W4.4, W4.5
Hornick, Gottfried, W32.15
Horst, Louis, W24.2
Horst, Steven, W14.64
Howard, Ann, W14.40
Howard, Greg, W3.63
Howard, Patty, W32.6
Howarth, Judith, W6.4, W6.5, W9.7
Howe, Janet, W72.9
Howe, Martha Jane, W44.3, W44.4
Howell, Margaret, W85.19
Howerton, Beverly, W3.70
Huddleston, Charles, W56.52, W80.25
Hudson, John, W4.14
Hudson, Mark, W56.27
Huffman, David, W32.22
Huffstodt, Karen, W30.1
Hughes, Karla, W80.32
Hughes, Kevin, W14.38
Hughes, Nan, W3.49
Hugo, Soraya, W3.47
Hukvari, Astrid Hellesnes, W14.46
Hullum, Nancy, W64.10
Hulse, Eileen, W32.16, W32.17

Hume, Alastair, W59.1
Hunt, Karen, W64.12
Hutagalung, Horas, W79.2
Hutagalung, Joseph, W79.2
Hutto, W. Benjamin, W53.6
Hynes, Elizabeth, W4.11, W4.11a, W4.11b

Ianni, Barbara, *Sister*, W56.22
Icelandic Opera, W56.32, W80.13
Illig, Annett, W32.21
Indiana University Opera Theater, W22.5
Irwin, Thomas M., III, W14.66
Irwin, Tom, W32.19
Isepp, Martin, W9.1
Israel Chamber Ensemble, W14.30
Ivanchich, Dolores, W32.6
Ives, Bill, W59.1

Jackman, Jeremy, W59.1
Jackson, Richard, W52.8, W52.8d, W52.10
Jackson, Simon, W53.5, W53.5b
Jacobs, Anne, W56.56
Jacobs, Lawrence, W84.1
Jacobsson, Sven-Erik, W14.20
Jaffe, Charles, W42.1
Jagust, Marian, W56.23
Jalbert, Madeleine, W14.52
Jamerson, Thomas, W60.1
James Sewell Ballet, W3.59, W3.59a
James, Carolyne, W14.43, W19.11, W56.25, W56.26, W56.35, W56.35a, W56.35b
James, Eleanor, W3.31
Jamroz, Krystyna, W14.33
Jang, Jinyoung, W3.50
Jarvis, Scott, W56.56
Jauhiainen, Brian, W14.61
Jeffers, Galen, W3.60
Jenkins, Neil, W14.30
Jenkins, Tammy, W3.54
Jennings, Harlan, W32.6
Jennings, Jerry J., W3.20
Jennings, Kenneth, W3.68

Jennings, Mary, W72.11, W72.12
Jennings, Ronald, W3.11
Jervis, Ian, W32.16, W32.17
Jette, Maria, W3.59
Jobin, Raoul, W41.1
Johanson, Erik, W3.57
Johns, Roy, W3.61
Johnson, Bessie, W52.11
Johnson, George, W3.53
Johnson, Maxine, W84.1
Johnson, Patricia, W14.23
Johnson, Penny, W56.52, W80.25
Johnson, Roy, W56.63
Johnson-Healy, Marian, W56.45
Jones, Delores, W60.1
Jones, Dennis, W3.32
Jones, Jennifer, W56.45
Jones, Roger, W3.31
Jones, Rowland, W14.22, W14.23
Jones, Steven, W14.44
Jones, Valerie Ann, W32.19
Jongeyans, George, W14.15, W14.69
Joselson, Rachel, W32.24
Juilliard American Opera, W4.12
Juilliard American Opera Center, W34.4
June, Ava, W14.23, W14.40, W14.40a
Jung, Jeanette, W56.25

Kahn, Madeleine, W3.18
Kahn, Philippe, W14.52
Kaldenberg, Keith, W72.27
Kale, Stuart, W14.40
Kalman, Mike, W14.65
Kaltenbach, Jérôme, W56.39
Kaptan, Miyase, W14.54
Karamu Lyric Theatre, W14.24, W56.13, W56.16
Karnakoski, Karl, W73.1
Karousatos, Nicholas, W7.1, W34.4
Kavafian, Ani, W10.1
Kay, Brian, W59.1
Kayan, Orrin, W85.8
Kearney, Sheila M., W14.44
Keefe, Robert, W7.1, W34.4

Keeley, James A., W46.1, W58.3, W80.12
Keene, Christopher, W3.22, W14.35, W14.36, W14.39, W32.9, W34.1, W60.1, W60.1i, W60.2, W79.2
Kehrig, Diana, W72.16
Kekanui, Van, W3.60, W3.60a
Keller, Evelyn, W56.10, W56.10f, W56.12, W56.14, W56.59, W56.8, W56.9, W56.9f
Kelley, Norman, W14.17, W14.21, W14.26, W52.3, W52.4
Kellogg, Cal Stewart, W14.51, W56.34, W56.36, W80.15
Keltner, Karen, W3.39
Kemp, Michelle, W56.46
Kendall, David, W34.1
Kendall, Gary, W80.12
Kennerley, Michael, W32.16, W32.17
Kent, David, W13.1
Kentish Opera Group, W72.10
Kermoyan, Kalem, W14.19
Kerski-Nienow, Claudia, W56.53
Kibler, Belva, W56.11, W56.64
Kidwell, Jody, W72.24
Kim, Sung Kil, W79.2, W79.3
Kimura, Yuriko, W24.3
King, Martha, W3.66
King, Paul, W56.14, W80.8
King, Wayne, W32.20
King's Singers, W59.1
Kinsey, Sam, W3.49
Kirk, Florence, W4.3
Kitchiner, John, W14.40
Kleinman, Marlena, W56.17
Klieme, Stefan, W14.56
Klimek, Zdislaw, W14.33
Klippstatter, Kurt, W56.53
Klosowska, Eligia, W14.59, W64.16
Kmentt, Waldemar, W3.27, W3.27e
Knetlar, Walter, W34.1
Knighton, Barbara, W56.16
Knoll, Richard, W3.28
Knoop, Laura, W56.49
Kobart, Ruth, W14.25, W52.2, W52.3
Koehn, Daniel, W3.51
Kogel, Richard, W56.21, W56.23
Kolganova, Elena, W14.63
Kolomyjec, Joanne, W14.64
Kombrink, Ilona, W52.4
Köppl, Leopold, W14.45, W56.41, W64.17
Kosbahn, Gerda, W14.55
Kotze, Michael, W14.65
Kouloumbis, Andreas, W52.9
Kova, Marija, W14.26
Kovács, Attila, W14.55
Kozma, Tibor, W4.6
Krabill, Dorothy, W72.14
Kraft, Jean, W32.5, W32.8
Kramar, John, W56.45
Kramer, Helmut, W14.54
Kraus, Otakar, W53.1
Kreklewich, Rick, W3.32
Kreste, Mary, W14.21, W64.7, W64.8
Krilov, Arthur, W84.1
Kronenberg, Kim, W52.11
Krooskos, Christina, W14.31
Krueger, Dana, W7.1, W22.1, W22.4, W53.5, W53.6
Kudo, Gary, W3.46
Kuethe, Kim, W32.6
Kuhlman, Rosemary, W3.10, W3.12, W3.13, W3.14, W3.16, W3.28, W3.28a, W3.64, W3.71
Kuhn, John, W52.3
Kühr, Klaus, W9.4, W10.5, W27.3, W63.3
Kungliche Hovkapellet, W14.71
Kuntzsch, Matthias, W3.20, W32.4, W32.10
Kurt P. Reimann Opera Studio, W72.23
Kurtze, Arthur, W3.70
Kutner, Michael, W80.16
Kuzmich, Andrea, W13.1, W13.2, W13.7
Kuzmich, John, W13.1, W13.7
Kwartin, Paul, W56.9

## Performer Index 325

Kyung-Hong, Hey, W56.29

La Jolla Civic/University Symphony
  Orchestra, W85.11
La Marchina, Robert, W19.10,
  W19.9, W19.9b, W19.9c,
  W56.17
La Rochelle, Jacques, W56.8
La Scala Orchestra and Chorus, W4.15
La Selva, Vincent, W14.28, W72.11,
  W72.12
Labarthe, Nicole, W14.52
Lachona, Chris, W14.19
LaCosse, Steven, W34.5
Ladsen, Lonnie, W53.6
Lafon, Brigitte, W13.4
Laghezza, Anna, W3.59
Lamartine, Nicole, W3.54
Lampl, Hans, W14.44
Landis, Barbara, W56.58
Lane, Gloria, W14.15, W14.17,
  W14.21, W14.69, W72.7,
  W72.7i, W72.13, W72.27
Lane, Louis, W3.67
Langford, Audrey, W72.10
Langton, Sunny Joy, W19.11
Lankston, John, W14.36, W60.1
Lanza, Manuel, W56.49
Lanzetter, Nicola, W14.38
Larsen, John, W14.22
Larson, Gene, W3.29
Las Cruces Symphony, W3.54
Las, Genia, W52.15
Lathroun, Juan Carlos, W3.47
Lawrence, Barry, W3.51
Lawson, Catherine, W64.9
Lawson, Charles, W3.38
Layman, Jennifer, W80.28
Le Sawyer, Mary, W14.26, W56.15
Leaf, Helen, W56.47
Leak, Alice E., W3.60
LeBeaux, Eugene, W56.57
Ledbetter, William, W14.36, W60.1,
  W72.16
Lederer, Viktor, W14.55
Lee, Mary Ann, W6.3

Lee, Sung Sook, W79.2, W79.3
Legendre, Pamela, W14.66, W32.19
Leggate, Robin, W27.4, W53.7
Lehtinen, Pertti, W44.5
Leigh, Jack, W85.6
Leinsdorf, Erich, W18.2, W18.2b,
  W18.2c, W18.5
Lemon, Denise, W32.6
Lemon-Brundin, Benna, W14.20,
  W14.71
Lengfelder, Jacquelyn, W3.50
Lenkl, Siegfried, W14.41
Leonard, Lawrence, W53.1
Leonetti, Adrienne, W3.34
Leppert, Robert, W14.18
Lerner, Gloria, W56.24
Lescault, John, W56.52
Lesser, Lawrence, W26.1, W26.2
Leue, Edina, W14.54
Levitt, Joseph, W22.5
Lewenthal, Raymond, W70.5
Lewis, Marguerite, W15.1
Lewis, Michael, W3.26
Lewis, William, W37.1
Leyser, Christine, W64.16
Lichter, Cheryl, W56.41, W64.17
Lichtfuß, Martin, W14.59
Lichti, Dan, W56.22
Lieber, Dean, W14.18
Lief, Arthur, W56.24
Lièvre, Geneviève, W13.4
Lim, Jee Hyun, W89.1
Lind, Joanna, W56.58
Lindevald, April, W56.56, W56.56a
Lindquist, Karen, W63.1
Linford, Jon, W3.54
Lipinska, Pola, W14.33
Lishner, Leon, W3.10, W3.14,
  W3.64, W14.15, W14.16m,
  W14.29, W14.32, W14.69,
  W45.1, W72.7, W72.27
Litevsky, Tzvia, W56.50
Littel, Thomas, W6.1
Little Orchestra Society, W3.40,
  W46.3, W73.5, W88.3
Livingston, Kimberly, W34.5

Livingston, William, W19.13
Llorca, Adolfo, W14.51, W52.13
Loca, Jean-Louis, W56.38, W56.39, W56.42
Locke, Randy, W14.43
Lockhart, James, W3.19
Loftin, Nat, W3.60
Lombardi, Riccardo, W14.45
London Symphony Orchestra, W18.2b, W72.9, W73.6, W84.2
London, George, W18.2, W18.2d, W18.5, W18.6, W19.8, W19.8k
Long, Charles, W52.9
Lopez, Ilca, W14.59
Lopez-Cobos, Jesus, W3.26
LoSchiavo, Joseph A., W14.58
Louisville Orchestra, W80.37
Loup, François, W19.13
Low, Stephanie, W56.24, W64.11
Lowe, David, W3.40
Lublin, Eliane, W56.19, W56.61
Ludgin, Chester, W14.25, W14.27, W14.37, W52.4
Luening, Otto, W56.8
Lugar, Peter, W6.1
Luketich, Richard, W14.65
Lusmann, Stephen, W14.61
Lutz, Alfred, W9.4, W10.5, W27.3, W63.3
Lynch, Olive, W56.45
Lyon, Robert, W44.6
Lyric Opera of Chicago, W14.63
Lyric Opera of Kansas City, W3.48, W3.48a, W13.6, W56.18, W56.26, W72.14
Lyric Opera of Kansas City Honors Chorus, W13.6

Mackin, Robin Lehleitner, W9.3
MacNeil, Cornell, W14.15, W14.69
MacWatters, Virginia, W64.5, W64.6
Madison Opera, W32.24
Madison Symphony Orchestra, W32.24
Magallenes, Nicholas, W85.7
Maggio Musicale Fiorentino Orchestra, W80.21
Magnani, Anna, W36.1
Majercik, Cheryl, W4.13
Makino, Seiji, W14.54
Malakova, Petra, W44.6
Malaspina, Gianpiero, W4.20
Malfar, Lanny, W56.55
Malfitano, Catherine, W72.16, W72.16c
Maliponte, Adriana, W19.7
Malkin, Seth, W4.13
Mallery, Denise, W64.13
Mandia, John, W85.7
Manford, Barbara, W47.1
Mangin, Noel, W3.20, W32.4, W32.10
Manitoba Opera, W14.64
Manring, Lesley, W32.15
Manson, George, W3.55
Manzari, Robert J., W79.2
Manzo, Andrew, W85.11
Marcello, Michael, W3.61
Mark, Peter, W3.34
Marlo, Maria, W14.15, W14.21, W14.25, W14.26, W14.69, W72.7, W72.27
Marrazzo, Randi, W72.24
Marschner, Kurt, W32.4, W32.10
Marsee, Susanne, W44.3, W44.4
Marshall, William, W3.30
Martelli, Edith, W4.9
Martha Graham Dance Company, W24.3
Martignoni, Robert, W14.50
Martilotti, Nelson, W14.41, W44.5
Martin, Ethel, W85.6
Martin, Marvis, W61.1, W63.1, W63.2
Martin, Philip, W66.6, W66.6a
Martin, Steven, W3.53
Martin, Thomas P., W64.5, W64.6
Martin, William, W4.2
Martineau, Malcolm, W9.7, W27.4
Martinez, Ana Maria, W74.1
Martini, Mary Ann, W72.18
Martinovich, Boris, W14.39, W44.6,

## Performer Index   327

W46.2, W58.5, W58.7
Marty, Jean-Pierre, W3.23, W32.11
Marx, Jacqueline, W56.37
Mashburn, Laura, W56.45
Masini, Gianfranco, W56.38
Maslova, Lisa, W73.1
Maslow, Leslie, W64.13
Massey, George, W4.10
Mastice, Catherine, W56.59
Masuda, Takako, W80.19
Mather, Debra, W64.13
Matherine, Karl, W32.13
Matheson-Bruce, Graeme, W34.2, W34.3
Mathis, Edith, W32.4, W32.10
Matiakh, Ivan, W14.50
Matranga, Deborah, W32.13
Matteini, Giuliana, W14.34
Matthews, James T., W73.11, W73.12
Matthews, Valerie, W3.41
Mauceri, John, W44.4, W79.3
Maxara, Maria, W32.21
Maxwell, Donald, W3.65
May Festival Chorus, W18.1
May-Humes, Stefanie, W32.18
Maynor, Kevin, W3.40
Mayo, Conrad, W4.2
Mazzara, Gina Marie, W56.56
Mazzoni, Elena, W4.15
McAlpine, William, W53.1
McCann, Dolores, W56.16
McCauley, Barry, W14.63
McClintock, Susan, W80.9
McClusky, Eric, W74.1
McCollum, Jerrald D., W64.10
McCollum, John, W3.66
McConnell, Regina, W22.1
McCorvey, Everett, W3.51
McCoy, Robert, W14.18
McDermott, Sheila, W14.66
McFall, Terry, W47.1
McFarland, Joan, W32.20
McIntyre, Donald, W53.1
McIver, William, W3.14, W3.16
McKenna, Jim, W32.6

McKerrow, Rita, W72.9
McKinley, Andrew, W3.10, W3.14, W3.64, W14.15, W14.69
McKinley, George, W3.11
McKinney, Tom, W3.39
McLaughlin, Cele, W15.1
McLaughlin, Marie, W14.40
McManus, Catherine, W52.11
McNamara, Gloria, W3.63
McRee, Theresa, W56.27
Meade, James, W64.13
Mega, Giuseppe, W80.21
Mehta, Zubin, W21.1
Meier, Eduard, W32.18
Meier, Gustav, W32.5
Meistre, Barbara, W72.18
Melendez, Manuel, W14.51
Melone, Roger, W43.1
Meloni, Claude, W14.52
Menges, Diane Julin, W80.29
Menotti, Francis, W22.4, W56.28, W56.29, W56.33, W56.34, W56.35, W56.36, W56.43, W56.45
Menotti, Gian Carlo (as performer), W65.3, W82.1
Menut, Nicole, W56.61
Mercurio, Steven, W30.2, W72.24, W72.24b, W72.25, W72.26
Meredith, Morley, W19.8, W19.8k
Merrill, Christopher, W3.36, W3.36b
Merrill, Kenneth, W27.1, W27.2
Merriman, Dan, W14.25
Mesplé, Mady, W19.7
Messingschlager, Joe, W32.6
Messingschlager, Kathy, W32.6
Mester, Jorge, W56.60, W64.19, W66.8, W80.37
Metropolitan Concert Band, W19.14
Metropolitan Opera, W4.4a, W19.8, W19.8k, W19.9
Metropolitan Opera Orchestra, W48.1
Meyer, Chris, W47.1
Meyer, Jennifer, W47.1
Meyer, Kerstin, W3.20, W3.23, W32.11

Miazza, George-L., W3.23
Michel, Solange, W19.7, W56.19, W56.61
Midland Music Makers Opera, W3.41, W4.14
Migenes, Julia, W14.29, W72.12
Milian, Tomas, W37.1
Miller, Catherine, W14.18
Miller, Sarah, W22.5
Miller, Valerie, W3.51
Milnes, Sherrill, W14.28
Milstein, Fredric, W14.26
Milwaukee Symphony Orchestra, W46.1, W58.3, W80.12
Mims, James Alexander, W52.13
Minde, Stefan, W14.37
Mindizova, Elena, W9.6
Minnesota Opera, W3.28
Minnesota Orchestra, W3.28
Minton, Sara, W32.6
Miranda, Ana Maria, W72.13
Misner, Ferne, W14.18
Misselwitz, Mathias, W3.20, W3.20c
Mitchell, Arthur, W85.7
Mitchell, Hannah, W56.55
Mitrica, Rodica, W52.12
Mitropoulos, Dimitri, W73.10
Mock, Joe, W32.6
Molese, Michele, W19.7
Moll, Clare, W14.38
Molzer, Felix, W3.38
Monachino, Francis, W3.10, W3.14, W3.64, W14.15, W14.69
Moncion, Francisco, W73.1
Monette, La Vergne, W14.29
Monici, Gabriele, W72.22
Montelius, Yvonne, W85.11
Moody, Robert, W80.9
Moore, Fanchon Angela, W56.54
Moore, Nancy Carol, W56.43
Morais, Nathalie, W14.64
Morales, Juan Carlos, W6.2
Morasch, Herbert, W14.54
Morelle, Maureen, W6.4, W6.5, W52.8, W52.9, W52.10
Morelli, Adriana, W72.22

Morgan, Donald, W56.11, W56.64
Morgan, Josephine, W56.47
Morgan, Mark, W14.62
Morgan, Morris, W32.14, W32.18
Morgan, Tywon, W14.66
Moriarty, John, W56.37
Morrissey, Jeffrey, W4.12
Motyka, Sally Mitchell, W64.14, W64.14a
Mouch, Camille, W14.62
Mourier, Marc, W52.11
Movroson, Denise, W64.11
Moynagh, Joan Marie, W52.5
Muckler, Zanice, W56.52
Munch, Charles, W88.6
Munzer, Cynthia, W56.52, W58.3
Mura, Bernard Jean, W6.2
Murano, Maria, W56.30, W56.30a
Murashima, Sumiko, W79.2, W79.3
Murphy, Kathleen, W14.55
Murray, Matthew, W22.1, W22.4
Muselescu, Dan, W14.59
Muti, Lorenzo, W3.62, W7.1, W52.2, W52.3, W52.15, W56.33, W72.18, W72.20, W73.3, W80.14, W88.2
Mutsumi, W14.62
Myers, Michael, W72.25
Myers, Pamela, W44.5, W44.6, W44.6d
Myrick, Korby, W14.57, W44.7

Nachmias, Rachael, W14.32
Nadeau, Lise, W84.1
Nadell, Rosalind, W4.5
Naneris, Nikiforos, W45.1, W56.17
Nantes Opera, W3.33, W56.30
Narducci, Daniel, W72.25
Nathan, Regina, W56.47
National Music Camp High School Symphonic Band, W19.16
National Symphony Orchestra, W18.3, W52.5
Nave, Maria Luisa Bordin, W60.2
NBC Opera Company, W52.2, W52.3o

NBC Symphony Orchestra, W64.4,
    W73.7
NBC Television Opera Company,
    W45.1, W45.1e
NBC Television Opera Theatre,
    W3.14, W72.7f
Neff, Yves, W13.4
Nelson, David, W56.46
Nelson, Munroe, W80.27
Nelson, Steven, W22.5
Neufeld, Lynda, W56.22
Nevada Opera, W56.44
New England Conservatory Chorus,
    W18.2, W18.5
New Israeli Opera, W56.50, W56.50a
New Jersey's American Boychoir,
    W74.1
New Philharmonia Orchestra, W4.21
New York Chamber Ensemble,
    W80.23, W80.38
New York City Ballet, W85.7,
    W85.7b, W85.17
New York City Opera, W3.12,
    W3.13, W3.15, W3.16, W4.4,
    W4.5, W4.8, W14.21, W14.25,
    W14.26, W14.28, W14.29,
    W14.35, W14.36, W44.4,
    W44.4a, W44.4e, W44.4k,
    W52.4, W56.15, W56.17,
    W58.12, W60.1, W64.5, W64.6,
    W64.7, W64.8, W72.11, W72.12
New York Lyric Opera Company,
    W56.24
New York Philharmonic, W21.1,
    W21.1b, W66.4, W73.2
New Zealand Symphony Orchestra,
    W3.69, W3.82, W73.8, W73.19,
    W73.22
Newark Boys' Chorus, W81.1,
    W81.1d
Neway, Patricia, W14.15, W14.16a,
    W14.16f, W14.16o, W14.16s,
    W14.17, W14.17f, W14.21,
    W14.25, W14.25a, W14.26,
    W14.26a, W14.28, W14.29,
    W14.69, W14.72, W47.1,
    W52.2, W52.3, W52.4, W52.5,
    W52.15
Newell, Julie, W56.40
Newman, Arthur, W14.21, W56.15
Nicholas, Roger, W53.1
Nickerson, E. Lynn, W34.4
Niemisto, Paul, W19.15
Nierlé, Jacques, W3.23
Nikodem, Zdzislaw, W14.33
Niles, John, W32.20
Nilsson, Raymond, W72.9
Noel, Rita, W52.10
Nolan, Lisa, W3.45
Noll, William, W14.43
Nordin, Birgit, W14.42, W14.42a,
    W14.46
Norick, Cecilia, W6.2
Norris, David, W56.51, W56.51a
North Carolina Dance Theater,
    W85.10
North Texas State University Opera
    Orchestra, W34.5
North Texas State University Opera
    Theatre, W52.11
Northern Sinfonia Orchestra, W53.7
Norwegian Opera, W14.46
Noseworthy, John, W56.37
Nosotti, Angelo, W44.6
Nottingham Music Theater, W22.2,
    W22.2a, W22.3

Ocasio, Jorge, W3.47
Okerlund, David, W3.48
Oklahoma State University Concert
    Chorale, W43.1
Olin, Jennifer, W85.12
Olivares, Maria Helenita, W60.2
Olsen, Carl, W4.8
Olson, Christian, W3.36
Ommerlé, Jeanne, W56.35, W80.23,
    W80.38
Opera Colorado, W3.35, W3.36
Opera Company of North Carolina,
    W3.62
Opera Company of Philadelphia, W34,
    W34.1, W56.38, W72.24,

W72.24a
Opera Company of Philadelphia
  Orchestra, W34.1
Opéra de Marseille, W52.6, W64.15
Opéra de Monte-Carlo, W14.61
Opéra de Paris Orchestre, W52.7
Opéra du Rhin, W14.52
Opera Kansas, W80.32
Opera North, W14.49
Opera of Central Kentucky, W3.51
Opera Society of Washington, W52.5,
  W56.60
Opera South, W3.45, W3.45a
Opera Theater of Boston, W56.37,
  W56.37a
Opera Theatre of Northern Virginia,
  W32.20
Opera West, W3.43
Opéra-Comique, W56.19
OperaDelaware, W6, W6.1
OperaFunatics of the Miami Valley,
  W3.63
Opie, Alan, W53.7
Orchestra da camera di Milano,
  W80.34
Orchestra of Eduard-von-Winterstein,
  W32.21
Orchestra of Rome della Radio-
  televisione Italiana, W56.11,
  W56.64
Orchestra of St. Luke's, W64.22
Orchestre de la Suisse romande,
  W3.23, W32.11
Orchestre régional Cannes-Provence-
  Côte d'Azur, W6.6
Orchestre symphonique de la
  R.T.B.F., W5.4, W73.9
Oregon Symphony Orchestra, W5.5,
  W5.6
Orenstein, Janis, W56.22
Orlando Opera Company, W3.39
Orlando, Danielle, W56.49
Ormandy, Eugene, W4.18, W78.1,
  W88.1
Orpheon Chorale, W3.40
Orselli, Raimonda, W37.1

Ortale, Ricardo, W56.42
Orth, Robert, W56.53, W80.37
Ory, Gisèle, W14.52
Ostendorf, John, W32.9
Oswald, Belinda Thayer, W64.18,
  W80.26
Otey, Louis, W14.47, W14.48,
  W14.60, W19.13, W30.1,
  W44.7, W52.13, W52.14
Owen, Richard, Jr., W13.5
Owens, Diane, W14.57
O'Briant, Pamela, W52.11
O'Donnell, Jerry, W47.1
O'Malley, Muriel, W64.6
O'Neill, Alicia, W72.18
O'Reagan, Beverly, W14.68
O'Reilly, Breffni, W13.1

Pabón, Rosalín, W3.47
Pacific Symphony Orchestra, W88.5
Padgett, Jesse, W3.53
Padoan, Carlo, W60.2
Paige, Norman, W14.37
Painter, Christopher, W3.65
Palencia, Mary Jo, W14.44
Palm Beach Civic Opera, W4.10,
  W56.28
Palmour, Deidra, W4.11, W56.35
Pálsdóttir, Thurídur, W56.32
Palzer, Uta, W14.45
Pandowa, Galina, W14.59
Panerai, Rolando, W4.7, W4.15
Panizza, Ettore, W41.1
Parcher, William, W56.48, W80.20
Pardoe, Toby, W3.45
Paris, Myrna, W14.57
Park Lane Opera, W52.8, W52.8e
Park Lane Players, W52.8
Park, Mi-Hae, W79.4
Parks, Marcia, W56.24
Parnas, Leslie, W10.1, W63.1, W77.1
Parrott, Julia, W14.49
Passen, Adrienne, W14.54
Patenaude, Joan, W72.14
Patrick, Julian, W3.66, W34.2,
  W34.3, W56.60

*Performer Index* 331

Patterson, Russell, W56.18, W72.14
Patterson, Susan, W56.39
Patterson, Willis, W3.66
Patterson, Yvonne, W73.1
Paul Hill Chorale and Orchestra, W85.16
Paul, Thomas, W72.11
Paulionis, Vytautas, W3.31
Paxton, Adèle, W14.49
Pease, James, W4.5
Peden, Margaret, W80.9
Pederson, Monte, W56.39
Pehlivanian, Elisabeth, W14.44
Pelle, Nadia, W56.33, W56.34, W56.36, W56.38, W56.43
Perez, José, W56.15
Perez, Mario Antonio, W3.60
Perreault, Geneviève, W14.41
Perriers, Danièle, W32.11
Perry, Douglas, W3.22, W3.62, W32.5, W32.8, W32.9, W79.2
Perusso, Mario, W56.42
Peters, Keith D., W14.44
Peters, Roberta, W19.8, W19.8f, W19.8k, W19.9
Peterson, Phillip, W6.1
Pfeffer, Bruce, W47.1
Phelan, Francis, W47.1
Phelan, Frank, W22.1, W56.19, W56.20, W56.21
Philadelphia Chamber String Sinfonietta, W65.3
Philadelphia Orchestra, W4.18, W4.19, W5.2, W5.3, W76.1, W78.1, W78.1b, W88.1
Philharmonia Orchestra, W3.26
Philharmonisches Staatsorchester Hamburg, W32.25
Phillips, Betty, W14.27
Phillips, Gerald, W32.6
Piane, Michael, W3.48
Piatigorsky, Gregor, W77.1, W77.1a
Piccola Scala, W56.55
Piccolo Teatro Dell'Opera, W3.49
Pierce, Judith, W14.23
Pierson, Edward, W3.22, W14.36

Pihl, Elizabeth, W32.19
Piitz, Lori, W56.62
Piland, Jeanne, W72.16
Pistone, Roberto, W37.1
Pittsburgh New Music Ensemble, W14.57
Pittsburgh Opera Theater, W14.57
Pittsburgh Symphony Orchestra, W5.1
Plowright, Rosalind, W52.8
Podic, Baldo, W19.13
Poffenberger, Jennifer, W56.62
Poleri, David, W72.7, W72.8, W72.27
Polezhayev, Yelena, W56.56
Polizzi, Robin Robertson, W14.66
Poljakow, Alexander, W14.59
Poll, Melvyn, W72.20
Pollack, Anna, W14.22, W14.23
Pollock, Michael, W3.12, W3.13, W3.16
Pomponi, Franco, W14.63
Poole, Thomas, W3.36
Popper, Felix, W4.8
Porrello, Joseph, W27.1, W27.2, W27.2a
Porretta, Frank, W45.1
Porter-Gaud School Boy Choristers, W53.6
Portland Civic Opera Association, W14.18
Portland Opera, W14.37
Portland Opera Association, W14.39
Portnoy, Donald, W56.48, W80.20
Pothier, Fabrice, W13.4
Povia, Charlotte, W14.29
Powell, Alvy, W3.42
Powell, Angela, W32.22
Powell, Deborah, W34.5
Powers, Marie, W14.15, W14.16h, W14.17, W14.69, W56.9, W56.9b, W56.9f, W56.10, W56.10c, W56.10e, W56.10f, W56.11, W56.12, W56.12a, W56.50b, W56.59, W56.64, W64.5
Prandelli, Giacinto, W4.7, W4.15

Preston, Ritchie, W52.5
Prewitt, Richard, W85.10
Price, Leontyne, W4.21, W19.9a
Price, Olwen, W14.22
Price, Percival, W75.2
Priestley, David, W3.43
Princeton High School Choir, W22.4
Prior, Beniamino, W58.4, W58.6
Probyn, John, W14.22
Proctor, Sondra, W85.12
Providence Opera Theater, W72.18
Pryor, Brett, W3.53
Prytz, Eva, W14.20, W14.71
Puffer, Monica, W56.44
Puleo, Robert, W3.21, W3.21a, W3.22

Quensel, Ida, W14.20, W14.71
Quezada, Guillermo, W3.54
Quilling, Brenda, W58.3

Rabbai, Joseph, W84.1
Racz, Teresa, W14.26
Rada, Susan, W4.10, W4.10a
Radcliffe, Stephen Rogers, W80.23, W80.38
Radio-Torino Orchestra, W64.21
Radulescu, Paul, W32.24
Rafanelli, Flora, W14.34
Ragains, Diane, W56.53, W56.58
Ragonetti, Marcia, W3.35, W3.36
RAI Orchestra, W26.1
Rainbird, James, W3.37, W3.65
Raithel, Ute, W14.55
Rakusin, Fredda, W14.39, W32.6, W34.1, W34.4
Ramlet, James, W3.28, W3.59
Randall, Gary Lee, W14.66
Rapchak, Lawrence, W56.58, W56.71
Raphael, Dani, W56.49, W56.49a
Raschio, Violet, W14.18
Raskin, Judith, W45.1
Raymond, Bob, W80.31
Raynal, Florence, W6.2
Reardon, John, W4.8, W19.10, W32.5, W45.1, W52.5, W64.19, W72.27
Reaux, Angelina, W3.62
Redd, Paul, W22.5
Reed, Janet, W85.7
Rees, Vernon, W14.22
Regency Opera, W80.24
Regger, Hans Gunter, W80.10
Reiner, Fritz, W4.2
Reinhold, Jonathan, W34.1
Reiser, Cheri Lynn, W32.20
Reist, Paul, W3.32
Remmert, Leslie, W14.62
Renan, Emile, W14.21
Renn, John, W85.6
Rescigno, Joseph, W14.60
Rescigno, Nicola, W4.11, W56.35
Resnik, Regina, W56.60
Revelli, William D., W19.17, W19.18, W19.19
Revzen, Joel, W14.68
Reynolds, Anna, W64.19
Reynolds, Frank, W6.1
Reynolds, Hilary, W14.38
Rheault, Gerald, W56.55, W80.31
Ricci, Gian Luca, W80.34, W80.43
Ricci, Ruggiero, W88.5
Rice, David, W14.56
Richards, Leslie, W72.21, W72.25, W72.25c
Richardson, Elizabeth, W14.65
Rickard, Laurie, W56.57
Rickner, Bob, W45.1
Ricks, Robert, W61.1
Ridge Quartet, W10.3, W63.2
Ridoni, Relda, W37.1
Riggs, William, W14.18
Rights, Marilyn, W3.11
Rinaldi, Alberto, W53.2
Rinaldi, Maurizio, W80.11
Rishon Letzion Symphony, W56.50
Rispal, Georgette, W56.19
Ritch, Bud, W47.1
Rizzotto, Leah, W34.5
Robbins, Julien, W72.21
Roberts, Paul, W32.16, W32.17
Robertson, Malcolm, W72.10

Robin Hood Dell Orchestra of
    Philadelphia, W73.10
Robinson, Elisabeth, W14.22
Robinson, Forbes, W3.19
Robinson, Madeleine, W15.2
Robson, Martin, W14.49
Roche, Sarita, W80.27
Rödin, Margit, W14.42
Rogers, Alyce, W14.37
Roggero, Margaret, W4.6
Rogier, Frank, W56.10, W56.59,
    W80.6, W80.7, W80.36
Rohrbaugh, David, W3.30
Roller, A. Clyde, W56.27
Rolli, Lucio, W60.2
Romaguera, Joaquin, W60.1
Rome Opera, W4.9
Rommel, Mildred, W14.18
Roocroft, Amanda, W14.49
Root, Scott, W3.35, W3.36
Rosen, Carole, W14.30
Rosendorff, Friedhelm, W3.25
Rosenstock, Joseph, W56.12
Roslak, Roålana, W3.31
Rosso, Camille, W7.1
Rostropovich, Mstislav, W26.2
Roszel, David, W3.38
Rouleau, Joseph, W72.24
Rousse, Sally, W3.59
Royal Opera House, W3.37, W3.65,
    W6.4
Royal Opera House Orchestra, W6.5
Rubin, Christina, W19.13
Rubin, Chuck, W47.1
Rubinfield, Penny, W56.46
Rubstein, Ariel, W14.18, W14.18b
Rudel, Julius, W4.4, W4.5
Rudolf, Max, W18.1
Ruffini, Alessandra, W80.21
Ruggiero, Gabriella, W72.7, W72.8,
    W72.27, W72.30
Ruggles, Sandra, W80.20
Rural Musicians Forum, W3.55
Ruskiewicz, Janina, W14.33
Ruspoli, Tao, W56.48
Russel, Margaret, W14.55

Russell, Rebecca, W52.13, W52.14
Russo, Vincent, W44.3, W44.4
Ryan, Byron Dean, W3.44, W56.26
Ryder, Mark, W24.2
Ryerson, Greg, W4.11

Sachs, Evelyn, W14.25, W14.26,
    W14.28, W14.29
Sadler's Wells, W3.37, W6.4,
    W14.22, W14.22a, W14.22b,
    W14.23, W14.23a
Salevic, Mischa, W9.4, W10.5,
    W27.3, W63.3
Salvemini, Benedetto, W60.2
Sammarco, James, W3.13
Samsonov, Rema, W14.30, W14.32
San Diego Chamber Orchestra,
    W10.4, W43.1
San Diego Opera, W44.3, W44.3b,
    W72.17
San Francisco Opera, G82; W56.39
San Francisco Spring Opera, W14.31
San Jose Community Opera Theater,
    W3.30
Sanders, Samuel, W77.3
Santa Fe Opera, W32.5, W32.7
Santana, Carlos Manuel, W4.10
Santi, Nello, W4.21
Santy, Chris, W64.14
Sanzogno, Nino, W4.15
Sapolsky, Robert, W3.26, W3.26c
Sarfaty, Regina, W14.25, W52.4,
    W56.15
Sarjeant, Greg, W3.39
Sarnoff, Dorothy, W64.4, W64.20
Sarris, Timothy, W4.13
Sarroca, Suzanne, W52.6, W52.7,
    W52.7a
Saskatoon Opera Association, W3.32,
    W13.3, W13.3a
Saunders, Arlene, W32.4, W32.10
Scaglia, Ferruccio, W26.1
Scarborough, Michael, W64.14
Scharley, Denise, W52.6, W56.19,
    W56.61
Scheib, Curt, W14.57

Schenck, Andrew, W3.69, W3.82,
    W24.4, W73.8, W73.19, W73.22
Scheunemann, Leona, W56.12
Schexnayder, Brian, W44.6
Schippers, Thomas, G79; W3.10,
    W3.12, W3.13, W3.14, W3.15,
    W3.16, W3.64, W3.71, W4.16,
    W4.17, W14.17, W14.34,
    W19.8, W19.9b, W56.11,
    W56.64, W64.7, W64.8, W72.7,
    W72.8, W72.9, W72.27,
    W72.28, W85.17, W85.6,
    W85.7, W85.8
Schmandt, Mark, W32.24
Schmidt, Helga, W14.41
Schmiedner, Helmut, W34.2
Schnitzler, Claude, W14.52
Scholz, Andreas, W32.21
Scholz, Edwin, W19.12
Schonberg, Seymour, W4.10
Schooten, Frank, W14.52
Schowalter, Mark, W3.59
Schreurs, Jean-Jacques, W34.2
Schroeder, John, W56.53
Schürmann, Werner, W19.12
Schwartzman, Seymour, W14.30
Schwarz, Reinhard, W3.27, W32.15,
    W32.15e
Schwarzkopf, Elisabeth, W9.1, W9.1a
Scottish Chamber Orchestra, W14.48,
    W56.34, W80.15
Scribner, William, W84.1
Sech, Svetlana, W14.64
Sechler, Craig, W52.4
Seel, Thomas, W56.31
Seibel, Paula, W80.37
Selwyn, David, W72.19
Semilian, Sorin, W56.50
Sena, Joan, W72.11
Senator, Boaz, W30.2
Serebrier, José, W73.6
Servant, Gregory, W14.39
Serviss, James, W3.11
Setian, Dorothy, W56.26
Sevitzky, Fabien, W65.3
Sewailam, Ashraf, W14.62

Sewell, James, W3.59
Shade, Nancy, W34.1, W34.1h,
    W34.2, W34.3
Shafer, Susan, W72.24, W72.26
Shamos, Jeremy, W3.35, W3.35a
Shapp, Richard, W34.1
Sharp, Frederick, W64.9
Shaulis, Jane, W4.11, W72.16
Shaw, Robert, W28.1
Shay, Gayle, W14.62
Sheperd, Sarah, W14.62, W14.62a,
    W14.65
Shepherd, Lynda, W4.14
Sherwood, Wayne, W56.24
Shin, Young Ok, W79.4
Shinall, Vern, W14.39
Shipley, Bill, W47.1
Shires, Marjorie, W14.22
Shook, Terence, W81.1
Shoor, Paul, W3.30
Shoup, Robert, W80.30, W80.30a
Shuard, Amy, W14.23, W14.23a
Sibley, Fred, W32.12
Sidney, Robert, W85.12
Siena, Jerold, W14.39, W72.16
Sigurvinsdóttir, Elín, W56.32,
    W80.13
Silberstein, Jascha, W84.1
Sills, Beverly, W44.3, W44.3a,
    W44.3d, W44.4, W44.4d,
    W44.4f, W44.4h, W44.4j,
    W44.4k, W44.7a
Silverman, Alan, W84.1
Silverstein, Joseph, W88.2
Silvestri, Anna Maria, W3.52, W72.21
Simmons, Calvin, W44.3
Simonetti, Alfredo, W64.21
Simson, Julie, W14.62
Sinclair, William, W52.11
Singer, Anna, W14.57
Sippy, Francis, W80.22
Sirmans, Sean, W81.1
Sitarski, Christof, W19.12
Skok, Heidi, W56.49
Skrowaczewski, Stanisław, W76.1
Slagel, Don, W3.11

## Performer Index 335

Small, David, W32.24
Smallens, Alexander, W73.1, W73.2
Smart, Sidney, W56.16
Smith, Carol, W56.31
Smith, Cary Archer, W22.4, W53.6
Smith, David, W14.28, W14.29, W56.17
Smith, Elaine, W47.1
Smith, Henry Charles, W3.28
Smith, Julian, W3.41
Smith, Malcolm, W72.12
Smith, Matthew, W34.5
Snook, Brandon, W3.50
Société des concerts du Conservatoire Orchestre, W66.7
Solem, Robert, W3.32, W13.3
Solomon, Nicholas, W14.65
Sosa, Chantal, W3.53
Sosnowski, David, W6.2
South, Pamela, W14.60, W14.60a
Soviero, Diana, W72.16
Speight, John, W80.13
Spillman, Robert, W14.62
Spivakovsky, Tossy, W88.6
Spoleto Festival Orchestra, W19.13, W30.2, W44.6, W58.6, W58.7, W72.22
Spoleto Festival Orchestra U.S.A., W19.11, W44.7, W46.2, W52.13, W52.14, W52.9, W53.6, W58.5, W72.21, W73.4
Spotts, Melissa, W64.13
Sprenger, Ulrich, W32.21
Squires, Shelagh, W14.40
St. Joseph's High School Glee Clubs of Boston, W18.2, W18.5
St. Louis Grand Opera Association, W4.3
St. Mary Redcliffe Secondary School Chorus, W53.1
St. Olaf Choir, W3.68
St. Olaf College Norseman Band, W19.15
St. Paul Chamber Orchestra, W3.59, W3.59a
St. Paul's Parish, Baltimore, W18.3

St. Stephen's Chamber Orchestra, W3.62
Staahlen, Torhild, W14.46
Staatsoper Warschau, W14.33
Staiger, Dorothy, W56.14
Stanciu, Virgil, W56.41
Stanley, Rachel, W64.10
Stannard, Ralph, W3.60
Stapp, Olivia, W14.35, W14.36
Stark, Molly, W64.14
Starling, William, W3.12, W3.13, W3.16
Steber, Eleanor, W4.6
Stedman, Nancy Eaton, W6.3
Steele, Brian, W3.48
Steffan, Sofia, W14.36
Stein, Wolfgang, W14.41, W44.5, W52.12
Stella, Martin A., W19.14
Stensvold, Terje, W14.46
Stephen Crout Chorus, W72.25
Stephen, Pamela Helen, W53.7
Stephens, John, W72.25, W72.26
Stephenson, Donna, W64.18
Stern, Gerald, W14.32
Stevens, Linda, W80.31, W80.31a
Stewart, Cal, W72.16
Stewart, Terese, W14.62
Stilwell, Richard, W52.6, W52.6c, W52.7, W52.7a, W60.1
Stoakes, Paul, W47.1
Stockholm Opera, W14.20
Stojkovic, Johanna, W14.54
Stokowski, Leopold, W66.4, W73.7, W84.1, W84.1a
Stone, Donna Elizabeth, W32.18
Stone, William, W14.51, W19.11
Storck, Helga, W9.4, W10.5, W27.3, W63.3
Storm, Richard, W14.58
Strassel, Johannes, W3.27, W3.27d
Stratas, Teresa, W3.26, W3.26e, W3.26d, W19.8, W19.8k, W19.9
Stratford Festival Orchestra, W56.22
Strauss, Jay, W3.61
Stringer, Mark, W4.12, W79.4

Strother, Martin, W22.5
Strummer, Linda Roark, W14.45
Strummer, Peter, W14.45
Suart, Richard, W14.38
Subashi, Xander, W3.63
Summers, Lydia, W14.15, W14.69
Surais, Martine, W14.50
Susca, Vito, W60.2
Swain, William, W64.18, W80.26
Swanson, Stephen, W14.54
Swanson, Tricia, W3.44
Swenson, Jan, W3.55a
Swenson, Swen, W85.6
Swensson, Evelyn, W6.1, W6.3
Swepston, Paula, W56.41, W64.17
Sydow, Jack, W47.1
Symphony of the Air, W66.5, W66.5a, W66.8
Syracuse Opera, W56.40
Syrus, David, W3.37, W3.65, W6.4, W6.5
Szczepanska, Krystyna, W14.33
Szell, George, W45.1e

Taddei, Giuseppe, W4.9
Tadeo, Giorgio, W4.9
Taghadossi, Mario, W14.55
Tai, Gleni, W56.57
Takada, Michael, W79.2
Tanner, Eugene, W85.7
Tardue, Marc, W56.32, W80.13
Tartaglia, Tony, W47.1
Tate, Sheila, W3.58
Taylor, Christine, W14.38
Taylor, Patricia, W14.40
Taylor, Ted, W56.52, W80.25
Taylor, Todd, W34.5
Tchereskaya, Ljuba, W32.9
Teal, Jean-Anne, W14.45
Teatro comunale "Giuseppe Verdi," W64.19
Tees Valley Boys' Choir, W53.7
Teeters, Donald, W85.18, W85.23
Telese, Maryanne, W72.25, W72.26
Terry, Samuel, W79.2
Tetzlaff, Stephan, W14.55

Texas Christian University Concert Chorale, W43.1
Théâtre Musical de Paris, W56.39b
Theatre-in-the-Dale, W15.1
Theyard, Harry, W60.1, W72.12
Thibaudet, Jean-Yves, W9.2, W77.2
Thieme, Helga, W32.18
Thomas, Benjamin, W4.6
Thomas, Carlo, W22.4, W53.6
Thomas, Richard, W85.7
Thomas, Suzanne, W80.31
Thomas, Thomas, W32.13
Thomas, Todd, W14.57
Thomas, Vickie R., W14.66
Thompson, John, W3.54
Thompson, Patti, W56.40
Thorn, Penelope, W52.12
Thorsen, Stein Arild, W14.46
Tian, Hao Jiang, W3.35, W3.36
Tillett, Kevin, W3.43
Tipton, Thomas, W64.8
Tirrel, Joan, W14.58
Titus, Maxine, W56.16
Tiziani, Aldo, W19.12
Tobias, Roy, W85.7
Todd, Alexander, W56.46
Todd, James, W3.56
Toone, Tina, W64.13
Torigi, Richard, W14.21, W72.17
Torkanowsky, Werner, W14.25, W14.26, W56.15
Tóth, Tibo, W14.55
Tozzi, Giorgio, W3.26
Trahan, Corey, W3.58
Trakis, Christopher, W50.1
Trampler, Walter, W10.1, W63.1
Travis, Dale, W14.63
Traynor, Robert, W3.43
Treash, Leonard, W4.2
Trego, Brian, W22.5
Trego, William R., W22.4
Truran, Dusty, W47.1
Truschel, Timothy, W3.46
Tucker, Gene, W22.1, W22.4, W53.5, W53.5b, W53.6
Turgeon, Bernard, W14.27

Turnage, Wayne, W32.9, W80.14, W80.15, W80.15a, W80.17, W80.18
Turner, Claramae, W56.8, W56.15, W56.15a
Turner, J. Michael, W14.66
Turner, Randal, W14.61
Turner, Rebecca, W52.11
Turri, Ida-Maria, W14.49
Tveten, Vesla, W14.46
Twitchell, Noel, W3.29
Tynes, Linzie, W13.5
Tyree, Mildred, W14.56

Ubukata, Bruce, W13.1, W13.2
Uecker, Korliss, W4.12
Ulloa, César, W14.61
Ulster Orchestra, W66.6
University Circle Singers, W85.12
University of Cincinnati Chamber Choir, W85.8
University of Colorado University Singers, W85.13
University of Houston Concert Band, W73.11
University of Houston Symphonic Wind Ensemble, W73.12
University of Michigan Band, W19.19
University of Michigan Chamber Choir, W85.15
University of Michigan Choral Union, W76.1
University of Michigan Symphonic Band, W19.17, W19.18
University of New Orleans Opera Theater, W32.13, W32.19, W56.46
University of Wisconsin — Eau Claire Concert Choir, W43.1
Upshaw, Dawn, W64.22, W64.25
Upton, Greg, W80.29
Urbanek, Hans, W32.14
Urrila, Irma, W14.46
Utah Chamber Orchestra, W3.44
Utah Opera, W3.29, W3.44, W3.44a

Vaccarri, Melanie, W80.30
Vaglieri, Paolo, W80.34, W82.34
Valentin, Bernd, W80.22
Valentine, Leslie, W56.51
Valentino, Francisco, W4.6
Van Amburg, Nick, W13.5
Van De Graaff, Peter, W56.58
Van Demark, James, W21.1, W21.1a
Van Dorsten, John, W6.3
Van Geldern, Harold, W32.9
Van Ginkel, Peter, W14.27
Vancouver Opera Association, W14.27
Vandever, Joy, W6.1
Vanelli, Adriana, W44.7, W72.24
Vanzelli, Gianni, W19.13
Varnay, Astrid, W41.1
Varon, Lorna de, W18.5
Vekshtein, Semyon, W14.64
Venable, Jacqueline, W44.7
Vennard, William, W14.19
Venora, Lee, W56.17
Ventura, Clyde, W72.11, W72.12
Verdehr Trio, W83.1, W83.1a, W83.2, W83.3
Vergera, Victoria W30.1, W72.24
Verkerk, Willem, W32.14
Vermeersch, Jef, W14.56
Vernhes, Alain, W14.50
Vernon, Derrick, W3.58
Verrier, Gillian, W72.10
Vespasiani, Ambra, W19.13
Virgil, Marcos, W3.54
Virginia Opera Association, W3.34, W3.34b, W56.51, W56.51b
Visca, Claudia, W14.56
Vogel, Don, W3.11
Voketaitis, Arnold, W4.8, W14.25
Voli, Albert, W14.52
Volkman, Elizabeth, W72.20
Vorrassi, John, W22.6
Votapek, Ralph, W70.6
Vote, Larry, W54.1
Vrenios, Anastasios, W22.1, W22.4

Wächter, Eberhard, W3.27
Wadsworth, Charles, W77.1

Waglechner, Erich, W64.16
Wagner, Alan, W6.1
Walchshofer, Alois, W64.16
Walker, Clyde Phillip, W32.5, W32.8
Walker, Henry, W3.43
Walker, Ian, W3.45
Walker, Michael, W80.31
Walker, Richard, W22.5
Walker, Sandra, W14.35, W14.36, W14.39, W14.64
Wallace, Robert, W72.23
Walt Whitman Middle School, W18.3
Walters, Jess, W72.9
Walters, Mark, W80.28
Walton, Huck, W3.61
Wang, Kewei, W79.4
Ward, Joseph, W3.19
Warren, Elinor, W14.17
Warren, Leonard, W41.1
Warren, Susan, W72.23, W72.23a
Warwick Symphony Orchestra, W4.19
Washington Opera, W14.51, W30.1, W56.33, W56.34, W56.36, W56.36a, W72.25, W72.25b, W80.14, W80.15, W80.17
Watson, Anne, W64.13
Watson, Chester, W14.15
Watson, Curtis, W3.37, W3.65
Watson, David, W14.64
Watson, Lois, W14.64
Watts, Clive, W72.19
Watts, Jonathan, W85.7
Weaver, John, W69.2
Weaver, Jonathan, W3.34
Weaver, Susan, W72.19
Wedekind, Johannes, W3.25
Weede, Robert, W4.3, W64.4, W64.20
Weigmann, Knut, W32.21
Weiler, Sherri, W3.56
Weisberger, Julien, W34.2
Weisel-Capsouto, Robin, W56.50
Wells, Mary, W72.10, W72.10a
Wells, William, W85.19
Welting, Ruth, W19.10
Wendelken-Wilson, Charles, W72.15

Wengerd, Tim, W24.3
Wennink, Michael, W53.1, W53.2
Wentworth, Richard, W3.12, W3.13, W3.16
Wentzel, Andrew, W30.2
Wermine, Bette, W14.20
Werner, Alfred, W14.45
Werner, Carolyn, W47.1
Wesemann, Marlene, W56.18
West, John, W45.1
West, Kevin, W3.45
Westbrook, Jane, W44.3, W44.4
Westbury, Marjorie, W64.9
Western Opera Theater, G82
Westminster Cathedral Choir, W19.11, W19.13, W30.2, W44.6, W44.7, W46.2, W58.4, W58.5, W58.6, W58.7, W72.21, W72.22, W85.10
Wettergren, Gertrud, W14.20
Weyman, Judith, W56.33, W56.34, W56.48
Wheatley, Patrick, W14.40
Wheeler, John, W52.2
White, Lois, W14.45
White, Richard, W18.3
White, Robert, W45.1
White, Sandra, W64.10
White, Willard, W3.26
Whitehead, Dara, W56.57
Whitehouse, Richard, W32.16, W32.17
Wicherek, Antoni, W14.33
Wickenden, Lynne, W14.56
Wiener Kammeroper, W80.10
Wiener Philharmoniker, W3.27, W32.15
Wiener Staatsoper, W3.27, W32.15
Wiener, Frances, W86.1
Wild, Earl, W66.8, W66.9, W66.10
Wilgar, Cheryl, W64.10
Wilkes, Jocelyn, W72.14
Willauer, Marguerite, W32.5
Willeke, Michael, W14.41
Willen, Niklas, W66.6
William Ferris Chorale, W22.6,

W85.9
Williams, Elaine, W14.38
Williams, Howard, W14.40,
  W14.40b, W14.40c
Williams, Nancy, W3.22
Williams, Paul, W56.44
Williams, Shawn Marie, W56.55
Williams, Valarie, W13.1, W13.7
Willner, Brenda, W3.30
Willoughby, Bob, W3.55
Wilmington Opera Society, W6
Wilson, Catherine, W32.11
Wilson, Charles, W3.21, W14.29,
  W14.31, W32.8
Wilson, Fred, W56.55
Wilson, George C., W19.16
Wilson, Illinois, W56.16
Winant, William, W13.1
Wind, Ursula, W14.54
Windle, Erin, W32.24
Wingard, Ellen, W6.3
Winnipeg Symphony Orchestra,
  W14.64
Winter, Paul, W32.14
Winter, Peter, W3.25
Winters, Lawrence, W3.12, W3.13,
  W3.16
Wirén, Arne, W14.20
Wise, Jennifer, W14.66
Wittges, Max, W18.3
Wojciechowski, Marek, W14.56
Wolansky, Raymond, W32.4, W32.10
Wold, Susan, W80.10
Wolf, Sibylle, W80.22
Wolfes, Helmuth, W14.24
Wolff, Beverly, W45.1, W60.1,
  W72.11, W72.12, W72.17
Wolff, Hugh, W3.59
Wolff, William, W14.30
Wood, Kenneth, W34.5
Woodley, Arthur, W3.34
Woodman, Thomas, W3.40
Woods, Sheryl, W80.14, W80.15,
  W80.15a, W80.17

Wooten, Germaine Darrell, W3.60
Workman, William, W3.20, W3.23,
  W32.4, W32.5, W32.10, W32.11
Wren, Sam, W15.1
Wright, Benjamin, W3.28
Wright, Sarah, W32.16, W32.17
Wrynn, James, W47.1

Xiberras, Maurice, W13.4

Yaghjian, Kurt, W3.66
Yale Opera, W3.46, W3.46a
Yeakey, John, W3.70
Yeend, Frances, W4.4, W4.5
Yenne, Vernon, W80.32
Yoder, Paul, W52.12
Young, Aaron, W3.56
Young, Norman, W64.5, W64.6
Yule, Don, W14.36, W60.1
Yung, David, W3.31

Zakai, Mira, W56.50, W56.50a,
  W56.50b
Zambalis, Stella, W52.13, W52.13c,
  W52.14, W52.14a
Zambrana, Margarita, W14.27
Zamkochian, Berj, W18.5
Zanolli, Silvana, W4.15
Zarins, Laura, W13.1, W13.7
Zeani, Virginia, W14.34, W14.34a
Zechnacker, Serge, W34.5
Zemp, Robin, W6.3
Zerial, Dario, W60.2
Zerlinger, Roman, W14.45
Zhang, Jianyi, W4.12
Ziegler, Shelley, W3.38
Zielski, Cynthia, W3.46
Zilio, Elena, W14.63
Zimbalist, Efrem, W88.1, W88.1a
Zinman, David, W64.22
Zitnik, Mary, W14.65
Zonta, Marcelle, W14.27
Zuccarelli, Ernesto, W72.23

**About the Author**

DONALD L. HIXON is Librarian Emeritus from the University of California, Irvine, where he served as Fine Arts Librarian from 1968–1992. He is the author of *Thea Musgrave: A Bio-Bibliography* (Greenwood, 1984) and serves as Series Adviser for the Greenwood Press series, Bio-Bibliographies in Music.

**Recent Titles in
Bio-Bibliographies in Music**

George Whitefield Chadwick: A Bio-Bibliography
*Bill F. Faucett*

William Schuman: A Bio-Bibliography
*K. Gary Adams*

Malcolm Arnold: A Bio-Bibliography
*Stewart R. Craggs*

Manuel de Falla: A Bio-Bibliography
*Nancy Lee Harper*

Elvis Costello: A Bio-Bibliography
*James E. Perone*

Carole King: A Bio-Bibliography
*James E. Perone*

Joachim Andersen: A Bio-Bibliography
*Kyle J. Dzapo*

Alfred Reed: A Bio-Bibliography
*Douglas M. Jordan*

Phil Ochs: A Bio-Bibliography
*David Cohen*

George Gershwin: A Bio-Bibliography
*Norbert Carnovale*

Paul Simon: A Bio-Bibliography
*James E. Perone*

Vladimir Ussachevsky: A Bio-Bibliography
*Ralph Hartsock and Carl Rahkonen*

ISBN 0-313-26139-3

90000>

EAN
9 780313 261398

HARDCOVER BAR CODE